The Social Production of Urban Space

The Social Production of Urban Space

By M. Gottdiener

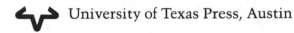 University of Texas Press, Austin

First Paperback Printing, 1988

Requests for permission to reproduce material from this work
should be sent to Permissions, University of Texas Press,
Box 7819, Austin, Texas 78713-7819.

Library of Congress Cataloging in Publication Data
Gottdiener, Mark.
  The social production of urban space.

  Bibliography: p.
  Includes index.
  1. Metropolitan areas—United States.   2. Suburbs—
United States.   3. Urbanization.   4. Sociology, Urban.
5. Marxian economics.   6. Land use.   I. Title.
HT334.U5G66   1985   307.7'6'0973   84-29125
ISBN 0-292-77586-5
ISBN 0-292-77614-4 pbk.

Portions of chapter 2 published by permission of Transaction,
Inc., from *Comparative Urban Research*, Vol. 10, No. 1,
copyright © 1983 by William John Hanna.

Contents

Preface

Several years ago I published a case study of metropolitan regional development. My purpose was to understand comprehensively the processes producing contemporary patterns of spatial restructuring and urban deconcentration. Although wishing to combine theory with empirical research, I discovered that existing approaches to urban development were inadequate for an understanding of the sprawling, polynucleated nature of metropolitan growth. It seemed to me that, in particular, urban ecology and marxian political economy were both limited, although the latter had overcome successfully the ideological constraints of the former and was certainly on the right track. I, therefore, embarked on an empirically inspired theoretical journey into new approaches to spatial analysis; a trip which required that I cross over to the literature of another continent. In the end I was surprised at unexpected attempts to discourage the appearance of new ideas by institutionalized forms of orthodoxy from both the conventional and the critical camps. Such incidents reinforced my desire to complete this project of reconceptualization despite the delays they caused.

Portions of chapter 2 have appeared in *Comparative Urban Research*, and portions of chapter 4 in M. Smith, *Cities in Transformation* (1984). I wish to thank the publishers, Transaction Press and Sage Publications, Inc., respectively, for their permission to reproduce this material. Research and writing were aided by several grants from the Academic Senate of the University of California, Riverside. I wish to thank Charles Bonjean for his early support of this project and Holly Carver and Scott Lubeck of the University of Texas Press for their editorial assistance. I would also like to thank Charlotte Stanley for her assistance in the translation of demanding French texts—a task whose difficulty can only be appreciated by those who have also attempted such readings. Finally, I wish to thank my wife,

Jennifer, for her daily support of my work and my struggle without which this book would never have appeared.

This book is dedicated to the memory of two men responsible for my intellectual development. Both were victimized by forms of oppression—the first, religious, and the second, academic. To my father, Moshe Ovadiah, and, my cousin, Professor Seymour Fiddle.

—M. G.

The Social Production of Urban Space

1. Introduction

In 1946, just one year after the end of World War II, three hundred acres of Hempstead Plain were converted to single-tract suburban housing. The area was situated less than twenty miles from the center of Manhattan, in a section of Long Island long renowned for its potatoes. This project, built entirely by a privately financed developer called Levitt and Sons, was one of the first mass-produced suburban developments in the United States. Up to that time, individuals wishing to live outside of the central city but within commuting distance from it moved to "exurban towns" such as the quaint New England–style villages dotting the north and south shores of Long Island. Such "exurbanites," as they were called, commissioned custom-built homes or remodeled old farmhouses. In contrast, Levitt and Sons gathered independent backing, created early forms of modular home construction, hired large numbers of nonunion workers, and completed several thousand Cape Cod–like houses which sold at the very beginning for the remarkable price of $6,990. Unlike the exurban homes of the "organization men" which preceded this form of development, Levitt's products were pitched at the untapped market of returning GIs who could take advantage of recently enacted federal legislation which subsidized home purchasing and financing by veterans. The demand for the new tract housing was voracious. By 1951 the community, now called Levittown, was comprised of 17,544 homes, selling at that time for $9,900 (an appreciation of $3,000 in four years in 1950's dollars). The massive tract development made a multimillion-dollar corporation out of Levitt and Sons, which went on to build similar Levittowns in New Jersey and Pennsylvania in areas once devoted to agriculture.

In a seemingly unrelated event almost twenty years later, in February 1970, the federal government, acting through its Department of Housing and Urban Development, awarded a 24 million dollar loan guarantee to the developers of yet another mass-produced community, Cedar-Riverside, in the central city section of Minneapolis. This project, called a New Town in Town by public officials, was supported under a government program of urban development which came into being as a consequence of the recently enacted Urban Growth and Development Act of 1970. Title VII of the act, the New Town legislation, targeted loan guarantees of up to $500 million for community development that aimed to contain a mix of housing and, in some cases, industry in a more balanced pattern of growth than the existing one of urban sprawl. Cedar-Riverside, however, was not built on vacant land. It expropriated the space belonging to a historical central city section of Minneapolis called Seven Corners or the West Bank. Most of the original residents, some of whom had lived there continuously for over half a century and all of whom were either working-class, retired, or young college students in need of low-income housing, were forced out by the new development. The developers satisfied the government's desire for mixed housing by building the first high-rise apartment buildings in the district. The rents in the new high rises were considerably greater than those existing prior to the project; consequently, the original residents were replaced by middle-class tenants. In an interview about New Towns for *Fortune* in 1971, Henry T. McKnight, a real estate speculator and the principal stockholder of Cedar-Riverside, stated: "In new cities nobody is an expert. We're all learning." He cheerfully admitted that he had no prior experience in community development.

Unlike the privately bankrolled and successful Levittown, this project has enjoyed mixed results. It has created a slum out of the single-family homes abandoned to make room for the development. The apartment high rises have provided housing for a new middle class taking up residence there, but they have also provided increased opportunity for street crimes and apartment burglaries. At present the project has displaced many more people than it now houses, and it has been halted due to lack of funds for completion. In short, it seems typical of most urban renewal projects built in the 1950s and 1960s.

The two communities, Levittown and Cedar-Riverside, are comparable although seemingly unrelated. Before we make the point we are developing, however, one further illustrative example is still necessary. Preliminary results from the 1980 census indicate that outlying areas once considered rural are growing at a faster rate than those communities closest to the metropolitan centers, although the major urban regions continue to contain the bulk of the U.S. population. In California, for example, the counties north of the mountain range marking the border with southern California grew faster in population than did all the counties to the south for the first time in the state's history (18.6 percent compared to 17.1 percent). According to a newspaper report on the 1980 results:

> The growth of the 50 counties north of the Tehachapi was led by the explosive growth in the rural counties from Plumas to Fresno. And within those counties, unincorporated communities grew faster than incorporated cities. Surprisingly, studies of the new residents in rural areas indicate that most are not counterculture flower children left over from the 1960's, but established professionals and other skilled workers who in midlife decided to start anew. (*Los Angeles Sunday Times*, January 18, 1981)

The report went on to summarize the characteristics of this demographic shift for the 1980s. Part of this population is comprised of retired people who have cashed in on property ownership equity in more developed places and are presently living off the proceeds in less expensive outlying areas. In addition, a recent survey of 550 new residents indicates that the middle-aged individuals are all highly educated and skilled. A significant proportion (40 percent) started their own businesses in these areas within the first five years of being transplanted. While they realized that their prospects of making money were not as great as in the larger cities, these people expressed a strong preference for life-style over economic considerations. Thus, in several ways, their personal profiles suggest the type of American who thirty years ago would have moved from the city to suburbia while still retaining a corporate job (Bradshaw and Blakeley 1979).

According to the state Office of Planning and Research in Sacramento, the new trend is expected to greatly affect representation in the state legislature during the coming years. It has also had an immediate impact on local public institutions within the small towns, due to such big-city effects as taxation pressures, traffic congestion, and rising prices. Once again, we may note that these features seem very reminiscent of patterns established early in the stages of suburbanization shortly after World War II. Differences lie in the facts that the current population is, on the whole, slightly older and that, instead of commuting to city jobs, residents are forming the nucleus of a more portable, less industrially related economic infrastructure. Just as early suburbanization was merely the prelude to massive regional growth, however, we can assume that such trends indicate the initial phases of a more comprehensive pattern of development for the years to come. In fact, let us not make the mistake, committed in the past by suburban analysts, of stating that this population shift represents a new, nonurban style of life. On the contrary, it is very urban in nature, and it signifies the next stage in a process of metropolitan deconcentration which has been occurring since the 1880s and which will no doubt continue over the coming years as regional expansion reaches out to land located in the most distant areas of the country. We can expect in a short time, therefore, to see the appearance in these peripheral regions of large-scale residential and shopping mall construction—of the social organization of space more typical of the fringe area metropolitan development that is presently characteristic of suburbia.

The more rapid growth rate of outlying areas compared to the central city has been a constant feature of urbanized regions since at least the 1920s (Hawley 1956). Beginning with the 1970s, however, this growth took place for the first time in areas *outside* the boundaries of the metropolis, signaling what has come to be known as the population turnaround. For the first time in history the outer reaches adjacent to urban areas are the recipients of migration at the expense of the central city, thus reversing the long-standing process of the urban implosion (Fuguitt and Beale 1978).

Our three examples provide us with different instances of one fundamental aspect of present-day sociospatial growth: urban life has become portable and, thus, so has the "city." In place of the compact city form which once represented a historical process years in the making, we now have a metropolitan population distributed and organized in ever expanding regional areas that are amorphous in form, massive in scope, and hierarchical in their scale of social organization. The margins of this development seem to be filled in almost overnight, and it has become progressively more difficult to escape the circumscribed built environment. As people attempt to move away from higher-density development in order to pursue a satisfying life-style in a locational way, they expand the reaches of this massive population dispersal still further. At present, developers and real estate speculators can single out a tract of wilderness or agricultural expanse, or even strike within the heart of a metropolis, and assemble market, government, and construction forces that will raise an "urban" development within a short period of time. The fact that a large regional mall, an office building complex, or an enacted residential community can be built virtually anywhere, anytime, and around almost anyone, despite the existence of zoning controls or the local residents' desire for "no growth," is somewhat disconcerting. Furthermore, as early as the 1880s, when Pullman, Illinois, was built outside Chicago to house the great railway works in a company town, capitalist industrialization has shown itself capable of such feats. This ease of construction has resulted in the total transformation of the landscape: virtually every American lives within a sprawling urban matrix of cities, towns, commerce, industry, heterogeneous strangers, and large public institutions.

The current patterns of development and their associated social, economic, and political implications have been noted, but as yet precious little has been advanced by urban scientists in the way of understanding them. Pick any textbook in urban sociology, for example, and you will be told about the "city" as *the* form of urban settlement, about "urbanization" as involving the concentration of people within bounded areas, and about the "differences" between the "urban way of life" and its "suburban" or "rural" counterpart. Despite the obsolete nature of these concepts, they remain the central focus of urban texts, even though most Americans have been living in polynucleated metropolitan areas outside the central city since the 1970s. Perhaps the emphasis on the city as the urban form persists because so much has already been said about it. For example, lengthy explanation in texts is usually devoted to reviewing decades of research on the central city: its genesis in history, how its compact form represents a unique type of community, and how variation in urban factors (mainly population size) produces different sociopsychological effects. The lists of terms and the alleged contrasts between them seem endless, yet such taxonomies provide little help in understanding current spatial transformations and the life lived in sprawling regions because the appropriateness of the terms and theories has diminished over the years.

In virtually all sociological texts, little attempt is made to cast off a dependency upon outdated paradigms of thought and to analyze contemporary spatial morphology, which is not just the city grown large but a qualitatively new form of settlement space. For example, Gist and Fava identify three urban stages—the preindustrial, the urban-industrial, and the metropolitan—without providing the reader with a discussion about aspects of the social organization which may have produced them. The authors note that "the metropolitan period represents a community form whose significance is still somewhat unclear, particularly in social terms, despite the fact that we already seem to be moving toward a fourth period of development" (1974: 60). Thus we get the impression from this text that the metropolis is already giving way to a new transformation, that periods of development appear through some static categorical process, and that most of what we now know about the city in its present form remains unclear. Such texts do not advance our understanding.

It also in this sense
that past disappears—
it was an earlier era.

They merely catalog the large numbers of facts learned about spatial changes, labeling them arbitrarily while remarking only that there are problems with city-focused concepts and theories because they are now less useful than they were in the past.

The present discussion meets the current spread city form head-on. I am interested in the type of social organization which can produce and sustain (or reproduce) such land-use patterns. I am concerned not with an urban past based upon the bounded city form but with the present regional organization of everyday life—I believe that previous urban thought has neglected this task for too long. I am interested less in bringing the reader up to the present by submitting a lengthy treatment of mainstream approaches to urban growth than in forging a new synthesis of fresh ideas on the subject of modern life and its megalopolitan habitat. For example, our three illustrations above indicate the variety of ways in which large areas of land can be converted quickly to satisfy many of the functions of urban life, such as housing and commerce, without possessing little else that once characterized the city. The scope and tenor of such development were made possible in part by the mode of home construction pioneered by Levitt and Sons, which was virtually unforeseen prior to World War II. In part, however, such development was also made possible by active government intervention, either indirectly by the subsidization of mortgages and homeowner tax shelters, as in the case of Levittown, or directly as a willing partner of real estate speculators and developers operating within the city limits of Minneapolis. Thus the production of regional space involves the state as much as it does the economy, and we are compelled to understand this relation.

In addition to examining the intersection of economic and political processes in space, I wish to investigate the use of planning and construction technology to encapsulate the physical act of land conversion in a language of sophisticated architectural rhetoric. This process involves the ideology of growth which always accompanies development and change. As a New Town in Town, Cedar-Riverside, for example, displaced linguistically as well as physically the community space which it then occupied and dominated. The conversion of physical space can proceed with its own ideology and rhetoric as well as with the urban bulldozer. In fact, the ideologies which obfuscate or mystify this development, such as technological or environmental determinism or pro-growth boosterism, and which make it more difficult for us to understand the genesis of spatial patterns, are prime subjects of my concern. Thus I will discuss the following areas: the dynamics of present-day societal processes of

metropolitan and regional development, the role of the state in constructing and sustaining spread city growth, the role of ideology and
semantic fields in obfuscating and masking the real processes at
work in restructuring settlement space, and the patterns of social organization responsible for the production of space in modern society.

In the past urban science has been focused on a particular image
of urban spatial deployment, namely, the bounded city form. While
the exact internal differentiation of this image has been a subject of
debate, especially between the early monocentric view of Burgess
and more recent polycentric approaches, urban science has retained
its belief in the organizing abilities of the central city as the source
of regional sociospatial dominance (see chapter 2). In a case study of
a metropolitan region adjacent to New York City (Gottdiener 1977), I
observed that this model of urban development was inaccurate. Regional sprawl is much less dependent upon central city agglomerations than is often believed and considerably more dependent on social forces operating at the level of society itself for its internal
patterns of functional differentiation. In consequence we presently
possess a new form of settlement space, one which is polynucleated
and functionally integrated by the three-dimensional matrix of social organization. Because the latter feature depends less upon horizontal relations of spatial integration emphasized by concentric
zone pictures and more upon hierarchically structured linkages to
global system processes, such as capital accumulation and the new
international division of labor, it is not possible to diagram the new
model of urban space—we can only imagine its appearance. I prefer
the term "polynucleated metropolitan region" for this form of settlement space in order to distinguish it from the analyses of those who
persist in perceiving it merely as a larger version of the city (Long
and DeAre 1983; Gordon 1984). By focusing on spatial patterns as
products of deep-level forces residing in modes of social organization, we can do away with all obsolete theories that reify the physical features of space themselves but that ignore the instrumental and
hierarchical manner by which all settlement spaces are integrated
through the actions of systemic forces.

The basic features of the new form of sociospatial organization
have been noted for some time by geographers, who are most attuned
to physical changes in the built environment. According to Vance
(1977), for example, urbanized areas, especially those encompassing
our larger cities, should be conceived of as multinodal *realms*. One
advocate of this approach, Muller, indicates that "the extent, character, and internal structure of the metropolitan region and the
number of its realms is a function of four properties: physical ter-

rain, the size of the metropolis itself, the robustness of regional economy, and the transportation network" (1981: 8). For example, the greater Los Angeles area can be studied profitably in terms of five realms, of which the original downtown section is but one district. Empirical evidence for Vance's descriptive model of the contemporary form of settlement space has been corroborated elsewhere (Green 1980; Guest 1975). In contrast to the picture of the city held by mainstream urban analysts, these polynucleated regions are no longer organized by the sociospatial activities of the historic city center. Words, such as "urban" and "rural," which were once used to categorize places have now lost their analytical value. In the present discussion I have abandoned any attempt to rescue these comparative concepts in favor of developing a generalized approach to settlement space (for an alternative which seeks to retain the term "urban," see Castells 1977; Saunders 1981; Dunleavy 1980).

The fields of urban science require reconceptualization because the patterns of spatial organization have changed. Several additional implications follow from this claim. Urban science in general rests on a basic premise that the spatial patterns of settlement space correspond to the action of deep-level forces of social organization. If a qualitatively new form of space has developed, as I contend, this implies that the very mode of social organization has also changed. Thus, the call for an appreciation that urban morphology has altered from the picture presently held by mainstream urban scientists possesses two fundamental implications. First, it is necessary to completely replace the existing mainstream paradigm of urban science. In the next chapters I shall prove this assertion and present an alternate paradigm which derives from marxism and which I call the production of space perspective. Second, it is necessary to specify explicitly the manner in which the structure of social organization has changed. Thus, it is simply not sufficient to say, along with many marxists, that it is "capitalism" which has brought about the changes restructuring space. Nor is it sufficient to subscribe to mainstream views which rely fundamentally on the role of technological change in explaining contemporary growth patterns. In contrast, the present discussion will also specify both the precise manner in which capitalist social organization has evolved and, more important, how aspects of the present social formation have produced the new form of metropolitan polynucleation.

In emphasizing the almost disembodied way in which urban development can take place as well as its far-reaching scale, I am interested in capturing a generalized view of the patterns of urban growth characteristic of post–World War II America. In this regard I assert that the new form of settlement space characteristic of the United States has not really appeared yet in a qualitative sense in other countries, even in industrialized Europe. Elsewhere central cities have continued to retain many of the organizing functions which have been performed historically for hinterland development. Consequently, the present discussion addresses the experience of one country, the United States, in the hope that this leading edge of capitalist development may serve as an example which other countries can avoid.

One important descriptive term for contemporary development patterns is "deconcentration." I shall define this in a manner which contrasts somewhat with mainstream use. Deconcentration refers to the absolute increase of population and density of social activities in areas outside traditional city regions and population centers. In the past this term has been used to describe a general demographic leveling of population density across metropolitan regions (Berry and Kasarda 1977). However, I wish to emphasize social activities as well as population dispersal, on the one hand, and the shift to the sunbelt from the frostbelt, on the other. Furthermore, in this view the process of deconcentration involves both a socioeconomic movement from the older central cities to outlying areas, or decentralization, as well as the appearance of citylike agglomerations and the buildup of social density in outlying areas, or concentration. In general, agglomeration effects are the consequence of decentralization either indirectly through endogenous sources responding to an increase in socioeconomic activity or directly from the exogenous effects of centrifugal relocation outside the central city. In summation, I choose "deconcentration" as the descriptive term for present-day patterns of polynucleated growth because it captures the massive regional dispersal of people, commerce, industry, and administration along with the contemporary restructuring of such regions into multicentered realms—sprawling for miles and miles and located everywhere in the country, especially in those areas once thought immune from urban development. In what follows, our concern will be focused on understanding the relation between deconcentration and Late Capitalism. We shall come to see that deconcentration is both a form—that is, a product—and a process—that is, a producer—which helps effect changes in Late Capitalism. In short, spatial patterns and social processes are dialectically related rather than being linked through cycles of cause and effect.

At its core deconcentration has been the consequence of many years of suburban growth outside the central cities at distances increasingly more removed from them. What is most striking to an observer of this phenomenon is the way in which over time suburbia, as a form of settlement space, has been evolving faster than our conception of it. Presently it is clear that early analysts, especially those who were struck by the relative uniqueness of individual developments, were mistaking a long-term process of change for a stable pattern of community life. Suburbanization, however, can be understood only as part of a global process of development which has evolved through a series of stages. During each period of development, academic activity managed to isolate key aspects of deconcentration without quite conceptualizing the broad features of settlement space growth that have emerged as characteristic of the post–World War II boom years. Let us examine these stages of growth as they have been demarcated by research interests. I shall focus here on the changing academic conception of deconcentration.

Initially, the phenomenon of development outside the central city was called exurban. The areas of Westchester and White Plains counties adjacent to New York City are good examples of regions invaded during the late 1940s and early 1950s by affluent executives, who converted old farmhouses for "modern" family use or commissioned architects and builders to produce custom-built homes. Such early movement out of the city for residential purposes gave rise to the first image of suburbia as the bedroom commuter shed of the central city; it also introduced an upper-middle-class status to the separation of home from work by making commuting fashionable. This image was amplified further during the height of suburbanization between 1950 and 1965, when mass-produced single-family home construction was introduced and millions of Americans took up residence in suburban areas. At this time suburbia came to be viewed as a conformist mode of settlement space organized around consumption, with a split-family life-style involving an absentee father off at work in the city and a self-possessed mother making the rounds of kaffeeklatsches with other female neighbors in between trips to the shopping center in her station wagon.

In retrospect, what was most important about this period was not the comments of spatial fetishists convinced of the apparent differences in this life-style from that of central city living, which were produced by environmental change (Fava 1956), but the clear identification of the pull factors which lured people away from the city to suburban communities. That is, at this time the city was also considered a decent, good place to live. Suburban relocation developed into a mass movement primarily as a consequence of attractive supply-side features made available to the majority of citizens, who happened to be white. For example, at this time many people were provided with the possibility of single-family homeownership in communities where, in many cases, the developer also provided a community image and infrastructure involving religious, recreational, and educational facilities (Gans 1967). The continuing importance of pull factors as the main determinant of demographic deconcentration independent of the vagaries of city living has been corroborated in recent research on white flight (Frey 1979; Marshall 1979). This long history does not seem to suggest that the famous American antiurban bias was as responsible for large-scale suburbanization as were the supply-side effects of a combined state-economy marriage which promoted fringe area development for the postwar housing needs of the white population. I shall return to this topic in chapter 7.

The second stage of suburban research is perhaps exemplified best by Dobriner (1958, 1963) and Schnore (1957, 1963, 1965). During the early 1960s the monolithic view of suburbia (to be abandoned later) was argued against for the first time. Suburban communities were differentiated with regard to class: they were stratified by income and life-style much as were central city neighborhoods. In short, there were many different kinds of suburbs, and this variety was captured once a regional, metropolitan view of urban development was adopted. Schnore in particular advanced the fruitful notion of functional differentiation for suburban communities. The metropolitan region was conceived of in areal terms and the internal complexity of the division of labor among settlement spaces was brought to the surface of analysis. Following the pioneering work of Douglas (1925), Schnore applied the notion of the employment-to-residence ratio by which different communities outside the central city could be classified. He identified three categories: the residential or bedroom community, the industrial suburb, and an intermediate type with mixed housing and commerce or industry (1965).

Several important consequences of suburban research followed from this work on functional differentiation. First, the complexity of community social orders implied that the totality of the suburban impulse could no longer be captured by the particularized single study, such as Whyte's Forest Park work (1956). Suburban research required the multiplication of cases and the aggregation of individual attributes in the manner of macrolevel census analysis (Riesman 1957). At this time, a conceptual disjuncture between aggregate data analysis and micro case studies appeared, and this matched the very same limitation of city-based work which had characterized the rest of urban sociology since the early Chicago School.

Second, a core line of convergence was introduced by which

both cities and suburbs were considered part of an expanding metropolitan region possessing ongoing processes of internal differentiation and growth, as conceptualized first by McKenzie (1933). The research focus, therefore, shifted to quantitative and largely descriptive areal analyses of aggregate census data on metropolitan morphology. Such studies, now legion, comprise the bulk of published journal research on a wide variety of urban topics to this day. Precisely through this mode of inquiry the shift to the sunbelt was also discovered, and by the 1970s it had become clear that fundamental changes were occurring interregionally within the United States, even if mainstream analysts misunderstood their nature (Watkins and Perry 1977).

Third, the metropolitan perspective forced researchers to consider the interactive effects of deconcentration, that is, the effects of suburbanization on the city and the effects of central city decline on suburban differentiation. This located suburban research within the broader tradition of urban-rural comparisons and the ecological analysis of metropolitan social spaces (Duncan and Reiss 1950; Wood 1959; Shevky and Bell 1975; Greer 1965). Accordingly, a picture of the metropolitan social order emerged by which suburbanites were considered to be relatively more middle-class, affluent, conservative, family-centered, white, professionally occupied, and politically active than were central city residents. In turn, central city populations were characterized as comprising greater proportions of minorities, ethnics, lower-income residents, the working class, and liberals; the central city was also the site for machine politics, primarily of the Democratic variety. Consequently, the metropolitan region as a whole in the 1960s came to be viewed as *ecologically* segregated by income, race, and life-style. An ambitious research agenda continues to be carried out which is concerned with the dimensions of this territorially manifested uneven development (Edmonston 1975). In fact, this research, which is almost wholly descriptive and which has not seemed in any way to have helped public policy lessen the inequitable nature of this segregation, has dominated the field of urban sociology for at least the past twenty years (Frey 1979; Jiobu and Marshall 1969; Bradford and Kelejian 1973; Coleman, Kelly, and Moore 1975; Kasarda and Redfearn 1975; Schnore and Winsborough 1972; Taueber and Taueber 1964). Such work has also illuminated the functional differentiation which has taken place between regions, especially the frostbelt and the sunbelt (Sternlieb and Hughes 1975; Burchell and Listokin 1981; South and Poston 1982).

Finally, research on the morphology of functional differentiation within metropolitan regions provided urban science with a range of special social problems which are viewed one way or the other as a consequence of metropolitan spatial differentiation. That is, the functional complexity of modern society arrayed according to demographic, economic, political, and cultural dimensions is viewed presently as deployed in space—thus the *spatial* arrangement of people and activities is said to lie at the core of a wide variety of contemporary problems associated with metropolitan life. However, these are viewed through the ideological spectacles of the dominant mainstream paradigm, discussed in the next chapter, which sees such deployment as an inevitable consequence of socioeconomic competition and functional differentiation. For example, urban inequities of all kinds have increasingly become viewed as a function of spatial deployment, so that social problems are seen to be caused by differences in location. Thus, the issue of racial segregation is viewed in terms of the spatial mismatch between job opportunities and available housing (Kain 1968); the issue of educational quality is viewed as a function of community segregation (Coleman 1976); the fiscal well-being of the city has emerged as an issue of spatial differentiation (Hill 1974); economic growth has become increasingly organized around inter- and intrametropolitan locational processes (Sternlieb and Hughes 1975); and the quality of community life is progressively viewed as an issue of regional community income segregation (Logan and Schneider 1981). The available evidence indicates that contemporary sociospatial patterns are increasingly inequitable with the segregation of races and income groups deployed throughout the metropolitan region. Consequently, sociospatial inequities are progressively more salient as public policy issues for local governments (Fainstein and Fainstein 1980; Megret 1981). While mainstream analysts have devoted considerable energy to describing these patterns, as we have seen, they have not come to terms with the fundamental connection between the ways in which our present society produces social inequities and its spatial manifestations (Thurow 1975; Gordon et al. 1982; Bluestone and Harrison 1982). One purpose of this discussion is to demonstrate the deep relationship between these two structural features of uneven development.

In summary, the study of the economic, political, and social problems comprising the bulk of the urban research agenda, which was always nominally or discursively labeled as ecological, has presently become dominated by an underlying spatial perspective which is regionally constituted and which is perceived as an analysis of locationally specific deployment patterns. This research is characterized, on the one hand, by the progressive use of spatial deployment as a means of discussing urban problems but, on the other hand, by a reluctance to question the way in which these sociospatial patterns are produced by the combined actions of systemic forces in society. It is precisely this latter issue which I wish to address in the following chapters and which calls for a new, critical paradigm of explanation for contemporary urban science. Currently, therefore, research on the massive restructuring of settlement space has grown into a global inquiry into the processes and activities associated with deconcentration: the internal differentiation of the metropolitan region, the differentiation of socioeconomic activities between entire regions of the country, and the massive deployment of uneven sociospatial development both within and between metropolitan regions in an aggravating cycle of boom-and-bust growth periods. These contemporary patterns, however, are currently described by a mainstream approach to urban science which holds an inaccurate image of settlement space and an ideologically distorted grasp of the forces which have produced it. As I shall discuss in chapter 2, there is a convergence of thought between each of the fields of urban science—that is, sociology, geography, and economics—around a core of assumptions associated with the theory of ecology. In what follows this approach will be unmasked as a weak way of understanding the sociospatial forces structuring and transforming settlement space.

In the most contemporary phase of deconcentration, suburban realms dominate the multicentered metropolitan regions throughout the United States. According to Muller (1981), in 1977 39.1 percent of the U.S. population resided in suburbs; 28.5 percent lived in central cities. In the largest metropolises, those containing more than 1 million residents, 61.3 percent of the population lived outside the central city (vs. 56.8 percent in 1970). Although rural areas contained 32.7 percent of the U.S. population in 1977, the greater proportion must be considered nonfarm and little different in life-style from other suburbanites (Fischer 1983). In fact, as observed above, current demographic trends reveal that rural areas are the fastest-growing of all the regional sectors and that the smallest towns are experiencing the greatest increases in population. This is a decidedly nonfarm, urban phenomenon (Kasarda 1980; Fuguitt and Voss 1979; Fuguitt and Beale 1978). Accordingly, if the polynucleated urban realm model is best at describing the current form of settlement space, then the urban growth of that space is presently unbounded. Deconcentration is affecting the farthest reaches of available land in the United States, and associated processes of internal differentiation within already developed regions, such as the central city, continue to dominate the growth patterns across the metropolitan continuum (Fuguitt and Heaton 1980; Vining and Strauss 1977; Berry and Dahman 1977).

No doubt the current depression in the housing industry has caused a considerable decrease in the rate of conversion of fringe area land. Metropolitan expansion has presently reached a stage where it has slowed down. However, this is merely a relative change in what has *always* been a cyclical phenomenon (see chapter 3). As I shall discuss in chapter 4, investment in real estate is always attractive, and there is some evidence to suggest that it retains its appeal even in times of depression. When studying investment in land it is important to be aware of the form that investment takes, as well as the level of funds which are cyclically being pumped into this activity. The uses to which land can be put, for example, are almost infinitely mutable. Consequently, the current slowdown in what was once a rapid expansion of metropolitan regions must be viewed as one part of other processes associated with the turnover in land which will now assume greater importance, such as changes in the internal differentiation of the metropolis—central city condominium conversion and mall construction, for example—and the shift to other, more intensive means of land development, such as office building. These latter processes are also part of what is meant by deconcentration, in addition to fringe area growth, because they transform the city and the sociospatial organization of the metropolitan region. In particular, one of the most dramatic consequences of deconcentration has been the massive restructuring of central city areas, especially in the Northeast and Midwest following two decades of urban renewal.

In the next chapters, I will demonstrate the need for new modes of thought which can address an understanding of the powerful forces that have altered settlement space in general and central cities in particular. Most mainstream analysts take the appearance of highrise office construction, for example, as a sign of the historical continuity of the central city's dominating influence within metropolitan regional organization. This misconception reveals the inherent weakness of mainstream thought, because it is dependent upon an outmoded interpretive paradigm. Since World War II, however, central city areas have been restructured as a consequence of the very same social forces which have caused the population dispersal to the suburbs and the sunbelt. In fact, this change within the city is part of the transformation of settlement space brought about by inter- and intrametropolitan processes of deconcentration. The eradication of ethnic enclaves, the growing marginalization of ghetto areas, the disappearance of manufacturing and of light industry from central cities, the flight of traditional commercial functions from the central business district despite the persisting signs of its redevelopment are all indicators that the central city of today differs greatly from what it has been in the past.

Despite the descriptive advances of ecology and geography and the proliferation of statistical analyses documenting the dimensions of deconcentration (soon to be exponentially increased as the 1980 census becomes available to the academic community), theoretical investigations into the reasons behind present sociospatial patterns are limited and weak. From a conventional perspective, we know what is taking place; however, we do not fully know *why*. This is not to say that urban theories do not exist. In fact, this discussion uses such work as a point of departure to forge a new synthesis of ideas about urban growth.

At present, by taking a state-of-the-art look at current theoretical modes of analysis for contemporary urban events and patterns, we can identify the following seven approaches: urban ecology, geography, and economics—which can be considered the mainstream view and which dominates academic production in the United States— marxian structuralism, urban political economy, neoweberianism, and the production of space perspective. Urban ecology, economics, and geography comprise the approaches typical of the overwhelming majority of urban analysts in the United States. The remaining perspectives have relatively fewer adherents; however, they are the consequence of intense intellectual activity occurring over the past decade by which the inadequacies of mainstream urban science have been exposed. The latter four formulations have emerged as alternatives to what is now perceived as the ideological stranglehold that mainstreamers have on the attempt to understand contemporary urban development. Even more fascinating, however, is the fact that the intense debate over proper perspectives has produced a kind of extended critique among alternate views. For example, urban ecology and geography remain severely hamstrung by a stubborn technological determinism through which urban deconcentration is explained largely in terms of innovations in the modes of transportation and communication.

Urban political economists, by contrast, in seeking to introduce a marxian interpretation of the urban process to replace the ideology of ecology, are constrained by an endemic functionalism. In essence, they view the mechanization of urban growth as a capitalist plot perpetrated by a select group of individuals on the bulk of the residents, who are called the working class (whatever that means in today's society). Urban ecologists scoff at the efforts of such marxists, while they in turn view the ecologists as ideological handmaidens of the ruling class. This is rather ironic because *both* views, as we shall see below, are essentially functionalist paradigms which are equally guilty of explaining causes by their effects and which share an over-emphasis on economic factors. One certain observation about this clash between equally limited versions of social science, however, is that ecologists of the technologically determinist variety dominate the institution of urban sociology at present. Consequently, alter-native approaches more interested in seeking the truth have been very slow to develop in the United States, because they have had to fight the forms of institutional constraint. When they have appeared they have come from *outside* the country. This is the case with the structuralism of Manuel Castells, who dismisses urban sociology as a bogus field of inquiry; with the neoweberian approach, which has developed in England as a response to the limitations of marx-ian structuralism but which shares Castells' ideological critique of ecology; and, finally, with the work of Henri Lefebvre in France on the production of space, which is at odds with the marxism of structuralists.

The following discussion introduces these alternate views but seeks to explain them by identifying the core analytical issues which have become responsible for such theoretical differences. That is, the focus of the present work will be on the issues that arise during the attempt to understand development patterns and sociospatial organi-zation. These issues will be isolated by discussing the seven broadly conceived approaches identified above. Thus, in addition to develop-ing a critical paradigm which can become the basis for a new urban science, it will also be necessary to encounter the debate between different versions of marxism and between alternate views on how best to analyze the contemporary mode of social organization. In short, the desire to forge a new approach to settlement space merges with the need to address long-neglected defects in the approach of historical materialism. By talking about settlement space and trying to understand the changes that have taken place there, we inevitably wind up talking about society in the same way.

In the final chapters of this discussion, I will present a synthesis of sociospatial analysis based partially upon the work of Lefebvre but incorporating the insights of other alternate approaches to under-standing sociospatial organization. And, by replacing the paradigm of mainstream analysis with an alternate critical perspective, I shall apply this synthesis to explaining the contemporary patterns of de-concentration in a manner which achieves a deep level of under-standing. This approach, called the social production of space, elevates the element of space to a principal focal point of analysis along with the workings of the economy and the state. This means that the contemporary form of metropolitan deconcentration can be approached principally as a historical and socially specific mode of *design* which can be understood by grasping the relationship between space and the elements of social organization, such as economics, politics, and ideological values. Urban analysis proceeds within such a context as a generalized understanding of the processes producing, sustaining, and reproducing settlement space.

Furthermore, the patterns of metropolitan regional deployment described by mainstream analysis are no longer accepted as isolated facts without design implications for social justice. That is, I seek not only to understand why the environment looks the way it does but also to appreciate the important fact that it does *not* have to look that way. There is nothing inevitable about the patterns of growth, despite the conservative thrust of mainstream theory which seeks to convince us of such inexorability. Although there are certain similarities in metropolitan development patterns between the United States and other countries, which we shall come to understand as being produced by the adoption of uniform practices of domination, there are distinct differences between the spread city, multiple-realm form of settlement space in the United States and the form of urban places elsewhere. Such comparative contrasts are merely indicators of a vast potential for design which remains unrealized by societies, rather than examples of spatial practices which I would like to see put into operation. That is, I am not advocating another society's approach as a counterexample to the current system in the United States, because urban planning in *every* society is a façade for power. My intent is to focus on the potential for the humanistic design of social environments, as yet untapped and unrealized, which can be made to guide the growth patterns of society—if a greater understanding of their malleability is accepted. Calling the contemporary form of spatial organization into question strikes at the very core of institutions and attitudes which perpetuate the myth that no genuine alternatives to the patterns of settlement space exist. Most important, I shall demonstrate below that not only is the form of space a social product, but so is its value. In short, space is a social construction in all its dimensions. This discovery means that what is presently accepted as accidental or epiphenomenal, the production of the environment, must become a directed object of social thought. Thus, the transformation of society must proceed by a conscious creation of new sociospatial relations linking the transformation of work with the transformation of community life.

The significance of the social production of space approach is that it seeks to unify the various fields of urban analysis by pursuing the observation that present-day problems of society seem increasingly to be articulated as issues of a spatial nature. Yet, if space is increasingly important today, why is this so? What is meant by spatial or territorial relations in society? How are the contemporary forms of settlement space produced? How can we understand the contemporary deconcentrated form? What is the relationship between space and class struggle, between the economy and space, between the state and space? In what ways does urban science fail, and in what ways is it revealed as an ideology? In what sense are marxian approaches similarly limited? Finally, how can we specify the articulation of social, political, and economic activities with space so as to capture the deployment patterns which produce the environment within which we all must live? It is this last, broad question, as we shall see below, which frames what I call the debate on the theory of space and which guides the organization of this discussion.

The main task before us involves the total reconceptualization of urban science, not merely the redefinition of its spatial forms. In chapter 2, I shall commence by considering the mainstream paradigm and its limitations. Most significant will be the realization that much of the work done by conventional analysts has long called its own explanatory foundation into question. In chapter 3, I shall consider the efforts of marxian political economists to provide an analysis of urban space appropriate to modern society. Early marxian research has challenged the assumptions and explanations of mainstream approaches. This perspective stresses the role of two separate processes which structure space: class conflict and the logic of capital accumulation. In the first case, the ecological emphasis on an equilibrating adjustment process has obscured the inequitable struggle over resources which patterns space, especially class conflict and the response of industries to labor militancy.

In the second case, marxian political economists have attempted to analyze urban development in more global terms by tracing the process of capital accumulation and its relationship to space. Instead of separating the city into nodes of functionally differentiated populations, as do mainstream analysts, marxists view it as an agglomeration which focuses the production of wealth spatially through the concentration of labor power and of capital. The sociospatial changes within the city are ruled by the logic of capital accumulation, and the end result of this process in a capitalist society is uneven development and social inequities which are deployed spatially as well as demographically. Inequalities of class and race along with differentials in the supply of social services are most characteristic of the metropolitan sociospatial milieu. The built environment has become the scene of boom-and-bust cycles in the property market, with blight and overconstruction existing side by side. Both these phenomena are produced by the very same process of city building under capitalist social relations; that is, uneven growth is intrinsic to the capitalist nature of development. In short, the approach of marxian political economy explains in a more truthful way the observable patterns of urban development by transforming traditional marxian concepts in a manner suitable to the analysis of space.

Despite the relative success of marxian political economy as an alternative to mainstream thought, it nevertheless possesses certain distinct limitations. These are identified as ones which have plagued marxism in general for quite some time. Thus, a desire to articulate a critical paradigm in the analysis of space forces us to face and resolve fundamental issues in the contemporary development of marxist thought. These include the inability of marxian political economy to break away from the ideological categories of mainstream economic reasoning, especially its shared emphasis on economic growth as the central social subject of thought; the scourge of positivism, in particular the penchant for replacing monocausal, deterministic arguments on the mainstream side with marxian versions of the same thing; and, finally, the imprecise way in which the state-society articulation is specified, which undercuts the ability of the marxian approach to address political phenomena within settlement space. Furthermore, marxian political economists have reproduced the spatial inadequacies of orthodox reasoning by focusing on the model of the bounded city form. Although some marxists have addressed deconcentration in certain limited ways, as we shall see, they persist in talking about the "built environment" instead of spatial organization and about the "city" instead of the polynucleated metropolitan region. More significantly, marxian political economists treat the city as a phenomenal form in the exact manner as do mainstreamers—namely, as the focus for accumulation tendencies which require, in a functionalist sense, a centralized agglomeration. In this way, spatial forms are little more than containers of economic and political processes. Consequently, much of the critique of mainstream analysis is also applicable to marxian political economy, even though the latter possesses a much more accurate theory of urban location.

In chapter 4 I shall examine more comprehensive approaches that address the issue of space in a generalized sense and from the marxian tradition. The question which is faced involves the need to go beyond the ideological trap of equating urban analysis with detailed economic investigations by specifying the articulation between the system of social organization in its totality, on the one hand, and the organization of space, on the other. The need for a marxian approach which takes into account the many levels of social organization, including the political and the cultural as well as the economic, has pushed analysis toward very broadly based conceptualizations of the society-space articulation. Consequently, important contributions to marxian analysis have been made through this endeavor; it has sharpened the critical grasp of sociospatial organization in modern society. In a section called "The Debate on the Theory of Space," the two main theories connecting social with spatial organization are contrasted: the Althusserian reading of urban science by Manuel Castells and the sociospatial dialectical approach of Henri Lefebvre. The contrast between these alternative perspectives, each deriving from different conceptions of marxism, is quite explicit because in many ways the work of the former can be interpreted as a structuralist rejoinder to the work of the latter.

Castells' approach demands attention both for its critique of mainstream urban ecology and for the unique way in which the state-space articulation is specified. In contrast to conventional urban analysis, which ignores the role of the state in structuring space, Castells asserts that the city is as much a product of the state as it is of the economy. His work focuses on the unique aspect of urban social processes, namely, the conjunction between the supply of social services provided by government and the reproduction of the labor force according to the needs of capital. Through the analysis of this intersection, which Castells calls collective consumption, urban social movements and politics within the locus of the bounded city form are explained.

Despite the many strengths of this formulation, the Althusserian reading of Marx commits serious conceptual errors, and Castells has fallen victim to these in his analysis of the city. In essence, a concern for space and for a marxian political posture with regard to Late Capitalist development processes has been sacrificed in favor of the analysis of certain theoretical questions divorced from praxis. Through the influence of Castells, especially his theory of collective consumption, the marxian approach to space has been transformed largely into an academic exercise. It has become a mode of discourse, however insightful, which has replaced the call for sociospatial political action by Lefebvre that was once used as an effective instrument of praxis during the events of May 1968 in France.

According to Lefebvre, the basis of capitalist hegemony is the existing property relations underlying society at its deepest level. Only by addressing the nature of these relations and by transforming them can the class struggle succeed in creating a humanist society. Lefebvre, however, is no pamphleteer. Like those of other marxists, his political assessments are grounded in a well-articulated theoretical analysis of contemporary life. In fact, Lefebvre today is perhaps the elder statesman of marxian social philosophy. For over a decade in France he has been applying himself to the analysis of urban life. The end result of this work is his 1974 *La production de l'espace*, which has never before been analyzed in the English-speaking world. In chapter 4 the entire intellectual production of Lefebvre on space is compared and assessed along with that of Castells.

The confrontation between structuralism and marxian dialectics found in chapter 4 raises issues involving spatial analysis which are added to the ones emerging from the critique of mainstream urban science by marxian political economy. While Lefebvre, for example, has progressed far in articulating a theory of space for modern society which includes cultural and political factors as well as economic analysis, several issues central to the development of a critical paradigm which can replace the mainstream approach remain unresolved. In chapter 5 I address these issues, which include the manner in which it is possible to perform a class analysis of sociospatial organization and a specification of the process of capital accumulation in space. These particular discussions allow us to survey the contemporary literature on urban subjects by those analysts straining to break free of conventional thought. As a result it becomes possible either to address fundamental issues which have not been resolved so far or, if this task proves impossible, then to make seemingly intractable problems as clear as can be for future work.

The synthesis proposed in chapters 5 and 6 contains the following properties. It specifies the ways in which actions by social groups are involved in the production of space according to the interactive and dialectical correspondences established by the unique structural features specific to capitalist society. The synthesis argues against the common marxian notion that material relations are manifested directly in space and dismisses as simplistic explanations for sociospatial patterns which do little more than label them as produced by "capitalism" or, even more anthropomorphically, by "capitalists." In place of such assertions, spatial production is analyzed as the material manifestation of complex social processes associated with the phases of capitalist development. However, sociospatial patterns and interactive processes are seen as constituting contingent outcomes of the many *contradictory* relations interacting in the capitalist mode, rather than as direct products of either capitalist intentions or structural machinations. The leading edge of these relations, moreover, is conceptualized as uniquely embedded in the activities of the property sector, described in detail in chapter 6. Thus, spatial and social relations are dialectically related. If the needs of capital are manifested in space, then spatial changes are manifested in the needs of capital.

Having developed a conceptual way of analyzing the production of space which is based upon materialism, I devote chapter 7 to a discussion of the contemporary form of settlement space. The unique feature of present-day patterns involves the restructuring of sociospatial organization by the combined effects of Late Capitalist social process and the spatial process of deconcentration. Patterns of deconcentration and their internal differentiation are considered the central focus for urban science. Explanations for these features derive from the critical perspective, and these are contrasted with the limited attempts of mainstream science. At present the city-country opposition no longer characterizes growth in the United States, as it does in so many other industrialized nations which still possess precapitalist relations prevailing in rural settings. The deconcentrated, polynucleated region depends as much upon the operation of Late Capitalist relations in agriculture as it does in industry—so that space is transformed by "modern landed property" at both ends of the metropolitan region. Chapter 7 concludes with an analysis of the restructuring of urban functional integration across regions, sometimes known as the shift to the sunbelt, which is at direct odds with mainstream explanations. In particular, what is taken to be a natural process of societal evolution is unveiled as an uncoordinated form of profit taking aided by the state and involving the manipulation of spatial patterns by vested interests operating within the property sector. The thoroughness of this critique of conventional thought, along with the material developed in chapters 2 and 3, adds up to a formidable paradigm which sweeps away the last remaining credible threads of mainstream spatial theory.

The outcome of contemporary sociospatial restructuring has been the production of uneven development. While this concept as used here involves both a spatial and a social dimension, its most important feature is the toll taken in personal lives by the inequitable nature and dehumanized design features of the production of space under existing social relations. The mainstream notion of equitable adjustment generated by interaction between large numbers of relatively equal social actors is unveiled as a falsehood. Thus, the need for a new conceptual paradigm becomes more than academic when we examine contemporary urban policy. Mainstreamers wish us to believe that growth patterns reflect some efficient adjustment process involving demographic change and technological innovation. If municipalities have problems because of sociospatial disparities, for example, little should be done about them because the global view reveals that they are produced by social forces which are "natural." Tampering with the manner in which this society develops, it is alleged, can only hinder the organic way in which we are evolving. A reading of urban public policy documents in recent years exposes the shocking extent to which the above ideology has influenced administrative ideas. Yet, recent alternatives proposed by leftist liberals which have attempted to counter the sentiments of neoconservatives suffer from the very same limitations plaguing reformist approaches for quite some time, especially a shared emphasis on promoting economic growth at the expense of transforming all social relations. The choice between neoconservative and left-liberal alternatives to national public policy is really no choice at all.

In a concluding chapter on urban public policy, I will address ways in which a qualitatively new mode of sociospatial reasoning can present alternatives that break through the limitations offered by existing choices. Consequently, a reconstructed sociospatial policy is seen to depend upon work which refines further the critical paradigm analyzing sociospatial organization and which leads us to contemplate utopian approaches to design that have their roots in the nineteenth century, a prospect once considered anathema by marxists and mainstreamers alike. Such an inquiry redirects thought away from equating the quality of community life with economic growth and toward more transformative social actions.

2. Urban Ecology, Economics, and Geography: Spatial Analysis in Transition

Current knowledge about spatial environments in modern society is divided among the several specialties of urban science, including sociology, economics, and geography. I call these the mainstream or conventional approaches because, as institutionalized modes of inquiry, they draw upon a paradigm which I consider outdated. There are two distinct sources of criticism of these fields. The first is internal to mainstream or conventional thought itself and represents the process by which these fields have developed as academic disciplines. The second is the assault on conventional theory from the marxian tradition or, rather, from several distinct perspectives deriving from marxism. In the discussion below I shall focus on mainstream thought while leaving an extended look at the marxian challenge for the next few chapters.

URBAN ECOLOGY

From its earliest conceptions social thought, in general, attempted to connect community forms with the processes of social organization. Eventually in such early arguments the spatial array of the city itself would be invoked as illustrative of one aspect of this relationship, especially as its material manifestation. Thus Comte saw cities as the "real organs" of the social organism in a complex biological analogy which viewed other aspects of social life as cells, tissues, and so on (1875). It was Spencer, however, who articulated the first direct relationship between social form and function through his concept of species competition. He did so by utilizing Darwin's theory of evolution in order to explain the functional role that species competition played in the production of social organizations possessed of increasing complexity (1909). In particular, Spencer asserted that in both the biological and the societal cases physical size led to functional differentiation, conceived of socially as the division of labor (Turner 1978: 21). Such a view became the cornerstone of mainstream urban thought in the twentieth century and its first theoretical formulations in the approach known as urban ecology.

The early advocates of the sociological perspective (Spencer, Comte, and Durkheim) drew heavily in their theorizing upon the biological analogy between the structure of society and that of lifeforms. As Giddens has indicated, this fostered an early version of the systems perspective because collectivities were seen not as mere aggregates of individuals but as interdependent and as possessed of emergent properties which were considered to be equilibrium-seeking in nature (1979: 237). In this regard, the form which the social environment assumed could be treated successfully as a *physical* manifestation of the processes of social organization, a mode of thought common to all the urban sciences today. Furthermore, the biological analogy which became the basis for ecological theorizing was also carried over into urban sociology, economics, and geography. That is, these three fields possess a common basis in a theoretical dependency, however nonexclusive, upon human ecology. According to the ecological approach, the spatial arrangements of urban settlements represent the accommodation of social organization to its physical environment (Park 1925). For example, according to one pioneer of the urban sociological perspective, McKenzie:

> In the absence of any precedent let us tentatively define human ecology as a study of the spatial and temporal relations of human beings as affected by the selective, distributive and accommodative forces of the environment. (1925: 64)

This important correlation between ecological patterns and social processes is also a cornerstone of urban geography. As Herbert indicates, "A basic assumption in a geographical perspective is that spatial organization is in itself of some significance in understanding patterns of human activity" (1972: 19). Thus, a focus on the ecological approach to space grasps the theoretical underpinning of urban sociology, economics, and geography. In fact, early ecology at the Chicago School was in a real sense a fusion of these fields.

The first theoretical issue raised by the ecological perspective is already amply in evidence, namely, the usefulness of the biological analogy. The organicism at the base of ecological thought constitutes a serious limitation which prevails at present (Hawley 1950), even though its earliest pioneers treated such an analogy with considerable caution (McKenzie 1925). A second issue also surfaced relatively early in regard to the work of urban ecologists in the 1920s and 1930s, that is, the work associated with the early Chicago School. At that time two distinct traditions were articulated as part of the ecological approach. On the one hand, the behavioral emphasis, which was dominant initially, focused on the innate characteristics of the human species that compel interaction to assume specific forms of organization, such as the demographic deployment of people within the city. On the other hand, the social science emphasis was on objects of analysis considered as *sui generis* group reifications or social system attributes of formal living, such as the functional division of labor in the city. This distinction is difficult to comprehend in practice and often leads either to the misunderstanding of social theory or to the misplaced criticism of theory, as lacking an emphasis which it has chosen to lack (e.g., as in voluntarism's critique of structuralism because it ignores individual behavior). It is clear, however, that urban ecology can be separated into two phases by this distinction. The first constitutes the pre–World War II Chicago School approach to theory, which focused on behaviorist or sociobiogenic factors as the explanator of spatial patterns, while the second is the postwar perspective, located in several places, which emphasizes a systemic view of societal adjustments to the environment that are a consequence of fundamental social forces, such as economic competition. Our discussion of urban ecology, therefore, will be organized around these two phases.

The Chicago School

The principal practitioners of the early Chicago School approach to ecology were Robert E. Park, Ernest W. Burgess, and Roderick D. McKenzie. Although these three shared the same theoretical sensibility, they specialized in emphasizing different applications of the ecological approach to urban sociology. At the outset of inquiry in the 1920s, for example, there was an acknowledged understanding that concrete research of the city would uncover the organized operation of formal principles of human behavior. This meant that urban patterns were to be explained by what Park called human nature. Importantly, if this had been conceptualized as a constant influence, it could *not* have been able to explain the spatial variation observed in the different areas of the city. Instead, however, human nature was conceived of as the meshing of two distinct species-specific urges: the biotic and the cultural. The biotic urge gave rise to forms of spatial organization which were produced by the social Darwinist force of competition. According to Park, under a system of laissez-faire economics, the struggle for survival in a bounded space led to a functional division of labor: "The city offers a market for the special talents of individual men. Personal competition tends to select for each special task the individual who is best suited to perform it" (Park, Burgess, and McKenzie 1925: 2). In this way Park explains the spatial order of the city, as opposed to rural environments, as an emergent property of economic competition and its resulting division of labor. Thus:

> The multiplication of occupations and professions within the limits of the urban population is one of the most striking and least understood aspects of modern life. From this point of view, we may, if we choose, think of the city, that is to say, the place and the people, with all the machinery and administrative devices that go with them, as organically related; a kind of psycho-physical mechanism in and through which private and political interests find not merely a collective but a corporate expression. (1936: 2)

The cultural dimension, in contrast, which was also seen as differentiating space, followed from the assumption that human beings are communicating animals. According to the Chicago School, social interaction proceeded through symbolic exchanges, mutual understandings, and the exercising of freedom of choice—which compelled individuals to cooperate as well as compete with each other. This enabled collectivities to arrive at a consensus about personal conduct, called a moral order. The moral order was comprised of shared sentiments which evolved over time but which were locationally specific. Thus variation in the sectors of the city, which were tied together by an economic division of labor, was produced by the overlay of moral orders through competitive-cooperation. According to Park:

> In the course of time every section and quarter of the city takes on something of the character and qualities of its inhabitants. Each separate part of the city is inevitably stained with the peculiar sentiments of its population. The effect of this is to convert what was at first a mere geographical expression into a neighborhood, that is to say, a locality with sentiments, traditions and a history of its own. (Park, Burgess, and McKenzie 1925: 95)

In Park's urban sociology, therefore, the cultural dimension was fused onto a biotic base. In practice, however, urban ecology became progressively more reliant upon the sociobiogenic aspects of human interaction as a mode of explanation and theory. Thus, urban ecology came to stress economic factors as central to spatial organization. This occurred by conscious choice. As Berry and Kasarda have noted:

> Park was careful to point out that every human community actually was organized simultaneously on the biotic and cultural levels. He contended, however, that the proper focus for human ecology was the biotic level. Analysis of the decision to exclude ideational factors from the scope of human ecology eventually led to a substantial amount of polemics, and to a split among sociologists investigating ecological problems. (1977: 4)

Implied in Park's decision, however, was the belief that by separating out the cultural or "nonrational" values, which were commonly known to vary widely across the world's communities as well as within each city, the more universal aspects of human behavior at work in economic competition and natural selection could be isolated. In short, the early work of the Chicago School might qualify as a version of political economy, in the nonmarxist sense, because of its emphasis on the effects of economic organization and competitive processes in explaining aggregate patterns of social behavior. This affinity between social theorizing on the nature of urban space and neoclassical economic theories of location became the unifying impulse behind the diverse urban fields.

The early Chicago School maintained a behavioral perspective by connecting human behavior with economic competition and social order with the spatial deployment of the division of labor. In addition, its members turned their backs on the importance of cultural values in social interaction in order to strive for the isolation of specific sociobiogenic impulses which could be generalized to all cities as helping to structure space. The latter choice came to frame early criticisms of the Chicago School, as we shall see next. This perspective evolved within a framework which virtually equated urban sociology with ecology. In sum, the early Chicago School posed three theoretical assertions: the efficacy of the biological analogy, the use of social Darwinist principles to explain human behavior, and the relegation of symbolic values to the realm of social psychology as secondary to the primacy of economic competition.

These elements were brought together by McKenzie and Burgess to explain urban form, especially its land-use patterns. According to McKenzie, the fundamental quality in the struggle for existence was "position" or the locationally specific aspect of an individual, institution, or collectivity. McKenzie conceived of spatial relations as dependent upon the forces of economic competition and functional selection. These affected spatial position and, as physical locations altered under the sway of these forces, social relationships were also said to change. To this essentially laissez-faire economic framework, McKenzie added biological processes such as the "Internal Structure Cycle" of invasion, competition, succession, and accommodation— that is, a cycle of competition between populations of living organisms over spatial location. This was used to explain the way in which different ethnic groups or economic functions sifted spatially through the various areas of the city. In this way, McKenzie explained land-use patterns as the product of generalized ecological processes and an economic division of labor, which deployed objects and activities in space according to their functional roles. As he states:

> The general effect of the continuous processes of invasions and accommodations is to give to the developed community well defined areas, each having its own peculiar selective and cultural characteristics. Such units of communal life may be termed "natural areas," or formations to use the term of the plant ecologist. In any case, these areas of selection and function may comprise many subformations or associations which become part of the organic structure of the district or of the community as a whole. It has been suggested that these natural areas or formations may be defined in terms of land values, the point of highest land value representing the center or head of the formation (not necessarily the geographic center, but the economic or cultural center), while the points of lowest land value represent the periphery of the formation or boundary line between two adjacent formations. (1925: 7–8)

Thus McKenzie, as had Park, explained the spatial deployment of the city in a more developed ecological formulation. He converted the ecological forces which were functions of "position" into a spatial location theory derived from biogenic competition over land. It was left for Burgess to paint the picture of the Chicago School's theory of space.

In this work Burgess followed the earlier approaches of Von Thunen (1966) and Weber (1899) in developing his classic concentric zone model of urban form. In essence Burgess (along with McKenzie) was concerned with articulating an explanation for change in land-use patterns, especially by relating this change in the internal differentiation of the city to the process of urban growth. Over the years this theory of metropolitan expansion has become the central organizing topic in orthodox theories of space, as we shall see when we discuss the postwar school below. Essential to Burgess' picture was the notion of centrality—that is, the center of the city, by virtue of that position and as the result of a historical process of agglomeration, dominated the spatial competition around it. As the city population grew in size, competition and the increasingly specialized division of labor would trigger two additional ecological processes, called centralization and decentralization, which were a functional version of the invasion-succession cycle.

According to Burgess, the city grew by a dual process of central agglomeration and commercial decentralization, as new businesses arose in fringe areas as well as the central business district in order to meet the needs of the functionally differentiated activities throughout the expanding region. Thus the city grew outward because functions which lost out in central city competition were relocated to peripheral areas. This in turn led to further spatial differentiation as activities were deployed according to competitive advantages. Burgess hypothesized that in time the city would take on the form of a central business district which would be the area of highest competitive land prices, surrounded by four concentric rings (1925: 51).

The early Chicago School practitioners had a cultivated appreciation for the actions of land speculators less prevalent today among urban ecologists (see, e.g., Hughes 1928). Burgess believed that the undeveloped holdings of such agents surrounding the central business district, coupled with the unfavorable proximity of residential structures to industrial enterprises, created a neglected slum adjacent to the center which he called the zone in transition. Blighted homes divided up into rooms by speculator landlords waiting for redevelopment and the further expansion of the central business district drew the "seedier" elements of the population as residents. These included transients, hoboes, the urban poor, newly arrived immigrants, and "radicals." This served to further propel well-to-do elements of the population away from the central business district and, in short, gave the city a bad name.

In subsequent chapters, I shall indicate that the zone in transition is really one case of a phenomenon Harvey (1976) calls the devaluation of the built environment, which is viewed as a necessary part of the capitalist urban growth process. That is, along with growth there is an internal production of uneven development in the spatial patterns of the built environment. Rather than being an aberration in an otherwise equilibrating process of change, blight is built into the way in which urban development proceeds in this society

(Scott 1980). For Burgess the slum was not a residential shell produced by an uncaring group of renters but the direct product of land speculation and economic competition. In this way he also recognized an uneven development process which only later became important to marxian analysis but whose theoretical content was ignored by mainstreamers.

Behind the zone of transition in Burgess' model were located the residential rings of the city—determined by people's relative ability to afford commuting costs, because most jobs were conceived of as remaining tied locationally to the central areas. As he indicates:

> A third area is inhabited by the workers in industries who have escaped from the area of deterioration but who desire to live within easy access to work. Beyond this zone is the "residential" area of high class apartment buildings or exclusive "restricted" districts of single family dwellings. Still further, out beyond the city limits, is the commuter's zone—suburban areas, or satellite cities—within a thirty to sixty-minute ride of the central business district. (1925: 50)

The work of the early Chicago School on the relationship between social organization and space culminates, therefore, in Burgess' concentric zone model. This is both a picture of urban land use and a model of metropolitan expansion and internal differentiation; it represents the ideas of Park, McKenzie, and others in addition to Burgess. In short, it signifies the prewar Chicago School's ecological theory of urban space, and its contribution to that endeavor is threefold.

First, Burgess' model explains the urban residential, industrial, and commercial array in terms of the ecological theory of competition over "position" or location. This sociospatial approach was further extended by Burgess himself through the notion of centrality. Thus all positions are not equal in spatial competition—there exists a hierarchy of locations and the central position dominates this hierarchy by virtue of being at the center. Clearly, such a model implies that economic and political forces require centrality in order to organize social activities. Such an implication became the major debating point between Burgess' approach and that of others. Second, the model explains the expansion and internal differentiation of the enlarged metropolitan region by McKenzie's very same theory organized around the "Internal Structure Cycle," especially its processes of invasion and succession, along with two regional processes: centralization and decentralization. Finally, Burgess revealed that the internal differentiation of the urban land area represented a social pathology gradient from the center to the periphery. That is, personal attributes which were logically *unrelated*—such as mental illness, marital status, ethnic or racial background, and crime rates—were hypothesized as clustering in zones along the radial dimension of the city. Traversing the urban form from the central business district to the periphery, Chicago School researchers, using official city and census data, found that the incidence of social pathology decreased while homeownership and nuclear-family status increased. The inner zones, therefore, were discovered to be the areas of much crime, illness, gang warfare, broken homes, and virtually every other social indicator of disorganization. The vast bulk of this work became a distinctive part of what is presently considered to be urban sociology.

In sum, the Burgess model of urban form documented spatially the way in which the city was the playground of competition between social groups and economic forces, believed by the early Chicago School to be propelled by biogenic drives. This model provided evidence for an antiurban bias which connected seemingly unrelated aspects of social pathology to the deployment of the built environment; thus urban sociology came to be personified by the study of social problems. The collective contribution of the early Chicago School has been summarized succinctly by Martindale as follows:

> One may sum up Park's conception of the city in a sentence:
> the city represents an externally organized unit in space
> produced by laws of its own. The precise statement of this ex-
> ternal organization of the city in space—the badge by which
> the ecological theory is most quickly identified—was made by
> Ernest W. Burgess. The systematic statement of its inner
> "laws" was the work of Roderick McKenzie. (1962: 23)

In retrospect, the guiding hand of Park proves most interesting for our discussion to follow, in that for the Chicago School spatial organization emerged from the outcomes of social interaction in a manner akin to Darwin's evolutionary forces or Smith's "Invisible Hand." Ecological drives were self-regulating or equilibrating and thus by implication socially useful (Park 1936). According to Suttles, the urban mosaic was not "the planned or artificial contrivance of anyone." Park, Burgess, and McKenzie emphasized that spatial patterning developed out of the "many independent personal decisions based on moral, political, ecological, and economic considerations" (Suttles 1973: 8). There is a certain appreciation for social forces as playing an equal, interdependent role in the life of the city, as well as an implied understanding that interaction within a space conceived of as a container produces the patterns which we subsequently observe through the mechanism of some organic invisible hand. Regional patterns of growth, therefore, are believed to be the inevitable product of ecological competition among large numbers of *individuals*. To be sure, the early ecologists considered the group basis of interaction (Thrasher 1963). This was conceptualized, however, without benefit of class or consumption considerations and was distinctly focused on the individualistic nature of social collectivities. It is this doctrine which was carried forward explicitly in the later writing of ecologists and which serves to frame the ideological bias at the very core of ecological thought. Such a belief in the inexorable production of environmental design is, from the perspective of this discussion, the key point of contention between mainstream and alternative approaches to space.

The urbanization theory of the early Chicago School began to receive a critical response in the 1930s (Davie 1937; Hoyt 1933; Alihan 1938; Harris and Ullman 1945; Gettys 1940; Firey 1945; Form 1954). Contentiousness over theoretical assertions surfaced during this time, especially over the Chicago School's reluctance to recognize the important role which cultural values played in the determination of locational decisions and its reliance on economic competition as paramount in social interaction. In addition, however, Alihan raised another issue, namely, that taken as a whole ecologists used the term "community" to specify both an empirical reality and an abstract unit of ecological organization (1938). In this way the Chicago School confused the "real" with its "theoretical" object of analysis and thus failed to move in the direction of greater theoretical clarity. This limitation, in particular, proved fatal to Burgess' concentric zone model, which could not hold up under a comparative analysis and which, as its critics maintained, was misguided even as an ideal type (Hoyt 1933; Harris and Ullman 1945). It is Castells, however, who has clarified the debate touched off over human ecology's early beginnings. The opposition of "culturist" to "naturalist" factors by critics merely shifts the ecological approach's emphasis but does not solve the spatial problematic (1977: 121). A theory of space necessarily needs to select from a wide range of factors in order to develop internally consistent concepts and the analytical relations between them for an explanation of settlement space patterns.

It may seem ironic that a marxist would criticize nonmarxists for leaning too heavily on economics as an explanatory factor, yet this is precisely what Castells has in mind when he categorizes ecology as a form of "vulgar materialism." But, according to Castells, the voluntaristic criticism of ecology does not go beyond faulting the Chicago School for its choice of theoretical factors and its conscious process of analytical exclusion, however ill conceived it may be. This altered emphasis does not propel us any closer to a theory of settlement space production—except by showing the limitations of all one-sided approaches which do not take into account the multifactorial basis of social organization. As Castells states:

> In fact, the problematic proper to any theory of space does not consist in opposing values and "natural" factors but, on the epistemological plane, in discovering structural laws or the composition of historically given situations and, on the strictly theoretical plane, in establishing hypotheses as to the dominant factor of a structure in which, obviously, all schools include the totality of elements of social life. (1977: 121)

Thus our focus on developing a theory of space compels us to raise a series of analytical questions regarding the limitations of the early Chicago School. For example, what are the important factors in the production of space? What is the relationship between economic, political, and cultural interests? What is the relationship of these three to land-use decisions? To what extent does central location imply spatial dominance? What factors contribute to metropolitan expansion and what is the relationship between them in the production of space? What is the relationship between innate biogenic drives and territorial organization? Finally, what model of urban land-use patterns is closest to the empirical reality of modern American metropolitan regions? As we shall see, subsequent approaches to space have addressed these and other related questions in a framework of growing sophistication regarding the analysis of settlement space.

Contemporary Urban Ecology

Following World War II, the ecological tradition was resurrected. One important reason for this was that the urban areas of the United States had quite suddenly matured. Results from the 1950 census indicated to sociologists that a significant expansion of the metropolitan spatial reach was under way due to the process of suburbanization. A second reason arose from the growing awareness of economists and geographers that the progression of differentiation in city functions during the national effort of the war years had resulted in considerable regional, even international, integration of productive activities. Economists responded to such maturation by articulating a marginal theory of location and a regional approach to economics, while ecologists went in two seemingly related but different directions. On the one hand, they revamped the theory of human ecology (Hawley 1950), and on the other they proposed a formal scheme of analysis called the ecological complex (Schnore 1957, 1961; Duncan and Schnore 1959; Duncan 1961). The latter theory has been so well critiqued by others that I shall not discuss it here (Castells 1977).

Both of these refurbished approaches were organized around a response to the culturist critique. One important observation regarding this activity is that the new theory of human ecology proposed by Amos Hawley played a principal role in consolidating the efforts of orthodox urban economists and geographers into a unified mainstream approach to the built environment. Previous critiques of ecology from neomarxist (Castells 1977) and neoweberian (Saunders 1981) contexts have not appreciated the central role of Hawley's work in contemporary urban thought, nor have they sought to assess it with the same rigor devoted to the earlier, more vulnerable exponents of the Chicago School. In what follows I shall attempt to remedy this. Let us, therefore, turn to a consideration of Hawley's work.

By far the most ambitious theoretical project unveiled during the postwar years was the 1950 publication of *Human Ecology*. This represented a concerted attempt by Hawley to retain the core of biological organism in a purely sociostructural analysis of city growth and development which was divested of culturist elements. Furthermore, Hawley remained true to the original project of the Chicago School in that he proposed a theory of metropolitan growth which would explain urban form. In order to carry out this task he performed several conceptual operations on the Park-Burgess-McKenzie model. First, he deemphasized spatial form per se in favor of focusing on the interdependent functional network of spatial organization. This view was an extension of McKenzie's functional analysis of regional metropolitan growth (1933). Hawley drew directly upon McKenzie's use of functional interdependence and of the importance of locational position as central concepts in his model of ecological organization. I shall return to these ideas, since they complement the basis for urban economics' and geography's mainstream theories of urban location.

Second, Hawley upgraded the ecologists' object of analysis, the "community," to an abstract theoretical status, while retaining the organism at the root of ecological thought. This was done in order to avoid the conceptual confusion, pointed out by Alihan in the early Chicago School's work, created by the use of the community as both an empirical object of research and a theoretical concept employed to explain that same research. Hawley's approach was concerned with explaining the origin and development of community settlement space through the operation of abstract biogenic forces internal to the community itself. His is, therefore, a horizontal analysis which sees urban spatial organization as emanating from the center of the city. Focusing on the interdependence of Darwin's "web of life" rather than on the competitive aspects of the struggle for survival, Hawley identified a twofold relational consequence of spatial co-existence arising from the use by the same species of one community habitat. He thus elevated the "cooperative" aspect of Park's competitive-cooperation to a prime generative factor in the functional order of society.

Hawley's benign view of interaction depended upon "symbiotic relationships" or the "mutual dependence between unlike organisms," such as the predator-prey relationship or the less sanguine one between legumes and nematodes, and "commensal relationships" or the cooperation due to supplementary similarities within the same species because "we all have to eat from the same table" (1950: 36, 39). One limitation with this abstract approach to community spatial organization was that it neglected to explain the spatial form of the cities of that time. This need, however, went unfulfilled within the parameters of the model of the ecological community; it was met instead by a return to Burgess' picture of concentric zones. Hawley's work proceeded, therefore, in the same manner as neoclassical economics, with an abstract model of reality based upon simplifying assumptions—in his case all social relations could be reduced to the biogenically cooperative ones above; in the urban economists' case we possess among other things "perfect competition." In both instances, apparently, the need to make images of urban space conform to observable patterns of sociospatial organization was not as important as the abstract exercise of deducing models of the urban community floating in a reified, two-dimensional space organized by horizontally deployed forces emanating from the city center. Thus, the urban geographers' picture of the city, based as it was upon the charting of material forms, began to differ from the abstractions of ecologists and economists at this time, and such a division of labor has remained characteristic of these disciplines ever since.

On the basis of functional interdependence, spatial differentiation, and the biogenic relationships outlined above, Hawley derived an explanation for the internal stratification of the ecological community which avoided either the use of the marxian concept of class or the weberian concept of status; it offered instead an organicist explanation for the stratification of wealth and resources. Furthermore, this social order, as we have already seen, was based upon the symbiotic impulse instead of on the competitive struggle for survival, thus explaining the inequitable distribution of social resources without the need to mention conflict, indeed, as produced through "cooperation"! There is to my mind no clearer illustration of the ideological nature of conventional thought than this one. As Hawley states:

> Symbiosis, for example, does not exist uniformly among all individuals in the communal aggregate, and among those who are so connected the relation may occur in varying degrees of directness. The community presents the aspect of a cluster of symbiotic groupings through which are mediated the relations of individuals to the population at large. Likewise, commensalism is not at all times constant throughout the community. It appears mainly among individuals of similar functions. And, since functional differentiation is a fundamental characteristic of the community, commensalism tends to occur disjunctively in each functional category. From the standpoint of this relationship, the community may be conceived as a series of layers or strata. (1950: 209)

During the cold war period of the 1950s in the United States, therefore, we witness the appearance of an abstract formulation for stratified urban social organization which does not mention class, status, or power and which strips society of all conflict over the inequitable distribution of social wealth.

A third feature of Hawley's theory is his specification of the central focus of human ecology as the process by which the community adapts collectively to its environment. Because the latter was assumed to be constantly changing through endogenous and exogenous influences, community development was conceived of in a dynamic way. This replaced the more descriptive and static view of the community characterizing the early Chicago School. The emphasis on collective adaption pushed ecology into the Parsonian world of "equilibrium-seeking" systems which further denied a view of society as possessing various problems arising from its class nature and which ignored the effects of racism, economic inequality, and uneven spatial development in settlement space. This theoretical convergence with Parsonianism is one aspect of the more global convergence within mainstream urban science in the 1950s around a core of ideas which insulated itself against marxist thought. The focus on urban systems as being oriented principally toward adaption rather than a struggle over inequitable resources prevails as a central focus of the field of ecology even today, as Berry and Kasarda indicate:

The central problem of contemporary ecological inquiry is understanding how a population organizes itself in adapting to a constantly changing yet restricting environment. The adaption is considered to be a collective phenomenon, resulting from the population developing a functionally integrated organization through the accumulative and frequently repetitive actions of large numbers of individuals. (1977: 12)

The above is a perfect example of what passes for mainstream urban science today, namely, the use of mystifying abstraction and an emphasis on a noncontentious process of adjustment and functional integration to hide the important concrete issues of everyday life arising from the unequal distribution of resources, which both Weber and Marx recognized as a principal driving force of social history.

As I have indicated, the intent of Hawley's *Human Ecology* was to articulate a theory of settlement space. Thus, the dynamic processes of ecological adaption were used to explain the nature of community morphology and territorial expansion. In the pursuit of this central focus for his work, infused as it was with a benign view of the struggle over inequitable resources, Hawley launched a critique of the early Chicago School's reliance on Spencerian notions of species competition in favor of Durkheim's explanation of "organic solidarity." He thus opposed the former's perspective that social development was a function of increasing population size and "physical density" (the endogenous change in environment due to the birth rate), against the latter's notion that complexity of social organization arises due to "social density," that is, Durkheim's "moral density," or "the frequency of contacts and interchanges among the members of a population" (1950: 196). According to Durkheim it is moral density which leads to the competition necessary for the greater specialization of tasks, and this leads ultimately to the "organic" division of labor characteristic of societies possessed of a benign and integrated social order. Hawley utilized Durkheim's less sanguine concept of competition, as compared to that of Spencer or even the early Chicago School members, to derive his ecological principle of community adaption. The complexity and enlargement of the society necessary to sustain population growth can occur only with an increase in the range and frequency of interhuman contacts, that is, through increased social density itself. This effect, in turn, can be achieved only through the facilitation of physical *movement*. Thus community adaption means community expansion, and Hawley passed from his ideas about the social order to a theory of community growth. As he indicates:

The term movement is used here in a broad sense to include all forms of transportation through space, whether of individuals, materials, or ideas as such . . . In a very large degree the history of the growth of human organization is a record of the development and perfection of the facilities for movement. (1950: 200)

As we can see, therefore, Hawley's theory of the means by which societies progress to greater degrees of internal differentiation and functional complexity is based squarely on his idea of the importance of transportation and communication technologies, because these are the means by which the increasing moral density necessary to progressive levels of greater complexity can be facilitated. In this way we isolate the technological determinism at the very core of ecological thought which has been a constant explanatory device characterizing the field since then (Hawley 1956, 1980; Berry and Kasarda 1977; Street et al. 1977). This same explanation for the change in urban form or "the conquest of distance as a barrier to size" is utilized by other urban fields as well in a unified explanatory perspective on social and urban morphological change that serves as the core of these disciplines. According to this view, the spatial generating factor of complex modern social formations is the quality of movement abstracted as transportation and communication technologies. Thus transport, in particular, explains massive regional deconcentration, as we shall see in a subsequent chapter; the morphology of metropolitan development for urban geography (Borchert 1967; Adams 1970; Muller 1976); and the dynamics of locational economics conceptualized as the minimization of transport costs for urban economics (Alonso 1964; Wingo 1961; Perloff and Wingo 1968).

The limitations of contemporary urban ecology are already in evidence. It possesses a biologically reductionist view of human relations which ignores the influences of class, status, and political power. Thus, it disregards the healthy appreciation of the early ecologists for the competitive struggle—as reflected in space by gangs, crime, and so on—in favor of a cooperative view of all human interaction. Second, it is schematically conservative because of its focus on adaption and functional integration. Finally, it is technologically determinist in its reliance on innovations in transport and communication as the explanation for urban growth and change. Hawley's theory proceeds by logical exclusion to a level of abstraction possessing internal consistency but leaving out such factors as class conflict, the voluntaristic impulse in environmental decision making, the vested interests operating in space, the influence of government programs and policies, the changing nature of economic organization, and the production of uneven spatial development, all of which have proven over the years to be more important to an understanding of the contemporary urban environment than any of Hawley's insights.

Given the shortcomings of *Human Ecology*, we begin to beg for relief from alternate approaches. These appeared only quite recently. Perhaps the main reason for this slow response has already been indicated, namely, the ideological stranglehold of the conservative view on academic institutions. Our assertion here can be bolstered by calling attention to the analytical convergence of economics, geography, and ecology in the analysis of the urban structure. In essence, contemporary ecological theory combined with the economics of location to effect a unified mainstream approach to settlement space. This important aspect of theoretical convergence among mainstream urban approaches can be illustrated by considering urban economics and geography.

URBAN GEOGRAPHY AND ECONOMICS

The mainstream approach to urban economics and geography which has emerged since World War II takes for its organizing concepts certain statistical regularities regarding city size, function, and spatial organization which have been observed for many years. These include Walter Christaller's central place theory, first proposed in 1933, George Zipf's rank-size rule, presented in 1949, and Colin Clark's negative exponential density relationship, circa 1950 (Christaller 1966; Singer 1936; Clark 1951). These stochastic properties, expressing descriptively the distributional characteristics of population, were combined with the postwar, neoclassical economic analysis of location in two separate but related ways. On the one hand, the economics of location combined with Clark's distance-density ratio to articulate a two-dimensional analysis of intraurban spatial deployment which was dependent upon transport cost considerations (Alonso 1964; Wingo 1961; Muth 1969). On the other, this essentially horizontal view of economic spatial organization has been modified over the years to include noneconomic considerations, but only in a limited way (Mills 1972; Bourne 1971; Chapin and Weiss 1962; Goodall 1972).

In chapter 3, I shall consider the critique of mainstream location theory from a marxian perspective. At that time we shall transcend the limits imposed by the self-criticism internal to conventional analysis by opening up the discussion of location theory to include the *social* nature of land values and rent, the neglected effects of supply-side interests in determining the use and exchange values of land, the role of vertical or hierarchical forces of spatial organization, the determining role of monopoly rent and monopolistic control in patterning space, and the importance of state intervention in the production of the built environment.

Among the limitations of economic models of urban form, however, three are worth mentioning at this time. First, virtually every mainstream approach to urban land use follows Von Thunen by hypothesizing the primal role of the historical city center in organizing urban space. In recent years attempts have been made to overcome this limitation, because evidence exists that Von Thunen's model may not even explain the use of agricultural land under modern conditions of urbanization (Sinclair 1967). Second, there is a core reliance in conventional economic thought on the importance of technology, especially communication and transportation costs, in determining changes in the value of land. This principle has also been attacked from within the mainstream tradition in a limited way (Leven 1978b). Finally, conventional approaches ignore the most fundamental aspect of land value—its *social* nature. Consequently, conventional theory is an equilibrium theory which assumes the absence of externalities. Considering the complex, dense nature of urban life, this has always been an unreasonable assumption. Not too long ago the problem of externalities was also addressed by mainstreamers within the context of attempting to understand urban growth problems (Bourne 1971). Again this discussion was limited in its analysis and implications. In short, two observations can be made about mainstream urban science at this time. First, there is ample evidence from *within* this tradition to cause us to question its explanatory paradigm. Second, although mainstreamers address these shortcomings, they do so in limited ways. Before proceeding further, let us amplify the three inadequacies of conventional thought.

Centrality in Location Theory

According to Berry, central places constitute the economic base around which other urban activities agglomerate. The logic of location theory hypothesizes that there may be several reasons for location considerations, depending on industrial needs, supplies of production factors, market considerations, and administrative or organizational requirements. The perceived benefits of agglomeration are extremely compelling, according to the mainstream approach, as Berry states:

> The location theorist commonly classifies locally concentrated economic activities into those which are raw material oriented, those located at points which are intermediate between raw materials and markets, and those which are market oriented . . . The three classic principles of urban location derive from the three types of locational orientation of economic activities: cities as the sites of specialized functions; cities as the expressions of the layout and character of transport networks; and, cities as central places. Whereas cities are central places providing retail and service functions to the surrounding area, not every city has the first two aspects . . . The central business district is a point of focus about which land uses and densities, the spatial patterning of the urban population, subsidiary retail and service locations, transportation and commuting patterns and the like, have evolved. (Berry 1971: 97)

Mainstream urban economists vary with regard to how they determine the importance of centrality, while accepting the premises of central place theory. Some focus on economic considerations arising from competition within perfectly functioning markets. Others consider the economic decisions of city residents. Following Losch (1954), a tradition was started of general equilibrium models combining resident with business location decisions; Alonso's household location model was the first of these (Alonso 1964; Beckmann 1968; Muth 1969). Essentially, both business and household decision makers are assumed to face a trade-off between high prices for land at the city center and relatively higher costs of commuting as one moves out toward the periphery, that is, in the direction of lower land costs. Such a trade-off makes sense only if one assumes that the center of the city is a concentrated point both of employment opportunities and of marketing (see Wingo 1961). This approach follows directly from early ecological reasoning in that it assumes that space is produced by the interaction of countless individuals rather than social groups. Thus, it is basically a demand-side view which elevates individual consumer and business preferences to a primal place among those social forces articulating with space and which neglects the social factors that structure the differential supply of attractive locations, such as government programs. This same limitation is characteristic of mainstream explanations of interregional shifts (Sternlieb and Hughes 1975; South and Poston 1982), as we shall see in chapter 7.

The concept of centrality as it is used in conventional economic analysis seems untenable and unsupported today. Quite clearly, mainstream location models possessed some currency when the city center performed in the manner assumed above; however, this period has been surpassed by spatial transformations over at least the past thirty years. As Romanos notes:

> By assuming concentrated employment in the CBD, two biases will influence the results of monocentric models: (1) In explaining urban structure and the location of households, the CBD is given more importance than it really deserves; and, (2) The analysis of the rest of the urban area becomes inadequate because the homogeneity of residential land is interrupted by the presence of non-residential uses. (1976: 79)

Work has progressed in recent years among mainstream location analysts only by the introduction of several distinct points of agglomeration within the same urban region in so-called polycentric models. Such work remains limited. On the one hand, location analysis in polycentric models no longer possesses the kind of unique credibility for its explanations that was once enjoyed by monocentric theory. Once the existence of many agglomeration points is acknowledged, there can be any one of several reasons for determining location decisions. On the other hand, the presence of multiple nuclei points to the progressively more complex functional differentiation of urban space *within* metropolitan regions. This calls into question the primal assumption of dominance for the historical central city. As we shall see below, once the concept of dominance is struck down there is really little left of conventional explanations for urban form.

Technological Determinism

Mainstream urban economics follows ecological theory's explanation for spatial change very closely and is just as technologically determinist. Most location analysts focus on transportation considerations as the determining factor in spatial patterns, as we have already noted. More recently, communication innovations have received attention in structuring space (Pye 1977; Pred 1973; Gottmann 1972). Ironically, conventional analysts have developed an appreciation for the role of technological innovation as a force of production in the marxian sense. Their analyses, however, never tie this important source of social change to other factors, especially institutional ones, which are more important as explanations of urban morphological transformations. For example, Leven explains industrial decentralization from cities to suburbs solely by tracing the ways in which technological change, as a force of production, has influenced the industrial production process in recent years. As he states:

> Locating economic activities near the core of an urban area or within a metropolitan area at all is much less important today due to more recent technological developments. Most significant has been the steady reduction in the bulk of raw materials associated with many occupations. At least two-thirds of American workers are not involved with any raw materials, due to expansion of the service sector. For the remainder there has been a fairly steady drop in bulk-to-value ratios for most commodities. At the same time, the need for large individual production units has been reduced, since the extent of economies of scale at the establishment level is much more limited for services than for goods. (1978a: 102)

The above astutely singles out the effect of innovation on the social relations of production. Implicit in this analysis, however, is the status of technological change as the sole cause of industrial transformations which take place seemingly without an institutional context. In effect, spatial patterns of organization change because social relations of industrial development change. These, in turn, have been altered due to technological progress. A distinct chain of causality, therefore, is present in the above argument, which emanates from the alleged effect of technology as a prime agent of change in society. This is an example, therefore, of the type of reasoning which can be called technologically determinist.

In the next chapter we shall see that the monocausal argument of ecologically inspired reasoning explains away the most critical factors operating for social change, factors which are institutional or structural in nature. To be sure, technological innovation has provided the means by which socioeconomic transformations have occurred. However, the causal interconnections between forces of production and the higher levels of society are much more complex than mainstreamers would lead us to believe. This is especially true for the effect of space itself on those same industrial transformations often attributed to the blind force of technological progress. In chapter 4 we shall examine Lefebvre's claim that the interests of capitalists are advanced by using spatial organization itself as a force of production. In such a social system, technological innovations in communication and transportation technology are merely aspects of a much larger complex of sociostructural forces which have transformed space-time relations in modern society.

Equilibrium Theory

Mainstream theory is an equilibrium theory. That is, by assuming a systemic view stressing functional differentiation and integration, it asserts that all the parts of the urban system fit together into a smoothly run social whole. This view does not recognize the existence of conflict or its role in bringing about change. It is a familiar position adopted by mainstream social science in general as a means of eschewing considerations raised by marxian analysis.

According to conventional analysts, the impersonal forces of the market act as a sort of invisible hand which sorts out users of land in a functionally differentiated deployment according to their individual preferences and as constrained by their relative ability to afford locations. The following is an example of how mainstreamers, by an argument which stresses functional equilibrium, explain away the uneven competitive struggle for the use values of space:

> Every urban function and every establishment has its own set
> of requirements for centrality. Since urban land derives its
> value from its potential use, and the competition among users
> therefore drives up the cost, the highest land costs are at the
> points of maximum accessibility to the most prospective
> users. There is, thus, a sorting out of the land users and estab-
> lishments with respect to the ability of each to benefit from,
> and hence to pay for, central location. (Mayer 1969: 37)

The concept of equilibrium severely constrains the ability of mainstream analysis to grasp the processes of metropolitan development. In fact, there is considerable evidence that regions develop by a process best described as uneven and best analyzed by so-called imbalance theory (Myrdal 1957; Holland 1976). These authors reject the notion of equilibrium in favor of an analysis that focuses on the way resources flow between regions that are differentially successful in promoting growth. According to Holland:

> Imbalance theory has greater scope than the theory of regional
> self-balance in explaining why regional problems occur. There
> are various reasons. One is the artificial assumptions de-
> manded for most self-balance models of regional resource al-
> location. These abstract from internal and external economies
> of scale, neglect asymmetry in the response of labor and capital
> to interregional differences in potential earnings and so on. In
> other words, regional self-balance theory starts with a blindfold

to the main features of the regional world, and introverts into
an idealized unrealistic analysis. (1976: 54)

The very same remarks made by Holland about conventional regional analysis also apply to conventional equilibrium analysis of
the internal structure of the city. Mainstream theory cannot explain
social problems, the differential way in which city areas grow, or the
relationship between the two. It has no way of grasping the forces
producing uneven social development, such as class conflict, conflict between separate capitals, or even fractions within the same
class—not to mention the pathologies associated with city living,
such as crime, split families, and drug addiction.

The models of mainstream analysis which have private and social costs coinciding in competitive optima have been critiqued by a
number of analysts, some of whom are also mainstreamers (Koopmans and Beckman 1957; Solow 1973). Solow, in particular, considers the assumption of equilibrium in urban location models to be
"silly," because the built environment is so durable as to play a primary role in determining the location of economic activities despite
the operation of other forces. Only a small step is necessary to go
from Solow's insight to the greater revelation that location choices
are dependent upon the supply-side activities of special interests in
the real estate market, yet Solow and other mainstreamers have not
taken it. In subsequent discussions, I shall bring out the crucial role
of supply-side considerations in understanding the form of settlement space. Furthermore, the next few chapters will focus on the essentially uneven way in which urban development proceeds, thus arguing strongly for a marxian version of imbalance theory. In this way
I can demonstrate the need for an interventionist state, whose presence mainstreamers all but ignore, to correct the inequities of uncoordinated growth.

The three limitations of conventional urban economics, discussed above, revolve around a central organizing concept, namely,
the importance to mainstream analysis of a city center that dominates its hinterland, one whose location is somehow more important
to the process of domination than that of other, noncentral places.
This concept has undergone a transformation among mainstream urbanists. Initially, dominance meant the control of socioeconomic activities by the city center as manifested in its *spatial* ability to
organize activities in its own hinterland. This view of dominance is
attributable to all Von Thunen–like models, such as that of Burgess;
it pictures urban integration as a set of horizontal linkages deployed
across space. Consequently, when contemporary ecologists refer to

dominance, they sometimes imply this meaning. In contrast, beginning with the work of Gras (1922) and Duncan and his colleagues (1960), dominance has come to signify the ability of any single city to *functionally* organize linkages to all other cities that are lower down on a hierarchy of city types. This "systems of cities" approach constitutes the perspective of urban geography and economics today. It is important to note that the one version of dominance does not preclude the existence of the other and that together they define a three-dimensional network of urban places organized vertically as well as horizontally in space. Thus, when contemporary ecologists speak of dominance they tend to use these terms interchangeably. The "systems of cities" approach, however, is a central concept in urban geography and economics, and thus it requires more of our attention.

The Systems of Cities Perspective

In retrospect, it can be asserted that both urban economists and geographers advocating the systems of cities approach to urban organization followed the ecologist McKenzie's functional orientation to location. In McKenzie's analysis of the built environment, he pictured the city very much as Burgess had, except that by focusing on economic functions and the interdependent network of trade McKenzie came to appreciate the broad-based regional nature of urban influence. Consequently, he introduced the notion of the *metropolitan* community with a regional emphasis (1933). Furthermore, in place of Burgess' notion of dominance, which was a function of central location alone, McKenzie substituted the notion of dominance by economic influence. In an embryonic version of central place theory, he dissected the regional deployment of places according to their economic functional influence within the surrounding area. Thus he identified a hierarchy of domination which included industrial, commercial, primary service, and recreational areas (1925). Geographers and economists combined the notion of functional economic differentiation and interdependence due to trade with the more developed version of central place theory from Christaller to explain the location patterns of space (Berry 1968).

The systems of cities perspective combined all the elements above, that is, central place theory, functional interdependence, a regional perspective, and the importance of economic activities in the analysis of both the horizontal and the hierarchical integration of space (Losch 1954; Isard 1956; Berry 1968). The regional economy was viewed as a hierarchy of urban places which comprised a functional matrix of marketing, transport, and administrative networks supporting a nest of cities from small outlying ones to larger, centrally located agglomerations. The key aspect of the larger cities was their ability to perform a variety of functions on a regular basis for the other urban places located in the surrounding region. Furthermore, these network arrangements were shown by Walter Isard (1956), in particular, to be highly dependent upon transport costs, so that spatial competition became the single most important factor in the economics of location. Thus the interurban analysis of the city was brought into a consistent theoretical framework along with intraurban considerations by virtue of the primacy of transport costs in the economics of location. In addition, the dominant descriptive idea in this unified theory was that cities were functional nodes in a society thought of as a large social system performing essentially economic tasks. Thus, in the early 1960s, Wilbur Thompson and Brian Berry published articles which consolidated this view as the systems of cities perspective (Thompson 1965b; Berry 1962). This approach is the dominant one in urban geography today. In functionalist terms reminiscent of Hawley and McKenzie, Berry emphasized the interdependence between urban places, their economic specialization, and their hierarchical organization, which thereby structures space. Such an array comprised a system, as he indicates:

> It is clear that cities may be considered as systems—entities comprising interacting interdependent parts. They may be studied at a variety of levels—structural, functional, and dynamic—and they may be partitioned into a variety of subsystems. The most immediate part of the environment of any cities is other cities, and sets of cities also constitute systems to which all the preceding statements apply. (1962: 132)

Modern urban geography advanced by assimilating the theoretical approaches of human ecology, central place theory, and the economics of location. The compelling nature of its systems of cities perspective was its ability to link up with the overarching approach of general systems theory, which was fashionable at the time. There was, therefore, a soft underbelly to this field which would later be exposed by such marxian geographers as Harvey (1973).

Urban geography and economics were able to provide two advances to the theory of space. First, the formidable years of orthodox analysis resting on the convergence of ecology, geography, and economics produced a series of descriptive interdisciplinary analyses of the contemporary structure of space. Several comprehensive studies of regional urbanization were carried out under foundation or government auspices in the 1960s, beginning with Duncan and his colleagues (1960) and culminating in the six-year effort sponsored by the Social Science Research Council (Hauser and Schnore 1965). These combined the talents of geographers, economists, historians, and ecologists in documenting the extent of urban functional differentiation and regional metropolitan development. They also served to signify the theoretical compatibility of these separate fields.

Second, the power of the systems of cities formulation was revealed by its ability to explain certain network flows of resources along vertical axes—from linkages between individual places to national and even global linkages of urban activities. As one example, cities of the same rank in the systems hierarchy, although spatially separated, were found to be affected by the spread of technological innovation first, before change filtered down to the hinterland areas adjacent to the initial site of innovation (Pred 1973; Berry 1972). That is, by generalizing from Zipf's rank-size rule to the systems perspective, the flow of resources, ideas, and people between equivalent cities on the vertical ranks was discovered to be as important as or more important than the horizontal linkages between urban places in proximity to each other (Bourne 1975; Pred 1977; Bourne and Simmons 1978).

Some of the most important limitations of the systems approach to urban science have already been noted, including its reliance on a competitive model of demand-side land-use location theory and its conservative view of functional economic integration. In addition, the systems of cities perspective raises descriptive classification to the primary focus of urban studies. It categorizes without analysis in much the same manner that the rank-size rule persists, some thirty-five years after its discovery, as a stochastic observation with little theoretical impact. The major flaw of this approach is that it is an example of what Anderson calls spatial fetishism (1973) and Alonso calls the geographical fallacy (1971), that is, the assignment to cities themselves of the powers and attributes which belong to institutions and to the activities deployed within these places. The theoretical importance of these *social* forces becomes reified into spatial attributes of cities through a debatable process of aggregation, and we are blinded by the definitions of geographers for spatial units—prevented from seeing that the functional organization of the economic system is a social product not of places but of concentrated institutional power (Williamson 1975; Green, Moore, and Wasserstein 1972; Baran and Sweezy 1966; Mandel 1975). In addition, geographers' and economists' models of cities obscure the important social characteristics of urban organization *within* such places. As Anderson remarks, "The fetishism of space is the geographer's particular conceit. Rela-

tions between social groups or classes are presented as relations between areas, obscuring the social divisions *within* areas" (1973: 3).

The systems of cities perspective is an example of spatial fetishism because it condenses intraregional metropolitan organization
into a spaceless node, the named city. Thus the most salient features
of the contemporary urban form are ignored—namely, their massive,
dispersed, and almost unbounded reach and their inequitable or uneven pattern of socioeconomic development. By the internal structure of this regional array and a vertically oriented systems approach,
spatial fetishism is given free rein and allowed to prosper. As indicated in the preceding chapter, it is often very difficult to identify
where individual cities end and others begin. The study of functional
differentiation is predicated upon a procedure of aggregation according to the institutional practice of the census and by virtue of certain
definitions for spatial forms which simply do not hold up under
close empirical scrutiny (Edmonston 1975; Mazie 1972). None of the
definitions for regional development adequately captures the sprawling nature of growth. As Bourne, one of the advocates of the systems
approach, admits:

> The problem of defining the levels of such (national) systems
> in reality still remains unresolved. While the national urban
> system may be easily recognized, the differentiation of levels
> within that system is not. Nor are the levels likely to remain
> fixed over time. Rapid growth and the spread of urban life
> styles have blurred traditional boundaries between urban and
> rural, and even between small and large cities. Consequently,
> traditional attempts at boundary definitions, for individual ur-
> ban regions and urban hierarchies, have been brought increas-
> ingly into question. (1975: 14)

Thus, while no one can deny the descriptive knowledge acquired by
the sophisticated statistical techniques of urban science, the conceptualization of this information into a theory of space is artificial: it
fetishizes the abstract definitions for space which it itself imposes
upon the reality of the built environment, ignoring the real forces
which are at work producing the observed forms of spatial organization. Whenever we have the opportunity to reexamine the defini-
tional schemes of the abstract empiricism characteristic of mainstream geography and ecology, we discover that spatial distinctions
are the categorical artifacts of this research rather than the real objects of spatial analysis.

This review of mainstream urban science has indicated ample
reason for alternative approaches to be articulated. Yet the neat ideo-

logical package of orthodoxy has been slow to unwrap. Alternate views on space seek to discard the mechanical and fetishized perspective of mainstreamers, which gives the impression that the sociospatial environment is produced by the inexorable effect of the invisible hand. In its place they propose a theory of interests and actions by which certain forces of social organization and/or certain groups of individuals possess the ability to control space and alter its patterns of development in support of special interests. Our built environment assumes the form that it does because of the interplay between these separate vested powers, while the majority of individuals and competitive businesses are left to fend for themselves in the space which these significant others have produced.

Up to this point I have been concerned with indicating the areas in mainstream analysis that have been opened up to contention from sources internal to it as well as from the marxian tradition. Generally these have framed theoretical issues which, therefore, require theoretical analysis. This need will be addressed in subsequent chapters. There is, however, a second way in which to assess mainstream analysis, namely, by examining its ability to explain urban development. In the interests of brevity, I shall be concerned below with one aspect of ecological theory—its assertions regarding its understanding of the process of metropolitan expansion. In what follows I shall examine this theory on its own terms.

The Theory of Metropolitan Expansion: A Reexamination

The ecological theory of metropolitan expansion was articulated by Hawley (1950), following the work of McKenzie (1933), as an explanation for growth in city size. As Schnore (1965) has noted, the central thrust of the early Chicago School, culminating in Burgess' theory, was to explain the shifting internal differentiation and expansion of metropolitan areas. In its pre–World War II form this theory relied heavily upon social Darwinist ideas, especially the "Internal Structure Cycle" of invasion, succession, and so on. This early variant exists today in a reified and functionally deterministic form (Sly and Tayman 1980). Hawley, however, focused upon the central role of population pressures as the endogenous engine for growth. As the population of the sociospatial community increased, Hawley believed that settlement space would expand in order to adapt to this change. One aspect of this process of expansion is accomplished by virtue of concentrating administrative and coordinative functions within the community center, much as the nucleus of a biological cell enlarges as the cell itself grows. The second aspect of this process involves an extension of the community at the periphery, so that the spatial area of the entire ensemble of community organization increases. This particular way of conceptualizing the center-periphery relationship relies upon an organic analogy explained through the mechanism of countervailing processes of centrifugal and centripetal growth (Hawley 1950: 348). The following discussion focuses on the first part of this argument, on the centripetal process, while in chapter 7 I shall consider the second aspect, namely, the explanation for urban deconcentration.

As Hawley has stated in a recent formulation:

> The centripetal movement has concentrated administrative tasks, and the retailing of expensive and fashionable commodities in the central business district of the central city. This movement has been associated with a less conspicuous centralization of control over the metropolitan system. The spatial rearrangement is an external manifestation of a functional reorganization of an enlarging community. (1981: 183)

Hawley did not provide any proof of this assertion, while also acknowledging that administrative functions are presently dispersing to the periphery—but to a lesser extent than are other urban activities (Hawley 1981: 178; Sly and Tayman 1980). Nevertheless, the ecological explanation for the concentration of administrative functions within the city center remains a principal aspect of the orthodox theory of urban ecology which is responsible for the persistence of fallacious notions about city centrality. Furthermore, Hawley's theory was tested and confirmed by Kasarda (1972) and again by Berry and Kasarda (1977: 195–209), using data from 157 census SMSAs. In the latter case, the authors postulated a consistent pattern of positive relationships between the size of metropolitan areas and the development of organizational functions within the central city, even when effects of population size, SMSA age, income, and racial composition for the central city were controlled. In the following, therefore, I shall dwell at some length on the work of Berry and Kasarda with regard to the topic at hand, not because I wish to single them out as particular examples but because Hawley himself has not provided a test of his theory while the former two have.

Berry and Kasarda used 1960 data to test Hawley's theory, ignoring the 1970 data which were also available at the time they published their results. We can only wonder why a major period of suburban growth and urban dispersal was ignored. Even with the 1960 data, however, there are several reasons to reconsider their results. First, their data set consisted of figures on employment from 157 monocentered SMSAs with populations of 100,000 or more, in seven occupational categories hypothesized as being related to administrative functions: professional, managerial, clerical, communication, finance, business services, and public administration. That is, they hypothesized that figures from standard white-collar occupational categories were adequate proxy measures for administrative functions. However, while some of the white-collar occupational categories, such as public administration, refer directly to organizational functions, others, such as the professional category, are not strongly related at all. A more accurate approach would attempt to measure the precise number of white-collar jobs that are located specifically in administrative activities. Second, the Berry and Kasarda method ignores classification techniques of organizational functions that are more direct and that possess greater clarity. For example, we might consider the locational patterns of corporate and government headquarters in metropolitan regions and compare the central city with areas adjacent to it. A focus on the construction of office buildings and the location choices of both private and public administrative enterprises would sharpen our ability to test the Hawley theory.

An alternative approach to assessing organization location patterns has been utilized by Armstrong in two separate studies (1972, 1979). Working for the Regional Plan Association of New York, with the aid of census data, she constructed a measure of office employment that provides an index of administrative functions more accurate than the broader white-collar classification used by Berry and Kasarda. Armstrong's category deletes occupational groups that are not organizationally connected, such as artists, musicians, pharmacists, dentists, and physicians—groups that are counted by the Berry and Kasarda method.

Using this measure for the same year, 1960, Armstrong chose to study the twenty-one largest SMSAs in the nation with populations of over a million, thus making her work more useful for our purpose of examining the Hawley hypothesis because the largest cities, according to Hawley, should exhibit the greatest concentration of administrative functions. Armstrong found that, in this sample, 65 percent of all office employment was concentrated within the central cities. However, more than 33 percent of the office jobs in 1960 were accounted for alone by Manhattan, the New York City central business district. Thus:

> . . . leaving Manhattan and the New York SMSA out produces a fairly even allocation between the downtowns and the suburbs: 1.84 million office jobs in the suburban ring against 1.6 million in the downtowns, with the remainder—1.28 million

office jobs—located in the central cities outside the downtown business district, at various office, factory, institutional, and commercial sites or in smaller subcenters. (1972: 49)

Using a second measure, for the years up to 1965, of the extent of the concentration of office headquarters in central cities, Armstrong's analysis can also call into question the work of Berry and Kasarda. Focusing on the twenty-one largest metropolitan areas, she indicated that before 1965 only one of seven firms had located their headquarters in the suburbs. However:

By 1969, nearly one in six headquarters were housed in the suburbs. It is apparent that industrial headquarters preferences for suburban locations are mounting with large metropolitan areas, and that they initially appear as the size of the metropolitan area increased beyond a population of about two million. (1972: 52)

Armstrong's study seems to disprove Hawley's theory of metropolitan expansion, especially for the larger cities, upon which the theory most depends. On the basis of her analysis of 1960 data and the trends in office location since then, she considers that administrative and control functions are related to the role of the metropolitan area in the national and global economic system and that these functions have very little to do with the relationship between the central city and the expansion of the urban hinterland. Administrative activities can be divided into headquarters, middle market, and local market functions. The local functions that are most dependent upon the particular urban region are also least likely to be concentrated within the local central business district. In contrast, those administrative and control functions symbolized by corporate or banking headquarters buildings are concentrated in large central business districts but have little to do with the metropolitan coordinating needs of their city. They possess, instead, administrative connections to global enterprise. In short, once we disaggregate data so that more objective measures of office employment are used and more objective distinctions are made between the central business district, city areas adjacent to it, and suburban rings, there is little evidence to support the theory of metropolitan expansion as conceived by contemporary urban ecologists—and there are substantial reasons to abandon the perspective entirely. This is especially the case for the largest SMSAs with populations of over a million people.

A number of separate studies on trends since 1960 indicate that administrative and coordinating functions are dispersing, along with all other socioeconomic and political activities, despite the continued viability of the central city as a site for office construction (Cassidy 1972; Manners 1974; Quante 1976; Pye 1977). In fact, the most recent report on the construction of office buildings indicates that the bulk of office construction and relocation activity in the 1980s will take place *outside* the central business district (*National Office Market Report* 1980). Thus, the data and analyses since 1960 show a curvilinear relationship between the concentration of administrative functions and the growth of metropolitan regions. In the initial stages of urban growth, central areas acquire a greater concentration of coordinating functions, hence the importance of the central business district for the Burgess model. However, as the peripheral land areas become developed for alternate uses, under the play of hierarchical, global forces of sociospatial organization, urban administrative functions begin to disperse along with other activities (Sly and Tayman 1980). While the ascendant phase (approximately up to the 1960s) of this curvilinear relation is a function of population size and the level of economic organization, that is, of classical ecological factors, we need to look elsewhere to discover the reasons behind urban dispersal. Since the 1960s, Hawley's centripetal base of development simply does not appear to exist.

In summation, then, it is clear that there is a locational "division of labor" with regard to coordinating functions. Those firms choosing the central city are more likely to be involved in global administrative activities, while those firms with distinctly regional ties to the metropolitan economy seem to be dispersing along with other activities to the urban hinterland in recent years. Finally, government employment and other public sector–related employment, a major source of administrative activities, seem equally prone to recent deconcentration trends.

Our evidence suggests that around 1960 a significant change in the social formation of U.S. society began to manifest itself materially in settlement space. This does not necessarily mean that such changes occurred that year. In fact, it is presently apparent that qualitative transformations in the structure of American society have been occurring since the late nineteenth century, although these accelerated their impact after World War II. While marxists are not the only academics concerned with these transformations—such nonmarxists as Bell (1973) and Galbraith (1969) have written on the subject—a concern for systemic transformations in the mode of production is the essential hallmark of the marxian analysis of American society, which exists as a paradigmatic alternative to the orthodoxy of ecological reasoning. The marxian analysis of post–World War II capitalist transformations, called Late Capitalism by Mandel (1975), spans a significant number of analysts and conceptualizations, including mainstream contributions. In general, three essential features of Late Capitalism differentiate this phase from the previous period in the United States.

First, we have witnessed the rise to hegemony of the corporate-bureaucratic form which has transformed the business enterprise in America to one dominated by multiproduct, multiplant, multinational corporations (Chandler 1977; Holland 1976; Hymer 1979). This change is characterized by the global integration of the capitalist system, by an international division of labor (Frobel, Heinrichs, and Kreye 1980) and finance, and by the growing concentration of industry, as exemplified by the increased frequency, since 1950, of business and banking mergers (Zeitlin 1970; Heilbroner 1965; Minty and Cohen 1972; Wallerstein 1979; Baumol 1959; Berle and Means 1932; Means 1964; Baran and Sweezy 1966; Schonfeld 1965; O'Connor 1974; Menshikov 1969; Green, Moore, and Wasserstein 1972; Hymer 1972; Amin 1976; Palloix 1975; Mandel 1975).

The second transformation involves the structural role of the interventionist state as an everyday participant in economic activity and as a supporter of capitalist relations of production through spending, regulatory, and legislative policies. The perception of this change has evolved from early work on the Keynesian connection to present-day analyses of the fiscal crisis and the socialization of capital (Lerner 1944; Klein 1947; Dillard 1948; Crosser 1960; Baran and Sweezy 1966; Mandel 1975; Castells 1980; O'Connor 1973; Hirsch 1981; Holloway and Picciotto 1979; Crouch 1979).

The third transformation concerns the rise in importance of knowledge and technology as organized forces of production in capital-intensive enterprise. On the one hand, studies in this area point to the organized and accelerated way in which a knowledge "industry" is now articulated with economic activity (Rosenberg 1972; Silk 1960; Mansfield 1968; Mandel 1975). On the other hand, this transformation has been assessed as altering the economic structure itself, especially by shifting labor force needs to white-collar jobs and information processing and away from blue-collar, manual laborers (Carter 1970; Gillman 1957; Poulantzas 1976; Bock and Dunlap 1970; Fuchs 1968; Singelmann 1977; Braverman 1974; Blau and Duncan 1967; Gartner and Reissman 1974).

These fundamental transformations have affected spatial morphology in a variety of ways, including the promotion of suburbanization (Walker 1981; Gottdiener 1977); the transformation of agriculture into agribusiness (Hightower 1975; Shover 1976; Danborn

1979; Berry 1972); the rise of the interregional shift to the sunbelt (Sternlieb and Hughes 1975; Watkins and Perry 1977); and the restructuring of the central city environment (Fainstein et al. 1983; Smith 1984). It is the last aspect which we need to address at this time. I shall leave until chapter 7 a full explanation of the ways in which these transformations have affected all of settlement space. Our discussion here requires that I focus on concrete examples of these processes as they have changed the nature of the city center and points of agglomeration in the suburbs.

While my approach derives from a marxian perspective, it is not necessary to be a marxist to appreciate its main conceptual focus. Unlike mainstream analysts, I assert that the important changes in spatial patterning and urban restructuring have occurred because they are functions of changes in the larger social system, not because they are products of processes internal to places themselves. The mainstream ideological position can be summed up neatly by an early observation of Robert Park's: "The city is an externally organized unit in space produced by laws of its own" (Park, Burgess, and McKenzie 1925: 4). The social production of space perspective which I advocate rejects this view and seeks to replace it with an understanding of the ways in which settlement space forms are structured by forces from the larger system of social organization. To be sure, there are a number of key interactive processes which also play themselves out within urban environments that possess purely local origins, and it is equally important to appreciate their role in generating sociospatial patterns. These, however, are produced by needs that have little to do with places as such and are more affected by the systemic processes operating everywhere, that is, in rural and suburban as well as urban environments.

In order to illustrate this conceptual shift, it is necessary to explain the actual patterns of spatial use from within this more hierarchically conceived model of social organization. Consequently, let us return to a consideration of the ecological theory of metropolitan expansion. We are already in possession of enough counterfactual evidence to cause us to abandon this approach. It is now appropriate to use our theory in order to specifically address the same question, namely, what are the factors underlying the distribution of administrative functions within the metropolitan region? The changing patterns in urban morphology can be explained as being produced by the operation and requirements of the larger social formation, which have affected administrative location patterns.

Our first example involves the shift to a tertiary (service) and quaternary (information) service-oriented economy specializing in information processing, with a labor force transformed by the need for white-collar skills. The question which we are addressing here is, in what way is the increase in white-collar employment related to the distribution of administrative functions across the metropolitan region? Second, we shall look at the role of the interventionist state with regard to the construction boom in central city office buildings. In particular, we will focus on the case of urban renewal efforts in order to address the question of why the central city has been able to retain a significant percentage of administrative functions, given the presence of a strong centrifugal trend working in favor of urban deconcentration and against agglomeration in the central business district.

White-Collar Employment and Administrative Location Patterns

Beginning with the post–World War II period, but especially since 1960, the American labor force has undergone a profound shift away from manufacturing and toward white-collar occupations. This qualitative change has affected the central city directly, especially those located in the Northeast and Midwest (Sternlieb and Hughes 1975). Between 1950 and 1975, for example, 70 percent of new labor force participants offered white-collar skills, and nearly 20 percent of these were in service categories (Armstrong 1979: 64). A 1979 estimate by the Department of Labor claims that, by 1990, white-collar positions will account for more than 50 percent of all new jobs, thus indicating the shift in the economy away from industrial production and toward process- and service-related business.

There is little question that the increase in office employment is a special case of this more general social transformation of the labor force. As indicated above, however, understanding the location patterns of administrative functions requires that we correct white-collar employment figures so that they specifically reflect the office component in the manner of Armstrong (1979). For example, a study by Berry and Kasarda reveals that between 1960 and 1970 suburban areas received a greater share of white-collar jobs for each of four major categories: professional, managerial, clerical, and sales (1977: 228–247). Thus the evidence would suggest that since 1960 administrative functions have been *decentralizing*, along with the other aspects of the economy, to the suburbs and away from the central city. This suggests that no one particular area of the metropolitan region is specialized in administrative activities, although there is a clear division of labor between cities and suburbs with regard to the focus of those activities. It is necessary, however, to adjust these figures in order to represent more adequately the changes in office employ-

Table 1. Office Workers as a Percentage of the Total White-Collar Employment, 1950–1975

Year	Professional			Managerial			Clerical			Sales		
	Total	Office	%	Total	Office	%	Total	Office	%	Total	Office	%
1950	4,867	1,563	32	6,646	1,863	28	7,292	6,657	91	3,785	988	26
1960	7,280	2,293	31	7,140	2,574	36	9,655	8,965	93	4,386	1,333	30
1970	11,287	3,781	33	8,002	3,281	41	13,791	12,757	93	4,982	1,605	32
1975	13,032	4,457	34	8,386	3,682	44	15,384	14,230	92	5,756	1,920	33

Adapted from Armstrong 1979:66.

ment, before we can entertain this conclusion. Armstrong (1979: 66) has compiled national figures for office jobs as a proportion of white-collar employment for the same four categories above and for the years 1950, 1960, 1970, and 1975. Using her figures for total white-collar employment for the sake of consistency, it is possible to depict the percentage of office workers as a fraction of the total for each category. This is illustrated in table 1.

Table 1 reveals that office employment varies greatly between white-collar occupational categories. The percentage is highest for clerical positions, categorized as belonging to office employment, which average over 90 percent; professional and sales occupations, categorized as administrative functions, each involve under 35 percent of all white-collar employees. A comparison with the Berry and Kasarda data (1977: 236) reveals that the suburbs scored their single greatest increase in employment precisely in the clerical category. In addition, the central cities lost in an absolute way thousands of managerial positions during the decade between 1960 and 1970, while the suburbs gained in this area by almost 50 percent. According to Armstrong's figures, the 1970 proportion of office workers in managerial occupations was 41 percent. Together these measures suggest that since 1960 the suburbs have captured *more* than their share of administrative office workers, besides enjoying a more rapid surge in white-collar employment than have the central cities.

These figures suggest the impact of sociostructural transformations on the entire expanse of settlement space across metropolitan regions. They indicate that administrative functions, far from concentrating within the central city districts, have been dispersing since the 1960s to the suburbs at an impressive rate. What is important here is that such results provide additional evidence for our view of settlement space as understood through its interconnection with national and global forces of social organization, as opposed to the localized and horizontal conception of ecology which sees regional growth as coordinated by a single city center.

By way of concluding this section, let us speculate on the reasons for the strength of suburban office worker employment. As I have indicated, this must be understood as a special case of suburbanization in general after World War II. Perhaps the most interesting aspect of contemporary regional growth is the increasing problem of governance for suburban areas. In fact, political coordination and integration have been made difficult by the proliferation of local governments within metropolitan regions in a segmental, polynucleated pattern of administrative decentralization that is strikingly opposite from the concentric picture Hawley seems to possess. In a 1967 survey of 227 SMSAs, Campbell and Dollenmeyer found a total of 20,703 different local governments, an average of 91 per SMSA (1975: 364). More important, Bollens and Schmandt (1965) note that the larger the SMSA the greater the number of local governments and, therefore, the greater the fragmentation of coordination and administration for the region. In 1962, for example, SMSAs with a population between 300,000 and 500,000 averaged 76.6 governments; those with 500,000 to 1,000,000 citizens averaged 98.5; and those with 1,000,000 or more averaged 301 different governmental units.

According to such studies, the greatest increases in local jurisdictions have been in suburban special service districts, which provide such public goods as water, sewage disposal, sanitation, police forces, and fire protection. In 1962, such districts grew five times faster than the next fastest-growing type of local government (Bollens and Schmandt 1965: 147), and between 1962 and 1967 their increase was almost ten times greater (Campbell and Dollenmeyer 1975). The employees providing such services are classified as white-collar, and each decentralized district requires its own administrative staff, also white-collar, to supervise their work. Suburbs have had to adopt a decentralized solution to the provision of these special services, because in almost all cases regional growth has proceeded within a politically constrained system of separate jurisdictions, inflexible city boundaries, and jealously guarded public employee agencies. While many may lament the pattern which has evolved (e.g., Wood 1961), the structure of governance within expanding metropolitan regions is so balkanized that any central coordination seems like wishful thinking or romantic ideology on the part of its advocates and theoreticians. Let us now turn to our second example, the central city growth which illustrates our perspective, namely, the case of urban renewal.

Urban Renewal and Central City Transformations

Although suburbs have clearly increased in importance as the locations for administrative functions, most central cities have also experienced massive office building construction since 1960. During the decade following that date, 44 percent of all money spent on such buildings went into the twelve largest metropolitan areas, and the total square feet of office space in the nation as a whole doubled between 1957 and 1970 (Armstrong 1979: 67). This trend was as evident in such older central cities of the Northeast as Boston (40 percent increase in office space) and New York (24 percent increase) as it was in such sunbelt metropolises as Dallas (23 percent increase). In a survey of the thirty largest cities in the United States, for example,

O'Brien and Ganz reported that between 1960 and 1970 these cities averaged a 44 percent growth in office space (1972).

Ecologists mistake the appearance of newly constructed high-rise office towers as a validation of organicism. This restructuring of the historic central business district, however, has resulted from the combined efforts of urban public policy and programs and the monopolistic interests at work in the economy. Although a case-by-case analysis of each city with regard to the state-economy relationship might be instructive, let us instead try to illustrate this articulation with regard to central city space by summarizing the effect of the wide variety of efforts which fall under the general heading of urban renewal, keeping in mind that not every project was supported by federal funds. As Michael Smith states: "In central cities affected by the loss of manufacturing jobs, population, and tax base, the chief governmental response has been to subsidize speculation in office and luxury apartment buildings through 'urban renewal'" (1979: 239).

Beginning in 1958, the national allocations for projects aimed at central city renewal increased greatly each year, even though federal urban renewal legislation had been enacted since 1949. For example, combined expenditures came to $706 million in 1960, $1.8 billion in 1966, and $3.8 billion in 1970, or an increase of over 500 percent in ten years (Mollenkopf 1975). Most American marxists attribute this sudden increase in renewal activity to the perceived need for social control following the ghetto riots of the 1960s (Mollenkopf 1975: 261). An alternative explanation stresses the needs of capital accumulation and the role of central city real estate investment in combating the falling rate of profit in the primary sector of production (Harvey 1981; Hirsch 1981), starting with the recovery from the recession years of the 1950s (Mandel 1975). Such an approach has been used within a structuralist framework by analysts of the British and Canadian central city building boom (Massey and Catalano 1978; Scott and Roweiss 1978; Longstreth 1979); however, this type of analysis is lacking for the United States. Nevertheless, the history of urban renewal efforts has been documented by a vast literature (Greer 1965; Wilson 1967; Bellush and Hauschnecht 1967; Mollenkopf 1975; Anderson 1964). Case studies indicate that the need for greater social control of downtown areas was coupled with a municipal desire to respond to the loss of manufacturing jobs as well as to the devastation visited upon central cities by the phenomenal health of suburban commercial districts.

According to virtually all urban analysts running the political gamut from the conservative Anderson (1964) to the more liberal

Hartman and Kessler (1984), the urban renewal program has had only limited commercial success, and it has failed as a social measure to provide low- and moderate-income housing for the poor. Nevertheless, it has contributed greatly to the process by which huge sections of the city have been removed, despite resident appeals, to be replaced by high-rise office towers and luxury apartments. That is, the restructuring of downtown centers was a direct result of the actions of special interests, operating through an articulation between the state and the real estate sector and associated with urban renewal, even if some projects were privately initiated (Friedland 1980; Mollenkopf 1983). In Minneapolis, for example, a civic coalition working with only $4 million leveraged $400 million in federally supported new building and rehabilitation projects, including federal loan subsidies covering as much as 90 percent of the total costs of development to rescue the economically depressed downtown area. The project included constructing an eight-block mall in the very heart of the city's dying commercial district, as well as building the fifty-seven-story Investors Diversified Services skyscraper; the latter was an extramural effort built adjacent to the federally subsidized development area. In a second example, Boston was able to spark an office building construction boom on land that was leveled by redevelopment. During the 1960s, 7 million square feet of office space were added to the central city's skyline, including the fifty-two-story, privately financed Prudential Tower and the New England Merchants Bank Building (O'Brien and Ganz 1972), thus preserving the central city's office function.

These examples point to what Scott calls the state-land nexus (1980), the articulation between government programs, urban planning, and monopolistic interests within the city. These have combined to devalue the infrastructure represented by the built environment of the past (Harvey 1981), to remove its physical presence, which has acted as a barrier to new investment (Lojkine 1977b), and to clear large sections for new construction—much of which represents monopoly capital and banking interests, as we shall indicate below. In addition, private capital combined effectively with publicly supported efforts to take advantage of the useful effects of agglomeration (Lamarche 1977) and exploit the social, interactive creation of value in space based upon the externalities of growth. Thus, revitalization is a social product subsidized by the state, rather than some magical, organic initiative of place.

It is virtually impossible for a single researcher to discover the behind-the-scenes process involved in the joint business-government partnership which has rescued the value of central city land. The

Nader group, however, comprised of a team of researchers, has un-covered the case history behind the building of the World Trade Center in New York City. The twin towers of 110 stories each were con-structed in 1972, adding 4.5 million square feet of office space to the downtown area all at once. The project was conceived initially by the Downtown Lower Manhattan Association "to provide a sound foun-dation for the expansion of lower Manhattan as the dominant center of finance, world trade and shipping" (Leinsdorf et al. 1973: 143). Belonging to the association were presidents or chairmen of the fol-lowing banks: First National City, Chase Manhattan, Manufac-turers Hanover Trust, Morgan Guaranty Trust, Chemical Bank, Bankers Trust, Irving Trust, Marine Midland Grace, and the Bank of New York.

The trade towers were not, however, built by this group. Instead, the project involved an independent public agency, the Port of New York Authority, which has the "government's power to condemn pri-vate land and borrow money at low, tax-exempt interest rates" (Leinsdorf et al. 1973: 141). The project, therefore, combined the ex-traordinary tax-exempt powers of the public authority with the pri-vate sector interests centered around *international* finance and world trade. As the Nader report indicates, such a partnership was most effective, despite the fact that local residents were opposed to the project, that New York City commercial needs did not require either such a massive increase in office space or an increase at that location, that there were limited transportation facilities servicing the site area, and that commuters using the bridges and tunnels op-erated by the Port Authority paid for its operating capital by their daily tolls without receiving any benefit from the towers or any re-duction in tolls because of the financial well-being of the Authority.

In order to finance the project, the Authority borrowed $210 million from a consortium of thirteen banks, using its revenue-generating monopoly control over Manhattan's bridges and tunnels as collateral. Ten of the banks were also members of the same associ-ation that had proposed the project. The Nader report concluded its assessment of this project by stating:

> On December 31, 1968, the Port Authority had 276 million
> dollars, or 93 percent of its time deposits in the same banks
> that were receiving tax-exempt interest on the 210 million dol-
> lar loan. Citibank, and probably the other banks as well, was
> also receiving tax-exempt interest on the bonds issued by the
> Port Authority. The Authority deposited the proceeds from its
> bonds in the same banks that were receiving its tax-exempt

interest payments. If the banks took tax deductions for the interest they paid on the Port Authority's time deposits, then they were violating the law. (Leinsdorf et al. 1973: 148)

There is some evidence to support certain generalizations from the Nader group study on the central role of international finance capital in channeling investment into central city real estate (Ratcliff et al. 1979; Sbragia 1981), even though there is a tendency for those studying the problem either to simplistically lump fractions of capital together (Friedland 1976, 1980) or to mistakenly consider such interests as an entirely separate class (Molotch 1976). Burns and Pang (1977) predict, for example, that while corporate headquarters will continue to decentralize, banks will keep their headquarters within the historic central city. Longstreth (1979) indicates that the financial capitalist fraction of the capitalist class, including banking and insurance, is in effect equated with central city interests in the United Kingdom, especially in the case of London. More evidence for the importance of the finance capital fraction in restructuring the central city comes from a recent report on Los Angeles, which indicates that banks, insurance companies, and foreign financial investors presently own the most valuable properties in the historic central city. According to the report: "Federal law prohibits banks from speculating on real estate, but they may own property they use for bank business. Such bank holdings account for perhaps one-fifth of total property values downtown" (*Los Angeles Times*, April 25, 1982). I may add that these properties, giant office towers with many nonbanker tenants, have changed the historic skyline of the city.

The picture of spatial morphology as a product of Late Capitalism which is emerging in the United States is one in which the downtown sections of cities have been reserved for the finance capital fraction, along with the headquarters functions of corporations that have taken up tenancy in the giant office towers built by the state–finance capital coalition, while manufacturing and commercial activities have either dispersed throughout the metropolitan region or been exported elsewhere. This makes the former fraction, along with real estate developers and speculators, the primary beneficiaries of urban renewal (Carruthers 1969; Boyer 1973). Such an observation raises important theoretical questions regarding the differential deployment of capital's needs in space, given the presence of a fractionated ruling class. In the main American marxists perceive capitalism's influence in space as a monolithic corporate presence, because they fallaciously assume a direct link between capitalism's transformations and spatial forms (see Gordon 1977a, 1977b; Tabb and Sawers 1984). The contentious issue of specifying the relation between capitalism and space is one of several that I shall return to in the next and in subsequent chapters.

The view advocated here regarding central city restructuring differs from technologically determinist mainstream explanations, such as that of Gottmann (1972), which explain the agglomeration tendencies of finance capital as the result of the close proximity of "transaction spaces" required by information-processing needs. To be sure, such needs are real (Burns and Pang 1977), but they do not explain the supply-side aspects of the state–real estate sector articulation, which constitutes the leading edge of spatial transformations; the extent of *concentration* of the major financial interests, which promotes agglomeration; or the construction by banks, under the guise of building accommodations for themselves, of massive office towers which house other corporate tenants.

Government spending continues to support central city revival and office building construction in the United States. In 1979, for example, over two hundred separate federal programs provided financial and technical assistance for central city revitalization. Federal agencies such as HUD, possessing a budget authority of over $30 billion, earmarked a significant percentage of their expenditures for such work. The general pattern of urban development, then, has involved the replacement of retail and residential sections of the central city with newly constructed commercial and administrative facilities, thus preserving, in part, the city's central location in the expanding metropolitan spatial array, despite more "natural" pressures operating in favor of dispersal. Much of this activity has been speculative, resulting from the ease of financing due to government subsidies for central city projects but not for suburban ones (Boyer 1973; Fellmuth 1973; Lindemann 1976; Hartman 1974). Throughout the central city building boom, the state made it easy for developers in every city to build by providing a variety of incentives, including federal tax benefits, local tax abatements, and direct subsidies to cover land costs (Goodman 1971; Marcuse 1981).

Once monopolistic development interests have worked their changes in space, other societal actors, including businesses and residents, must adjust to the new priorities of the metropolitan landscape (Davis 1980; Rosenthal 1980; London 1980). As a rule, government-business coalitions operated with little regard for resident desires as they forged pro-growth networks which pushed for downtown redevelopment (Mollenkopf 1975; Anderson 1964; Bellush and Hausknecht 1967; James 1977; Davies 1966). I shall discuss the exact nature of these coalitions in more detail in chapter 6, since their presence raises a number of important theoretical issues for the marxian analysis of space.

As an upshot of such endeavors, central cities across the country have begun to resemble office parks—a large-scale, high-rise version of the suburban administrative land-use pattern. Characteristically, such areas possess high densities during the day but become devoid of any population after working hours. There is an absence of manufacturing and of the previous low-income residents. Consequently, all downtown areas, such as those in San Francisco, Boston, Atlanta, Houston, and Phoenix, have begun to resemble grander versions of office parks located in suburbs as the multifunctional, historical city center disappears off the face of the earth.

CONCLUSION

It is a far cry from the joint government-business boosterism that produced the sparkling high-rise office centers of downtown municipal districts to Hawley's biologically pristine theory that the centers of organisms grow because their periphery expands in size. Yet Hawley, Berry, and Kasarda, as well as other urban ecologists, would be the first to agree that complex social system processes nurture the development of metropolitan regions, especially in technologically advanced modern societies. The shortcoming of their perspective lies not in their denial of such facts but in their reluctance to abandon the last vestiges of the biological organicism first popularized by Park and Burgess as the Chicago School approach. The ecological patterns discovered by the sophisticated statistical techniques of factorial and social area analysis are open to question. More important, their explanations for inductively discovered features seem hopelessly limited.

The production of space perspective leads to a greater understanding of these patterns and events, because it explains them as products of fundamental societal processes, structures, and transformations. Both the cities and the suburbs are sustained and nurtured by national, even global processes of advanced industrialization. Business, finance, and government at all levels converge on urban space to alter or transform it, because in most cases class fractions of capital require it, the property sector produces it, and the government has made it profitable to do so. Although local areas still grow "by themselves," the really broad aspects and problems of contemporary urban expansion, conceptualized as massive systems of regional growth, require the societal view argued for in this volume.

The above discussion of metropolitan agglomeration and re-structuring has merely introduced aspects of the marxian approach to space, without a great deal of theoretical specificity. Some of the elements of this alternative argument are already in evidence and will be taken up in subsequent chapters. These include the role of class fractions in space, especially those within the capitalist class; the relationship between spatial development and social control, that is, class conflict as deployed in space; the relationship between the state and space; and, finally, the role of pro-growth networks in restructuring settlement space forms. In the next chapter I shall examine these and other issues within the context of their treatment by marxian political economy.

3. Marxian Political Economy

The theoretical baggage of mainstream urban science has been carried, as we have seen, by the ecological perspective and its functionalist paradigm. Elements of voluntarism clearly play a role in this scheme—the economics of location emphasizes the demand-side role of consumer and business preferences in a world free of monopoly constraints. The epistemological thrust of such work, however, remains compatible with the ecological emphasis on sociobiotic forces manifested at the structural level of society rather than at the level of individual behavior. The dynamic focus of this approach is a form of ecological functionalism viewed as a collective process of adaption. That is, society is conceived as a formal system, undoubtedly integrated by Parsonian mechanisms of value consensus, which collectively adjusts to environmental perturbations in a balanced manner. From such a perspective, metropolitan development is understood as a *natural* process flowing from the inexorable pressures for social change produced by technological innovation and the increasing societal scale which that innovation makes possible.

By the 1960s, a rude awakening was in store for any urban analyst willing to believe in such a reified, conservative version of the realities of city life. The ghetto riots of the middle sixties exploded across the United States, thus belying the theoretical value of ecological adjustment processes. The most significant fact to arise from the multitude of investigations which followed the central city insurgency of the sixties was evidenced by the explicit documentation of the many years, in fact the intergenerational nature, of deprivation suffered by the growing number of urban poor in all our large cities, even those located in the sunbelt. This "other America," to use Michael Harrington's phrase about rural as well as urban conditions, involved over 20 percent of the United States population, whose everyday life was hemmed in by poverty, unemployment, rac-

ism, substandard housing, malnutrition, violent crime, family disintegration, and inadequate medical and educational care.

At the time, the split between critical and conservative social
scientists which followed was really over their respective sensitivity
to the inequitable development of U.S. society and the social violence affecting the very core of everyday life in America. Critical
analysts expressed a desire to understand such attributes rather than
neutralize them conceptually as falling outside the limits of accept-
able topics for urban analysis. In retrospect, it is probable that a
marxian version of urban analysis would never have been articulated
had mainstream work been able to advance an understanding of the
social inequities permeating life in our metropolitan regions.

During the 1960s, the marxian analysis of modern society received a lift from abroad. In May of 1968, the "explosion" rocked
France and indeed all of Europe. Over 20 million French workers
took to the streets in a general strike, placing that country on the
very precipice of revolution. By a fortuitous decision the unrest at
the core of European society was identified, in part, as urban in
nature, and the state threw its support behind a social science effort
to analyze what came to be known as the urban revolution. The prolific amount of work on urban topics which came out of France after
1968 eventually cross-fertilized the efforts of marxian urban analysts
in the United States at a time when such an alternative approach
was sorely needed. The fundamental aim of all marxian work which
followed was the replacement of what had become a tired application
of descriptive urban factorial correlations with a vibrant synthesis
that could, on the one hand, uncover the processes by which the urban environment had assumed its current form and, on the other,
explain the features of uneven spatial development and the social
crises associated with it. This critical perspective concerned itself
not only with the poor and with social justice but also with the presence of dehumanizing architectural design and inadequate urban
planning. Marxian urban analysis, therefore, was at once an economic, a political, and a social commentary on city events and city
form, called into existence by the inadequacies of conventional
approaches.

The problem facing the early proponents of the marxian perspective was that the legacy of the master featured precious little in
the way of urban analysis. In fact, it was Engels, not Marx, who
seemed to be most interested in writing on the subject (Engels 1973,
1979; Lefebvre 1970). However, certain comments in Marx's *Pre-
Capitalist Economic Formations* suggest the essential structural

point: the form of settlement space must be considered as tied to its mode of production (1964: 78). In a brief passage, Marx develops the notion that the four stages of society identified by the technique of historical materialism as separate forms of social organization could be linked to an urban analysis:

> Ancient classical history is the history of cities, but cities based on land ownership and agriculture; Asian history is a kind of undifferentiated unity of town and country (the large city, properly speaking, must be regarded merely as a princely camp, properly imposed on the real economic structure); the Middle Ages (Germanis Period) starts with the countryside as the locus of history, whose further development then proceeds through the opposition of town and country; modern history is the urbanization of the countryside, not, as among the ancients, the ruralization of the city. (1964: 77–78)

This concise formulation was utilized as an organizing thought in the work of others, who filled in the details of the diachronic process outlined by Marx. Such writing served as the only marxian urban analysis available until the 1970s. In passing we should note the extraordinary prescience characteristic of much of Marx's thought: as we have indeed seen, present-day patterns of expansion involve the urbanization of the countryside. Yet it will also become clear that, in contrast to Marx's assertion and the view of marxists who have followed him, postulating a direct correspondence between a mode of production and a specific form of settlement space is too simplistic.

By the 1970s a good many marxists in the United States had turned their attention to urban space. In order to understand their work it must be viewed as an ongoing project, as a many-voiced discussion wishing to refine the critical approach so that it analyzes contemporary life with greater and greater fidelity. For this reason, while it is possible to fault individual examples of this intellectual production for being incomplete or in part undeveloped, it must be borne in mind that we are dealing both with an ongoing project and with the emergence of a new sociospatial paradigm. At present, because of the fecundity of marxist thought and the variety of its interpretations, a number of separate approaches are applied to urban analysis. These must be evaluated by a close look at the questions they raise, the issues they highlight, and the answers they supply.

The central problem engendered by the application of marxism to the case of the United States is, can such an approach be circumscribed within the perspective of political economy? This is so because marxian political economy dominates, at present, the mode of thinking most characteristic of marxism in this country (as I shall demonstrate below, the answer is in the negative). Even this distinction, however, presents certain difficulties, because there are several separate perspectives all calling themselves political economy. In the main, we can distinguish between those analysts who stress class conflict and its processual consequences for determining urban form and those who are more concerned with the logic of capital accumulation. Quite clearly, the two aspects are part of the very same process, namely, the hegemonic domination of capitalist social relations in modern society. Nevertheless, it is fruitful to distinguish between them.

In what follows I have refrained from performing a review of the literature on marxian political economy. Instead, I have focused on a select group of four exponents. My purpose in doing so is to isolate the underlying mode of reasoning characteristic of political economy along with the issues raised by its limitations, rather than trying to summarize the scope of its concerns. To do otherwise would fail to acknowledge the critical inadequacies of this approach, which can never be surmounted from within this paradigm.

CLASS CONFLICT THEORISTS

This approach fails to develop the important distinction between capitalism as a totality, as a systematically organized mode of production, and capitalism as a form of society within which the behavior of individuals follows class lines. Much of this work eschews dialectical analysis and merely reproduces conventional thought within a marxian form, because it possesses the same positivist emphasis on discovering one or two factors that "cause" urban phenomena. Invariably in this mode of analysis, the factor of labor is imputed to be the primary determinant of capitalist location decisions. Hence, the urban form is "explained" as a product of the class struggle.

In its earliest articulations, the class conflict approach was used to substantiate a social control view of land-use decision making (Gordon 1977a, 1977b; Mollenkopf 1975; Katznelson 1976). It hypothesized the existence of a capitalist class which was capable of behaving monolithically in order to orchestrate events so that they better fit the needs of that class. In some cases the capitalist class is endowed with a prescience capable of making its politically orchestrated decisions functional for the survival of the system (Boulay 1979: 615). This approach suggests that everything which enhances the ability of the capitalist class to control society has been willed into being, or, if that sounds too conspiratorial (and many marxists prefer things to sound that way), then capitalism itself can be anthropomorphized so as to act *as a whole* and determine what is best for it as a system in an evolutionary fashion by weeding out whatever is not. The functionalist heights which such arguments have sometimes reached have not gone unnoticed by marxists themselves. As Edel remarks:

> If phenomena exist because they are needed by an accumulation process, and they are themselves part of the accumulation process, what is being said is that they exist because they need themselves. How the accumulation process can exist as a thing apart to determine the characteristics of its component parts is unclear. (1981: 39)

An approach which stresses the equilibrating powers of capitalism or the capitalist class, which singles out labor considerations as determining land-use form, and which explains events by functionalist arguments is little different from mainstream social science, as we shall soon see. In certain ways, however, class conflict theorists have made substantive improvements in our understanding of the urban location process and have contributed to a greater clarification of the dynamics of that process while, nevertheless, remaining within the constraints of conventional thought. Two arguments, in particular, should be singled out at this time. The first is Gordon's explanation for the decentralization of industry; the second is Storper and Walker's labor theory of location.

Social Control Theory and Urban Form

Conventional urban ecology and geography explain the changes in city form as a consequence of changes in transportation and communication technology (Hawley 1956, 1977; Schnore 1957, 1961; Borchert 1967). Such an explanation illustrates what marxists wish to avoid: the discussion of urban change divorced from the larger systemic aspects of economics, politics, and history. As it stands now, ecologists and geographers seem to suggest that the urban form takes shape as the inevitable consequence of technological innovation. Thus, there was little any one of us could do, for example, to alter the spread city pattern once the automobile was introduced in a mass way. In contrast to the technological determinism of ecologists, David Gordon, in a series of three separate treatments of the same theme, has advanced an early marxian explanation for the spread city form (Alcaly and Mermelstein 1977; Watkins and Perry 1977; Tabb and Sawers 1984). According to Gordon, technological innovation is important in the development of urban space, and the automobile is particularly critical to this process. However, such technological factors provide the means but *not* the incentive for spread city growth and urban dispersal. He notes that urban deconcentration was occurring in the United States as early as the 1880s, when even railroad commuter lines were relatively new.

In carrying out his critique of technological determinism, Gordon marshals the following arguments. First, he creates nominalist categories, conforming to various periods of capital accumulation, which he elevates to the status of stages *within* the historical development of the capitalist system without any demonstration that these are qualitatively unique modes of organization. He refers to commercial capital, industrial capital, and monopoly capital. Each stage then has a unique form of city correlated with it: the commercial city, the industrial city, and the present form, the corporate city. Thus he tells us that these three stages in the history of capitalism are reflected in distinct forms of settlement space. Further, these forms were produced by the variety of spatial responses that the capitalist system (or sometimes the capitalist class) had to make in order to maintain its social hegemony over the production process. Each stage is viewed as being dominated by capital in general insulated from conflict between fractions. During the period of industrial accumulation, in particular, the profit-making process shifted qualitatively to the factory mode of production. At this stage the economy "required" a system of mass production in large factories and a stable work force in such plants on a regular basis and for long hours at one time. This stage is distinguished from the previous one, which focused upon the global trading and colonizing process that "required" well-run port cities with markets; it is also distinguished from the corporate city stage, which "requires" the need for administration and office headquarters.

Gordon then argues that, in the industrial city built up of factories around the turn of the century, the class struggle turned into open conflict of a violent nature. He indicates this in a table which shows the number of strikes from 1880 to 1920. Because the capitalists were concerned with accumulation through the factory process, they needed to protect their factories and the work regime from this labor unrest. Consequently, the primary agent contributing to early deconcentration was the need to isolate the labor force from unrest and collective agitation. That is, the capitalists' collective decision to move their factories outside the heavily populated central cities to adjacent areas was caused by their need for greater social control of the labor force.

According to Gordon, therefore, factory owners responded to the class struggle in this very direct way. Such a trend created the infrastructure that supported the beginning of metropolitan decentralization, as city growth expanded to link up with satellite towns and industrial sites located in suburban areas. This centrifugal growth was aided greatly by the construction of railroad lines that enabled workers to commute, for example, from the congested Chicago slums where they lived to the steel plants of Gary, Indiana. However, because mainstreamers concentrate on the technological aspect of this growth, they ignore the historical record of class conflict and the incentives operating to impel such trends and use innovation for social purposes alone.

We have dwelled upon Gordon's demonstration because it illustrates some of the best and worst aspects of marxian analysis. It provides a missing element for the complete study of urban expansion in a society that experiences events as shaped by people and their respective conflicts or desires, not by reified mechanical inventions which mysteriously appear to bend wills to their bidding. Its limitation lies in the fact that such economic and political labels as "corporate city"—invented on the spot and thrown about only as nominalist categories—lack substance because they assert that capitalist development passes through qualitatively distinct changes which automatically reflect themselves in distinct spatial forms. Gordon creates a series of stages as typologies and accompanies these with a series of surface correlations, but absent from this approach is a marxian model that demonstrates in detail the specific ways in which the capitalist processes of accumulation, production, and reproduction dictate a decision-making procedure which creates material changes in the urban form. This shortcoming can be raised as the first issue facing marxian urban analysis: the procedure by which we can specify the relationship between social structure and spatial structure. In chapter 6, I shall argue against the view of qualitatively separate historical forms of capitalism in favor of the historical continuity of this mode. Furthermore, I shall also argue against the view of distinct capitalist processes as reflected in space, in favor of a more dialectical relation between spatial and social organization.

It takes little to substantiate the fact that the turn of the century was a period of sustained class struggle characterized by the open presence of worker militancy and violent forms of social control. The question which must be addressed, however, is whether this struggle alone caused a number of factory owners to seek suburban plant locations. By failing to see this as only part of the answer, Gordon fuses complex historical processes into a linear, causal chain which exhibits both a conspiratorial view of change in city form and a functionalist analysis of capitalism. As we shall see in chapter 7, a number of factors are important for the decentralization of industry, including land speculation; the pro-growth ideology, which supports the incentives for migration; cycles in the accumulation of capital; and, finally, conflicts between fractions of the capitalist class itself. Thus Gordon's analysis raises several more issues. How can we specify a marxian analysis of space which treats the many factors operating there? What is the relationship between the need to control the class struggle and the built environment? What is the relationship between capital accumulation and class conflict as they affect the built environment? How can marxian analysis avoid functionalism while specifying the need for the capitalist class to dominate the system? In short, what is called for by an assessment of Gordon's work is not an abandonment of the urban marxian approach but, rather, a need to make it more sophisticated. As it stands it seems a functionalist correlate of ecological theory, in that it also seeks monocausal explanations and confuses behavioral with sociostructural phenomena. A similar limitation afflicts the second class conflict approach that I wish to discuss, Storper and Walker's labor theory of location. Let us consider this next.

The Labor Theory of Location and Urban Form

All marxist urban thought represents a critique of mainstream location theory, even if it is developed only in limited ways. Michael Storper and Richard Walker (1983, 1984), however, have decided to face the neoclassical approach head-on in a thorough critique of industrial location logic. It is easy to grasp the inadequacies of mainstream theory, emphasizing as it does transport and communication technology, because mainstreamers themselves recognize that such factors no longer count for as much in location decisions as they once did (Massey 1977a, 1977b; Richardson 1972; Watkins 1980). Storper and Walker have sought to move quickly from acknowledging this limitation to proposing an alternate approach, which they claim is rooted firmly in marxian thought. Their argument proceeds by analyzing the complex way in which labor force and labor power considerations have progressively emerged as *most* important in contemporary industrial location decisions.

To begin with, Storper and Walker call attention to the increased capacity of industrial enterprises to locate in a greater variety of places. The factors they single out as being responsible for this can hardly be argued with from any perspective; they merely bring location analysis in line with present-day realities. These factors include innovations in transport and communication technology, of course, as does conventional location theory, along with such transformations associated with Late Capitalism as the growth and development of global capitalist organization, which has incorporated peripheral areas in a general deepening of industrialization and marketing processes; global integration, which has opened up new sources of labor and raw materials; proliferation of multiple-plant, multiple-stage industrial processes, "making the idea of a single best location outmoded"; new forms of automation and synthetic production technology, which have attenuated previous raw material and labor market dependencies; growth in the importance of large corporations for general economic well-being, which has enabled them to elicit attractive infrastructural and financial conditions; and, finally, the increased scientific capacity of firms in calculating optimal locations and optimal component structures for their production purposes (Storper and Walker 1983: 2–3).

Together these transformations have made the traditional limitations on location less important today. Consequently, as Storper and Walker note, labor considerations have naturally risen to greater importance: "As capital develops its capability of locating more freely with respect to most commodity sources and markets, it can afford to be more attuned to labor force differences. Under the pressure of competition, this becomes a necessity" (1983: 3–4). Up to this point their analysis is most conventional, indeed! However, recognition of the important industrial transformations associated with Late Capitalism becomes a mere prelude to a more marxian approach to location theory.

According to Storper and Walker, while conventional analysts might agree with their assessment of greater locational flexibility, they are *incapable* of treating labor within the conventional framework in a manner adequate to its role in location decisions. This is so because all neoclassical thought reduces labor ideologically to the reified status of a commodity. For mainstreamers, labor power is merely one input among several which is obtained from a market by the capitalists for use in production. As they suggest:

> To confuse labor with true commodities means adopting the following incorrect assumptions: the worker is the same as the objects of work; production is a purely technical exercise, a system of machinery that workers do not in any sense direct or contribute to . . . ; the production process is devoid of

social relations and social life that affect worker behavior . . .
(1983: 4)

By focusing on the unique aspects of human labor in the industrial process, Storper and Walker articulate a critique of conventional
location theory which is distinct from mainstream thought. They
divide their analysis between factors affecting changes in the supply
of labor and those affecting demand. Most important to their view is
the recognition that labor-specific factors vary from place to place.
Hence location decisions must take labor's geographical specificity
into account even if other location-specific factors have become less
important. In the case of the supply of labor power, factors affecting
it are said to be idiosyncratic and dependent upon a number of separate considerations which individual industries assess differently.
These include the conditions of purchase, which depend not only
upon wages but also upon whatever other costs of labor's reproduction workers require employers to bear, such as those of health, security, housing, prospects for advancement, and so on; the quality of
labor, which includes skills, creativity, and regularity and which is
"known to vary markedly between regions"; the control of labor, because "the most fundamental difference between labor and true commodities is that there is no guarantee that you will get what you paid
for, even in the fairest exchange"; and, finally, "reproduction in
place," or the variable dependency of labor on locationally specific
aspects of community and home life, which also vary geographically
(1983: 5–6). In short, the reason why labor force considerations have
become more important in location decisions lies in the unique
qualities of labor power as an input to production, an aspect mainstream analysis cannot recognize due to its ideological constraints.

In the second case, corporations' *demand* for labor has also
changed but remains geographically constrained. Storper and Walker
suggest that industries locate where the supply of labor best fits
their own demand. This, in turn, is primarily a function of the dominant technology used in the production process, which includes six
separate types: craft-type batching, continuous processing, automated materials processing, mechanical assembly, mechanized processing, and manual assembly. Certain common characteristics of
labor are increasingly looked for in determining demand, such as
workers who are vulnerable to accepting corporate controls on wages,
who have little support for collectivized forms of protest, and who
are under pressure from similar workers who are unemployed. Such
factors help keep wages down wherever plants are located.

However, by singling out dominant technologies, Storper and

Walker have introduced differentials determining the regional specificity of some industries as opposed to others. For example, a plant
assembling automobile engines by processing automated materials
requires large numbers of skilled machinists to operate effectively.
Such plants tend to be located in the industrial heartland of the Midwest, which has an overabundant supply of such workers. In contrast, the textile industry is an example of a mechanized process industry; it requires workers with minimal skills and much patience
who can attend machines without complaint. These industries tend
to locate in rural areas of the South, away from union influence, and
in areas where large numbers of low-skilled workers are readily
available.

In effect, Storper and Walker show that, because mainstream
theory fails to understand the true nature of labor's effect on location
decisions, it lacks an appreciation of marxian anthropology and,
therefore, it fetishizes the nature of labor power. In addition, conventional thought has left unexplored the differential relation between
labor power and industrial technologies as forces of production,
along with their greater locational dependency on specific places. As
they observe:

> One must not only analyze the common forces acting on differ-
> ent branches of industry but study what makes them *distinct*.
> Otherwise, aggregation can mask as much as it reveals. This
> approach retains the idea of systemic, structural forces driving
> industrial evolution, but escapes the excessive generalizations
> of the product cycle; that is, it considers the particularities of
> industries as a necessary prism through which the structural
> forces are refracted into specific outcomes. The common forces
> of competition; class struggle, etc., have led industries down
> different evolutionary paths because each one faces fundamen-
> tally different sets of possibilities and limits in marketing, pro-
> duction and organization. (1983: 25)

That is, the specific qualities of each industry's product prevent
mainstream analysis from aggregating all qualities effectively and require instead an industry-by-industry look at specific determinants
for location decisions. This is the case even after we acknowledge
the primary role that labor force considerations do play. In fact, technological production constraints and labor force needs are tied together by Storper and Walker's analysis of location decisions through
a central focus on the technology of production. As indicated above,
once a typology of such production technologies has been specified,
geographical distinctions regarding location decisions can be made

on the basis of finding a labor force in an area that best fits production needs.

Finally, Storper and Walker move their analysis from an emphasis on the determining quality of industry-specific technology to an explanation of the historical trajectory of industry development. They conceive of the latter as being determined by three separate processes linking respectively the relation between capitalists and workers, between industry and the surrounding community, and between industry and regional growth. As they suggest:

> Breaking out of a static conception of employment means rethinking industrial location. Location is more than matching plant labor demands to appropriate labor forces scattered about the landscape. It is entwined in the reproduction of capital, labor and the pattern of industrial geography. (1984: 39)

It is at this point in their argument that the major contribution of the labor theory approach to location can be highlighted. The heart of Storper and Walker's approach is their introduction of the class struggle to location theory, which is specified as the employment relation, that is, the struggle between capital and labor over the conditions of employment. On the one hand, capitalists are constrained in this struggle not only by their own profit margins but by the external operating environment, including sectoral competition and the "stability of an area's industrial base" (1984: 40). Industry health often means promoting regional growth as well. On the other hand, the stability of the local labor supply is dependent to a great extent on the well-being of the community and the localized process of labor reproduction. For this reason the fortunes of industry and of community life are often intertwined. In the end, the struggle at the core of the employment relation will regulate both the supply of and the demand for labor and in turn will affect specific industry expansion as well as regional development. However, this process plays itself out against the larger operating environment of industry, sector, and society as a whole.

In this sense, stable solutions to the employment relation "cannot be maintained forever," as the contradictions of capitalist development penetrate the peace between boss and worker. Disequilibrating impacts force companies to rethink location and to shift spatial arrangements as a means of managing both labor costs and sectoral competition. As Storper and Walker observe:

> In sum, location and relocation are essential means of shaping and changing the employment relation in a continuing effort by management to remain competitive and contain the class

struggle in the workplace. Mobility in space is not a luxury for capital, but a necessity. Over time the intersection of labor and capital in space, as a critical dimension of employment, feeds back into the fortunes of capital, the evolution of technology, and, of course, the history of the working class communities. (1984: 41)

There can be little argument with most of Storper and Walker's assertions, even from mainstreamers. Their contribution, which follows from marxism, is the manner in which they prove that labor is not like other inputs to production but involves a contentious process which affects its supply, quality, and cost. This approach illustrates the fallacious premises of contemporary location theory, which reduces labor to a lifeless commodity offered at a price. In this way the marxian approach again shows its superiority to mainstream urban science by being better able to explain societal change, especially the present, highly fluid environment of location shifts.

Storper and Walker like to leave their readers with the impression that they have explained everything. This is in keeping with one ideological limitation of marxian political economy, namely, its aping of mainstream positivism. Thus, they acknowledge that other factors not related directly to labor also play a role in location decisions. Yet, we are asked to place such considerations in the background in favor of a causal model of decision making which relies exclusively on technological and labor force constraints. Thus factors involving circulation or marketing, industrial organization, sociospatial amenities, international competition, financial constraints, and competition between capitals—in short, changes in the social relations of production—become second-order phenomena of less importance than the two factors stressed by Storper and Walker, because they are conflated by vague terms such as "sectoral environment" and industrial "structure." In essence they have articulated a causal, empiricist theory of location which is *compatible* with mainstream thought because it asserts that a select few factors, which are not dialectically related, determine the location of firms in specific places. In fact, they share with mainstreamers an emphasis on technological considerations and a vulgar emphasis on the deterministic effect of the forces of production (that is, labor power and technology) at the expense of production relations.

Regardless of how little Storper and Walker's capitalists value the human worth of laborers and how much they seek to employ "vulnerable" elements of the population in the industrial process, they are conceived by them as still seeking to maximize their profits in a *rational* manner, much like the capitalists of the neoclassical location model, that is, by controlling the forces of production so as to minimize their costs. When any contradiction appears in their argument, it is dropped in from outside of what is essentially a rational process of capital's management of the class struggle at the workplace. In short, Storper and Walker's analysis complements conventional work by supplying a marxian version of human capital theory which does not move beyond marxian anthropology to articulate the contradictions and conflict between the forces of production and capitalist relations of production and reproduction. In opposition to their approach, this intersection is not only contingent and anarchic in its outcomes, but the relations of production and reproduction are also organized hierarchically and globally, a feature which Storper and Walker neglect in favor of a more limited view of social structure (1983: 31–33, 1984: 38–41). By centering, instead, on class conflict at the workplace, they ignore aspects of capitalist hegemony which manage the reproduction of labor from the larger system of sociospatial organization, that is, from *outside* the factory.

One aspect of the present discussion, in addition to exorcising the scourge of positivism from marxian analysis, is its attack on political economy for its reductionist tendencies, especially its placement of economic factors as central to sociospatial analysis. In the present case, this becomes a need to highlight the hierarchical structure of the relations of production which support the new relations of sociospatial organization. Thus, Storper and Walker's approach is limited because of the way in which they conceptualize the employment relation. It is seen as structured by what are basically straightforward, almost one-dimensional relations between workers and capitalists *within* industries, communities, labor markets, and, especially, the context of work itself—or what they call the relations in production, using a new term coined by a recent fashion of industrial sociology. This neglects those social forces, hierarchically structured, which mediate the employment relation from the outside. Both the demand and the supply of labor, to use the same categories in their analysis, are affected qualitatively by relations of production and reproduction exogenous to the particularized employment relation.

First, and with regard to supply, the relatively well paid, highly skilled segment of labor is professionally trained and marketed increasingly by national systems of education and employment, while the progressively marginalized secondary segments have been so deskilled that the differences between workers themselves are secondary to the relative extent of their organization by labor unions. This makes the supply of skilled labor dependent on a reproduction process which is serialized by location over time, while the supply of semiskilled labor is regulated by general conditions of labor marginalization and impoverishment, such as the need for two family incomes and the busting of union power. National labor marketing and geographic mobility in educational careers both provide a more footloose base to the trained labor force than Storper and Walker seem to suggest. When this affects male household heads in our society, women and children, who constitute the mainstay of the low-wage labor force, seem to tag along. In short, labor, in addition to capital, has been made more mobile by contemporary social relations.

The willingness of labor, comprising all segments of the market, to move is amply demonstrated by the rapid influx of people in boom areas, such as California and Texas. Underlying this phenomenon is an allied willingness on the part of most Americans to travel from place to place, so that prospective employers are not as tied down or as dependent upon particular locationally specific sources of labor power supply as they once were.

Second, Storper and Walker forget the principal exploitable feature of labor power relative to other inputs in production, namely, its ability to absorb its own costs of supply. There is no inventory when it comes to labor, only a reserve army of the unemployed and the choice of accepting the wage bargain or absorbing the costs of conflict. In this regard labor acts, when the reserve army has grown to a critical mass, as a perfect competitor—with the struggle at the core of the employment relation being regulated by the exogenous features of the larger society's level of class consciousness and its willingness to subsidize labor's reproduction. Thus, the supply of labor can be orchestrated in its favor only if the labor force assumes such noncompetitive collective forms as unions, employee organizations, and the like. At present the level of the organization of labor supply in the interests of workers is at one of the lowest ebbs in U.S. history. Consequently, employers are less concerned about managing the supply of labor through all means, including space, than Storper and Walker suggest. In fact, in recent history the white-collar work force in particular—upon which most of the new industries depend—has shown itself eager to absorb the costs of capitalist location decisions. This is so with regard to moving to new employment opportunities as they open up nationally and paying for the increasing costs of commutation with money and time. When we consider the present, a kind of reverse Say's law is in operation for labor. Demand creates its own supply, even for skilled occupations. One has only to follow the course of events after the announcement of job openings, from positions in academia to municipal fire fighting, to be convinced of the new mobility of labor. Thus, while industry is dependent upon sources of labor, contemporary conditions which have operated to reduce class conflict in general, such as the sheer volume of job loss, have made labor almost as mobile as capital—running scared, as it were.

Third, the contemporary employment relation, which is weighted heavily in favor of the capitalist class, benefits by hierarchical systems of domination. Quite effective in attenuating class conflict in recent years, these include most especially the role of the state and that of mass culture. In fact, all three aspects of social organization—economics, politics, and culture—have been tied together in the discussion of class conflict by the theory of Fordism, especially its French school (Aglietta 1978). This approach has been broken down into stages, that is, periodized, to address changing aspects of the present, called neo-Fordism (Aglietta 1978; Hirsch 1983) or global Fordism (Lipietz 1982). According to this approach, the employment relation can be specified by the adoption on the part of, respectively, the capitalist class in particular and the society as a whole of mass production techniques and the culture of mass consumption. According to Davis, these processes were manifested most especially by the twin drivers of "automobilization" and household "mechanization" (1984: 14), both of which have affected sociospatial organization through the promotion of suburbanization and deconcen-· trated metropolitan change. Viewed from this perspective, the relation between capital and labor is regulated less by the contradictions in the forces of production or within the confines of the direct confrontation between capital and labor at the place of employment, as Storper and Walker claim, than by the concerted efforts of a combined public-private sector system of priorities which integrates the working class into the very core of capital's needs. Fordism, therefore, represents a delicate meshing of political and cultural behaviors orchestrated hierarchically to fit the logic of capitalist development. For Davis this confluence supported the sociospatial changes which are the subject of the present discussion, namely, deconcentration.

According to Storper and Walker, the working-class community is the site of the reproduction of unique labor pools. Thus the classic community promotes the stability of capitalist-worker relations and the meshing of industrial and social development. Yet, under the forces of metropolitan deconcentration, Fordist ideologies, and state intervention in the field of consumption (see chapter 4), the tightly knit working-class community of the past has increasingly disap-

peared. This has made capital less dependent on such classic mechanisms of labor's reproduction and more dependent upon the state.
Further, the disappearance of such communities has been occurring
for quite some time, well before the recent phase of deindustrialization and plant closings, as it is intimately connected to the process
of suburbanization in the United States. It is not by accident, therefore, that Storper and Walker choose to support their theory of labor's
reproduction by citing sources which tend to address the British
rather than the American case.

The principal locational implications of metropolitan deconcentration, state intervention in the reproduction of labor, and Fordist strategies, which Storper and Walker fail to consider, involve
both the liberation of labor demand from particularized locations
and the regulation of industrial development less by the class struggle
than by the contradictions deployed across space, in fact, globally, of
the Fordist orchestration itself. As Lipietz (1982), Hirsch (1983), and
Davis (1984) all suggest, the shifting locational choices of capitalism
and the complete, global sociospatial deployment of production are
dictated by the contradictory realities of Fordist logic and its current
crisis, an issue which must be bypassed here. Suffice it to say that
the limited, nonhierarchical view of the class struggle conceptualized by the labor theory of location requires revision from the
larger perspective suggested by the more global view above. This
takes into account the political and cultural as well as the economic
contradictions of the Late Capitalist process of global accumulation
and labor sourcing in determining the changing locational needs of
industry. Both metropolitan deconcentration and the social production of space are more clearly grasped from the latter perspective
than from class conflict approaches, which limit the management of
the clash between capital and labor to the site of work itself. Consequently, the variant of marxian political economy focusing on class
struggle as an explanation of changes in spatial form, as discussed in
the previous two sections, is too causally constrained, and we must
search elsewhere for a more dialectical approach. Within the confines of marxian political economy, such a need is met by the theory
of capital accumulation in urban environments.

CAPITAL ACCUMULATION THEORY

All marxian analysts would agree that the study of capitalism requires a focus on the accumulation process (Edel 1981; Hill 1977;
Harvey 1975a). According to Hill, for example:

Capital accumulation, the production of surplus value, is the driving force of capitalist society. By its very nature, capital accumulation necessitates expansion of the means of production, expansion of the size of the wage labor force, expansion of circulation activity as more products become commodities, and expansion of the realm of control of the capitalist class. (1977: 41)

From such a perspective, capital accumulation theorists explain the process of city development or urbanization as the spatial manifestation of the accumulation process. As Harvey remarks, "Urbanism involves the concentration of surplus (however designated) in some version of the city (whether it be walled enclave or the sprawling metropoli of the present day)" (1973: 237). Or, as Hill suggests, "In a capitalist society urbanization and the structure and functioning of cities is rooted in the production, reproduction, circulation and overall organization of the capital accumulation process" (1977: 41).

The accumulation perspective aims at a more global grasp of the societal development process than does the class conflict approach. Clearly the two aspects are related and, as Edel observes, at any time "the reproduction of capitalist relations and the accumulation of capital may be interrupted or may be affected by the ongoing struggle between capitalists and the working class" (1981: 37). In practice capital accumulationists stress the structural aspects of this process and relate them to urban development. For the most part, analysts invoke the signifier "capitalist" without specifying precisely what the accumulation process is like, deployed spatially. The very best examples of this approach, however, locate the genesis of urban phenomena *within* the development process itself by showing how capital accumulation is manifested in space and how it is affected by that very deployment. This is very much like a dialectical theory of sociospatial relations, the focus of this book; consequently, its articulation requires our detailed attention. Among all analysts working in this vein, David Harvey and Allen J. Scott stand out in their attempts at capturing the interrelated nature of capitalist development and spatial form. Let us consider their approaches to space.

The Role of Finance Capital and the Interventionist State

David Harvey's approach to the built environment is spread out over several articles and one book (1973) which apply the marxian method to urban analysis. Even his 1981 article, which offers a framework and comes closest to a complete statement of his perspective, is meant more to guide further urban analysis than to bind together his previous material. For this reason any assessment of Harvey requires a reading of all his papers rather than his most recent book (1983), which is meant more as a general analysis of capitalism than as a study of urban phenomena.

Harvey starts from the same place as Gordon does. The urban form can be explained in a marxian sense if we focus on the two drivers: capital accumulation and the class struggle (1973). At once, however, we leave simplified arguments to face the full complexity of an attempt to integrate institutional with economic factors in the analysis of capitalist development. Harvey begins his explorations by applying classical marxian concepts to urban development, such as surplus value, overproduction, the falling rate of profit, and the accumulation crisis. To these he adds current arguments explaining the rise of Keynesianism or the interventionist state and the hegemonic thrust of finance capital—all aspects of Late Capitalism not treated by Marx. Over the course of these papers, five central arguments of political economy are developed.

First, Harvey specifies the city's functional role—the accumulation process—and the consequences of that role for the class structure of society. He defines the city as an intersection node in the space economy, as a built environment that arises from the mobilization, extraction, and geographic concentration of significant quantities of surplus value (1973: 246). Capitalism depends first upon the concentration and then upon the circulation of this surplus product. The city is produced by the spatial patterning of these processes, and the role that the urban form plays in them is a function of the social, economic, technological, and institutional possibilities that govern the disposition of the surplus value concentrated within it. A different combination of those possibilities, therefore, would result in a different role for the city as a node in the space economy. In this way Harvey explains the functional differentiation underlying the systems of cities approach.

Much as any other marxian geographer would, Harvey argues that the city form depends for its survival upon an adequate functioning of the spatially organized social system. As he states:

> The flows of goods and services throughout this space economy are a tangible expression of that process which circulates surplus value in order to concentrate more of it. This conception of the space economy is more instructive than the conventional one extant in geography and regional science which rests on Adam Smith's notion that everything can be explained by an insatiable consumer demand and mutual gains from trade. It

is more realistic, therefore, to model an urban-space economy as a surplus-creating, -extracting and -concentrating device. (1973: 238)

Using this conceptualization, and following Lefebvre (1970, 1972), Harvey articulates a theory of the production of space which covers much the same ground as does mainstream geography but also serves as a marxian alternative to it. He provides an explanation for the rise of the city from an undifferentiated agricultural plain in the manner of Von Thunen. He then gives an explanation for the shifting spatial patterning of the city, as specified by qualitative changes in the social formation from feudalism to the modern metropolis. His analysis, however, is much more specific than that provided by the labor conflict perspective, and it is tied more directly to his model of the city as an accumulation node in the system of extraction and circulation of surplus value.

In particular, Harvey demonstrates how the drive for capital accumulation through the realization of surplus value and its confrontation with labor in the class struggle has created a complex social structure with fractions *within* the capitalist class as well as a shifting relationship between labor, capitalists, and the state. In two articles, in order to address this topic more specifically, he turns his attention to the changes that have occurred as a consequence of capital's intervention in society due to the crisis of the Great Depression of the 1930s, especially the effects of Keynesian transformational measures (1975b, 1976). According to Harvey, the very same features arising from the need to stimulate effective demand and prevent widespread unemployment also turn out to function as a means of producing urban deconcentration and the rise of the regional metropolitan form. This functionalist argument will be assessed below, as it differs from the Fordist theory discussed above.

In a subsequent article (1976), Harvey turns his attention to specifying the manner in which capital accumulation takes place in space. He and Scott are the only two urbanists in the United States to have assumed this chore. Using the categories of classical political economy, Harvey distinguishes between three conditions under which capitalists realize surplus value in space; these involve forms of rent, interest, and profit. Various fractions within the capitalist class operate by appropriating any one or a combination of these three forms. Hence, Harvey begins his discussion of the role of capital accumulation in space by rejecting a monolithic view of the capitalist class. Such a qualification becomes important because he indicates that there seem to be at least three fractions of capital oper-

ating in the built environment, according to the various forms of realizing surplus value.

The first fraction of capital concentrates on rent and appropri-
ates it either directly, as in the case of landlords, or indirectly, as exhibited by financial interests which operate through real estate speculation. The second fraction of capital seeks both interest and profit
through construction—adding directly to the built environment either by engaging in construction or financing the work of others.
There is a third fraction of capital that operates in the interests of
the class as a whole. Harvey calls this "capital in general," because it
regards the built environment as a site for the effective appropriation
of surplus value, which supports capital accumulation. This last
fraction is interventionist by nature, and it has operated since the
1930s at least, most directly through state-supported and state-
administered programs which attempt to insure the survival of the
capitalist class.

This conceptualization illustrates not only the advances made
by Harvey but also some of the limitations of his analysis. On the
positive side, these papers attempt an explanation of the production
of urban form by the capital accumulation process and, next, a specification of that process in space. On the negative side, two points can
be noted at this time. First, the fractions of capital in the accumulation process do not correspond directly to the components of capital
identified as rent, interest, and profit. Capitalists can work with any
one or with any combination of these elements to realize surplus
value in space. However, the activities of capitalists can be divided
into separate fractions of capital, which Harvey identifies as corporate, financial, and landed interests. The distinction between the
fractions of capital constituted as parts of the capitalist class and the
forms of surplus value constituted as rent, interest, and profit is *not*
made clear in Harvey's analysis. In addition, marxists differ with regard to considering these as truly separate fractions (see chapter 5).
If, as Harvey does imply, they are to be viewed as distinct, he does
not supply us with a class analysis that can defend such an implication. Consequently, Harvey had a need for a more structural way of
specifying the process of accumulation. This was accomplished later
on by his introduction of Lefebvre's idea of capital's circuits.

Second, Harvey conceptualizes the interventionist aspects of
the capitalist class as "capital in general." This assumes that the
state operates as an agent of the capitalist class, a view belonging to
orthodox marxism. Recently, however, it has been profitable to consider the state as possessing what Poulantzas (1973) terms "relative
autonomy," or as being "autonomous" according to the work of the

neoweberians (Saunders 1981), and as pursuing political as well as economic interests not always capitalist in nature. This view of the state imputes more degrees of freedom to political actions than does the functionalist perspective adopted by Harvey. This is so despite the fact that the state can also be viewed in the sense which he intends, as well as in a more "autonomous" mode of action.

Harvey then proceeds to a third topic—building a theory of the relation between the state and capital with regard to intervention in space. His analysis integrates class conflict into the contradictory relation between the state and civil society. He notes that labor "uses the built environment as a means of consumption and as a means for its own reproduction." This focus for labor's use of the urban form will become important below when we consider the approach of Castells. It is, however, also essential for Harvey's analysis because he situates the class struggle within matters associated with *living* arrangements, in addition to those issues that arise in the workplace. As he indicates, "Labor, in seeking to protect and enhance its standard of living, engages in a series of running battles in the living place over a variety of issues that relate to the creation, management and use of the built environment" (1976: 268). Such a perspective on the importance of the quality of everyday life for workers is also addressed by Fordist theory, as we have seen, and is especially fruitful for an understanding of urban politics. For Harvey and for Castells, this struggle is theoretically specified as a displacement of class conflict to the local community. As I shall argue in chapter 5, this is a limited view of sociospatial conflict and a reduction of local politics to a neomarxist variant of economism.

The fourth aspect of Harvey's work addresses the need to explain changes in urban form. His argument for the transformation of the urban pattern from the city to the expanding metropolitan region focuses on the interconnections between the fractions of capital and the class struggle. He contends that the built environment is transformed essentially by interventionist capital acting through government. This is so because appropriators of rent and builders working for profit do not necessarily enjoy a confluence of interests regarding how each should use the social surplus. Furthermore, labor at the place of residence struggles with these separate fractions of capital over the quality of life as development schemes are proposed. Therefore, Harvey contends that "capital *in general* cannot afford the outcome of struggles around the built environment to be determined simply by the relative powers of labor, the appropriators of rent and the construction fraction" (1976: 272). Capital must intervene, and it usually does so through the agency of the state.

Harvey indicates several aspects of this interventionist feature, including the socialization of the labor force by the imposition of work discipline, the management of collective consumption as part of Keynesian crisis measures to prevent a recurrence of depression, and the fundamental shift to homeownership as the dominant mode of worker residence. As in Fordist arguments, these three responses by capital have converged over the years to produce a complex internal differentiation of government, business, and labor that is characteristic of society today; however, Harvey has a much more functionalist version of this approach. At this point in the discussion of his work, it is possible to underscore its central limitation. Just as do other marxian political economists, Harvey ascribes far too much rationality to the capital accumulation process as well as, more significantly, to the state-capital articulation. In particular, the abstraction "capital in general" as the chosen means of specifying the nature of state intervention leads Harvey down a terminally functionalist path. His endemic functionalism is perhaps illustrated best by his discussion of the social control nature of state intervention, especially the support of private homeownership.

According to Harvey, the urban fiscal crisis is but one aspect of a general debt-financing pattern assumed by the capitalist system principally since World War II, which coincides with the rise of finance capital as a hegemonic capitalist fraction. He highlights a special case of this process, the phenomenal growth of private homeownership, as indicative of one additional way that "capital in general" has intervened in society to protect the accumulation process from the class struggle. Single-family housing is perhaps the only major element of suburbanization and, consequently, the main constituent of regional population dispersal. It emerged against the wishes of what used to be a significant fraction of capital, the landlords with investments in rent-bearing properties within the central city.

Harvey explains the switch to private homeownership in terms of social control. He notes that, in a capitalist system with only rental apartments or rental houses available to the working class, a well-developed struggle between tenants and landlords can potentially call the entire system of private property into question—because of the relative ease with which living quarters can be expropriated initially by their residents. By extending homeownership to a segment of the working class, this segment's allegiance to the system of private property can be acquired in a fundamental way. In this sense, such an extension is "functional" for the continued survival of capitalism. Furthermore, moving a segment of the working class into property ownership splits workers into fractions comprised of those who can afford the cost of a home and those who cannot. As Harvey observes, "This gives the capitalist class a handy ideological lever to use against public ownership and nationalization demands because it is easy to make such proposals sound as if the intent is to take workers' privately owned houses away from them" (1976: 272). Although such ideas are attractive, they can hardly explain the phenomenon of state housing policies; we need to search for other factors. In addition, the social control explanation for suburbanization is an essentially weak one, as we shall see in chapter 7.

The fifth and final feature of Harvey's work focuses on the infrastructural changes in contemporary capitalism which support the circulation of capital and aid its realization in space. Using Baltimore in a 1975 study, for example, Harvey details the precise way in which the complex, highly specialized system of capital circulation links changes in the urban spatial pattern with the process of financial investment (see also Hula 1980). Such a system is differentiated into a variety of institutions, including savings and loan associations, commercial banks, credit unions, life insurance companies, pension funds, real estate investment trusts, and financial brokerage houses. Each of these operates with different objectives in mind, and each has an impact upon different aspects of the construction industry. Harvey demonstrates that in Baltimore suburban growth and central city decay were both linked directly to the incentives and relative ease of financing provided by this system. The channeling of resources to the Baltimore region had a differential geographical manifestation which supported regional expansion but also engendered uneven development, with its consequent inequities. Harvey concludes:

> There is abundant evidence that the financial superstructure plays an important role in the organization of local housing markets and that many of the "urban problems" with which we are familiar—racial and class segregation, housing abandonment, neighborhood decay, speculative change, fiscal inequalities between cities and suburbs, inequality of access to services (such as education and health care)—are in some way tied to residential differentiation in cities which is, in turn, tied to the way in which investment is channeled into local markets. (1975b: 140)

For this reason, Harvey indicates that the contradictions experienced in the built environment are reproduced because of the steps taken to make finance capital the "mediating link between the urbanization process (in all of its aspects including the building of built environments and urban social movements) and the necessities dictated by the underlying dynamic of capitalism in the United States" (1975a: 40). In the next section, we shall see that Allen Scott explains the very same results using a different, neoricardian model.

In summation, David Harvey's work has five main arguments. He has set out to explain the production of the built environment by providing a detailed picture of the ways in which the capitalist system works and is transformed in response to its crises. He ties the class struggle to more fundamental aspects of capital's desire to socialize the industrial labor force, manage collective consumption, and pursue Keynesian interventionist measures. Finally, he indicates that these efforts have resulted in a social formation dominated by finance capital—with society dependent upon the adequate functioning of a complex monetary structure that keeps capital circulating as *investments* in the city. In the end, Harvey arrives at a realization that the nature of urban space has been altered. Originally an engine for concentrating and appropriating surplus value through industrial production, the urban environment has become a place created to stimulate consumption and maintain a high level of effective demand within a debt-encumbered framework. In agreement with Fordist arguments, he states:

> The American city is now designed to stimulate consumption. The emphasis upon sprawl, individualized modes of consumption, owner-occupancy, and the like, is to be interpreted as one of several responses to the under-consumption problems of the 1930's (military expenditures being another). And it is in these terms, too, that we can interpret how the financial superstructure, itself created in response to the crisis conditions of the 1930's, so mediated the flow of investment into the urban infrastructure, including housing, that its mediations served to transform cities once fashioned as the "workshops of industrial society" into cities for the artificial stimulation of consumption. (1975a: 139)

In this way we can trace the rather dramatic shift in Harvey's emphasis as he has developed his ideas, beginning with the publication of his 1973 work. From an engine for growth, the city has become an organized space for consumption and capital investment. From a view of the city as a concentrated production node, we have moved to the more decentralized space of the built environment which functions primarily as the site of capital circulation rather than production (for a better approach, see Scott below). Finally, from a view of society which sees the capitalist class as intervening monolithically through the state to avoid crises of underconsumption, we see a fraction of capital, finance capital, achieving hegemony. Thus the process of capital investment becomes the central focus in the production of the built environment.

These changes represent more a refinement of Harvey's approach through his several articles than a transformation of ideas. However, through them he seems to have abandoned the role played by the production of surplus value in the capital accumulation process, a role which is considered central to analysis by most marxists. Furthermore, by seeming to ignore production, Harvey can develop only a very attenuated version of class conflict, which is another key process for marxists. The central problem in his analysis is the lack of connection between the focal process in the production of the built environment, which he has identified as capital accumulation, and the larger social formation, which performs other functions as well. Thus, his theory of the relation between capital and the state leaves much to be desired (see the discussion on Castells in chapter 4). To be sure, while Harvey's analysis of class conflict seems more sophisticated than social control theory, for example, it nevertheless requires greater amplification, especially with regard to conflicts between separate fractions of the class structure and the role of the state in space. As Mingione (1981) has recently remarked with regard to Harvey's approach, there is far too much emphasis on the built environment in his work—to the neglect of explaining spatial patterns both in general and as the result of the complex mode of production under Late Capitalist relations. In short, Harvey has specified in considerable detail the relation between capitalist processes of development and sociospatial organization; however, each of the topics which he addresses requires considerably more work if marxian analysis is to overcome its functionalist, positivist limitations.

As a means of recovering a more theoretical overview of the connection between space and the mode of production, Harvey (1981) has proposed a general framework for analysis, drawing upon his previous studies, which integrates the arguments above. According to him the central focus for urban analysis is the production of the built environment, and as we have seen this process reduces to one which involves the dynamics of capital investment. Harvey's task is then to explain in some detail the connection between this process and capital accumulation for the society as a whole. He proceeds to specify this relationship by abandoning his earlier returns-to-capital argument (see above) and by identifying three separate circuits of capital accumulation. The primary circuit, which is based upon Marx's analysis of capital, refers to the organization of the productive process itself, such as the application of wage labor and machinery to produce commodities for profit. The secondary circuit—Harvey derives this distinction from Lefebvre (1970), as we shall see in the next chapter—involves investment in the built environment for production or fixed assets and consumption goods or the consumption fund (1981: 96). Finally, the tertiary circuit in Harvey's model refers to investment in science and technology and "a wide range of social expenditures which relate primarily to the processes of reproduction of labor power" (1981: 97).

The immediate question for marxists raised by such a scheme is that, since all value is created by labor power through the process of production, how can the secondary and tertiary circuits be considered a means of acquiring surplus value for capitalists? In what sense is there an incentive to invest in other capital circuits, or, rather, what is the place of those circuits in the creation of surplus value? Harvey attempts to answer this question by dynamizing capital production, that is, by viewing the operation of the mode of production across several time periods. In this way investment in the secondary circuit enhances capital's ability to produce more by installing more fixed assets and also by stimulating consumption through the production of commodities for the consumer society. Tertiary circuit investment also results in greater surplus value being created over time, both because technological expertise is a force of production which amplifies labor's power and because investment in education and health improves the intrinsic quality of labor power. However, as we shall see, Harvey's functionalist faith in the productive nature of capital's articulation with space is unwarranted.

The next task of Harvey's framework is to explain the connection between the production of the built environment and the capital accumulation process. Following Marx, Harvey notes that competition between capitalists results in overaccumulation: "Too much capital is produced in aggregate relative to the opportunities to employ that capital" (1981: 94). A temporary solution to this problem becomes a switch of capital flow into the other circuits. When this is done involving the secondary circuit, we have the production of the built environment. However, as Harvey is quick to point out, despite the benefits to future production periods, individual capitalists will tend to underinvest in the built environment. Consequently there is a need for two structural aids to insure investment of overaccumulated capital in the secondary circuit. On the one hand, capital requires a freely functioning financial network and market (1975b). On the other hand, capital requires a state willing to supply the backing to long-term construction projects (1975a). Both the financial network and state intervention become the mediating processes for the accumulation relationship between the first two circuits of capital.

Interestingly enough, the state in this framework is specified as an investment coordinator between the circuits of capital. We know from Harvey's previous writings, however, that there should be more to the state than this with regard to the built environment, and we shall come to this inadequacy below. In fact, it is at this point that we reach the limits of his theory of capital flows. According to Harvey, as overaccumulation is siphoned off into the secondary circuit, a system limit is reached and such investments are no longer profitable. Harvey explains this phenomenon by recourse to a theory of capital devalorization. In fact, his entire approach to the relation between capital and space comes to rest on this very concept. He states that, when investment in the secondary circuit reaches its limit, "the exchange value being put into the built environment has to be written down, diminished, or even totally lost" (1981: 106). However, he fails to explain why secondary circuit investment reaches saturation, a point of disagreement, as we shall see in chapter 5, explaining only that the dead labor represented by the built environment must be periodically swept away in order for new investment to occur. Accordingly the old built environment becomes a barrier that can be overcome only through periodic devalorization. Thus, what can be viewed as the product of unanticipated socio-spatial outcomes (see Scott below), that is, the uneven development of space, becomes for Harvey a functionalist theory of devalorization.

In Harvey's approach, the periodic investment rush and the subsequent devaluation of the built environment are clearly indicated in the cyclical rhythms of the capital investment process in space. The cycles include especially the Kondratieffs or fifty-year-long waves and shorter, fifteen- to twenty-five-year movements. These serve to document the cyclical nature of periodic crises in capitalism as a whole. The dynamic behind the investment cycles of capitalism, therefore, explains the stages in the construction of the built environment, and Harvey backs up this claim with impressive empirical evidence from Britain and the United States, gathered by Gottlieb (1976). The logical conclusion of his approach, however, is that uneven spatial development and the periodic devaluation of the built environment are "functional" for future capital investment. For every "zone of growth" representing an area attracting investment, there is a "zone of transition" where fixed capital is devalorized before speculators can cash in on redevelopment. As Harvey indicates:

> The devalued capital in space functions as a free good and stimulates renewed investment, under capitalism there is, then, a perpetual struggle in which capital builds a physical landscape appropriate to its own condition at a particular moment in time, only to have to destroy it, usually in the course of a crisis, at a subsequent point in time. The temporal ebb and flow of investment in the built environment can be understood only in terms of such a process. (1981: 114)

Most important, and according to Harvey's theory, this process occurs because of the saturation of investment in secondary circuit activity, a view which I do not share and which subsequently calls his entire theory of capital into question.

A discussion of the limitations of Harvey's theory of accumulation will help frame the issues which still need to be considered by a marxian analysis of space. First, his approach is limited because it fails to specify the relationship between the state and space. In the entire corpus of Harvey's writing, the state's ontological status is as the agent of capital in general. Thus Harvey's view does not progress beyond a traditional marxist notion of the state as the agent of the ruling class. At his most sophisticated, this state is a partner of a particular fraction of the capitalist class—finance capital—but in this sense Harvey progresses little beyond specifying the nature of the state in capitalism as did Rudolf Hilferding or V. I. Lenin. We shall see in subsequent chapters that a theory of space requires a detailed understanding of the relationship between the state, the society, and space itself, and only Castells and Lefebvre have provided us with such a connection.

Second, Harvey sees the creation of value in society as dependent upon the switching of capital flows between circuits, which is driven by the crisis base of capitalism, that is, the tendency of the rate of profit to fall. He specifies the mechanism for such switches as external to the capitalist class itself and as located in a combined state–finance capital framework. However, this *cannot* explain the operation of the law of exchange value in society, nor can it explain why capital can counter the falling rate of profit by such investment. Harvey does not explain why it is that overinvestment occurs in the secondary circuit because he has not specified the operation of the law of value in space (see Lipietz 1977, 1980). Instead, the secondary circuit is not perceived by Harvey's capitalists as necessarily attractive for investment, except during overaccumulation crises. Thus, the flow of capital into the built environment is orchestrated from outside the capital-labor relation and by the state–finance capital framework. In the case of Lefebvre, however, space itself has been elevated in importance to a force of production by a theoretical argument which can be used to overcome this limitation and explain why investment in land is *always* attractive; I shall take this matter up again in the next chapter. Suffice it to say that Harvey has not explained how capital can be made to switch to other circuits of capital, the state and financial networks notwithstanding—and this is especially important for an understanding of Late Capitalism, where the productive circuit is dominated by concentrated forms of monopoly capital that, through global networks, certainly can modify the kinds of overaccumulation crises Harvey claims still prevail. In fact, Harvey's analysis of Late Capitalism as a form of social organization and its global process of accumulation is surprisingly undeveloped in general, as Mingione observes (1981), and I shall try to remedy this shortcoming in chapter 6.

A third limitation of Harvey's work is the strain which views all interventions in space as advancing the capital accumulation process in a functionalist manner. For example, he claims that eventually the built environment is devalorized so that uneven development can play its role in the future process of accumulation. This is a very limited view of the process of uneven development and the role it plays in space (for a critique of devalorization theory see Theret 1982; Mandel 1975). Furthermore, the assertion that such devalorization occurs because it is needed once again succumbs to the functionalist fallacy—trivializing Harvey's more sophisticated empirical analysis, where he documents the role of the fragmented financial structure in devaluing the central city sections of Baltimore (1975b). Throughout Harvey's intellectual production there is a tendency to revert to a manipulated city argument, in which a capitalist class dominates a monolithic working class and its everyday space. This confuses the operation of capitalism as a structural system with the voluntaristic actions of individuals as members of classes. By asserting that outcomes of processes eventually serve the interests of the system, Harvey claims for capitalists as individuals a prescience which, as Boulay has already remarked in another context, "strains the limits of credulity." Consequently, Harvey's analysis of the important process of uneven spatial development leaves much to be desired. In the very next section, we shall see that Scott has proposed an alternate explanation for the uneven nature of central city development, one which specifies the production of such a pattern in much more detail without recourse to devalorization theory.

Fourth, and following from the above, Harvey's analysis of class structure in modern society and its relationship to land requires further explication. We agree here with a wide variety of other analysts, to be discussed more fully below, that an understanding of such a relationship demands greater detail regarding the nature of stratification under Late Capitalism. In particular, by identifying the separate interests operating in the built environment we can understand spatial conflict which, on the one hand, is more complex than Harvey would have us believe and, on the other, has results not necessarily functional for anyone, such as environmental inefficiency, rampant violent crime, the spatial reproduction of racial segregation, and so on.

Finally, I note that Harvey's main contribution seems to be his elaboration of Lefebvre's and Gottlieb's work on the relationship between the empirically verified periodic investment cycles, producing the built environment, and the capital accumulation process conceptualized in terms of circuits. This same capital logic argument, however, seems to assert that such a relationship has remained invariant for hundreds of years, that is, since the advent of capitalist hegemony. Thus, Harvey's theory does not really explain the production of different urban *forms*, a matter of central concern for our analysis. Furthermore, as Mandel has shown (1975), since such cyclical changes vary according to particular social formations, they must be examined today from an overall perspective which periodizes the features of capitalist development as a whole. It is at this point that we can come to appreciate the great need of all marxian political economists for a theory of social organization that can tell us about the way in which all the elements of society articulate together in space (and with space). That is, despite Harvey's best efforts so far, it has become apparent that the growing sophistication of the marxian method requires a more comprehensive theory, one which details the nature of social organization and indicates the processes by which the elements of that system come to be deployed in space.

A Neoricardian Approach to the Built Environment

Allen J. Scott has worked out his theory of the "urban land nexus" in a series of articles which culminated in a single monograph (1980). This work requires our attention because he has supplied us with the only coherent model of central city growth from a neoricardian perspective which is more detailed than marxian analyses of production. This approach is noteworthy because neoricardian analysis overcomes the limitations of marxist method specifically with regard to the latter's inadequate theory of value and Harvey's devalorization of capital flows. Scott's essential task has been to ascribe an epiphenomenal status to such concepts as rent, wage, price, and interest in connection with the built environment by demonstrating that all market relations are reified manifestations of underlying relations of production and reproduction specific to capitalism. In this sense Scott's work is much closer to Marx's own thought on the critique of political economy than to that of Harvey. As Scott and Roweiss remark:

> In relation to urbanization processes and urban land problems, then, the essential point of departure for us is not the phenomenon of competitive bidding for land (rents, prices, etc.), but the deep structure of urban property relations in relation to which the competitive bidding for land is only the faintest and most superficial pulsation. (1978: 54)

The significance of Scott's work, therefore, is its appreciation for the ideological nature of all political economy, even in its marxian versions, and its desire to grasp urban processes through an understanding of "totality" or the process of production under capitalist social relations and through the commodity form. There are two key conceptual aspects of this perspective. First, Scott wishes to emphasize the *contradictory* nature of the value of urban land, acknowledged first by French marxists (1976). The use value of land is dependent, on the one hand, upon "the aggregate effects of innumerable individual, social and economic activities" (Scott and Roweiss 1978: 58) and, on the other, upon the social intervention of the state, which provides for infrastructural improvements and public services. According to Scott, the first phase "is unplanned as a whole, and socially undecidable at the outset. In the other phase, land-use outcomes are the result of the political calculations of the state, which exerts direct control over the quality, location and timing of public works" (1980: 136).

Because the overall process of development is driven by the first, privately controlled phase, state intervention cannot rescue the use values of space from the externalities of private expropriation. Yet, state intervention regulates this process in a variety of ways with varying degrees of ineffectualness. Consequently, a second feature of land development under capitalism is its uncoordinated nature. As Scott remarks: "From this it follows inevitably that the urban land development process as a whole in capitalism is anarchical, and leads persistently to outcomes that are neither intended nor socially decided" (1980: 137). As we shall see, I am in agreement with this view—which argues squarely against the assumptions made by Harvey and other marxists that intervention in space by capitalists is always productive and logical, even when it chooses new locations on the basis of available labor.

Scott's analysis points out the contradictions internal to the land development process itself. These are captured by what he calls the urban land nexus—the dense, embedded system of practices by which private and public decision making interact in a pattern which is contingent in nature. On the one hand: "This *contingency* of land-use outcomes in capitalist cities is the direct result of the existence of private, legal control. In brief, precisely because urban land development is privately controlled, the final aggregate outcomes of this process are necessarily and paradoxically out of control" (1980: 137). On the other hand, the state intervenes to offset the irrational nature of market processes, yet it is itself constrained by the social relations of capitalism from coordination in a way which can correct such inadequacies in the general interest.

As Scott indicates, the total effect of these contradictions produces an urban landscape which is the result of a contingent, non-functional process of uneven development. Phenomena such as blight, speculation, property booms and busts, pollution, the differential spatial patterns of residential areas, and so on are produced by the capitalist land development process itself, because that process is uncoordinated and anarchical. As we have seen above, Harvey explains the same effects, through devalorization theory, as being functionally produced by capital flows which are mediated and channeled by the finance capital fraction of the capitalist class. The difference, then, is that Scott explains uneven development as something internal to the production process of capitalism—as something compelling dysfunctional location decisions without recourse to other circuits of capital—while Harvey's focus explains how uneven development becomes intensified by the functionalist "need" of the capital accumulation process to devalue its past investments.

Scott's unique contribution is that he has demonstrated the inexorable nature of uneven development by an economic model of location which integrates the neoricardian approach of Sraffa (1960) with marxian premises regarding the dynamics of surplus value production under capitalism. In this way he has applied the cumulative knowledge of contemporary political economy toward a most sophisticated grasp of the determination of urban land rent within the bounded city form. As Bandyopadhyay has stated:

> Scott follows Steedman in treating real wages as exogenously determined in order for the commodity producing economy to yield determinate prices and profits. In this context the originality of Scott is twofold. Firstly, as indicated, he goes beyond the analysis of exploitation and class struggle presented in a labor-value reference system by orthodox marxists. The latter have concentrated on the process of monopolization and over-accumulation of capital in the sphere of production and have invoked the role of the State as primarily responding to the crisis of falling rates by removing a portion of social capital from the valuation process through public financing of collective consumption and housing for the labor force. Whilst a rich analysis of the partial socialization of the costs of reproducing labor power is provided, such studies, with few notable exceptions, have ignored the formation and appropriation of urban rents and the role of the latter in accounting for the pattern of location of various productive and socially reproductive activities. Scott concentrates on the former problem but has relatively little analysis of the production and location of collective consumption . . . This focus on production processes and consequently on the importance of the utilization of land, and therefore, of rents is closer to Marx's own practise than is the analytical importance given to problems of injustice and inequality as regards access to services, housing and amenities, i.e., a set of distributive results, in much of the recent marxist and radical literature. Non-marxists have had little difficulty with the latter work because a few declarations regarding fiscal remedies or redistributive measures have sufficed to meet such claims. (1982: 278)

I have quoted this summary of Scott's work at length because it helps isolate the important arguments to be considered in the next chapter. Scott raises two issues for a marxian analysis of space. First, his approach to urban land rent, while sophisticated political economy, is merely a model of urban form. As such it is limited by the very nature of deductive reasoning. To be sure, Bandyopadhyay is correct in asserting that this analysis is closest to Marx's own because Scott seeks to model the capitalist development process as it is deployed in space by isolating its internal contradictions. Yet, we may well ask whether this model does an accurate job of depicting the form that that development process actually takes. The answer is no, as it was also for mainstream location theory, because any approach modeling the built environment as a monocentered, bounded form has been rendered obsolete by current history. The neoricardian analysis of land rent determination depends heavily on agglomeration tendencies at the city center, with space itself being fallaciously assigned the status of a commodity (see Scott 1980: 31–41). Quite simply, this cannot explain contemporary determinants of land value in a polycentric metropolitan region, even for the case of land development at the site of the old central business district (see the previous chapter). Throughout his work Scott is crippled by a reliance on Von Thunen and concentric zone models. Thus, this approach has limited value as the basis for a theory of the production of spatial forms, because space is not simply reducible to a commodity produced by capital, as neoricardians might suppose. Scott's approach does, however, succeed well as a refutation of devalorization theory and as a demonstration that uneven growth is a phenomenal effect of capitalist production relations.

Second, in order to show that uneven development is an internal contradiction of the capitalist growth process, Scott assumes a simple two-class model of society which is devoid of class fractions and, consequently, of the differential determinants of wages, interest, and rent. While this is in keeping with his desire to transcend the ideological categories of political economy, Scott throws out the critical phenomenal status of class fractions based upon the contentious division of the surplus product. Inductive analyses of social structure carried out by contemporary marxists all indicate the importance of class fractions in the struggle over surplus value appropriation—as the discussion of Harvey's work has indicated, competition between separate fractions within the capitalist class is particularly important in determining the differential flow of resources throughout the metropolitan region. More specifically, and as I shall specify in chapter 5, the law of value in space operates not only through the aggregate effects of collective actions, as Scott indicates, but also through the monopolistic efforts of specific fractions of capital, sometimes in conjunction with the state. Without recognition of the factors of concentration that stand outside the market, analyses of the land development process, such as Scott's, merely reproduce the competitive form of bourgeois political economy.

It is most ironic and ultimately debilitating that, in an effort to ignore other marxian analysts who focus on the effect of monopo-

listic interests in the determination of urban land-use patterns, Scott
has articulated a neoricardian version of perfect competition. To be
sure, his model points out the contradictions of that process, especially as they derive from externalities; however, his approach is
closer to mainstream assumptions regarding the differential extraction of surplus value, or profit, than to a marxian analysis more attuned to the ubiquitous presence of monopolistic forces and their
supply-side production of space. Such a preference is revealed in his
earliest work on the urban land-use question, where he criticized
voluntaristic approaches that focus on elite coalitions in the development process as being too simplistic and conspiratorial (Scott and
Roweiss 1978). For Scott such interests stand *outside* the structural
logic of surplus value appropriation or are merely epiphenomenal
products of that process. This antivoluntaristic bias exists in his
most recent formulations because he wishes to specify the fundamental nature of the uneven development process, which is independent of the actions of such coalitions or the alleged need for
devalorization.

I disagree with this approach, while appreciating the restricted
way in which Scott specifies the nature of uneven development as
internal to capitalism. In what follows I shall show that no picture of
metropolitan development under capitalism can be complete without a grasp of the role of agency as well as structure, especially the
manner in which monopolistic forces and growth networks operate
in space. Scott has leveled the land-based interests of the property
sector, reducing them to mere replicas of the capitalist interests operating in the same way everywhere. As I shall demonstrate in the
next chapter, this neoricardian, capital logic approach is absolutely
valid for the production of any other commodity except space. Thus
the analysis of the multiple ontological statuses of space in the Late
Capitalist formation requires a mode of inquiry which surpasses the
limits of the capital logic school or one which reduces space to a
commodity. More specifically, Scott does not consider the qualitatively distinct properties of Lefebvre's secondary circuit, which
unites structural processes with group actions organized around the
property sector, and which Harvey has amplified to great benefit. It
is precisely the operation of specific class fractions in the secondary
circuit, the role of the state at all levels in assisting real estate sector
activity, and the contradictory consequences of these interventions
which explain spatial form.

In short, Scott has modeled the urban environment, but his image approximates some of its real features and ignores others. While
his view of the production of land values is essentially correct for a

monocentered city without monopolistic interests in land development, there are properties of space and separate fractions of capital
which enter into the collective determination of exchange and use
values in ways that are qualitatively different from those analyzed by
Scott or, for that matter, by mainstreamers. Finally, Scott's analysis
of the state is too limited. His notion of the urban land nexus is in-
tellectually attractive, because contemporary marxists all acknowledge that the state has some integral role to play in Late Capitalism.
Yet, his specification of the state–civil society articulation is rather
ill defined. In fact, what Scott means by the urban land nexus is
never made very clear.

Scott's analysis has what I consider to be a fatal error of misplaced concreteness for the case of the United States. He virtually
equates state intervention with urban *planning*. As can be shown,
however, while a good many ideological and bureaucratic resources
are devoted to the "idea" of urban planning in the United States,
there is, in fact, very little urban planning in this country (Gottdiener 1977, 1983). State intervention in this society is more a
matter of public *policy* and indirect regulation than of planning, although some land-use control is carried out at the local level. Neo-
marxian analysis, especially collective consumption theory, has
been most effective in providing us with an understanding of urban
policy as the primary mode of state intervention. In particular, the
state–civil society articulation has been analyzed according to the
historical nature of reactions to accumulation crises, of the necessities of social control, and of structural transformations over time in
response to capital's needs.

One might consider Scott's conceptualization of the urban land
nexus as an accurate representation of the land-use regulatory powers of the local state. Zoning and other home rule devices, such as
restrictive covenants, are certainly instrumental in determining patterns of settlement space development. Yet this aspect of intervention is specified by Scott in a particularly static way, one which ignores the class struggle over land use. As any analyst of municipal
decision-making processes can attest, land-use policies are a volatile
area of political conflict. At times state policies are contested between working-class fractions, such as homeowners, and capitalist
fractions, such as large-scale developers. At other times, however,
the state becomes an arena for a clash of capitals themselves or a
confrontation between local public bureaucrats and monopoly capital interests, as in the case of environmental conflicts. In all sociospatial disputes, the relationship between the state and civil society

is considerably more contentious than that portrayed in Scott's analysis.

Finally, Bandyopadhyay, in the above review of Scott's work, is wrong when he asserts that nonmarxists easily dismiss problems with inequitable differentials in the supply of social services by resorting to reformist countermeasures as a solution. As Castells (1978) has remarked in connection with the analysis of collective consumption, the intervention of the state in civil society at any level is not simple but complex and contradictory. As an expression of a class society, it can never adequately correct the uneven nature of the private development process which it is functionally called upon to assist. In contrast to Scott, who sees the state as some pristine urban planner standing apart from the class struggle, Althusserian structuralists such as Castells view the state as a political system of social practices homologous to the capitalist private economy itself and consequently suffering from similar contradictory tendencies. In particular, while not always apparent, state intervention is the product of the class conflict in civil society; its interventions always tend to reproduce the problems of a class society rather than alleviate them.

In the next chapter I shall devote more time to the theory of collective consumption, which makes this argument most forcefully. In addition to discussing Castells, we will also examine the work of Henri Lefebvre. With regard to state intervention and what Scott might consider as urban planning, Lefebvre possesses an even more critical view. For Lefebvre, the state not only intervenes *in* space, it helps produce it. It creates an "abstract space" through such intellectual and bureaucratic practices as urban planning, which then becomes an administrative framework of social control aligned against the uses of space by the working class in everyday life. Furthermore, this spatial framework of state domination is not confined to capitalist societies alone but is present as an instrument of control in every nondemocratic social system and is most characteristic of totalitarian regimes.

Before moving on, it is worthwhile to contrast marxian political economy with mainstream theory. The former improves on the spatial theory of the latter in at least four ways. First, it replaces a simplistic theory of location, focusing on the equilibrium between land and transport costs, with a more accurate picture of locations mediated by the class struggle and the needs of the capital accumulation process, which is at present deployed as a global structure of profit taking. Second, in place of a spaceless version of capitalist growth,

based upon the equilibration of large numbers of producers and consumers within a space which merely contains them, marxists have
specified the role of the built environment in the capital accumulation process and its connection to periodic accumulation crises.
Thus, space becomes an integral part of the relations of production.
For neoricardians, in addition, space is produced by the contradictory nature of the production process, which involves disequilibrating tendencies that contrast with the placid mainstream picture of
efficient growth. Third, mainstreamers act as if the state does not
exist. Marxian political economists address explicitly the role of
the state in space, although this work requires greater elaboration.
Fourth, in place of the hierarchical network of spatial integration,
known as the systems of cities approach, marxists transcend the reified vocabulary of place by showing how location is the site of production relations which are then integrated by a global system of
capitalist accumulation and a world-scale process of production, including an international division of labor.

The marxian political economic approach, however, seems limited by at least three aspects, some of which are shared by neoricardians. First, it possesses a positivist strain which seeks to advance
its explanatory argument by denying the operation of other factors,
so that distinct causes can be linked to distinct effects. Second, its
endemic functionalism suggests that the needs of capital are ser-
viced by historical events, so that the beneficial effects become identified ex post as the causes of change, thereby explaining causes by
effects. Finally, the approach focuses analysis on the patterns of economic development in society, rather than on the revolutionary
project of transforming it. Marxian political economy shares this
same ideological limitation with mainstream urban science, namely,
a penchant for concentrating on ever more detailed economic de-
scriptions of society. This equates the understanding of social well-
being with the inquiry into the wealth of nations. It is necessary to
break away from economism, and we shall do so in the next chapter.

It can be said that Continental marxism's main contribution to
the inquiry into the production of space lies in its insistence that
marxian analysis possesses an epistemological disjuncture from the
analytical categories of bourgeois thought. After all, that was what
Marx really meant when he subtitled *Capital* a "critique of political
economy." In this sense Continental marxism is an antidote to political economy. This more philosophical approach deemphasizes
what Marx himself said in favor of concerted attempts to grasp how,
in fact, he thought. For these reasons the approaches which I shall
consider next stand apart from political economy, even though they

rely on it for insights deriving from the concrete analysis of spatial forms. Both marxian structuralism, as exemplified by Castells, and sociospatial dialectics, as exemplified by Lefebvre, strain to reproduce Marx's own mode of thinking and establish a permanent disjuncture between the creeping tendencies of mainstream social science and the dialectical epistemology of Marx. Furthermore, both Lefebvre and Castells aim at a more global perspective on the production of space and its relationship to social organization than does marxian political economy. Such an approach must consider those aspects of the social formation that we have already identified above as important to any analysis of space: the state, the class struggle, the capital accumulation process, uneven development, ideology, and the reproduction of the relations of production. While Manuel Castells' influence on urban marxian analysis has been second to none in the United States, Henri Lefebvre has published prolifically on the same subject. Unfortunately, much of the latter's work has yet to be translated. As I shall demonstrate below, the difference between these two is less one of analytical content per se than a fundamental question over the true nature of marxist analysis. If it is not already obvious to the reader, in this clash I strongly favor Lefebvre, although I shall take great pains to indicate how spatial analysis must bid adieu to all such sectarian conflict in order to forge a coherent marxian theory that rises above the influence of single personalities.

4. Floating Paradigms: The Debate on the Theory of Space

Because of the inadequacies of mainstream formulations, marxian urban analysis has emerged to explain the important urban events since World War II. Similarly, but within a different nonspatial context, the structuralist enterprise among marxists can be understood as a long-awaited theoretical response to the inadequacies of orthodox marxism. According to a view codified into a dogma by stalinist propaganda and a generation of "vulgar" political economists, the economic mode of production or the "base" determined the processes of politics and culture, the "superstructure." In such a model the state was nothing more than the capitalist class dressed up as corrupt politicians, while every musical or artistic event, for example, was an exercise in bourgeois brainwashing. Beginning with the Frankfurt School of the 1920s and 1930s, as dialectical reasoning replaced the deterministic, causal modeling of the vulgar materialists, an attempt was made to open up marxian political economy to a more interdependent viewpoint. In particular, the Frankfurt School stressed "neohegelian" critical thought, which was philosophically grounded in the German-historicist notion of "totality." The action of society and all of its elements operated as an ensemble or dialectical "moment," wherein aspects of economic necessity were related to cultural and political needs and vice versa (Horkheimer 1972).

While the Frankfurt School specified the existing social formation as a capitalist system, it did so by way of showing how "superstructural" phenomena, such as politics or culture, operated much like the "base" did, as all were aspects of the very same contradictions that characterized the whole of the social formation. In this view, self-liberating individual actions were constantly being pressured to turn aside by the encapsulating totality of the capitalist mode of production. Domination operated not only through the relations of production but also through ideology, which masked reality, and through the mechanisms of alienation, which siphoned off the potential unrest that could threaten the workings of the system into personally destructive forms of everyday life. Such ideas were also developed by Lukács (1971) and Gramsci (1971), who independently pursued the ways in which cultural and political attitudes could, on the one hand, serve to "reproduce" or legitimate capitalist relations of production or, on the other hand, constitute a springboard for action which could overcome the system through collective struggle. These theorists believed that so-called superstructural phenomena were just as important in their own right for transforming capitalism as the vulgar marxists' view that capitalism was organized in and through the mechanizations of the economic base. Among Althusserians such a conceptualization of marxian theory became known as the ideology of historicism, because it asserted that the present moment could be captured by thought and that radical intervention could be based on such an analysis. For this reason, historicism was distinguished from the evolutionist perspective of orthodox marxism, which asserted the inexorable destruction of capitalism as a consequence of crisis.

In the final analysis, the anti–vulgar marxist impulse aims to grasp through dialectical analysis the full complexity of social phenomena, extending from the level of abstract, *sui generis* structures such as economics and politics to the individual, behavioral level of alienated everyday life. For this reason both the active members of the Frankfurt School and early associates such as Lukács or independents like Gramsci all deemphasized "political economy" and developed cultural analyses of modern society, or even a marxian "social psychology," in order to bridge the gap between the individual and society in a dialectical conception of capitalism as a totality.

In the 1950s and 1960s, orthodox marxists struck back at the Frankfurt School by claiming that it had turned marxism into a hegelianism. Marcuse, Horkheimer, Adorno, Benjamin, et alia, it was claimed, had grafted a humanist impulse onto the inexorable laws of marxism by reasserting the importance of the individual mind as an autonomous actor in society. This critique grew out of the ascendancy of structuralism, a philosophical movement in the social sciences dominating French intellectual life for a score of years beginning with the 1950s. Under the influence of structuralism, an antihumanist, antihistoricist marxism arose which analyzed social phenomena in a manner distinct from that of a reliance on (or even much interest in) the behaviorally situated condition of the individual, existential subject. This structuralist reading of Marx was spearheaded by Louis Althusser, who preserved the Frankfurt School's notion of totality, as well as the insight of critical theory regarding the relative independence of political and ideological factors from the economic base, while at the same time reasserting the importance of political economy. More significantly, however, while the dialectical approach focused on contradictions, structuralists tended to follow orthodox marxism's emphasis on the crisis base of capitalism.

At present the structuralist enterprise is on the wane; Althusser's thought, in particular, has been assailed from a variety of directions, most of which derive from marxism itself (Thompson 1978; Lefebvre 1973; Glucksmann 1974; Hirst 1979). There is a great temptation to dismiss Althusser's effort entirely, without understanding its place in the historical development of marxian thought. This would be a mistake. While Althusser's project has had only limited success, its main assertions deal with issues that are fundamental to the marxist enterprise. There are at least three aspects of his approach which bear mentioning at this time, because they will emerge in other contexts below. First, as Althusser suggests (1970b), Marx's work is constrained by the dislocation in the semantic field of Hegel's concepts with Marx's own, so that the latter's ideas are not articulated in a theoretically precise language divorced from hegelianism. Had Marx lived one more decade, it would have been conceivable for him to have made his concepts in *Capital* clearer, through an innovative terminology, so as to be more consistent with the removal of his thought from hegelianism. Consequently, understanding Marx requires textual interpretation. In order for such an analysis to illuminate marxism, it is necessary to understand how Marx himself *thought*, not just to know what he said. Thus, interpretations of Marx's own texts depend greatly on how the latter view is formulated in the mind of the interpreter. Asserting this much, however, does not necessarily justify the structuralist reading of Marx, as we shall see below.

Second, historicist and humanist positions vis-à-vis marxism can be reduced to variants of idealist philosophy. This limitation delegitimizes those perspectives as bases for radical political action. According to Althusser, only a truly "scientific" mode of marxian reasoning can overcome idealism and provide a legitimate mode of praxis. Althusser's structuralism aimed at achieving this level of "science" by transforming historical materialism into a theory of social organization. Every social formation was a structure comprised of economic, political, and ideological systems (or EPI) that were relatively autonomous. Thus, in place of the empiricist causality of vulgar marxism, which held that the base (relations of production) determined the superstructure (politics and culture), Althusser sub-

stituted a more complex picture of determination consisting of practices, levels, and instances As the many critics of this approach have
demonstrated, the attempt to articulate a more scientific marxism
based upon this structural approach has largely failed. Without a demonstrable claim to an exact science, there is little left of the structuralist project and its ideological critique of other marxisms. Presently, marxists have been thrown back on living with historicism.
Such a fate may not be as bad as die-hard structuralists would like it
to sound because, in part, this implies that political action must
be responsible for its own underlying principles (Hirst 1979; Gottdiener 1984).

Finally, Althusser asserted a particular version of marxian dialectics, as exemplified by his discussion of the epistemological break.
This refers to the alleged total disjuncture between the thought of the
early Marx, before the publication of the *Contribution* in 1857, and
the later Marx, embodied in *Capital*. According to Althusser, the
young Marx's theory centered around anthropological or humanist
concerns, while the mature Marx was preoccupied with the structuralist problematic of the laws of motion of capitalism. This interpretation of Marx's development has also been called into question
(see Mandel 1971; Séve 1978). After perhaps a decade of being dis-
credited by the structuralist project, the place of humanism in marxian thought is slowly reasserting itself (Séve 1978), especially since
the philosophical nature of marxian inquiry has failed to be transformed by the structuralist assault.

With the collapse of support for Althusser's method, the need is
currently not met for a systematized or codified technique of marxian analysis applicable to social formations as a whole, especially
Late Capitalism. While we may agree with Lefebvre that the desire
for a scientific marxism is itself questionable (Martins 1982), due to
the lack of formalism in the dialectical method, marxist thought is
presently plunged into a crisis because structuralism has failed to
answer the critical questions it has raised. Several analysts, such
as Mandel (1975) and Hindness and Hirst (1975), have recently responded with their own global analyses. Yet these efforts have not
enjoyed the compelling support of other marxists, which should indicate to us that some underlying unity of conceptualization remains to be worked out. More recently Giddens (1979, 1981) has
called the entire marxist project into question as being unable to circumscribe completely an analysis of Late Capitalism or advanced industrial society. In consequence, it is my belief that history will be a
good deal kinder to Althusser than present circumstances would
suggest, if only because his challenge has forced marxian thought to

engage in a battle over issues which are quite central to its needs as a would-be interpretive paradigm of modern society.

Given the largely successful critique of Althusser, the persisting importance of his disciple, Manuel Castells, is something of an enigma. His major work, *The Urban Question*, is a direct application of Althusser's general approach to social organization, in the particular context of the "urban system" or the "specific articulation of the instances of a social structure within a (spatial) unit of the reproduction of labor power" (1977: 237). The justification for an Althusserian reading of urban analysis comes from Castells' assertion that all structural systems, such as Late Capitalism, contain within themselves subsystems of practices homologous to the larger structure because they operate by the very same laws. Consequently, if the larger social order can be analyzed according to the threefold schema of economics, politics, and ideology (EPI), so can its subsystem, the urban complex. For this reason, the legitimation of Castells' analysis rests completely with accepting the validity of the assertion that "urban" constitutes a unique "subsystem." Such an assertion, however, possesses no material basis.

In what sense, then, can we identify the contributions of Castells? At present there appear to be three somewhat separate areas in which he has advanced marxian urban analysis. First and foremost, Castells took on mainstream urban science, especially sociology, in a head-to-head critique, first published in 1968. He articulated in a well-defined way the dissatisfaction which had been felt by many before him but which, until Castells, had not been expressed in so forthright and devastating a manner (1977). Second, Castells provided a marxian framework for the study of urban politics and social movements where before only the clichés of vulgar marxism seemed to prevail (1975, 1977). Finally, he specified a *theoretical* relationship between the concept of "urban" and the marxian view of the state (1977, 1978). This relationship is provided by his theory of collective consumption, which remains at the center of much debate, especially among the neoweberians in England. It is this third area, the specification of the relationship between the state and the "urban," which is the most central to Castells' approach and which subsumes the other two—urban social movements and the critique of urban sociology—within a theoretical framework. Consequently, I shall focus on this last aspect in a review of his work.

In order to understand Castells' theory of collective consumption, it is necessary first to deconstruct it by providing a reading which illuminates the circumstances of its production. The central focus of *The Urban Question* is section 8, in which Castells broaches the subject of "the debate on the theory of space" (1977: 115–128). That there was such a debate should have been news to English-speaking analysts; however, few recognized that implicit in the organization of this work was an underlying intent to respond in an Althusserian manner to the formidable work on urbanism carried out by an archenemy of structuralism in France, Henri Lefebvre (for exceptions, see Soja 1980; Martins 1982).

The debate on the theory of space, therefore, is one initiated by Castells in contradistinction to Lefebvre. In the previous chapter I demonstrated the limitations of marxian political economy as a means of grasping the nature of spatial organization. In effect this approach remains limited by its failure to throw off the ideological nature of bourgeois categories of thought. Both Castells and Lefebvre aim for a more global view of the articulation between society and space, and they both employ separate epistemologies which are uniquely different from those of the political and economic analyses we have just considered. For these reasons, both Castells and Lefebvre provide alternatives to more commonly encountered marxian thought on the analysis of space. In what follows I shall review each of these theories and then compare them, so as to revive the debate on the theory of space in a manner which transforms the "absence-presence" of Lefebvre into an active alternative to the structuralist project.

THE DEBATE ON THE THEORY OF SPACE

Castells' Theory of Space

The focus of Castells' theory of space is the same as Lefebvre's: Castells analyzes space as a material product of a given social formation. This emphasis frames the marxian approach to space. Castells begins with an evaluation of the Chicago School, which, as we have already seen, he finds crippled by the ideology of "evolutionary organicism." Nevertheless, he asserts that its approach was possessed of the right idea because it viewed space as determined by "the productive forces and the relations of production that stem from them" (1977: 123). What is needed, however, is not to abandon this materialist focus but, rather, to develop it by specifying a more marxian view of the vulgar materialism of the Chicago School and by conceptualizing the other elements of social organization which articulate with the economic aspects of society. Thus the theory of space consists of a specification of a general theory of social organization as it articulates with space. That is, "there is no specific theory of space, but quite simply a deployment and specification of the theory of social structure, in order to account for the characteristics of the particular social form, space, and of its articulation with other, historically given, forces and processes" (1977: 124).

Thus, in opposition to Lefebvre, who has developed a marxian theory of space in order to frame what he calls a sociospatial praxis, Castells wishes to assert the primacy of Althusser's theory of social structure, which can then be used to explain (to account for) spatial forms. That is, it is at this juncture in *The Urban Question*, after an extensive critique of mainstream urban science, that Castells proposes to apply a structuralist paradigm in the debate. "To analyze space as an expression of the social structure amounts, therefore, to studying its shaping by elements of the economic system, the political system and the ideological system, and by their combinations and the social practices that derived from them" (1977: 126). In short, Castells' response to Lefebvre is to apply the EPI framework not to the social system as a whole, as Althusser has done, but to a homologous part of it, the urban system. It is this exercise which he acknowledges in his afterword as presenting the "most serious difficulties," because of the overburdened structuralist typology and its classification grid of elements, subelements, and so on ad nauseam (1977: 438).

Compelled first and foremost by a desire to render a theory of space in Althusserian terms, Castells requires a theoretical object of analysis which can serve as a "conceptual delimitation of the urban, within a theory of space, itself a specification of a theory of social structure" (1977: 128). Quite clearly the first question which must be posed involves whether such a delimitation is necessary in "urban" terms. Castells himself has raised doubts about whether such a desire can be realized (Pickvance 1977a), because of the theoretical "vagueness and the historical relativity of the criteria concerning the urban" (Castells 1977: 234). However, he realized that, if he did not specify in theoretical terms what he meant by "urban," he would be left merely with the concept "space," and this would place him on an equal footing with Lefebvre—a prospect Castells, in his Althusserian passion, surely disliked. As he indicates, "Since physical space is the deployment of matter as a whole, a study 'without a priori' of any 'spatial' form and manifestation will amount to establishing a history of matter" (1977: 234). By this observation Castells calls for a return to the theoretical question posed by the nature of urban space—that is, the *form* of space particular to modern society, where space itself merely covers the underlying social relationships at work producing it. This is done, however, within the structuralist framework, as he indicates:

> To pose the question of the specificity of a space, and in particular urban space, is equivalent to conceiving of relations between the elements of the social structure within a unit defined in one of the instances of the social structure. For more concrete terms, the delimitation "urban" connotes a unit defined either in the ideological instance, or in the political-judicial instance, or in the economic instance. (1977: 235)

According to what is now the familiar scheme of three relatively autonomous structures, the search for an urban unit requires Castells to conceptualize EPI in a way which provides a unique urban focus for analysis. In an argument which Saunders mistakenly calls a logical process of elimination (1981: 184), Castells settles on the economic structure as specifying the key conceptual link to a theory of space. That is, the urban as an ideological (cultural) unit is rejected because of the arguments marshaled in his critique both of urban sociology and of Lefebvre, namely, his view of the fallacy of asserting that the nature (essence) of any particular society can be characterized as urban, as opposed to the marxian view that identifies societies according to their mode of production. Similarly, the political structure is rejected, despite the fact that the city is a political-judicial entity. This is so because the spatial organization of relations under modern capitalism has increasingly become a product of economic processes rather than political ones. As Castells indicates, "And this is no accident, for it is as if the spatial units were defined in each society according to the dominant instance, characteristic of the mode of production politico-juridical in feudalism, economics in capitalism" (1977: 235).

As the above quote reveals, we are confronted not with a logical process of elimination at all but, rather, with the teleological reflex of structuralist functionalism. Thus aspects of sociospatial relations are dominated by the economic structure because this is precisely the structure dominating the capitalist mode of production, according to the Althusserian schema. That is, the economic element is used by Castells to define the urban because such a definition is needed to conform with the Althusserian requirements of analysis. In his search for a unique urban object of analysis, Castells distinguishes two fundamental elements of the economic structure: the means of production and labor power. A search for the theoretical specificity of the urban in the first case leads to an analysis of regional problems. This regional question is rejected because it represents more the contradictions resulting from the articulation of all three structures in space than a pure product of one single dominating instance and because the space of production forms a continuous network which seems to ignore urban idiosyncrasies (1977: 236). Consequently Castells settles on specifying the urban unit as defined by the processes relating to labor power "other than in its direct application to the production process" (that is, the regional problem). As he states:

> I propose the following hypothesis: in advanced capitalist societies, the process that structures space is that which concerns the single and extended reproduction of labor power; the ensemble of the so-called urban practice connotes the articulation of the process with the social structure as a whole . . . The urban units thus seem to be to the process of reproduction what the companies are to the production process, though of course, they must not be regarded solely as loci, but as being the origin of specific effects on the social structure (in the same way, for example, as the characteristics of the company— production unit—affect the expression and forms of the class relations that are manifested in them). (1977: 237)

Thus the urban for Castells is a spatial unit of the reproduction of labor power. The production of the built environment occurs through the processes by which the entire ensemble of EPI structures articulates with this spatial unit. This is defined by what Castells calls the urban system, which he then specifies by an additional formal analysis consisting of elements and dominating instances, all of which have been disposed of in his subsequent analyses. In short, the discovery of the urban system takes place through a reductionist argument typical of the discursive nature of Althusserianism.

In summary, Castells' approach to the theory of space has the following characteristics. First, it is an application of Althusser's approach to an explanation of the production of the built environment. Second, it represents an attempt to rescue the term "urban" by defining it theoretically as a spatial unit within the structural system which produces the built environment. As early as the famous afterword to Castells' book, however, the failure of the first effort was absolutely clear. Consequently, he expanded on the second aspect by reassessing its usefulness. In this endeavor he discovered that his specification of the urban unit brings to the surface the problems associated with the process of collective consumption in modern society and its crisis base. As he states:

> It is in this sense that I say the essential problems regarded as urban are in fact bound up with the processes of "collective consumption," or what Marxists call the organization of the collective means of reproduction of labor power. That is to say, means of consumption objectively socialized, which, for specific historical reasons, are essentially dependent for their production, distribution and administration on the intervention of the state. (1977: 440)

The processes of collective consumption refer to the support by the state of certain public goods which Castells sees as being essential to the reproduction of labor power—he is concerned with "the organization of the means of collective consumption as the basis of the daily life of all social groups: housing, education, health, culture, commerce, transportation, etc." (1978: 3). This shift of analytical focus, however, means that Castells is no longer interested in a theory of space per se—rather, he is developing a theory of urban problems. In effect he centers on the fact that most of the issues which have been classified as urban are connected to the problem of collective consumption, so that by this analysis he has retranslated urban concerns into a theoretically useful approach. Thus in place of a theory of the production of space, which continues to occupy the thoughts of Lefebvre (see below), for example, Castells returns us in one sense to the world of the Chicago School, which as Martindale (1962) has noted came to focus the analytical interests of urban sociology upon the city as a site of social pathology. The comparable line of reasoning we find in Castells involves his replacement of a concern with explaining how space is produced with a concern about how urban problems are produced—what will eventually become for him a crisis theory of capitalist society (1978, 1980). For Castells the concept "crisis" represents the same analytical focus as the concept "contradiction" in the thought of Lefebvre. Due to the inadequacies of structuralism, therefore, Castells has been forced to retreat further and further away from a theory of space and to seek refuge in evolutionist marxism, with its clichéd soothsaying about the inexorable ultimate crisis. As he states in his most recent work:

> I believe we are on the edge of a major socio-spatial catastrophe but not as the ecologists say, because of the process of metropolitanization and consumption of natural resources. It is because the new dominant interests and the new social revolts

tend to dissociate the space of organizations and the space of experience. (1984: 236)

The most important aspect of Castells' shift in thinking is that, by moving away from applying Althusser to a theory of space, he came to develop a specific aspect of that theory, namely, the relationship between the state and settlement space. The difficulty with appreciating this fact lies with Castells' unfortunate insistence on retaining the term "urban" in his analysis and on defining the city as a spatial unit of the reproduction of labor power. In the subsequent debate on the importance of collective consumption as an organizing element of urban analysis, these critical points regarding the origin of Castells' ideas and the shift in his thinking have not been recognized. Consequently, those interested in the marxian analysis of the relationship between the state and space have been afflicted with what seems to be an interminable debate on the significance of collective consumption as the focal point for urban analysis. The limited usefulness of this debate is revealed by its ability to cause confusion. Thus Saunders conceives of the urban as specifying uniquely the realm of urban sociology, while his U.K. colleague Dunleavy asserts that it is urban political science which is delimited by this same concept. In this way the theoretical usefulness of the concept is undermined by the very people wishing to employ it.

It is with some reluctance that I must warn prospective readers of the tediousness of this debate, especially the debate between neoweberians and neomarxists in the United Kingdom (Saunders 1981; Dunleavy 1980). While otherwise trenchant in many respects, at their core such analyses fail because of an unfortunate desire to retain the concept of "urban" as a theoretical object of analysis. In what follows, therefore, I wish to focus on the theory of collective consumption only as a means of clarifying the relationship between the state and settlement space. In our review of this literature, it is well worth remembering our discussion of the evolution of Castells' thought and retaining the import of what analysts such as Mingione have come to see, namely:

> Collective consumption theory is the result of two opposed intentions: to see urban social processes in terms of class needs and to redefine the urban sector as an autonomous object of social studies. I strongly sympathize with the first intention but disagree with the second. The consumption process itself is not definable in a purely territorial context, it does not correspond to any "urban question" but is rather an important part of the general social question. (1981: 67)

Before discussing the relationship between the state and space, which will commence my synthesis of the marxian approach to settlement space, let us consider the approach of Lefebvre.

Lefebvre's Theory of Space

At present, while recognizing the importance of space, urban analysts have enjoyed only limited success in formulating a sound approach to studying it. As we have seen, mainstream urban geography and ecology can be characterized as essentially spaceless, because locational relations are conceived of as operating *within* space—that is, within a space acting as a container, more often than not hypothesized as being a featureless plain. This is a minimalist variant of reflection theory, which asserts that social processes are deployed *in* space, so that space merely holds or supports them. In this way mainstreamers reify geographical locations and make them stand for social processes, as in the manner through which spatial terms, such as the "city" or "systems of cities," replace the socioeconomic and political mode of organization which comprises place. Both Anderson (1973) and Alonso (1971) have called attention to this fallacy of spatial fetishism characteristic of conventional thought. According to marxists, spatial analysis has to be tied directly to the transformations of society produced by the drive for capital accumulation and the class struggle. Such an approach would specify an analysis of space as "an expression of the social structure" (Castells 1977: 126), not as an independent or relatively autonomous set of spatial relationships.

In the previous chapters I have indicated the ways in which spatial concerns were introduced into marxian analysis—but introduced by being circumscribed within a framework which focused upon the deployment of economic, political, and ideological structures *in* space. The summary effect of the marxian efforts which we have considered so far has been to discount a separate emphasis on spatial considerations as an analytical fetish and to posture a mode of spatial analysis which is wholly contained within the perspective of marxian political economy, either in its eclectic mode or as Althusserian structuralism. That is, most marxists reject the need for a separate theory of space, in favor of a political and economic analysis of spatially deployed social relations based upon the two-class struggle between capitalists and workers (Edel 1981). The marxian approaches I have considered so far all share with Gordon the belief that the processes of capitalist development are materialized in space, almost through a one-to-one correspondence with the actual forms of the built environment. This is very much like mainstream reflection theory and is even closer to the belief of ecologists that sociospatial patterns are direct manifestations of sociobiotic drives. Thus, the features of space are little more than epiphenomena—and few marxists are interested in discussing a more dialectical view. As Martins observes:

> Implicit in this debate is the assumption that the spatial orga-
> nization of societies derives from more general features of their
> historical development, and, more specifically, from the evolu-
> tion of the productive forces and the associated division of
> labor. In this problematic, there is no room left for an indepen-
> dent theorization of the spatial organization of societies, as
> this is conceptualized as the mere territorial projection of the
> social relations, particularly of the social relations of produc-
> tion, and of their reflection in consciousness. (1982: 162)

We are left wondering whether a marxian theory of space as such is at all possible in the face of what Soja has termed an "increasingly rigidifying orthodoxy" (1980: 207). Such a concern leads us to the work of Lefebvre, who since 1968 has been addressing just this need in a prolific production of books on the urban condition (1968, 1970, 1972, 1973, 1974). For Lefebvre, the transformation of modern so-ciety into a humanist society must take place as an "urban revolu-tion"—as a revolution of spatial design organized around unalien-ated everyday life—in addition to the economic transformation called for by most marxists. In the thought of Lefebvre, therefore, "spatial praxis" is elevated to a radical activity alongside efforts to reorganize social relations, and he supports such a perspective by a marxist theory of space (such statements cannot make sense otherwise).

Lefebvre, however, is concerned with not only what is but what also might be. This mode of thought is labeled historicist by struc-turalists; hence, his work has not been well received by Althusser-ians. Furthermore, in the view of most marxists, Lefebvre is quite simply wrong: he has hypothesized a mode of analysis in his early work (prior to 1973) by which spatial relations are viewed as being independent of class relations in urban society. This judgment is in-accurate because it fails to consider Lefebvre's more mature work, especially *La production de l'espace* (1974). Without exception, cri-tiques of Lefebvre have been based on material published prior to this period (Castells 1977; Saunders 1981). In this sense, the politi-cal strategy debate and the intellectual fashions among structuralist marxists and humanists both in the United States and in Europe have become a formidable barrier to an informed appreciation of

Lefebvre's theory of space. In what follows I shall attempt to overcome this obstacle as well as the additional one of the lack of suitable translations In order to appreciate Lefebvre's approach.

Lefebvre and the Production of Space Perspective

As I read Lefebvre, the most important theoretical aspect of space is its multifaceted nature. Space cannot be reduced merely to a location or to the social relations of property ownership—it represents a multiplicity of sociomaterial concerns. Space is a physical location, a piece of real estate, and simultaneously an existential freedom and a mental expression. Space is both the geographical site of action and the social possibility for engaging in action. That is, on an individual level, for example, it not only represents the location where events take place (the container function) but also signifies the social permission to engage in these events (the social order function). This idea is fundamental to Lefebvre's notion of praxis, which stands at odds with other marxian attitudes toward political struggle. Furthermore, space possesses multiple properties on a structural level. It is simultaneously a means of production as land and part of the social forces of production as space. As property spatial relations can be considered part of the social relations of production, that is, the economic base. In addition, space is an object of consumption, a political instrument, and an element in the class struggle. These multiple aspects require clarification.

In the first case, and in distinction to Scott (1980) and Castells (1977), space cannot be reduced to the three realms of production, consumption, and exchange commonly used in marxian political economy. According to Lefebvre, these activities and locations when taken together as social space can constitute a *fourth* realm of social relations, namely, the production of wealth or surplus value. That is, space itself must be considered as one element of the productive forces of society, especially through the operation of form or design. Traditional political economy merely recognizes the importance of land as a means of production alongside that of capital and labor. According to Lefebvre, however, spatial design itself is one aspect of the productive forces of society—to be considered along with technology, human knowledge, and labor power as contributing to our "productive potential." As he indicates:

> The city, the urban space, and the urban reality cannot be conceived simply as the sum of the places of production and consumption . . . The spatial arrangement of a city, a region, a nation, or a continent increases productive forces just as the

equipment and machines in a factory or in a business, but
at another level. One uses space just as one uses a machine.
(1979: 287)

This assertion can be explained by a brief excursion into political economy. For marxists the means of production consist of two classes of material objects. These are the objects of labor, those objects which are processed by labor, such as raw materials, and the means of labor, the tools which are used in production. According to Oskar Lange, "Under this heading we place objects made for the performance of certain operations . . . other objects which, although not tools themselves, facilitate the use of tools, like buildings, stores, harbors, roads, and land, are also included in this group" (1963: 4). Thus the built environment, as political economists define it, is part of the means of production, specifically, the means of labor. The reduction of space merely to this aspect, however, such as in the work of Harvey (1981), results in certain important limitations in the ability of neomarxists and neoweberians to explain aspects of spatial production, as we shall see in the next chapter. In contradistinction to the reduction of space merely to the means of production, Lefebvre considers space as one of the forces of production alongside others recognized by orthodox marxists. As Cohen also observes:

> Space deserves membership in the set of productive forces.
> Ownership of space certainly confers a position in the economic structure. Even when a piece of space is contentless, its control may generate economic power, because it can be filled with something productive, or because it may need to be traversed by producers. (1978: 51)

In addition to this first nature of the role of space in production, spatial organization also possesses a second nature. This figures prominently, according to Lefebvre, in the social relations of production. More specifically, it is in part through the medium of space that society reproduces itself. For Lefebvre, the coherencies of spatial order control the inherent contradictions of capitalism for the benefit of the dominant interests in society. Capitalism, therefore, as a mode of production has survived in part through its use of space as a reinforcer of those social relations which are necessary for that survival (Lefebvre 1973). In short, the dialectical properties of spatial relations articulate with the externalized properties of the mode of production at a number of levels, in ways ignored totally by marxian political economists—who reduce the properties of space merely to a built environment. The question of control over spatial relations and design, therefore, represents the same revolutionary importance to society as the struggle over the control of the other means of production, because both ownership relations and relations of material externalization—that is, the production of space—are united in the property relations which form the core of the capitalist mode of production. Under the spell of structuralism, recognition of the need for praxis to address these property relations has been abandoned in favor of a theoretical effort divorced from direct action which seeks to study academically the operation of economic laws in space.

Furthermore, due to its status as a force of production, space possesses the very same contradictory relationship with private property (the relations of production) as does the ownership of machines; that is, the social relations governing the activities associated with space need to conform to the way in which space is used to acquire wealth. This relationship is contradictory since the uses of space to make money are continually coming into conflict with the institution of private property, that is, ownership relations, and the public regulation of economic activities. Thus, for Lefebvre, space possesses the same ontological status in the mode of production as capital or labor. And spatial relations represent a rich and constant source of social contradictions which require analysis on their own terms and which cannot be dismissed, as marxian political economists try to do, as a mere reflection of contradictions internally produced by the production process itself. In fact, space's status as a force of production implies that it is an essential part of that process.

Second, space is not only part of the forces and means of production, it is also a product of these very same relations. This property makes spatial design different from any other social factor or commodity, a concept which political economy ignores. Lefebvre notes that in addition to there being a space of consumption or, for that matter, a space as the impact area for collective consumption, there is also the consumption of space, or space itself as an *object* of consumption. This can be illustrated by tourism, where the environment itself is consumed through recreation, or by the relocation of business because of natural amenities. Thus spatial design itself can be converted into a commodity along with land, something that architects, city planners, and tourists have known for some time. In this way, sociospatial relations pervade the mode of production as both producer and product, relation and object, in a dialectical manner that resists reduction to either class or territorial concerns.

Third, according to Lefebvre, "Space has become for the state a political instrument of primary importance. The state uses space in such a way that it ensures its control of places, its strict hierarchy, homogeneity of the whole and the segregation of the parts. It is thus an administratively controlled and even policed space" (1979: 288). Spatial organization, therefore, represents the hierarchy of power. Spatial design is a political instrument of social control which the state uses to further its own administrative interests. The space of political jurisdictions and administrations thus provides the state with an *independent* instrument to further its own interests. Consequently, spatial relations figure prominently in the reproduction of existing social formations and in the hierarchically structured administrative practices of the nation-state.

Finally, Lefebvre sees class conflict as being deployed in space, that is, as being spatial conflict as well as a struggle between economic interests. This conflict arises because of the central contradiction of capitalist space: its pulverization by the social relations of private property, by "the demand for interchangeable fragments, and the scientific and technical capacity to treat space on ever more vast levels" (1979: 289). The state and the economy have reduced organic space to an abstraction—infinitely fragmented into parts. However, this process makes us aware of the forces reducing space to the reproducible, homogeneous building blocks of mass society required by the forces of domination. Consequently, in response to abstract space, which is fragmented, homogeneous, and hierarchical, the uniqueness of personalized and collectivized space reasserts itself, and such organic concepts of spatial integration arise as personal space, social space, the image of space, residential space, and even global space.

According to Lefebvre, this active naming of space, this parceling out and claiming of space by a multitude of actors and institutions, has produced an "explosion of spaces"—the multiple articulation of stratified social relations with space. This explosion of finely tuned spatial distinctions between people and groups in society results in a chaos of contradictory spaces that proliferate the boundaries at which sociospatial conflict appears. Such conflict cannot be reduced to mere reflections of the class struggle or its displacement into realms outside the work site, as many marxists contend, but represents instead concrete differences between people as a consequence of the domination of abstract over social space in our present society. Countless spatial irritations permeate social relations at every level: the personal, the communal, the regional, and the global. As Lefebvre indicates:

> Neither capitalism nor the state can maintain the chaotic, contradictory space they have produced. We witness, at all levels,

this explosion of space. At the level of the immediate and the lived, space is exploding on all sides, whether this be living space, personal space, scholastic space, prison space, army space, or hospital space. Everywhere, people are realizing that spatial relations are also social relations. At the level of cities, we see not only the explosion of the historical city but also that of all the administrative frameworks in which they had wanted to enclose the urban phenomenon. At the level of regions, the peripheries are fighting for their autonomy or for a certain degree of independence . . . Finally, at the international level, not only the actions of the so-called supranational companies, but also those of the great world strategies, prepare for and render inevitable new explosions of space. (1979: 290)

For Lefebvre the conflict produced by spatial antagonisms cuts across class lines, because it is not produced by relations of production alone. The essential spatial contradiction of society is the confrontation between abstract space, or the externalization of economic and political practices originating with the capitalist class *and* the state, and social space, or the space of use values produced by the complex interaction of all classes in the pursuit of everyday life (1979: 241). Thus, the contradictory basis of capitalist social relations is not merely projected onto space, as political economists contend. Because spatial patterns are produced by an antagonistic social formation, they possess a dynamic of their own and they involve contradictions which stem from the dialectical nature of sociospatial organization. In modern society, abstract space—a homogeneous, fragmented, hierarchical space—has come to dominate social space, or the integrated space of social communion, and the very productive potential of the latter has itself been attenuated. Consequently, social space has lost its organic unity in the cities of modern societies—it has become pulverized into separate ghettos. As Lefebvre notes, "Those of the elite, of the bourgeoisie, of the intellectuals, of the immigrant workers, etc., these ghettoes are not juxtaposed, they are hierarchical, spatially representing the economic and social hierarchy, dominant and subordinated sectors" (quoted in Martins 1982: 182). The hegemony of the capitalist class is renewed through this spatial segregation and through the effects of the "normalizing force" of state intervention in space.

On the basis of these properties, especially the peculiar nature of sociospatial conflicts resulting from the explosion of space in modern society, Lefebvre formulates a marxian approach to space which drastically departs from that of his contemporaries. He makes the bold claim that spatial phenomena, while produced in part by class antagonisms, cannot be approached through the traditional analysis of political economy. This is so because the latter only specifies theoretically an abstract space of marxian analysis, which contains relations of economic domination. But the importance of space for Lefebvre is captured by the dialectic between use value and exchange value, which produces a social space of uses as well as an abstract space of expropriation. As he states:

> Space is not merely economic, in which all the parts are interchangeable and have exchange value. Space is not merely a political instrument for homogenizing all parts of society. On the contrary . . . Space remains a model, a perpetual prototype of use value resisting the generalizations of exchange value in the capitalist economy under the authority of a homogenizing state. Space is a use value, but even more so is time to which it is ultimately linked because time is our life, our fundamental use value. Time has disappeared in the social space of modernity. (1979: 291)

For Lefebvre, the revolutionary transformation of society requires the appropriation of space, the freedom to use space, the existential right to space (*le droit à la ville*) to all be reasserted through some radical version of sociospatial praxis. This does not mean that space needs to be seized and dominated by some new order. Space is already socialized, but the present domination of abstract space hides this fact. We need to wipe out the system of property relations and institutional forms of regulating space which produces the domination of it both politically and economically, and we need to replace such relations by liberatory social relations which foster the ability to appropriate space for liberatory social uses. Thinking ahead to a radical political program, Lefebvre indicates:

> The production of socialist space means the end of private property and the state's political domination of space, which implies the passage from domination to appropriation and the primacy of use over exchange . . . In so far as we can conceive it, given certain tendencies, socialist space will be *a space of differences*. (1979: 292)

According to Lefebvre, space can be grasped only dialectically because it is a concrete abstraction—one of Marx's categories, such as exchange value, which are simultaneously a material, externalized realization of human labor and the condensation of social relations of production. The concrete abstraction is simultaneously a medium of social actions, because it structures them, and a product of those actions. For Lefebvre, understanding space requires us to grasp how space is produced as a multimanifested concrete abstraction. The concept of production in the marxian sense represents the way in which we can overcome the philosophical dualisms, such as the subject and object opposition, which lie at the heart of static structuralist or simplistic marxist analysis:

> In any product, however trivial, the subjective and objective aspects, the activity and the thing, are intimately linked. These are isolated objects that have been separated from Nature . . . And yet these products still remain objects of Nature . . . Every product—every object—is therefore turned in one direction towards Nature and in another towards man. It is both concrete and abstract. It is concrete in having a given substance, and still concrete when it becomes part of our activity, by resisting or obeying it, however. It is abstract by virtue of its definite, measurable contours, and also because it can enter into a social existence, be an object amongst other similar objects and become the bearer of a whole series of new relations additional to its substantiality. (1939: 119)

But space is produced like no other commodity. It has both a material reality and a formal property which enables it to constrain the material reality of other commodities and their social relations. Just as other commodities, it represents both a material object and a process involving social relations. Unlike other commodities, it continually recreates social relations or helps reproduce them; furthermore, these might be the very same relations which helped produce it in the first place. Thus space has the property of being materialized by a specific social process to act back upon itself and that process. It is, therefore, simultaneously material object or product, the medium of social relations, and the reproducer of material objects and social relations. In this way Lefebvre grounds the multiplicity of the society-space articulation in a dialectical relation. It is precisely this dialectical, ontological status of space which gives rise to its multifaceted nature in society. Space literally saturates society at every level.

To understand Lefebvre, we must dialectically overcome the functionalist thinking of marxian analysis and transform his concepts by introducing a spatial dimension. As he states:

> Today scientific and technological transformations of the modern world render inevitable a reconsideration of Marxian

> thought. Here is my theory: All Marxist concepts are taken to
> a higher level without any one stage in theory disappearing.
> The reconsideration of Marxist concepts develops optimally by
> taking account fully of space. (1974: 236)

According to Lefebvre, however, in order to carry out this theoretical
reformulation marxist thought must drop its emphasis on economism, and therein lies the reason for the lukewarm reception his
work has received from other marxists. Lefebvre does *not* wish to
dispense with political economy, merely to supplement it with a
nonreducible production of space aspect. He conceives of modern society as a postscarcity phenomenon produced by the organizational
efficiency of industrialization. Political economy, as a mode of analysis, can be viewed from this perspective as the "ideology of asceti-
cism." That is, in a world conceived of as dominated by problems of
scarcity, we need a science to tell us how to apportion our resources
to make production decisions for the greatest good. The marxian debate with "bourgeois" economists revolves around the preferred social organization for making those decisions, with the former arguing for a socialization of the means of production as the only
solution to the violence at the core of all other systems of distribution. Lefebvre does not see such a solution as being sufficient to
insure a humanist society or even one that would, say, by the nationalization of land do away with the contradictions of running an
economy in a modern society. In fact, he sees the humanist solution
as involving an end to alienation through a revolutionary approach
to everyday life and to the production of space.

For Lefebvre the modern period began with the Bauhaus movement, because there a total design concept was articulated for society which integrated the "inside" with the "outside" in a consis-
tently thought-out sequence of ensembles (from furnishings to the
home to the city). To date we have failed to carry on the Bauhaus
spirit—we have failed to create a humanist postindustrial space as
an integrated ensemble. Instead, capitalist relations have taken over
the elements of space and fragmented the environment through the
mechanism of the commodity into freestanding sculptures. This
pulverization of space into cities with individual buildings designed
as works of art produces the abstract space of domination and hierarchy (see Bookchin 1984). Capitalism has survived as a system by
producing its own space dictated by its mechanical needs and by its
need to reproduce the social relations of production. The system sur-
vives only because no other logic of space has emerged to challenge
it, although a nascent impulse along these lines has appeared in the

environmentalist movement, in what Lefebvre calls consumer movements, in street actions such as the People's Park incident, and in the squatter phenomenon of central city housing. As he states:

> Space, the land, the soil have not disappeared, absorbed by industrial production; on the contrary, integrated into capitalism they are affirmed as elements in its extension, an active extension. Not only has capitalism seized pre-existing space, the land, but it tends to produce its own space. Through urbanization, under the pressure of the world market. Under the law of the reproducible and the repetitive, by cancelling out the differences in space and time, by destroying nature and natural time. Economics, fetishized into world markets and its space, along with politics carried to the absolute, risk destroying their own foundation, the earth, space, the city and the countryside and consequently destroying themselves. (1974: 376)

In the final analysis, Lefebvre's critique of capitalism is based upon his supposition that its produced space destroys everyday life and the level of civilization once associated with the city. Furthermore, the destruction of nature which such a system engenders through industrialization (here in common with all western countries) threatens to disrupt the ecologically regenerating processes responsible for sustaining life on this earth. In place of a world in which relatively abundant natural resources are utilized to produce commodities under conditions of scarcity, we now have a potential abundance of all manner of commodities but a growing scarcity of natural resources—nature itself is presently being threatened with exhaustion. In place of the science of economics, founded as it is on the ideological notion of scarcity, therefore, Lefebvre feels that we need a revolutionary science of design which can preserve both everyday urban life and nature. Furthermore, this perspective is marxist and requires a radical political intervention. Its practice means the transformation of existing property relations and an end to the domination of social space by abstract space. But this domination cannot be overcome until the constraints on the technical ability to develop space by private ownership are removed by a socialized mode of production. As a first step in this project, Lefebvre proposes his theory of space.

There is little doubt that Lefebvre has developed a unique approach to the built environment. However, his approach raises many questions which he has ignored but which must be addressed for an adequate marxian analysis of space. In this sense we must grasp the central thrust of his theory, that all marxian concepts are raised to a higher level of understanding by taking into account the element of space. Unfortunately, Lefebvre himself has not addressed this task. In conformity with what has apparently become a division of labor fostered upon us by the style of French intellectual writing, it becomes our task to work through Lefebvre's ideas to articulate a marxian approach to space. It is thus necessary to discuss the important aspects of Marx's theory and to introduce spatial considerations in order to fully address the project which Lefebvre intends.

There appear to be at least four areas which need to be covered. Is there a class analysis of space? What is the role of space in capital accumulation? What is the relationship between the state and space? What is meant by urban space? In the next chapter I shall address the first two questions, as they will enable me to synthesize the material from preceding chapters. In what follows I will be concerned principally with addressing the relationship between the state and space, because it is this topic which frames the fundamental difference between the approach of Lefebvre and the trajectory of marxian thought represented by Castells. As it turns out, in addressing this issue it becomes imperative to also consider the essential differences between Lefebvre and Castells over what they mean by urban space. Consequently, I can begin to synthesize marxian ideas on an approach to space by examining the relationship between the state and space.

THE STATE AND SPACE

The nature of the state and state activity in Late Capitalism is a much debated and highly articulated topic. Its relevance to society is perhaps unparalleled by any other societal change associated with the modern period, because, since the Great Depression, the state has been intervening actively in the economic life of capitalism. As Clark and Dear have indicated, the starting point for a theory of the state focuses on such intervention because of the acknowledged inadequacies of the self-regulating mechanism of economic competition in recreating the production relations of society (1981: 46; Mandel 1975: 475). In the debate on the theory of the state, certain fundamental distinctions have been advanced, such as the distinction between political power and the political apparatus (Althusser 1971: 140); between the functions of the state in a capitalist society and the nature of the capitalist state (Clark and Dear 1981); between the state as a condensed structure of power relations (Poulantzas

1973) and as an instrument of the ruling class (Miliband 1973). Furthermore, both the nature of power or control and the functions of the state apparatus or decision-making framework have been scrutinized within the marxist tradition from a variety of well-defined positions (Holloway and Picciotto 1979; Miliband 1973; Offe and Rouge 1975; Therborn 1978; Jessop 1982).

Urban inquiries into the relationship between the state and space have preserved the same focus on the importance of intervention; however, most marxists seem to stress the role of the state apparatus as a public policy instrument managing society rather than as a purposeful means of spatial design. In this sense the relation between the state and space for political economists is epiphenomenal to the principal nexus—that of managing the crisis base of capitalism. Consequently, marxists transpose the two traditional functions of the state in capitalist society, namely, its accumulation and legitimation functions (O'Connor 1973; Habermas 1975), directly to their analysis of the state's relation to space. Thus, the latter is specified either as the action of government in managing the capital accumulation process as it is deployed in space or as the action of public policy in moderating class conflict (Scott 1980; Lojkine 1977a: 141). The last topic, in turn, has generated a third and separate area of inquiry involving the nature of the ideological relations controlling class consciousness by the state, which can be treated as intervening in space as well (Mingione 1977: 26; Althusser 1971).

In all cases, however, marxian political economy only assigns to space the status of a container, which is an indirect product of the state's management of capitalism's crisis base. The state is not perceived as moving directly to produce its own space. Thus, analysts of urbanism in totalitarian societies find a comparative difference between Eastern and Western European countries because in the former the state has a direct role in the construction of entire towns and cities (Misztal and Misztal 1984). Yet, as we shall see below, this difference is not as great as often supposed, because the capitalist state does play a more direct role in the production of space. This relation, however, is a subtle one and must be brought out by an analysis different from that of political economy. Furthermore, if space is epiphenomenal to the primacy of economic relations, as marxian political economists suggest, then urban politics is essentially a phenomenon of class relations. In the West, urban clashes are perceived from this perspective as confrontations produced by deep-level antagonisms between capital and labor, rather than stemming from some other source such as territorial inequalities in the supply of resources. In communist totalitarian societies, urban clashes are perceived as being produced by the conflict between workers and the state, so that conflict is once again perceived as a mode of class struggle. Thus, for marxian political economists, the importance of sociospatial relations for the understanding of urban struggles is always considered secondary to economic conditions. However, as we shall see next, this reductionist economism does not hold up when alternate approaches are considered.

In practice, marxian political economists have combined the three aspects of state intervention discussed above in their analysis of urban policies. Thus, Harvey reveals the multiple role of government housing subsidies for the home construction industry. First, state subsidies to the industry itself operate as a Keynesian support for the economy and as a key regulator of growth. Second, the ownership of a home is viewed as one way in which worker demands have been bifurcated between work-related and quality-of-life-related concerns, with the latter receiving greater emphasis by the state (socialization of capital). Finally, property ownership by a major portion of the working class serves to further fracture class consciousness and help ally the homeowning working-class group with capitalists and against those who rent (Harvey 1975b: 265–295).

This integration of the three functional roles for the state and their epiphenomenal effects on settlement space to the primacy of economic concerns is perhaps clearer for the topic of urban planning. A prevailing marxian view is that such policies serve to alleviate problems of capital accumulation rather than aiming at the conscious design of the environment (Preteceille 1973; Topolov 1973; Scott and Roweiss 1978). The metropolitan landscape represents a spatial array of structures and locations with varying degrees of efficiency. The urban land market operates imperfectly in clearing away the barriers to new development arising from uneven patterns of growth, and state intervention is required to free up land for more profitable investment. At the same time, the long history of urban planning can be viewed, in part, in terms of efforts to alleviate the environmental problems of working-class life and class conflict (Roweiss 1981). Planning, however ineffective, is viewed as a functional mechanism for controlling class conflict within industrialized cities. Finally, planning has also been viewed as an ideological mask which serves to seduce the working class into believing that state intervention in the environment actually promotes the representation of their interests in society, although this is not the case (Lefebvre 1973, 1974).

The three forms of state intervention in space are viewed as being encapsulated within contradictions which doom it to exacerbate rather than alleviate the problems of capitalism, because the problems of economic development can never be solved by the state. That is, the study of state intervention eventually leads to consideration of how the state manages the social contradictions of growth. Thus, a focus on the role of the state in space is transformed into a concern which returns us to the general question of the nature of the capitalist state itself by exploring the contradictions of its policy and planning interventions as a support of capital (Scott and Roweiss 1978; Lojkine 1977a; Mingione 1981). In general, this pursuit of a theory of the state by virtue of studying its spatial contradictions is handled best by returning to Mandel's notion of the state as a reproducer of the social structure, as Mingione says:

> The intervention of the state is concerned both with the immediate interest of capital accumulation and general social reproduction. However, this second field of intervention has recently come to be the main one and has come to condition the whole work of redistribution of surplus-value on the part of the state. (1981: 17)

In short, marxian political economy's approach to the relation between the state and space has two principal characteristics. First, it assigns to that relation an epiphenomenal status relative to the role of the state in managing the crisis base of capitalism. Thus both the production of space itself and urban politics are perceived as being produced by the manifestations of class conflict. Second, this approach is forced, eventually, to relate the analysis of sociospatial public policies back to the more fundamental question of the nature of the capitalist state itself, because such interventions are contradictory in their effects since crises can never be overcome politically under capitalist relations of production. However, this second aspect, namely, the role of the state in the reproduction of capitalist relations of production, is handled badly by political economy, as we have already seen in the case of the labor theory of location (chapter 3). Consequently, the relation between the state and space forces marxian analysis to consider alternate approaches which specify the state's role in the reproduction of social relations.

There appear to be two lines of reasoning, expressed specifically in terms of the reproduction of social relations, which strive for a *theoretical* understanding of the role of the state in reproducing relations through settlement space. The first follows Castells' urban question, and the second is Lefebvre's production of space. The question of the relationship between the state and space, therefore, leads us to confront the two most sweeping and most different marxian approaches to this relationship. In the remainder of this section, let us compare the two approaches.

Collective Consumption: Castells' Theory of the State

According to Castells' mature notion of collective consumption, the city is as much a product of the intervening state as it is of the economy (1978). Castells explains this growing intervention by an argument reminiscent of mainstream economics' theory of public goods, namely, that collective consumption goods necessary for the reproduction of labor power have to be supported by public expenditures because there is no incentive for private capital to supply them. According to the mainstream argument, the necessity of intervention arises from an intrinsic problem with the goods themselves, while Castells views this necessity as a historical product created by the maturing requirements of capitalism over time. As he indicates:

> As capitalism develops, the means of collective consumption at the basis of urban structure are required increasingly by the evolution of capital, production and consumption processes, and social demands. Now, at the same time it so happens that, usually, the production and management of most of these collective goods are not profitable for private capital—at least not unless an intervention external to capital has established the prior considerations necessary to capitalist profit. The reason for this is related to the historical relations between classes and not to the "nature" of these goods and services themselves. This leads us on to a major contradiction of capitalist development: the logic of capital cannot fulfill a diversity of fundamental demands. It is in an attempt to resolve this contradiction that the State decisively intervenes in the production, distribution and management of the means of collective consumption and spatial organization of these services. (1978: 169)

Hence, sustaining the urban form as the reproduction site for labor power has required, as capitalism has matured, the active intervention of the state in a way that is somewhat separate from the Keynesian program celebrated by Harvey. Castells formulates a more comprehensive notion here because he sees Late Capitalism as requiring active government involvement. This is necessary not just as a way to sustain the adequate living and social service arrangements which are needed for the sustenance and reproduction of the industrial-corporate work force but as a product of Late Capitalist transformations to counter the falling rate of profit and, in part, as a response to the organized class struggle which has made the state responsible for the quality of life—a burden the private sector has been reluctant to bear (Castells 1978).

Castells indicates that the intervention of the state in collective consumption performs a number of functions within the built environment that benefit capitalist interests. First, by supporting the needs of workers, intervention decreases the responsibility of the private sector to provide for the reproduction of labor power needs, thereby easing salary demands. This is especially true for state subsidies toward housing. Second, state investment in public goods, which is generally nonprofitmaking for the state, is considered a form of the devaluation of capital which is required by the capitalist class to counter the falling rate of profit over time: "By investing 'at a loss' the general rate of profit of the private sector holds steady or increases in spite of the lowering of profit relative to social capital as a whole." Third, Castells indicates that state investment in the built environment is always done with private capital, either by subsidizing the renovation of a lagging industry to make it more competitive or by assuring a certain framework of organization for the mobilization of capital through financial or functional aid so that private interests can amplify their ability to accumulate capital. "Thus the public highway infrastructure makes use of the automobile possible, and urban renewal operations permit the actions of private developers" (1975: 178).

This argument frames for Castells the essential contradiction of Late Capitalism. Active state intervention cannot resolve the crisis base of capitalism because it has been asked to sustain *both* the falling rate of profit through Keynesian measures *and* the quality of community life through the reproduction of labor power. Debt-financed public expenditures at every government level are increasingly required to overcome the progressively degenerating core of modern society, since social wealth is always privately expropriated and siphoned off by capitalist interests. It is by virtue of this formulation that Castells links up with the extensive analysis of the city fiscal crisis of the 1970s, which focused on the overwhelming social service burden placed upon the local municipality and its overtaxed, debt-financed nature. In fact, Castells' work on urbanism is merely a prelude to his examination of what O'Connor (1973) means by the fiscal crisis of the state, brought about by the progressive socialization of capital in modern society.

Starting from the identification of the city as the reproduction site for labor power, therefore, Castells has developed a full-blown crisis theory of capitalism, associated with the dual aspects of government's intervention in the private sector and its social responsibility to cover the increasing costs of reproducing the labor force and sustaining the quality of everyday life. Thus we see that Castells' view of urban social organization as being "explained" in terms of the fiscal problematic associated with collective consumption leads inextricably to a crisis theory of capitalism as a whole (Castells 1980). With the latter endeavor Castells has moved from a particularized conception of urban social organization to a generalized analysis of the social formation of Late Capitalism and the fiscal problems associated with the socialization of capital. It is beyond the scope of our present work to pursue an evaluation of this crisis theory of social organization, as it must stand alongside such other attempts at comprehending advanced industrial society as those by Lefebvre, Mandel, Galbraith, Touraine, Bell, Janowitz, Kahn, Baran and Sweezy, and many others.

Returning to the significance of the linkage between Castells and O'Connor, however, we can note that in the work of the latter the theory of collective consumption has been generalized to encompass the question of the socialization of capital, so that the urban question itself is but a special case of what Mingione calls the social question (1981). In contrast, Castells' work on urban politics has retained a city focus—he relates the general phenomenon of the crisis base of capitalism specifically to the urban milieu by conceiving of the city as an arena for collective consumption, as we have seen. Urban politics is then explained in part by the intervention of the state as an expression of a class society which cannot help but politicize the economic contradictions that necessitate this intervention. What is new and different about Castells' approach to urban politics, however, is that he sees the responsibility of the state for collective consumption as politicizing environmental concerns and as producing social cleavages between urban populations which cannot be reduced to class differences. That is, the contradictions in modern capitalism have expressed themselves politically in a ubiquitous fashion and are globalized or cross-class in their impact. Urban politics is no longer merely an epiphenomenon of class relations. Housing, education, transportation, and pollution and energy concerns have all become part of a growing and generalized political agenda shared by the majority of citizens, because the state instead of the private sector has assumed responsibility for the quality of life. The essence of these "new" forms of social cleavage is the fact that they are produced by state intervention rather than by economic relations, as most marxists might suppose. As Castells indicates, in the realm of urban politics we find these new disparities to be based upon the *sociospatial* inequalities of collective consumption:

They do not correspond to the position occupied in class relationships but to the position in the consumption process itself,
as well as in specific elements of this process and in the unities
of the urban system where it operates . . . such inequalities
among social groups are not entirely autonomous of the class
system since its logic determines the organization of consumption, but the positions defined in the specific structure of inequality do not correspond one-to-one to the structure of class
relationships. It is in this sense that there is specific production of new effects of social inequality. (1975: 191)

According to Castells, the urban social movements produced by
these new sources of inequality possess the potential of strengthen-
ing the working-class struggle through the addition of persons traditionally not integrated into the conflict against capitalist interests.
Such a view has been advocated primarily from a knowledge of the
French and Italian cases; it remains an untested assertion with regard to the United States. This hypothesis regarding the source of
new cleavages in urban politics is perhaps Castells' most interesting
contribution, but it raises a series of issues which he does not resolve. First, it represents a view of political conflict based upon consumption groups and classes, while the marxian approach to class
struggle is essentially defined in terms of production relations, as we
have seen. There is thus a strong need to clarify the relationship between conflict around the built environment and the class struggle.
This theme has been addressed more fully by the neoweberians, as
we shall see in the next chapter.
    Second, by making the state responsible for collective consump-
tion, we need to specify the way in which government operates in
response to social interests. That is, while Castells has progressed
far toward developing the relationship between the state and settlement space through his concept of collective consumption, he has
not addressed the question of clarifying the nature of the state itself
in modern society. State intervention, for example, is decidedly
more complex than that suggested by the notion of acting in the interests of "capital in general" (Pickvance 1982: 22). Castells' efforts
at specifying the nature of the modern state are limited because he
links up with Poulantzas' structuralist theory. There is considerably
more to the theory of the capitalist state than this (Jessop 1982).
Thus, one reason why Castells' theory of the state is weak is because
Poulantzas' theory is weak.
    Third, under an Althusserian compulsion for theoretical specifi-
city, Castells has categorized the essence of the urban in terms of

collective consumption, and this continues to haunt his entire project. Neither collective consumption nor the reproduction of labor power can seriously be viewed as specific to the city alone. In fact, in many cities of the United States child-rearing couples have fled this environment as being destructive to reproduction. Furthermore, the separation of production from consumption raises serious questions regarding the neglect by Castells of the relationship between settlement space and the capital accumulation process. This neglect is compounded by the important role of urban public policies in countering the falling rate of profit, which Castells does recognize but leaves undeveloped. The question of the relationship between space and the state in the production of surplus value is addressed only through the back door of underconsumption theory, that is, by virtue of Keynesian measures to support the level of effective demand.

This third weakness of collective consumption theory requires some amplification, as it bears on important questions in urban political economy and illustrates why Castells' theory of urban social movements is so limited for the U.S. case. In essence, state intervention in space has two key effects on the capital accumulation process. On the one hand, its activities can be viewed as transferring the costs for the reproduction of labor power to the society as a whole via the mechanism of public finance. On the other hand, according to Castells, state expenditures counter the falling rate of profit by investing at a loss in the public sector. But neither of these aspects can be addressed effectively within the confines of collective consumption theory, because it has been circumscribed by Castells to deal only with the provision of use values—public services and the reproduction of labor power through consumption. In effect, this is merely a transfer of income to the working class from the social surplus through the intervention of the state. According to Theret, however, such a perspective implies that intervention raises "expenses capital" corresponding to any given cycle of production of surplus value within the urban environment. Consequently, Castells, Lojkine, Preteceille, and others consider such transfers as devalorized capital, because intervention shifts it from productive to unproductive uses. In this way they conclude that collective consumption is investment at a loss. For Theret, however:

> Such a point of view constitutes a sort of revival of bourgeois theories of capital which deny the existence of contradictions between workers and capitalists. Indeed, it implicitly reduces the basic difference between these classes to a difference of degree in the development of their respective "capitals." There-

fore, it introduces an idea of continuity between the various classes, and implicitly negates the marxist conception of exploitation. The worker can thus be considered as the holder of a capital which is devalorized because it is assigned to consumption, an operation producing zero surplus value and zero profit. (1982: 356)

As Theret astutely observes, because of the initial decision to separate the creation of use values (collective consumption) from exchange values (the general conditions of production), collective consumption arguments split surplus value into separate streams of capital in the manner of bourgeois political economy. Consequently, the fundamental antagonisms constituting the capitalist mode of production which produce social movements and urban politics are masked, such as fractions within the capitalist class itself. The latter, in fact, have quite recently redefined the extent of state intervention toward decreasing support of such activities by recapitalizing and withdrawing support for extensive public sector involvement following the fiscal crisis (Tomaskovic-Devey and Miller 1982; Pickvance 1982). Despite some spirited defenses of this fundamental separation between production and consumption values (see Dunleavy 1980), approaches based on collective consumption are doomed to reproduce basic errors in marxian political economy. Thus Dunleavy (following Castells and Lojkine) includes, in his definition of collective consumption goods, highways and infrastructural improvements carried out through urban planning, which are more correctly part of the means of production regardless of their financing origin. As he remarks:

> The last two areas are not strictly concerned with consumption but with regulation or management of the urban system; but following Castells, I include them within the scope of urban analysis since their primary impact is on the development of collective consumption processes. (1980: 52)

However, the inclusion of the means of circulation, such as highways, and of state practices, such as land-use regulation, confuses the theoretical nature of state intervention in space. Dunleavy has lumped together elements which involve the state in the reproduction of labor power with those that serve to reproduce capital as a whole. Consequently, this definition cannot specify a unique consumption element in the quality of state intervention and the theory breaks down.

Finally, Castells' evolution in thought culminates in his neglect of settlement space itself, while at the very same time he has refused to let go of the term "urban." This has produced an overwhelming confusion in the writings of all those wishing to understand him. In his later work "urban" is referred to as belonging to the structural elements comprising social organization, which includes production, consumption, social classes, and the state (1977: 439), but it is *never* defined and assumes the shorthand connotation for "crisis." Thus Castells' "urban" has defied material specificity—being characterized more as a process which is at the heart of social problems than as a product of the deployment of social structure in space. This is the case despite the fact that he claims for it a certain locational specificity, because reproduction of labor takes place within a residence, an everydayness existing in settlement space. Yet the description of the spatial form within which everyday life transpires remains remarkably undeveloped, despite its extreme importance.

In contradiction to Castells, only a theory of the production of space can effectively explain social problems and the production of spatial forms. This is especially true for the United States. In this country questions regarding housing, transportation, recreation, leisure, and safety have become ubiquitous concerns of the population. They are no more city-based than they are suburban in nature; they are perceived clearly as a product of the general articulation between the social formation and space and as belonging to the general class of problems involved in the *reproduction* of capitalist social relations.

To be sure, Castells has made a fundamental contribution to the study of urban politics because he has identified the existence of non-class-specific conflicts under contemporary capitalist relations which cannot be reduced to traditional marxian categories; however, I do not see how this phenomenon can be completely understood by focusing only upon the nature of collective consumption. For example, Dunleavy acknowledges that services can also be supplied through private means. Thus the quality of life is also sustained by the private sector even for the case of services (1980: 52). Yet, it is extremely important for conditions in the United States to be differentiated even further from conditions in the United Kingdom in this regard: virtually all public services in this country can potentially be supplied through private means, including education, transportation, health care, and so on. The antagonism between public and private allocation of use values is an important one in the analysis of the state for the case of America and, possibly, elsewhere. Yet analyses in any one country do not exhaust an understanding of such conflict in the others (Pickvance 1982: 19). In fact, by developing his theory principally from the French experience, Castells has left himself open to the same charge of abstract empiricism which marxists level against mainstream positivists (Duncan 1981: 241). Collective consumption theory as an urban theory cannot hold up under cross-cultural comparisons.

In short, while Castells' approach to the relation between the state and space improves upon marxian political economy, his style of analysis must be disregarded in favor of the production of space perspective. In fact, because American marxists have virtually ignored Lefebvre, they have been denied access to an alternate approach to the urban, the state, and the nature of urban social movements. In the remainder of this chapter, let us consider Lefebvre's contribution to these topics. As I shall show, despite the all too sketchy nature of his writings Lefebvre's approach is not only more applicable to the case of the United States, but it also fits better the condition of the working class under totalitarian communist regimes. I shall begin the comparison with the contrast between Castells' and Lefebvre's approaches to the relation between the state and space.

Lefebvre's Approach to the State and Space

Lefebvre's approach to the state differs fundamentally from Castells'. Because they hold different views of the state, their respective approaches to urban political movements also contrast sharply. Castells draws upon Poulantzas' theory of the state, as we have seen, which treats it as a condensation of class interests. Accordingly, the state acts as a regulator of class conflict whose decisions and policies work in the long-term interests of monopoly capital but whose status is relatively autonomous of immediate capitalist needs. As Saunders summarizes, "It follows that the State does not itself have power, but rather reflects through its interventions the political relations between different classes. Power, in other words, is a function of class relations and is revealed through class practices" (1981: 191).

According to Lefebvre, however, the state is a framework for the exercise of power, which in the weberian sense cannot be reduced to economic interests alone. That is, the state can act, and most often does act, in the interests of capital, but it can also pursue its *own* interests, which tend to strengthen the hold of the nation-state framework on society. The creation of a space suitable to such interests is a *fundamental* and intrinsic part of state activity. In contrast to Castells, therefore, the state is a hierarchical form possessing the concrete abstraction of power in a domination-subordination relationship, which is then utilized by bureaucrats to control society. Furthermore, it realizes its essence, the concrete task of domination, in the same manner as it achieves economic power—historically by the destruction over time of social space and the substitution in its place of an instrumental, fragmented space and a hierarchical administrative framework deployed in space. As Lefebvre notes:

> What is the state? A "framework" say political scientists, the framework of a power which makes decisions. Yes, but we must add: a *spatial framework*. If we do not take account of this spatial framework and of its power, we retain only the rational unity of the state; we come back to Hegelianism. Only the concepts of space and of its production allow the framework of power to attain the concrete. It is in this space that the central power eliminates all other power, that a class in power claims to be suppressing class differences. This statist framework and the state as framework cannot be conceived without the instrumental space of which it makes use. (1974: 322)

For Castells the essence of the urban is arrived at by the application of Althusserian categories of analysis, which come to rest upon the functional importance of consumption and its supply through state intervention. The end result of this process of collective consumption is twofold. On the one hand, it maximizes the regulatory function of the state in society, as expressed through the process of planning, and on the other hand it politicizes the urban question and globalizes disputes over the demands for consumption goods as the quality of life deteriorates (1977, 1978). Castells' view (1980) places us inexorably on the analytical path to the fiscal crisis described by O'Connor (1973), where the growing inability of the public sector to support the system of collective consumption becomes manifest in a general breakdown of the capitalist social formation, a situation which by 1984 had reversed itself (Smith 1984)!

In contrast to Castells, Lefebvre arrives at the essence of the urban by a historical argument not dissimilar to that of Weber. According to Lefebvre capitalism as a totality is an unfinished historical project. As a mode of production, it has shifted and altered since Marx's day in order to survive. Lefebvre sees the survival of capitalism as a consequence of its ability to recreate all the social relations necessary to the mode of production on an ongoing basis. This has been accomplished over the years by capitalism's use of space—that is, it is by producing a distinctive space for itself that this process of domination through reproduction has occurred. As he indicates, "Capitalism has found itself able to attenuate (if not resolve) its internal contradictions for a century, and it has succeeded in achieving 'growth.' We cannot calculate at what price but we do know the means: by occupying a space, by producing a space" (1973: 21).

Lefebvre, therefore, also places his fundamental theoretical emphasis on the state's role in the reproduction of social relations. Unlike Castells, however, he is bound by historical argument to consider three separate aspects of this process: the biological reproduction carried out by the family, the reproduction of the work force, and the reproduction of the social relations of production (1974: 42). These levels and processes are maintained in a state of coexistence and cohesion by the action of social space, that is, by the organic community of production and consumption. For Lefebvre, the essence of this space is the everyday life which transpires in the urban center, a condition of social density associated more with the pre-capitalist, historical city: "The precise location of the reproduction of the relations of production is the pre-capitalist (historical) city, fragmented but inserted in a wider space" (1974: 66).

Thus the reproduction of the social relations sustaining the capitalist system is dependent upon the effects of agglomeration and is accomplished through a spatial form, the city center. In recent years this center has been fragmented, along with its functions, and deployed throughout the metropolitan region. This has produced certain problems for the effective reproduction of capitalist relations—a subject to be discussed immediately following. In summation, for Lefebvre, the essence of the urban is a spatial form which then supports the reproduction process of capital in general, while for Castells this essence is a process, the reproduction of labor power, which is embedded in a spatial form. This distinction becomes important because it divides these two theorists over the issue of political action or praxis. Most important, only Lefebvre among marxists sees the role of space as more than epiphenomenal, in fact, as essential to the functioning of capitalist social relations.

Lefebvre specifies the need for an interventionist state on the basis of the above conceptualization of the reproduction of the relations of production. For him, the fiscal crisis is only a special case of the general crisis of reproduction engendered by the pulverization of the historical urban form and the fragmentation of its center. Lefebvre would not be a marxist without his own crisis theory of capitalism, and he also possesses an apocalyptic vision. However, his is a general crisis brought about by the failure of the system itself to reproduce—a failure which has, in part, been engendered by the disappearance of the traditional social space associated with the city center.

The state's role in this process is contradictory. On the one hand, it must intervene in order to preserve the coherencies of social space in the face of their destruction by the capitalist transformations of use into exchange values—that is, of social space into abstract space. On the other hand, its interventions are all specified by the relationship of domination. Hence, the state's interventions do not rescue social space; on the contrary, it merely aids the hegemony of abstract space by producing some of its own through planning. Because the state is a framework of power, its interventions have inaugurated the destruction of social space and the compact, bounded city form. For Lefebvre, the state is allied not only against the working class or even against fractions of capital, it is the enemy of everyday life itself—because it produces the abstract space which negates the social space that supports everyday life and the reproduction of its social relations. According to Lefebvre this view of the state can be illustrated by the work of Georges Haussmann, who broke up the historic space of Paris for the benefit of a strategic space:

> When in the city the square (example: the Place des Vosges), a meeting place removed from traffic, changes into a thoroughfare (example: the Palais-Royale), urban life deteriorates unknowingly and profoundly to the profit of abstract space, the one that atoms of circulation (the auto) travel through.
> (1974: 360)

It is precisely because of Lefebvre's view of the state's role in the production of abstract space that the whole of urban planning (*urbanisme*) is called into question. For Lefebvre there can be no reformist urban planning. The destruction of the spatial ground upon which unalienated human existence transpires is accomplished by the domination of abstract space, brought about by state interventions masked by the ideology of planning. There is thus a radical rejection of all such activities by Lefebvre, who makes the bold claim that a truly liberating approach to the environment has yet to be worked out. In its place we have the analysis of abstract space in the name of political economy or structuralism, or we have debates on the relative merits of present-day urban planning from these various perspectives. For Lefebvre, however, "It is worth remembering that the urban has no worse enemy than urban planning and 'urbanisme' which is capitalism's and the state's strategic instrument for the manipulation of fragmented urban reality and the production of controlled space" (1973; 15).

Once we connect the elements of Lefebvre's argument, this total rejection of planning implies that radical activity, for him, must be concerned primarily with rescuing everyday life from domination by the abstract space of Late Capitalism's economic and state activity. It is at this point that we can begin to appreciate the forceful rejection of Lefebvre's ideas by Castells, who sees the former's argument at best as "a rather elegant way of speaking of the end of the proletariat and leads to the attempt actually to ground a new political strategy not on the basis of the structures of domination, but on the alienation of everyday life" (1977: 92), and at worse as a form of utopian anarchism. Thus Castells draws a battle line between himself and Lefebvre over the application of their thought to the political issues raised by their separate views of the urban, specifically with regard to the articulation between the class struggle and space. This is conceptualized as an approach to urban social movements. Let us compare these two contrasting perspectives next.

The Significance of Urban Social Movements for Castells

For Castells the study of urban social movements ties together the problematic addressed by a theory of space—the sociospatial context of the class struggle, the mode of production, the state, and so on. As he says:

> The heart of the sociological analysis of the urban question is the study of urban politics, that is, of the specific articulation of the processes designated as "urban" with the field of the class struggle, and consequently, with the intervention of the political instance (state apparatuses)—object and center of the political struggle and what is at issue in it. (1977: 244)

Castells shares with Lefebvre a focus on urban planning and its critique. Yet, for the former, urban social movements become the essential focus of urban politics. The difference between the two approaches can be expressed as follows. Whereas Castells studies what exists in the way of political action within the city and tries to explain it, Lefebvre wishes to consider what might occur in the manner of radical political action—hence the appeal of the former to an entire generation of academic marxists. For Castells, urban social movements represent the displacement of the class struggle from the work area to the communal living space (see also Harvey 1976; Cox 1981). This is specified theoretically as an organized claim on the part of the dominated class for more *indirect* wages. Thus the class struggle is deflected from its historical concern with the division of surplus wealth to one which addresses consumption needs, especially the means of reproducing the workers themselves. According to Castells, "Because no centralized regulation of the process is being set up in the economic sphere (by corporations), the state becomes the veritable arranger of the process of consumption as a whole: this is at the root of so-called 'urban politics'" (1977: 451).

In short, for Castells political conflict is at base a form of class conflict displaced to the community and involving concerns over needs tied to the reproduction of labor power. Due to the inability of capitalists working either independently or in concert to regulate this conflict, the state must intervene. As Castells points out in an extended discussion (1978), this local state intervention, far from resolving conflict, exacerbates it, but in a unique way: collective consumption produces new cleavages in society which at times cut across class lines and which globalize political conflict within the urban milieu to include many groups and widely disparate political positions.

Urban social movements for Castells reflect either class conflict or the intervention of the state in the field of consumption. Because state intervention is so broadly defined by Castells as spanning roles from regulation to such direct initiatives as public housing, this conceptualization of social movements is so broad that it encompasses everything and hence is nonfalsifiable, a limitation which has not escaped his critics (Saunders 1981; Pickvance 1982). According to Castells the new social movements produced by the state in particular possess great potential because they can reinforce the class struggle by joining with it. Yet, in his writings he does not identify the mechanisms through which such unity can come about, especially how protests organized around consumption interests in a modern society ruled by mass culture can link up with worker-based movements. This task is especially important in order to understand the case of the United States. Furthermore, as Pickvance has observed, Castells has underestimated the forces countering user revolts in society:

> Firstly, despite the expansion of state intervention there are strong ideological pressures against public provision generated by the fact that the public sector lies within a capitalist society . . . Users' revolts can only succeed if they break through the ideological stigma on public provision and insist that public provision is a right rather than a mark of failure. Secondly, there are organizational obstacles to users' revolts. In some cases like schools and hospitals users "consume" public services within organizations and this facilitates protest. But in others like public transport, refuse collection, etc., the service

is consumed outside an organization and this hinders collective action. (1982: 62)

In short, the political potential of the new movements organized around the collective consumption problematic of Castells' theory is overestimated by him, because of their reliance on the limited radicalizing nature of state intervention in consumption within the ideological context of capitalist society. No more devastating observation regarding this theory can be made than to recognize the present retreat of the state in supplying collective consumption and the remarkable acquiescence of users to this austerity, a development which has forced Castells to alter his entire approach to urban social movements in his most recent book (1983). While I cannot consider this material at this time (see below), it is important to observe that the study of such movements could progress only by an abandonment of the theory which specifies their source solely as the dynamic of collective consumption. This implies that Castells has also abandoned his theory of the relation between the society and the state. This has occurred without its replacement, making his new approach to urban social movements embryonic though not without considerable importance.

In contrast to Castells, Lefebvre does not seek to analyze and isolate the elements of urban politics. Instead, he is interested in promoting political struggle against the state and the property relations which sustain the capitalist mode, whether any manifestations of the struggle against the forms of domination exist or not. According to Lefebvre (see also Mingione 1981; Theret 1982), a theoretical emphasis on consumption both creates a false dichotomy in the study of capitalist relations of production and reproduction and eludes the essential focal point for thought which wishes to *change capitalist society*. As he states:

Thus for Engels in 1872 neither the cottage—today we would say the "suburban bungalow", nor, the workers barracks—we would say "high rise housing project", advances towards the solution of the fundamental problem, which is not that of housing. It eludes the problem of revolutionary transformation. (1970: 111)

That is, for Lefebvre the essential transformation point of power within the capitalist system is found in its existing property relations, not in the intervention of the state in the field of consumption. From this perspective the study of collective consumption is academic.

The Significance of Urban Social Movements for Lefebvre

Lefebvre is concerned to make clear that praxis requires a spatial component and that it is necessary to seize a space and control it at the same time that other seizures are carried out in the interests of the class struggle. This requires a certain boldness, a realization that the radical transformation of society can take place at any time because we exist in space. It is not necessary to travel to the revolution. The forces of expropriation and repression are externalized in the forms of space, and this abstract space of politico-economic domination exists everywhere. Thus, Lefebvre is not only interested in transforming everyday life, as Castells contends—he is interested in directing marxian thought to acknowledge the critical role of property relations in sustaining the capitalist system as well as the need for radical activity to produce a space of its own at the very same time that it intervenes strategically in the interests of the class struggle. The transformation of everyday life must proceed with the radical transformation of space because the one is bound up with the other. How different is this notion from the choices exercised by other marxists, who seem to separate their actions from space! They speed along past ghetto areas toward the "new" research sites chosen by their own mental "labor," thus reproducing by their actions both the spectacular commodity fetishism of society and its stratified social hierarchy. According to Lefebvre, "One of the most troubling problems in the urban problematic is the extraordinary *passivity* of the interested parties. Why this silence of the 'users'?" (1970: 239).

Could it be that we have been lulled with gifts? The present system has split us into homeowners and renters, automobile drivers and mass transit riders, the gainfully employed and the economically obsolete—in short, those who benefit from the existing property relations, whether they are mediated by public or private means, and those who are victims of these relations. Have we questioned the acquiescence of marxian academics in their chosen role as observers of these inequities? They have appropriated radicalism by fragmenting it, on the one hand, into a theoretical activity which becomes a career and, on the other, into a "praxis" which concerns some exotic Lacanian other—the minorities, the oppressed, the working class— far removed from their neighborhoods. The forms of oppression exist in our own everyday lives, not only at the end of some theoretically inspired journey. As Guy Debord remarks:

> To fail to criticize everyday life today means accepting the prolongation of the present thoroughly rotten forms of culture and

politics, forms whose extreme crisis is expressed in increasingly widespread political apathy and neoilliteracy, especially in the most modern countries. On the other hand, a radical critique in acts of prevailing everyday life could lead to a supersession of culture and politics in the traditional sense, that is, to a higher level of intervention in life. (1961: n.p.)

This higher level of intervention has yet to materialize. According to Lefebvre, the critique of everyday life must be linked to the transformation of space, yet there is a blockage which prevents us from perceiving the external contradictions in our immediate surroundings. The marxian project has become a mode of mental procrastination, a theoretical project separate from the externalization of radical action, an endlessly self-referencing project of a quality which Marx had specifically rejected. As Lefebvre notes, "The authors of projects do not seem to realize that (a) there is no thought without utopia, without exploration of the possible, and, (b) there is no thought without reference to a practice" (1970: 239).

Thus Lefebvre wishes to introduce two modes of reasoning into marxian mental activity, the utopian and the strategic. The former refers to an emphasis, not on what exists and its explanation in marxian terms, but on what is possible, what *might* exist in a humanist society; the latter seeks to address the application of marxian thought to politics in the ontological case, where the former is no longer a science. In such an epoch only strategic interventions have meaning (see Hirst 1979). According to Giddens (1973: 14), the historical dilemma of marxism has always been its tendency to assert itself as scientifically valid, on the one hand, and as a "moral guide to action" on the other. Yet Giddens is wrong to present the two choices facing marxists in this manner. He fails to consider the concept of the project in Lefebvre's and Sartre's sense—that is, the strategic intervention which overcomes the relativism of philosophy through political calculation (Hirst 1979: 3), which is aimed toward a well-defined goal and which proceeds through defensible means.

Within the contours of the debate on the theory of space, Castells objected to this line of reasoning because Lefebvre seemed, in his earlier work, to have divorced his concept of everyday life from the class struggle. Thus, Castells was perfectly willing to allow Lefebvre his utopian impulse regarding the humanistic vision of the urban as the mechanism by which alienated everyday life could be liberated from repression. He objected, however, that Lefebvre's concept was nothing more than a physical form which, it was claimed, produced social relationships and a liberating social content for everyday life, that is, a form that served as the spawning ground for radical political action. This placed Lefebvre, in the eyes of Castells, alongside the other environmental determinists such as Wirth and Fischer, who impute to the increased social density of urban interaction emergent properties which assume a *sui generis* nature. As Castells observes:

> What we have here is something very close to Wirth's thesis concerning the way social relations are produced. It is density, the warmth of concentration that, by increasing action and communication, encourage at one and the same time a free flowering, the unexpected, pleasure, sociability and desire. In order to be able to justify this mechanism of sociability (which is connected directly to organicism) that is quite unjustifiable: the hypothesis according to which "social relations are revealing in the negation of distance". And that is what the essence of the urban is in the last resort. For the city creates nothing, but, by centralizing creations, it enables them to flower.
> (1977: 90)

As Castells indicates, unlike other density theorists in the Wirthian vein, Lefebvre was aware of the crude organicism in this formulation. For this reason Lefebvre defined the active, revolutionary aspect of the urban as the right to the city, as the *seizing* of space by action which has been freed of repression and which is already part of a revolutionary praxis. Such action, informed by marxian reasoning, can be contrasted with intervention in space by the state in the form of urban planning. Yet this step, as Castells observes (1977), was not enough to rescue Lefebvre's original conception of the role of urban interaction from the fallacy of spatial determinism. It is because of the need to pass beyond mere environmental reductionism, beyond the limitations imposed by the concept of the urban in a rapidly deconcentrating social formation, that Lefebvre needed to generalize his theory to include space itself (1973, 1974).

As noted previously, Castells' criticism of Lefebvre was launched at a time when the latter's more mature version of space was not yet in print. In abandoning his concept of the urban, Lefebvre also abandoned the idea that any abstract spatial form could become a motive force in history. In its place he advocated the notion that radical activity tied directly to the class struggle required a spatial component to be truly liberating. In his later work, Lefebvre locates the transformational impulse in the act of appropriation that seizes the use value of social space from the dominating exchange value of abstract space. It is through a spatial praxis which is the concrete, material correlate of the more complex, multidimensional notion of class praxis that this abstract space can be destroyed. As Lefebvre indicates:

> To "change society", to "change life" means nothing if there is not production of an appropriated space. From the Soviet Constructionists between 1920 and 1930 and from their failure, comes this teaching: for new social relations there must be new space and vice versa. "To change life!" The province of poets and philosophers as a negative utopia. Now this idea has been taken up politically "live better", "the quality of life", etc. As long as everydayness exists in abstract space, with its very concrete constraints, as long as there are only technical improvements, as long as spaces (of work, leisure, residence) remain disjointed and re-joined only through political control, the project of "changing life" will remain a slogan, at times abandoned, at times taken up again. (1973: 72)

Implicit in Lefebvre's theory of space is the notion that the socialization of the means of production will not complete the humanist project of liberation from dominating social relations. He has in mind here the ill effects of state control in Russia. In addition to a class revolution, it is also necessary to produce a space within which a revolution of everyday life can be carried out. Taken outside of spatial practice, this radical activity can produce only signs, a "ridiculous folklore" of liberation which clings to marxian thought without benefit of experiencing the externalization of humanist social relations in everyday interaction. As Lefebvre observes:

> In the space of Modernity all groups lose their reference points. They dissolve or disintegrate. This is the "Modern Ordeal" which replaces the judgement of God. Groups, classes and fractions of classes are only constituted and recognized as "subjects" through generating (producing) a space. Ideas, representations and values which do not succeed in being inscribed in space by producing an appropriated morphology dry up into signs, are resolved into abstract ideas and changed into phantasms . . . Persistent morphologies (religious edifices, political monuments) uphold out-dated ideologies, while new ideas, not without power (eg. socialism), do not succeed well in generating their space. These ideas, to keep alive, nourish themselves with a peripheral historicity, a ridiculous folklore. In this light the "world of signs" results from a retreat, whatever is not invested in an appropriated space retreats into vain signs and significations. (1974: 479)

ASSESSMENT

Lefebvre's theory of space proposes a project, a strategy of liberation which is meant not to replace the class struggle but only to complement it by emphasizing the importance of producing a space concomitantly with radical action. Nevertheless, Castells' criticisms of Lefebvre possess a certain amount of validity because the latter has deemphasized the class struggle, without which there can be none of the possibilities for alternative everyday life. In fact, Lefebvre's very utopianism, by definition, is a signified for what does *not* exist. If such possibilities are meant to become the cornerstones of action, as Lefebvre intends, then some explicit strategy needs to be provided which demonstrates the affinity between class and spatial praxis. Castells' critique of Lefebvre's political position cuts to the very heart of the latter's limitations as a theorist of revolution because of his early emphasis on the liberating properties of urban social density, that is, of a spatial form, at the expense of the class struggle. Even in his more recent writings, however, Lefebvre pays little attention to specifying precisely what a spatial praxis coupled with the class struggle might look like, despite the obvious importance of such a concept. Furthermore, he provides precious little advice regarding just how a spatial praxis might be articulated, which differs from the kind of alternative to urban planning or humanist theories of spatial design that we presently possess. Thus, Castells' critique aside, Lefebvre's more recent work still leaves us unsatisfied with regard to sociospatial praxis.

Where does this put us? As long as marxian structuralism laid claim to the status of a science, it was possible to formulate a radical program through the interplay of some theory based on that science and the party, a political movement which possessed as its aim structural change (Pickvance 1977b). The collapse of Althusserianism compels a reexamination of marxism's status as a mode of liberation. Like it or not, we have been plunged back inside a Gramscian world where historicism and humanism reassert themselves, as trenchant political postures and as foundations for a marxian project. The death of structuralism leaves us orphaned without science, that is, without certainty, and with the hope of creating a humanist society as our only possession.

If we accept the revolutionary potential of sociospatial praxis as something which complements the class struggle, however, entire areas of social action which were once trivialized or even dismissed by orthodox marxists assume a new significance. Environmentalism, previously viewed as too fragmented and specialized a mode of strategic intervention, takes on immense importance. Such a movement cannot be understood as a manifestation of concerns covered by collective consumption theory or by a discursive expropriation of Lefebvre's theoretical concept of everyday life in favor of some nominalist reference to the quality of life (Castells 1984). From the perspective of sociospatial praxis, the environmental movement has invented an entire conceptual apparatus and vocabulary for specifying the nature of transformational interventions in space. Similarly, the actions of advocacy planners and the entire school of guerrilla architects (Goodman 1971) also assume a new light. Independent and spontaneous collective actions which have reasserted the primacy of social space over property exchange values acquire great significance, such as Ocean-Hill Brownsville (Berube and Gittel 1969), rent strikes (Weissman 1969; Lipsky 1970), resistance to renewal and redevelopment (Davies 1966; Rossi and Dentler 1961; Feagin 1983), and neighborhood activism (Boyte 1979). Collective attempts to seize space or to renegotiate the social costs of capitalist economic development exist everywhere. They fail or achieve merely limited success not because they ignore the class struggle or because they are displacements of that struggle but *only* because they are disparate in content.

By way of contrast, a massive intervention of space's users would probably take over society, as Lefebvre once supposed (1970: 239), yet this has never occurred except in the limited case of ghetto riots. In fact, we have yet to develop mental categories of analysis which would enable us to appreciate the type of liberating spatial logic contained in the unrestrained violence of ghetto insurrections (see, e.g., Pynchon 1968). The latter are not merely symptoms of racial deprivation, they are modes of action belonging to that particular genus of activity which can be called sociospatial praxis. They possess an origin in the holistic dependency of everyday life on the use value of community space.

The importance of communal space to everyday life cannot, as many marxists contend, be reduced to a category of political economy. Neither collective consumption nor exchange value will suffice. The concept of social space is dominated by culture, so that the analysis of any local neighborhood must focus on the confrontation between use and exchange values—on the complex articulation between symbolic universes of meaning, capital accumulation, and space. Consequently, the production of space perspective requires a synthesis between marxian political economy and Lefebvre's approach to space. This is not as difficult a task as might be expected, however, because the two seem to complement each other. It is my belief that the analytical issues raised in the current discussion of the relationship between space and the state, the class struggle, capital accumulation, and the urban can be a first step toward such a necessary synthesis. I shall attend to this task next.

One final comment: ultimately the study of urban politics focuses on the relation between state intervention and the users of space—its inhabitants. This must be specified according to a theory of the relation between the nature of the state and society as a whole. Castells' early work encapsulated user movements both within the dynamics of collective consumption theory and as produced by the phenomenal effect of the relation between the state and the Late Capitalist economy. Thus for Castells users were equated with consumers of state services and goods. In contrast, Lefebvre has identified a historicist domain of inquiry, the idea of everyday life, which is dependent in any given time on the development of social relations and their respective liberatory contents—contents which at present are relatively repressive. The dynamic of this concept of everyday life is controlled by culture itself.

In contrast to other marxists, therefore, Lefebvre understands the problematic concerning the users of space as some complex articulation between economic, political, and cultural forces, rather than as emerging solely from the political domain. Lefebvre's users of space, therefore, are users of everyday life. From this perspective it is clear that we are all potential candidates for sociospatial struggle. This new realization requires a new mode of thinking, as suggested above. I shall only begin to scratch the surface in supplying this need but will take up the topic again in chapters 5 and 8. In fairness to Castells, his latest book (1983) follows along the same path precisely because it also acknowledges the need for a transformation in the specification of the concept of user from his earlier approach. At present, Castells' users are similar to Lefebvre's, and new urban movements are considered as being produced by sociospatial arrangements which include instances of territory and culture (that is, ethnicity and race) as well as state intervention. It is my opinion, however, that the theoretical foundation for further development of the new approach has been supplied by Lefebvre, and it is this line of reasoning which will be developed.

5. Beyond Marxian Political Economy: The Trinity Formula and the Analysis of Space

Since at least the 1970s, marxian urban analysis has developed through the intellectual interaction of a variety of critical perspectives. This process has generated an increasingly more sophisticated set of concepts facilitating thought, which seeks to understand the deep-level relation between societal development and spatial change. Thus, from the view of an outsider, it is a mistake to suppose that some static, monolithic interpretation of Marx dominates critical urban thought.

In the United States, two distinct lines of marxist reasoning prevail: political economy and collective consumption theory. As we have seen, these remain limited for separate reasons. Those supporting the former line have failed to break out of the philosophical and conceptual straitjacket of positivist, neoclassical thought, while any advocacy of collective consumption theory seems almost odd in our present period of state retreat from domestic services and the limited reproductive role which urban areas play in society. As indicated, Lefebvre's theory of space presents us with a third, alternate way of thinking about urban affairs. His dialectical sensibility treats spatial relations as inseparable from marxian categories of analysis. Yet, this approach is not without its problems. In particular, because Lefebvre confines his intellectual production to a hyperbolic, metaphorical style of discourse, one is never quite sure how to replicate his reasoning. This effect is in keeping with his view that the dialectical method can never be formulized. However, the analytical specificity of his concepts remains his personal secret behind a suggestive façade, as does the epistemological basis by which he reduces all social relations to *triplicité*, that is, to sets of three—no more, no less. As time goes by, this list of threesomes scattered throughout his writings multiplies. Even among his most enthusiastic boosters, Lefebvre's ideas become little more than a nominalist discourse on "space" and its importance.

Until now Lefebvre's central idea has been ignored—namely, the need for a reevaluation of Marx's concepts by taking full account of the role of space in their formulation. Such a task will occupy us in the present chapter. As we have seen, space-time relations saturate society at every level. Spatiality in particular is part of the forces of production, the relations of production, and the manner in which the levels or structures of society interact. Contradictions between these levels multiply and complicate themselves further as they interact within the space-time matrix of social organization. But extant marxian approaches have failed to grasp this complexity because of their neglect of space itself in favor of temporality. Consequently, marxian analysis requires recasting. Precisely such a reexamination reveals, however, that the marxian approach is limited as an explanatory paradigm for contemporary societal development. It is my contention, to be demonstrated below, that by taking a full analytical accounting of space we push marxian analysis, no matter how sophisticated its conceptions, beyond a point where it then breaks down.

In order to venture into new terrain to study the interconnection between the space-time matrix of social activities and social relations, it is necessary to pass beyond marxian analytical categories. This does not mean, however, an abandonment of what can be called marxian thought, or even the dialectical method, but those who see in *Capital* a means of understanding the present development of society, even with the aid of a sufficiently astute rereading, are surely deluded.

Before plunging into the limitations of marxian political economy with regard to the analysis of space, I would like to frame the central objection to the material already considered in chapter 3 within its appropriate epistemological context. This can best be described in terms of the confrontation between positivist and realist approaches to what is meant by explanation, as well as the failure of marxian political economists to overcome the endemic functionalism of their thinking. Briefly, proponents of marxism place a distance between themselves and mainstreamers by asserting that Marx's fundamental contribution was his understanding, following Hegel, that appearances and empirically observed regularities were epiphenomenal reflections of underlying and largely invisible social relations. Whether they are conceptualized as collective consumption or political economic categories, all marxists subscribe to this notion, an epistemological position generalized in the philosophy of realism (Keat and Urry 1975; Bhaskar 1979).

Realists differ from positivists because, while the latter equate explanation with prediction, the former separate them and relate empirical events to deep-level causes which cannot always be observed. As Keat and Urry summarize:

> To explain phenomena is not merely to show they are instances of well established regularities. Instead, we must discover the necessary connections between phenomena by acquiring knowledge of the underlying structures and mechanisms at work. Often this will mean postulating the existence of types of *unobservable* entities and processes that are unfamiliar to us; but it is only by doing this that we get beyond the "mere appearance" of things, to their natures and essences. Thus, for the realist, a scientific theory is a description of structures and mechanisms which causally generate the observable phenomena, a description which enables us to explain them. (1975: 4)

In contrast, as is more well known, positivists focus only on what can be observed, treating all explanations hypothesizing deep-level primal causes as metaphysical.

Although the debate between realists and positivists is often misunderstood, recent writings on realism have helped greatly to clarify the issues involved (see, e.g., Thrift 1983; Pickvance 1984). The task facing marxists has always been both to identify the deeper social forces affecting surface events and to show how their laws of motion percolate, so to speak, through levels of social organization to determine empirically observed regularities.

Most marxian political economists, however, have failed to dissociate themselves from the last vestiges of positivist thought. In chapter 3 the functionalist reductionism of such work was highlighted. This limitation follows directly from a more basic one: the positivist desire of marxists to identify distinct causal chains which are said to fully determine surface events. In effect, a bourgeois sensibility has been retained as realist arguments regarding social forces which are not directly observable are grafted onto positivist, causal logic. Although such work has advanced our spatial knowledge because, by insisting on aping the bourgeois "science" of prediction, it has helped identify the underlying forces structuring social relations, reductionist functionalism prevails.

Critiques of marxian urban analysis, such as neoricardianism or neoweberianism, have been successful largely because they have isolated behaviors which marxists have not explained adequately. These phenomena include the differential political behavior of homeowners and renters (Saunders 1979), the autonomous role of local state managers in urban policy (Block 1980), and the primacy of political contingencies over economic needs within the city (Mollenkopf 1983). To be sure, some marxists have understood the need to make their tradition conform more closely with realist epistemology, especially with the latter's insistence that surface events are contingencies, a view which is fundamental to this discussion. Thus Pickvance (1984) observes that several marxists, such as Massey, have demoted this method to a "framework of analysis" (Massey 1977b: 32) rather than an empirically predictive paradigm, while others (Duncan 1981) abandon positivism entirely by asserting that marxism *cannot* deduce effects from deep-level causes. Political economists in the United States have mainly ignored such work, preferring instead to proclaim the causal role of economic forces while acknowledging the influence of other factors (e.g., Beauregard 1984; Hill 1984a).

In order to demonstrate the limitations of marxian urban analysis, it is necessary to proceed in realist fashion and assess the explanatory ability of the marxian spatial paradigm. Two distinct aspects of this perspective require reexamination: the role of class conflict in space and the manner in which the process of capital accumulation is said to produce the urban form. I shall argue below that, by integrating space fully into urban thought, both these perspectives fail as modes of understanding. This demonstration, in realist terms, will introduce space at the deep level of capitalist relations, then show how such processes of development affect spatial phenomena in ways marxists cannot explain. Such an approach requires us to return to Marx's concept of the Trinity Formula, because it is here that space as land is brought by Marx himself into the equation between capital and labor.

CLASS CONFLICT AND SPACE

As is well known, *Capital* was meant as a critique of mainstream political economy and its ability to mystify analytical thought regarding the nature of socioeconomic organization. In a remarkable fragment edited by Engels late in the third volume of *Capital*, Marx unveils what he refers to as the Trinity Formula: capital, labor, and land as the three components of the capitalist mode of production. Meant by Marx as a critique of bourgeois thinking, these categories represent the essential ideological mystification of surplus value production by mainstream economics. Under capitalist social relations of production, surplus value is divided three ways, thus obscuring the essential unity of its creation and thereby generating the basic antagonisms belonging to this mode. Marx states:

Profit (later interest), Land—ground rent, Labor—wages, this is the Trinity Formula which comprises all the secrets of the social production process . . . the alleged sources of the annually available wealth belong to widely dissimilar spheres and are not at all analogous with one another. They have about the same relation to each other as lawyer's fees, red beets, and music. (1967: 814)

As Rosdolsky (1980) makes clear, it is simply not correct to dismiss this tripartite division of society merely because it is a mystification. The various returns—profit or interest, rent, and wages—corresponding to the social fractions—capitalist, landlord, and laborer—represent social relations of production under the existing institutional arrangements of capitalism as a mode of social organization. Consequently, they are not mere illusions as long as capitalist practice remains intact, and they require our attention. As summarized by Marx:

We have seen that the capitalist process of production is a historically determined form of the social process of production in general. The latter is as much a production process of material conditions of human life as a process taking place under specific historical and economic production relations producing and reproducing these production relations themselves, and thereby also the bearers of the process, their material conditions of existence and their mutual relations, i.e., their particular socio-economic form. Capital yields a profit year after year to the capitalist, land a ground-rent to the landlord, and laborpower, under normal conditions and so long as it remains useful labor-power, a wage to the laborer. These three portions of total value annually produced, and the corresponding portions of the annually created total product may be annually consumed by their respective owners, without exhausting the source of their reproduction. They are like the annually consumable fruits of a perennial tree, or rather three trees; they form the annual incomes of three classes, capitalist, landowner, and laborer, revenues distributed by the functioning capitalist in his capacity as direct extorter of surplus-labor and employer of labor in general: (1967: 821)

It is one tragedy of the death of Marx that he was not able to develop his analysis of land as part of the capitalist Trinity Formula. This is so despite the fact that *Capital* does contain several extended discussions of rent. In this regard a ricardian approach was followed, as Marx conceived of rent as a return to a factor of production (land). However, he viewed this return not as some natural phenomenon but as a product of the capitalist relations of production, especially the institution of private property. The essence of this thought is that the ownership of land under capitalism is a means of acquiring wealth. As we can see from the above excerpt, this ability or potential ability is immutable as long as the capitalist relations of production remain hegemonic. Marx believed that historical circumstances surrounding the rise of the capitalist mode of production left land in the hands of a separate class (the remnants of the aristocracy). This is an important concept when analyzing development in third world countries (Rey 1982) and the landlord-peasant relation. It is also germane to certain parts of Western Europe, especially Italy and France. For the case of the United States, however, no such separate class of landlords can be said to exist, despite some arguments to the contrary (Molotch 1976). Nevertheless, the power of landholdings as a means of acquiring wealth exists in modern society for anyone willing to claim it—worker or capitalist—and such an ability must be contended with by urban analysis. Even in Marx's case, however, the hypothesized existence of a separate class organized around landed interests should not, as Fine (1979) notes, be taken to mean that landlords somehow stood apart from the capitalist relations of production merely because they were supported by agriculture. On the contrary, according to Marx, one essential precondition for the very existence of capitalism as a social system was the extension of its relations of production to the land and the consequent development of what he called modern landed property (1967: 275–279).

Consequently, the disappearance of a separate class of landowners for the U.S. case merely alters the conditions under which conflict over the total surplus of wealth occurs, but it does not imply the absence of such a struggle with regard to land. Furthermore, if by the disappearance of a landlord class certain contradictions of early capitalism have also passed from the scene, such as the symbiotic yet antagonistic relation between capitalists and landlords, other contradictions have been produced which have modern landed property as their source, such as the inability of capitalism to solve its housing problem for the less affluent. In the next section I shall return to Marx's concept of modern landed property, since it is important for an understanding of the accumulation process in space as well. In short, one reason why the antagonistic social relations and contradictions of capitalism play themselves out in space—there are others—is because ownership of land is a means of acquiring wealth under capitalist social relations whether a landlord class exists or not. While this may not provide the basis for a separate class, it does support the division of all classes into fractions, with some being organized around landed interests.

A central thesis of Lefebvre's concerns the distinction between use values and exchange values and the notion that, as capitalism develops, it requires the primacy of the latter over the former. Translated into spatial terms, this would mean a conflict between interests organized around social space, as the site of social use values and the deployment of communal relations in space, and around abstract space as the space of real estate development and government administration—the combined articulation between economic and political modes of domination. While this approach means that space involves many more aspects than those associated with landownership and development, most marxists have confined themselves only to analyzing abstract space expressed as the economic contradictions which are internal to the process of capital accumulation and externalized in real estate development—that is, in a space reduced to land—the political economists' built environment. The focus has been on the manner in which abstract space has fragmented class fractions, according to theories of rent and economic analyses of land, while the struggle over social space remains undeveloped by political economy even though it is a second source of spatial interests nonreducible to the first.

According to marxist analysts of abstract space, not only is there no separate landowning class for the case of Late Capitalist countries like the United States, but there is also no separate fraction of capital which is based solely on landownership (Massey and Catalano 1978: 186; Scott 1980: 100; Scott and Roweiss 1978: 52). However, because landownership remains a means of accumulating wealth under the capitalist relations of production, individuals throughout the social order have access to this means. Consequently, purely economic interests centered around the exchange values of land parcels proliferate throughout society, and these interests may or may not be compatible with others involved in the accumulation process. This is the case partly because of the complex social order of Late Capitalism itself and the presence of separate class fractions among both capitalists and workers with enough surplus wealth to invest in land. It is also a product of the peculiar nature of the capitalism-space articulation, which Lefebvre conceptualizes as the secondary circuit but which political economists view as a secondary form of appropriation rather than a direct source of surplus value (see the discussion of rent in the next section). In Late Capitalism, class fractions among workers as well as capitalists have progressively increased, and there is at least one "new" class, the new petite bourgeoisie (Carchedi 1975; Giddens 1973; Poulantzas 1973, 1976; Wright 1978). All these fractions are potentially free to utilize land in order to acquire wealth, because it is a commodity which has been pulverized by the real estate market. While a structural analysis of landed interests might reveal that only a limited number of factors circumscribe the actions of all these separate potential landowners, the proliferation of market positions with land as a means remains complex. Massey and Catalano, for example, have remarked with respect to the United Kingdom:

> Private land ownership of this nature—and specifically in present day Great Britain—does continue to pose structural problems and the increasingly capitalist nature of that land ownership will not remove those problems. It may indeed, as we have argued was possibly the case in Great Britain in the early 1970's, make those problems more intractable . . . The establishment of new forms of land ownership and the redefinition of property rights in land has not meant the end of the "land problem" for capital. (1978: 187–188)

In short, once we introduce land into the analysis of capitalism, several things occur. First, under capitalist relations of production, the owners of land have a claim on the surplus product in addition to the institutionalized returns to capital and labor. Second, because of this feature, any class fraction organized around land represents a separate interest determining the course of capitalist development regardless of how that fraction is constituted—that is, as a separate class, as a fraction of one class, as a coalition of several class fractions. Third, the interests organized around land are socially produced. That is, they are produced by the property relations of capitalism. Finally, the interests organized around land as a means of acquiring wealth represent only one aspect of spatial relations. This is land represented as the abstract space shared by both mainstreamers and marxian political economists. There is, however, another dimension of space, social space, which is defined more by culture and politics than by economics and which also requires analysis in sociospatial conflict. In sum, once we introduce spatial considerations into the analysis of capitalism, its social structure acquires a complex array of potentially contentious interests, because space is a multifaceted presence in the social structure of capitalism while the economists' "land" is only one of its manifestations.

The realization that landed interests complicate the logic of the class struggle alters the nature of marxian spatial analysis. Thus, it is important to specify accurately the precise nature of those interests organized around land. For example, most marxists follow Cox (1981) and Harvey (1976) and ascribe to developmental interests a separate class fraction of capital. Thus, Cox takes great pains to show how this class fraction pursues the secondary appropriation of surplus value from land at the expense of its users, the working class. Consequently, marxian political economy reduces the locational clash between the absolute space of exchange values and social space to that between a capitalist class fraction working in real estate development and the urban proletariat in pursuit of use values. That is, marxian political economy correlates abstract space and its interests with the capitalist class while reserving for the working class those interests organized around social space. In this manner sociospatial conflict is ipso facto a class phenomenon, representing either a clash of capitalist fractions or a clash between capitalists and workers over community space.

The present argument takes issue with these formulations. I assert that the antagonistic split between the forces structuring absolute space and social space actually cuts across class lines and cannot be specified by the capital-labor relation. There is no one-to-one correspondence between real estate and capital, on the one hand, and the use values of social space and workers, on the other. In order to support this contention, it is necessary to show that spatial interests in Late Capitalism represent neither a separate class, as Marx thought, nor a separate class fraction, as most marxists believe, but only a sector of class fractions which can include workers as well as capitalists. The exact nature of these interests will be detailed in chapter 6, because several introductory concepts need to be developed first.

Without a correspondence between landed values and social classes, political economic analysis breaks down. There are two main topics of discussion which illustrate this limitation well. The first concerns the debate between neomarxists and neoweberians on the existence of housing classes; the second involves the role of local community space based on *culturally* determined use values which manifest themselves independent of economic necessity. In both cases sociospatial interests divide not only the capitalist class into fractions but the working class as well. The complementary issue raised for marxists, then, involves whether or not it is possible to demonstrate the epiphenomenal nature of this crosscutting. As I shall show below, the answer to this latter issue is in the negative, so that sociospatial conflict cannot be reduced to the class struggle under existing relations, just as the action of space cannot be reduced to the economists' notion of land.

The Nature of Housing Classes

The concept of housing classes was broached by neoweberians in the United Kingdom to capture the manner in which the working class was split into political fractions according to homeowner or renter status. Neoweberians argued against the marxian assertion that such cleavages were more superficial than the forces essentially unifying the working class. According to Saunders:

> To the extent that Marxists have considered the problem of the spread of homeownership among the British working class, they have generally argued that the divisions it creates are ideological rather than economic. Put simply, the argument is that owner-occupation may serve to obscure class divisions, but it does not change them. This conclusion runs directly counter to the weberian approach developed by John Rex in his concept of "housing classes," for Rex sees tenure as an analytically separate basis for class formations. (1979: 18)

In a study of a working-class section in the United Kingdom, Rex and Moore confronted the inadequacy of marxian political economic analysis in explaining the interests of the homeowners, renters, squatters, transients, and immigrants located there. This compelled them to exploit Weber's twofold distinction between classes defined by the labor market, the traditional marxist view, and "acquisition classes" as defined by the commodity market. The latter group was distinguished from the former by its determination through relations of distribution rather than production. Using this weberian distinction, Rex and Moore were able to interpret their empirical results within a theoretical framework that stressed the social processes governing the distribution of scarce resources. These were only partly a function of marxian factors; in addition, access to such scarce resources, especially public housing, was partly a function of noneconomic, bureaucratic decision making.

Some of the earliest criticisms of Rex and Moore were quick to point out the sloppy way in which Weber's class distinction was applied (Haddon 1970). According to Haddon, their concept of housing classes was in reality considered by Weber to be a status group. The separate interests based on housing tenure are produced by the distributive relations of society and reflect consumption patterns rather than separate class distinctions. While such consumption groupings are important in understanding social behavior (Giddens 1979), an analysis of their origins does not pose a threat to marxian analysis, merely a complement to it. Thus status groups are added to class in the manner of Weber and we move away from reductionist marxism. Saunders, however, has persisted in a search for a demonstration that the cleavage between homeowners and renters is of a class nature. As we have seen, the ownership of real estate is a separate means of acquiring wealth under capitalism. Saunders departs from this observation with the claim that homeownership is a separate source of real capital accumulation. His analysis, based on the British experience, consists of three assertions. First, property appreciates faster than the general rate of inflation increases in metropolitan areas. Consequently, its *real* exchange value increases over time. Second, because homeowners acquire long-term debts at mortgage rates, they most often obtain interest at a level lower than that of the prevailing market. That is, they borrow at a negative rate of interest in order to finance their investment. Finally, homeowners receive tax write-offs on interest payments as well as additional tax advantages from the government. In sum, domestic property ownership is a source of real capital accumulation and constitutes a social class separate from work-related conditions.

Saunders' conceptualization can be applied to the United States as well. Unlike any other commodity, a home appreciates after purchase—it is worth more used than new. However, the increase in real value is contingent on other factors, most of which are economic in nature, such as the rate of interest and the operations of the housing market. Thus the question of the existence of housing classes can be resolved only by a look at the relation between the appropriation of wealth through landownership and its mediation by the state or the larger economy. For this reason analysts of the relation between political interests and homeownership have treated the neoweberian argument with some caution. Cox (1982), for example, takes pains to show that such a status, while constituting a well-defined interest in community political disputes, may be a function of the tight housing market, that is, homeowner activism is dependent on the inability to sell and move elsewhere. In contrast, when such market fluidity does prevail, homeowner activism decreases. Consequently, property-based interests are really produced by the field of market relations in housing, not by the operation of self-interest in preserving the exchange value of one's home—that is, not by the drive for capital accumulation. Dunleavy (1979) has attacked Saunders in a more theoretical way, arguing that for the most part the attractiveness of homeownership vis-à-vis accumulation is primarily a product of state intervention, thus adding political forces to the structuration of landed interests. A social division such as that between home-owners and renters is a product of collective consumption, which conforms to the picture of globalized political conflict in the city drawn by Castells (1977: 419). In such a view, housing interests are really products of the state-space articulation, representing as they do a displacement of the capitalist-worker antagonism through the mechanism of collective consumption, rather than a separate base of capital accumulation.

Such criticisms reveal that ownership of property can poten-tially produce multiple interests; they do not necessarily refute the neoweberian argument for the existence of fundamental cleavages in society produced by the ownership of land. However, Saunders' in-sistence on viewing this as a phenomenon of class is most unfor-tunate. Thus Edel is correct when he criticizes the need of neo-weberians to reduce the new cleavages produced by homeownership in society to class categories. As he states:

> A privileged fraction of home owners within the working class is a theoretical possibility according to the "reconceptualiza-tion" developed here. However, I conclude that an unprece-dented break with the past, involving the permanent creation of an advantaged group in the proletariat whose position is based on home ownership, is unlikely. (1982: 220)

Clearly this assertion is beside the point. The issue is one not of proving or disproving the existence of new classes but of new social cleavages which cannot be reduced to the concept of class. In a man-ner of speaking, Saunders, Cox, and Dunleavy are all correct in their analyses. By asserting a claim to exclusivity in the causal explana-tion of homeowner interests, however, they commit the positivist fallacy when an appreciation of spatial dialectics would be more fruitful. Thus, the category of class is not the only structural basis for political interests, as status and party affiliations, for example, have long been considered by analysts as *sui generis* forces. Recent research has uncovered an abundance of evidence that political ac-tivity organized around housing interests represents an important and volatile factor in local affairs (Heskin 1981; Hartman et al. 1982; Protash and Baldassare 1983; Pickvance 1984; Gottdiener 1983). To assert with marxian political economists that these spatially con-scious interests which cut across class lines are phenomenal products of traditional capitalist cleavages is to beg the entire question of why working-class political activism has itself virtually disappeared from the American scene in favor of divisions based upon other factors such as race, sex, and homeownership. Similarly, to follow neoweberians like Saunders and seek to argue for a separate housing class is to miss the real issue of spatial interests. As indicated above, it is only through an analysis of the interaction between class fractions and racial, gender, ethnic, and consumption groupings that the new sociospatial cleavages can be grasped.

Any analysis of spatially related interests must begin with Lefebvre's observation that spatial practice is one of the social forces of production which includes land as a means (1979: 287). Consequently, there are multiple manifestations of the society-space articulation. More specifically, the interests arising from homeownership do so for a variety of reasons, and they are constrained by a variety of institutional contexts. Some of these are related to capital accumulation, while others are more closely tied to the consumption process. In short, the homeowner-renter relation is a contingent product of deeper sociospatial factors which articulate with the social structure of capitalism to produce, in realist fashion, different interests organized around land, including the clash between cultural, political, and economic interests. If private interests are involved in producing these cleavages, then so too is the state. If class is important to an understanding of the interests deployed in space, then so too is the role of status or consumption groupings. Consequently, the multiple manifestations of space articulate in a contingent fashion with social interests at many levels, defying analysts to specify single causes for them. Modes of analysis such as political economy and neoweberianism, which seek to correlate classes directly to forms of landownership in modern society, falsely bypass the deeper social level at which landed interests are formed.

The issue addressed by the debate between neoweberians and neomarxists focused on the political basis of homeowner interests. This has obscured the more fundamental question of whether political interests in urban localities always reflect class differences. Clearly they do not. Simply put, for the case of the United States, the influence of class-based interests has grown less and less important in local politics, even if economic development has generated most of the contentious issues surrounding such disputes. Consequently, marxian political economy remains a limited means of grasping the complex range of political interests in the city (see, e.g., Castells 1983; Mollenkopf 1983). Sociospatial concerns about territoriality, race, neighborhood culture, and housing, in particular, are more complicated than the marxian two-class model of capitalism leads us to believe. This last assertion is best illustrated by considering the local community as a collective site of use values which have their basis in *non*-economic considerations.

The Community as Social Space

Without question social space and its use values have been neglected by marxian political economy, especially given the current lack of concern for the way space can be transformed. Community-based interests, or what Bell and Newby call communion (1976), constitute a separate source of cleavages in society, and these cannot be linked to the field of economic relations alone. Such interests derive from the sense of sharing produced by propinquity and from a recognition that important needs held in common are supplied by the local area within which individuals live. For the most part, communal ties are characterized by "reciprocity, stability, and affection" (Bell and Newby 1976: 191–192). What is most essential to the present argument is the realization, following Bookchin (1984) and Habermas (1979), that communal values and consociation possess origins in a mode of social organization which predates capitalism. Habermas, in particular, has argued that family ties represent an independent source of social movements in society, one that cannot be reduced to traditional marxian analysis. This mode of consociation based on kinship has been all but eradicated by the contemporary nature of social relations, yet it can be recovered by paying close attention to the cultural values of community life, provided that certain caveats are acknowledged.

Studies on the virtues of local community life are legion (Bernard 1962; Suttles 1973). Yet it is well known that community-based interests are not always supportive of the values associated with humanistic sentiments or communion. Territory-based conflict can exist within communities over life-style differences (Hannerz 1969) and between communities over space itself (Thrasher 1963). Thus, while such analysts as Lefebvre celebrate the nurturing role of community propinquity and the existential freedom of space, others lament the stultifying nature of its effects on the working class and the tyranny of social relations within small-town communities (Sennett and Cobb 1972). Consequently, analysts of communal interests must heed Suttles' warning against romanticizing the functional role of the community in fostering nurturing networks. Having established this proviso, it is nevertheless true that a domain of territory-based interests exists which cannot be reduced to exchange value commonalities and which can be observed influencing the political process. I wish to call attention, therefore, not to the benign nature of the social relations organized around the use values of space, as institutionalized in the ideology of community or expressed in Lefebvre's romantic optimism, but merely to the category of sociospatial action which has those relations as its source. As Mollenkopf observes, "The basic building blocks of community—ethnic and kinship bonds, geographic propinquity, voluntary associations, shared political connections—have far more to do with forms of political participation than does class" (1981: 321).

The common needs generated by child rearing, religious participation, crime prevention, and recreation are but some of the ways in which the qualities of communal social space can be appreciated and measured. To these must be added the more fundamental aspects of social relations isolated by Bookchin (1984), which form the basis for the "organic," nonhierarchical societies that place use values above exchange values: usufruct, complementarity, and the law of the irreducible minimum. Consideration of these features provides the antidote to the academic nature of prevailing urban marxian thought—namely, the need to transform space through praxis, not just to study it. It is not possible to pursue such topics here, but I shall do so in chapter 8. Suffice it to say that the basis of community is cultural and that the political transformation of society based on nonhierarchical, cultural values cannot be specified as an economic struggle alone.

In general, the distinction between group interests based on community or life-style considerations and those based upon market positions is a complicated one which cannot be resolved by marxian analysis in the case of modern society. It is necessary to show how consumption interests become articulated into separate political forces or party issues in ways that are distinct from class considerations, a task which neither neoweberians nor neomarxists have accomplished for the local community (Pickvance 1977b). For the most part, analysts have focused on conflicts pitting the desire to protect the use value of community space, associated principally with one class—the workers—against the interests of elite growth coalitions pursuing the redevelopment of real estate for a profit (Cox 1978, 1981; Molotch 1976; Mollenkopf and Pynoos 1972). In this way the conflict between abstract space and social space is reduced to a mere clash between workers residing in a communal space and that fraction of capital made up of urban developers. Due to the collective nature of local community life, however, the struggle between pro-growth and no-growth advocates does not reflect the class structure; rather, it cuts across it. Thus, community coalitions could also conceivably oppose development as easily as they could support it in order to protect their current quality of life. In fact, such non-class-specific clashes of pro- and no-growth coalitions are an increasingly common feature of the local political scene (see Gottdiener and Neiman 1981; Pickvance 1984).

A focus on the relation between social space as community and the quality of life, then, functions to isolate territory-based interests which transcend class, thereby passing beyond the relevance of political economy. Yet, this relation has been ignored in the main by the current crop of critical urbanists. Because community well-being in the United States is so closely tied to the ideology of growth, the issues involved here are complex. Initially, there is often some concordance between communal interests and economic development, as all public services require an expanding capital base for their well-being. On the consumption side, this is especially true of the need for shopping facilities, leisure activities, and commercial services. At a certain point in community development, however, the two trajectories of economic growth and the quality of life diverge. Such social problems of rapid and uncoordinated development as crime, pollution, traffic congestion, and fiscal crises appear (Baldassare 1980). Many local residents, regardless of class, therefore, can be observed to oppose growth once this point is reached. Yet other residents, especially renters in need of housing, as well as some developers may favor continued expansion. Consequently, it is not uncommon for both capitalists and workers to join together in camps aligned according to pro- or no-growth sentiments (Gottdiener 1983). Political disputes over the quality of life, therefore, involve an axis of social distinctions which shifts—sometimes following and sometimes cutting across class lines. This implies that the interests associated with the use values and with the exchange values of space are interconnected and contingently related.

In general, community struggles seem to manifest themselves as spatially based perspectives which emphasize fiscal administration, environmental quality, and the management of growth. Such broad concerns do not merely reflect elite ideology—they have a wide base of support among all groups within the community (Gottdiener and Neiman 1981; Protash and Baldassare 1983; Gottdiener 1983). If we can agree with Habermas (1979) that capitalists as well as workers have families and are equally aware that nurturing is dependent on the social basis of collective life, then it is also possible to see that workers as well as capitalists have an equal interest in the environment and also wish to manage the quality of societal growth. Consequently, a realistic consideration of what might be called an urban question would regard the quality of community life in general as the focal area of analysis (Lefebvre's "everyday life"), grounded within a specific milieu produced by the patterns of social development. The study of this problematic would involve a focus on the issues which threaten the quality of life, as well as on the various special interests mobilized around these issues in the development of the community space, such as the pro- and no-growth coalitions. Political organizing around this particular form of the urban question would necessarily have to face the dilemma of defining community interests, which could transform spatial development at the same time that liberatory social relations of production and reproduction are also advanced. This would then tie the need for radical design and planning directly to the liberatory transformation of social relations.

The role of the environment in sheltering socially useful benefits has emerged as a central political issue, one which transcends marxian political economy to connect with efforts Marx himself once dismissed as utopian (see chapter 8). On the one hand, the pro-growth versus no-growth opposition—or, more radically, the struggle over design and the space which will be assumed by development as well as the nature of the development itself—transcends the concerns of capitalist economies and applies equally to noncapitalist industrial and third world societies. On the other hand, the contentious needs of consumption groupings and the conflicting life-styles within localized territories raise issues which cannot be resolved through economic considerations alone but which also address fundamental questions of culture. Consequently, while it remains possible to speak of a class analysis of space, concerns organized around social space compel analysts to address issues of a sociospatial nature, which requires a more global approach.

The inadequacies of marxian political economy are even more apparent when we consider its second dimension of analysis—capital accumulation—and when we introduce the role of space into this process. In addition to addressing the central issue of the operation of the law of value in space, the next section is important to the above argument because it demonstrates that developmental interests are neither a separate class nor a class fraction. Thus the contentious nature of growth cannot be reduced to the opposition of classes alone.

THE VALUE OF LAND AND THE ROLE OF SPACE IN CAPITAL
ACCUMULATION

The Value of Land

The starting place for an understanding of determinants for the value
of land is Marx's Trinity Formula, as it is the place to begin any assessment of the mystification of surplus value production under
capitalism. This is the case in order to avoid the kind of analysis,
committed by marxists as well as nonmarxists, which assumes the
categories of political economy without addressing their ideological
nature. Regardless of the mode of production, according to Marx, all
value is produced by labor power harnessed to a social framework
with articulated relations of production. The wealth created by the
social forces linked to a particular economic base is divided up according to the institutional arrangements of that base, specifically
its ownership relations. If land by itself possesses a rate of return in
the production cycle, it is only because of those same relations. As
Ive observes:

> In other words, instead of having "land" and "capital" counter-
> posed as "factors of production" each with its own established
> claim to the net product, we have an "urban surplus" distribu-
> ted in "social (capitalist) space" which is fundamentally af-
> fected by the forms of spatial organization, particularly the
> kind of private property in "land." (1974: 28)

Yet, such an explanation suffices to determine only the price of
land, called rent by political economists of capitalism, *not* its intrinsic value. Clearly, the connection between the inherent qualities of
land and its price deserves analytical attention by anyone interested
in the value of land under capitalism. For this reason it is somewhat
astounding that the examination of urban land values by both mainstreamers and marxists is almost wholly limited to the determination of rent. According to the neoclassical view, for example, land
values are said to be produced by competition for a profit-making
factor which possesses a locational asset. As Gaffney (1967) has
noted, this view explains the price of land by a demand-side analysis
or as a product of competition over a commodity made scarce by demand. In this way, neoclassical analysis forged a link between location and rent theories through the notion of marginal utility. As we
have seen, the visualized outcome of such spatial competition and
its pricing structure looks very much like the Burgess model of

the concentric zone city, so that a mutually reinforcing perspective emerged among the separate fields of mainstream urban science.

The marxian theory of rent comes from Ricardo's notion of land as a material factor of production. According to this notion, land possesses an intrinsic agricultural fertility which can, however, vary. Rent is the price paid for the use of this resource. According to Marx, in contrast to Ricardo, the ability of land to command this rent arises from the class nature of society. In particular, landowners can lay claim to a portion of the surplus value produced by labor by virtue of the institution of private property, which legitimates their claim to receive payment for the use of their land. In this way, Marx analyzed rent from the perspective of the Trinity Formula and the class nature of capitalist society. Consequently, he envisioned rent as being differentiated in several ways by the nature of the landholding itself relative to the social organization of capitalist production (see Fine 1979).

In addition to Ricardo's conception, called differential rent by Marx, two other types of rent were envisioned: absolute rent and monopoly rent. These reflect the potential ability of landlords to act as monopolists under the existing relations of production and to *create* scarcities which manipulate location decisions to their advantage. Absolute rent involves the general ability of all owners in any natural resource industry (that is, an industry with a low organic composition of capital) to command a price for that resource regardless of market factors, because the resource is itself an essential ingredient of production. As Scott indicates:

> Marx suggests that the power of private ownership enables landlords to add a levy or absolute rent to the theoretical production price of agricultural commodities, so that those commodities will sell precisely at their labor value. As a consequence, and in opposition to Ricardian theory, even perfectly marginal land will always earn a positive non-zero rent.
> (1976: 114)

The importance of absolute rent remains somewhat vague, and in practice marxists tend either to explain it in an unclear fashion (Edel 1977: 6) or to use it interchangeably with the next concept, monopoly rent (Harvey and Chatterjee 1974; Walker 1975; Edel 1977). Monopoly rent, however, refers specifically to the ability of landholders to extract payment for land when demand for it is structured by a monopolistically produced scarcity, as in the case of competition over specific locations or specific pieces of land in the city. Monopoly rent, therefore, is the most useful to urban analysis because it expresses the social origin of location value. As Scott (1980) has indicated, since Marx's theory of rent was based upon Ricardo's analysis of agricultural land, it possesses limited use in understanding the urban land question, because in the city the value of land is based upon its location, not upon its intrinsic worth. Even for the case of agricultural land, however, Marx's analysis requires more work (Fine 1979). As in other places in his political economy, the labor theory of value possesses several breakdown points, such as the transformation problem (Sraffa 1960; Steedman 1977), which need to be addressed for the case of land.

It is interesting to observe that our two main theorists of urban space, Lefebvre and Castells, have effectively sidestepped these issues by choosing not to address the question of the determination of urban land values at all—and Lefebvre, in particular, has created certain problems, as we shall see, because of this strategic omission. In contrast, we have also seen in chapter 3 that the economic analysis of land value is the cornerstone of marxian urban political economy, especially in the work of Harvey and Scott. Each of their approaches to capital accumulation within the city was criticized at that time. Consequently, it is now necessary to propose an alternate approach. In what follows I shall sidestep the economic issue of the determination of the exchange value of urban land under capitalist relations of production, except by addressing it as socially produced. In part, this decision is prompted by the fact that it is far more important for an understanding of the urban environment to examine the way in which the capitalist relations of production operate to structure sociospatial organization, than it is to address the determination of urban rent by the labor theory of value. The former topic, as we shall see, compels us to consider the institutional arrangements producing the context within which the property market operates, what Marx calls modern landed property. In this way, the ideological and misleading separation of rent from the remaining fractions of surplus value is kept at the forefront of analysis. Most important, such an approach places an emphasis on understanding the process by which space itself is produced by capitalism, rather than aiming for better and better economic analyses of that environment for some unknown academic purpose without recognizing that economic categories, such as rent, are themselves social products of bourgeois ideology.

In short, I am not concerned with detailing the determination of rent according to either marxian or neoricardian economic analysis (see Scott 1980), as this merely provides another picture of how capitalism works but does not explain why it works. The latter is un-covered only if we follow Marx's critique and understand that the price of urban land is a social creation. Thus, it is important to show how the law of value in space is structured and manipulated by the capitalist class and its social relations to yield absolute and monop-oly rents within the metropolis. The social basis of this law of value means that urban land values can be creations of cultural (Firey 1945) or political (e.g., Brasilia; see also Misztal and Misztal 1984) as well as economic factors.

By focusing on the operation of fractions within the capitalist class in realizing returns to capital through the supply-side manipu-lation of land values, the distinction between rent and profit dissi-pates. This is especially true for those monopolistic interests which are capable of controlling the development of the built environment for their own purposes. As Harvey remarks:

> Rent is a transfer payment realized through monopoly power over land and resources conferred by the institution of private property . . . the blurring of the distinction between natural and artificially created scarcity makes it difficult to distinguish between rent and profit. (1975b: 147)

However, such an observation does not imply that the category of rent has disappeared or even that it has lost its material effect in the accumulation process. Clearly, location decisions by businesses are as affected by the price of land as are other components of society. Consequently, the price of land and rent has a strong effect on urban form. It is helpful to distinguish, therefore, between capitalists who own assets involved in the production of goods and services and capi-talists who wish to realize money by investing in land itself through its sale as a commodity. In this way we return to the central empha-sis on the process of surplus value production and the conflict over its division among all classes and class fractions. The distinction needs to be made, therefore, between the role of land in the produc-tion of goods and services and its role as a direct means of acquiring wealth. In the former case, we possess a picture of the city closer to the neoclassical view of competition between merchants for the right to locate enterprises at particular places within the built en-vironment according to the cost of location or rent. In the latter case, we have at the extreme those capitalists who manipulate land devel-opment through monopoly powers to create the conditions for the realization of rent and the production of an environment of land val-ues *within* which the neoclassical competitors will compete. This second activity, I believe, produces the forms of settlement space, and it is in this way that we can see that the value of urban land is a social product. Consequently, I prefer to stress its examination in more detail.

At this stage in the discussion I must switch from the analysis of land as a means of production to the analysis of space as a force of production and from the determination of land value, and its return—rent—to the social determination of location value in space and its return—profit. In order to address the issue of land and location values, we must first reintroduce Lefebvre's theory and pass from an analysis of land per se to that of real estate, because it is the latter which comprises capitalist as opposed to precapitalist space. I will define real estate here as the spatial environment—comprised of developed and undeveloped land—that is, the structures built upon land and the infrastructural improvements of harbors, roads, utility lines, and pavements surrounding those structures, which is supplied by a specific real estate market. Furthermore, real estate under capitalism is a social product which cannot be separated from the economic, political, and cultural forces or institutions, such as those of finance capital, which manage and regulate the uses of space.

Together these elements—the real estate market, its supportive infrastructure, and associated class fractions—comprise the property sector of Late Capitalism. The essential point about real estate is that it is a commodity which possesses its own market. Furthermore, its viability as an industrial commodity is a function of space itself, of the ensemble of location decisions, and not, as in the case of agricultural land, a function of the intrinsic value of the land. As Scott has indicated (1976: 115), both Walras and George, for example, discovered before Lefebvre that space is a social product and that its value is produced by the activities of society. Lefebvre locates his analysis of real estate within this Walrasian tradition. Its value is created by a sociospatial matrix of locations and activities associated with the production of wealth, which then endows particular urban sites with use value as a function of that socially determined spatial pattern rather than from an intrinsic quality of the resource itself. Individual businesses then compete for these choice locations, but this process is seen by mainstreamers as taking place as if a separate real estate market in control of those values did not exist. In this way we emphasize the social nature of space, rather than a labor theory of its value, by focusing upon the real estate market as the mediating mechanism which translates the use values produced by the spatial matrix of capital accumulation activities into commodity exchange values reflected in the price of real estate.

In short, the connection between the use value of location, which is a social product, and the price for the use of space, which is privately expropriated, is discovered by understanding the real estate market as a mediating link in the capital accumulation process. The rent of political economists is a mere epiphenomenon of the social production of space. The extraction of monopolistic returns in real estate is then a function of the ability of groups of capitalists working at times with the state to apply collusive powers in order to channel resources and development in particular spatial directions. The form of the built environment is then a function of this latter activity and of the many actions of other, nonmonopolistic interests which also indulge in the real estate market and contribute to the rapid turnover of land use. The property sector, therefore, involves both structural determinants and the social actions of groups; the synthesis which is to follow will capture the production of space in terms of this action-structure dialectic (Giddens 1979).

The importance of this last observation and of the emphasis on the social nature of real estate value is that this market is little understood by both mainstreamers and marxists. As Wallace Smith has observed about property:

> It is a very heterogeneous commodity, no two pieces of which are precisely alike. Because of this heterogeneity, there is no observable "price of land" or "price of housing"; these terms are meaningful only as index numbers, and there is no general agreement on how such index numbers should be calculated . . . "Who gets what" in the urban land market is more a practical thing to be concerned with than what the price of housing or land is, though the allocation of land and buildings is made essentially by means of price. (Smith 1970: 164)

As the above indicates, the analysis of the urban land market requires a focus on the distribution of surplus value by the real estate industry—on the operation of Late Capitalist relations in space—not on the determination of the price of land as such. This task, however, is made exceedingly difficult by the social nature of real estate value. Costs as well as profits are borne by a wide range of institutions and individuals associated with investment in the built environment. Thus the notion of urban land value as being produced socially presents us with a complex set of analytical choices. On the one hand, because the built environment already exists in any period, it presents a barrier to use as well as a potential for use. Consequently, we must examine the ways in which that barrier is removed and new investment interests penetrate the old. This requires a consideration of the ways in which land uses are controlled, which inexorably involves the relationship between capital and the state (see the preceding chapter). On the other hand, understanding the determination of the law of value in the built environment requires an examination of the role of space in the capitalist relations of production and reproduction, and I shall deal with this next.

In the *Grundrisse* (1973), Marx distinguishes between land as a feudal holding, therefore belonging to a precapitalist mode, and what he calls modern landed property. The latter commodity, transformed by capitalist relations, is held by landowners who themselves participate in capitalist relations of production. The importance of modern landed property as a form for Marx is that it is a precondition for capitalist industrial relations of production. In particular, the system of wage labor requires that land be held as private property and worked as a commodity. It is only through the mechanism of the capitalist social relations applied to former feudal landholdings that the masses having access to the earth as a resource in the previous social formation were driven off the land and transformed into wage laborers.

Thus, for capitalist social relations to be formed and reproduced in capitalist society so that those relations dominate previous modes, it was necessary for a certain space to be created—one in which people were denied access to the resource land *except* as wage laborers. Such a process occurred not only in England under the famous enclosure laws during the early part of the industrial revolution but also in the other countries of Europe as capital invaded land, turned it into a commodity, and made it expensive, so that the peasants were either driven to the cities or forced to work former feudal holdings as wage laborers engaged in producing a cash crop. Furthermore, the uneven development of this transition in third world countries and even in parts of Europe has been analyzed precisely from this perspective, which stresses especially the importance of the blocked transition in the change from feudalism to capitalism (see Rey 1982), thus preserving landlord-peasant relations. In short, modern landed property is an institutional transformation lying at the core of the bourgeoisie's usurpation of hegemony from the feudal aristocracy in the transition from feudalism to capitalism. Only when that transformation in space is complete can we say that capitalist relations prevail throughout the entire social formation. The essence of modern landed property as a precondition for capitalism is that it is a commodity which is traded on the real estate market—and, consequently, it is expensive. As Marx states:

The inner construction of modern society, or capital in the totality of its relations, is therefore posited in the economic relations of modern landed property, which appears as a process:
ground rent—capital—wage labor . . . The question is now, how
does the transition from landed property to wage labor come
about? . . . Historically, this transition is beyond dispute. It is
already given in the fact that landed property is the product of
capital. We therefore always find that, wherever landed property
is transformed into money rent through the reaction of capital
on the older forms of landed property (the same thing takes
place in another way where the modern farmer is created) and
where, therefore, at the same time agriculture, driven by capital, transforms itself into industrial agronomy, there the cot-
tiers, serfs, bondsmen, tenants for life, cottagers, etc. become
day laborers, wage laborers, i.e., that *wage labor* in its totality
is initially created by the action of capital on landed property,
and then as soon as the latter has been produced as a form, by
the proprietor of the land himself. (1973: 276)

For Marx, industrial capital depends for its very survival on
modern landed property, because land which has been transformed
into a commodity must be worked for cash crops and is costly for all
those who wish to live upon it. In both these cases, the feudal population categories all acquire the same status: that of wage laborers.
The existence of modern landed property, therefore, not only produces wage laborers for capitalism but *reproduces* people in that status because they are forever blocked from returning to the earth in a
precapitalist social world. As Marx summarizes:

There can, therefore, be no doubt that *wage labor* in its *classic
form* as something permeating the entire expanse of society,
which has replaced the very earth as the ground on which society stands, is initially created by modern landed property, i.e.,
by landed property as a value created by capital itself. This is
why landed property leads back to wage labor. In one regard, it
is nothing more than the extension of wage labor, from the
cities to the countryside, i.e., wage labor distributed over the
entire surface of society. (1973: 277)

In this early formulation, the connection is always established
between land and wage labor. This relationship, which grew and developed under capitalism, shows up as one of the ways in which this
system reproduces itself by reproducing the need of people to sell
their labor for a wage as their only means of support. That is, the

institution of private property, the high absolute price of land, and the industrialization of agriculture all reproduce the dependency of the population on wage labor. It is noteworthy that, with the exception of Lefebvre (1970), contemporary marxists have all but ignored the significance of landed property for the reproduction of capitalist social relations. Marx's discussion in the *Grundrisse* also establishes another important point. Capital accomplishes the reproduction of wage labor through modern landed property only by embodying a contradiction. While the conflict between the capitalist class and the workers is an internal one—it is articulated in the same place, the industrial site of the city—modern landed property assumes its form outside this process through the creation of a class of landholders distinct from capitalists and workers. Capital's creation, therefore, is externalized alongside the process of extracting surplus value in the factory, for example, and it exists materially *in space*. Landholders forevermore, according to Marx, can lay claim to part of that surplus value as absolute or monopoly rent, as we have already seen, thus interfering with the process of capital accumulation by reducing its net yield. Thus capital needs modern landed property but finds it, at profit-taking time, a luxury it cannot afford. According to Marx:

> After capital has posited landed property and hence arrived at its double purpose: (1) industrial agriculture and thereby development of the forces of production on the land; (2) wage labor, thereby general domination of capital over the countryside; it then regards the existence of landed property itself as a merely transitional development, which is required as an action of capital on the old relations of landed property, and *a product of their decomposition*; but which as such—once this purpose is achieved—is merely a limitation on profit, not a necessary requirement for production. It thus endeavors to dissolve landed property as private property and to transfer it to the state. (1973: 279)

Marx's analysis of land in the *Grundrisse* ends too quickly and with this contradiction: on the one hand, modern landed property is a precondition for the production and reproduction of wage labor, hence capitalism; on the other hand, modern landed property is a concrete relation outside of capital and hinders the accumulation process because the separate class of landowners can lay claim to part of the surplus value as rent. The essence of modern landed property is that it is both a necessity for capitalism and a luxury that it can ill afford. According to Marx, capital requires the state to intervene in this relation in order to manage the power of the landholding class. I have indicated above that we can no longer agree with Marx that such a separate land-based class exists in modern society. Nevertheless, it now seems clear that the contradictory relationship between capital and land is still very much with us. As we shall see below, the fundamental contradiction between capital accumulation and space is that the former needs to invest in the latter in order to combat the falling rate of profit; however, investment in real estate means that there is less money to pump back into primary capital production. Furthermore, as Edel has pointed out (1977: 2), under capitalist relations of production, housing has historically been relatively expensive, despite fluctuations in the real estate market. This has placed an upward pressure on wages, further aggravating the antagonisms between capitalists and workers. Consequently, Harvey's "faustian bargain" of labor with capital over living arrangements must be seen in a new light, one in which labor's dependency upon an expensive commodity forces capital to be dependent upon the state in order to control the societal effects of the opposition among industrial capital, labor, and investment by all fractions in real estate.

This contentious situation compels the capitalist class to enter into a faustian bargain of its own, this time with the state, as we shall see below. Furthermore, our understanding of such deep-level contradictions is enhanced because of Marx's own analysis of modern landed property. In chapter 7, I shall return to his dialectical analysis and apply the thought of the *Grundrisse* to the contemporary transformations in agriculture associated with Late Capitalism, in order to understand better how those property relations help reproduce everyday life in the metropolitan region. The role of land and the real estate market in the reproduction of capitalist relations, as Marx suggests, provides a structural reason for its expensiveness, in addition to the operation of supply and demand. Thus, what is important about the value of land is not how to determine its price by some economic analysis but how to appreciate that, under the contradictory nature of capitalist relations of production, the value of urban land is unnecessarily high and is socially produced. We now need to look elsewhere in order to draw out the full implications of the relationship between capital accumulation and space.

Space and Capital Accumulation

I am interested here in understanding the contradictory role of property in the capital accumulation process. It is at this point that Lefebvre's emphasis on the real estate market becomes helpful. As a commodity pulverized by the economic and political forces of abstract space, which is also supported socially in its value, property almost always offers an incentive to investors for personal gain, despite its well-acknowledged risk factors. Understanding this fact requires us to abandon the view of land as a component of the production process with its return, rent. In its place we need a supply-side conception of real estate sustained by the state and possessed of a wide variety of uses which are functions of the level of social organization and its locational needs—and with a return, profit. Despite fluctuations in the returns on real estate, property can always be shifted to other uses and can potentially be made to look like a profitable investment. It is this *potential* which is a function of social space and which is a socially produced value; thus investment in land is attractive even in hard times (Seldon 1975). In fact, during periods of depression or recession when all capital is devalued, the barrier presented by the fixed capital from the past in the existing built environment can be more easily broken down. Hence, real estate tends to draw investment even during times when primary production activities cannot.

One of the key conceptual contributions made by Lefebvre is his focus on the role of the real estate market in the capital accumulation process as a supply-side "second sector" of investment. It is this "parallel circuit" to industrial production which embodies the contradiction of capital's relation with modern landed property, which explains why real estate and housing are expensive, and which helps us understand the process of capital accumulation in space. Because of certain misconceptions that have already been propagated regarding Lefebvre's approach, this section of *La révolution urbaine* is reproduced in its entirety:

> "Real estate," as they call it, plays the role of a second sector, of a parallel circuit to that of industrial production working for the market of nondurable "goods," or at least those that are less durable than buildings. At times of depression capital flows in its direction. At first it makes fabulous profits, but soon it gets bogged down. In this sector the "multiplier" effects are weak: there is little secondary activity.
>
> Capital is immobilized in building. The general (so-called national) economy soon suffers from this. However, the role and the function of this sector never stops growing. To the extent that the principal circuit, that of the current industrial production of "movable" goods slows down, capital is invested in the second circuit, that of real estate. It can even happen that real estate speculation becomes the principal source, the

almost exclusive place of the "formation of capital," that is, of the realization of surplus value. While the part of overall surplus value formed and realized in industry decreases, the part of surplus value formed and realized in speculation and through construction increases. From the accidental it becomes the essential. But this is an unhealthy situation as the economists say. (1970: 211–212)

The importance of identifying the role of the secondary circuit of capital is that it explicitly introduces a spatial approach to capital accumulation. That is, it brings the analysis of the economy out of the factories and accounting rooms of industry and into the space of the built environment, which contains all such structures and their social relations. As we have seen in chapter 3, Harvey and his critics have focused upon refining Lefebvre's approach. In particular, Harvey has had to address the issue raised by Lefebvre's claim that investment in real estate constitutes a sector of capital formation and the realization of surplus value, especially when the primary circuit loses this ability. According to orthodox marxists, only the primary circuit, which exploits labor power at the workplace, possesses the ability to produce value.

Lefebvre, it would seem, has overextended himself in this statement. It is one thing to acknowledge that investment in real estate is profitable because existing institutional arrangements enable landowners to claim part of the social surplus produced in the primary sector. It is quite another matter, however, to claim, as Lefebvre does, that such a second circuit actually produces surplus value. As we shall see, this is true only within a specific context. Harvey dealt with this issue by dynamizing the process of production over time; he showed how the improved built environment both makes production more "productive" (see below) in future periods and stimulates consumption to match the necessities of the newly designed social space. This emphasizes the role of capital formation through the *circulation* of surplus value rather than its direct creation through work. In the conception of Marx, capital formed in one production period can be realized as capital only through its circulation over time in a future production period. Capital, therefore, needs to be reinvested and circulated to be increased. Using this conception, Harvey (1981) extended Lefebvre's analysis to a three-circuit model of capital accumulation over time. The role of space in this arrangement is reduced by Harvey only to its material form as the built environment. Consequently, in his capital accumulation model he merely addresses the form of space which acts as a means of production. In this sense, by reinvesting part of the surplus value from one production period in new infrastructural improvements, greater profits may be realized in subsequent production periods, and only in this sense for Harvey does the secondary circuit act as a source of capital formation.

The reduction by Harvey of space to the built environment is not what Lefebvre had in mind. By taking account of spatial design, there is an additional way in which settlement space can be viewed as the site of surplus value production. Marx considered transportation and communication technology as being distinct from the process of capital circulation per se for the case of transport to market. In such an instance these were included by him as part of the costs of production itself. This is so because, for Marx, the products of labor become commodities only when they reach the market and are distributed. Consequently, the spatial arrangement of and the communicative links between factories and markets themselves constitute a force of production, and space belongs to the general conditions of production, not only to circulation, as all marxian political economists assert. As Marx states:

> Economically considered, the spatial condition, the bringing of the product to the market, belongs to the production process itself. The product is really finished only when it is on the market. The movement through which it gets there belongs still with the cost of making it. It does not form a necessary movement of circulation, regarded as a particular value-process, since a product may be bought and even consumed at the point of its production. But this spatial moment is important in so far as the expansion of the market and the exchangeability of the product are connected with it. The reduction of the costs of this *real* circulation (in space) belongs to the development of the forces of production. (1973: 534)

Surely the above excerpt from the *Grundrisse* was what prompted Lefebvre to include spatial design in the social productive forces. Most marxists view the fight against the falling rate of profit as taking place within the work site and as leading to a reduction in labor costs by the capitalist. In this battle laborsaving technology is adopted. Rarely have marxists focused on the substitution of capital-saving techniques (Blaug 1968), because of a narrow fix on labor as the source of value. Yet a reduction in the costs of transportation represents just such a capital saving, hence its role in the formation of surplus value, however indirect. The difference between this view and Harvey's is that the former implies that bad design and uncoordinated planning can actually impede capital formation, being unproductive and, therefore, not functional for the capitalist class at all. Yet, it is clear that, following Lefebvre's argument (see chapter 4), the property circuit can be considered a site of capital formation just for the reason Marx suggests.

A second limitation of Harvey's approach, one which he shares this time with Lefebvre, is its inability to explain why investment is *more* profitable in the built environment; that is, both fail to show how the falling rate of profit in the primary circuit can make capital circulate as investment in space. Thus Harvey demonstrates how capital formation can occur through investment in real estate, but he doesn't explain why capital would want to invest in that market. In fact, he indicates that, in order to "bypass" some of the problems involved in conceptualizing the formation of capital in other circuits, it is necessary to switch from a consideration of investment profitability when talking about capital flows between circuits to "investment productivity" (1981: 100). In general, Harvey indicates that individual capitalists find it difficult to switch investment flow from the primary to the secondary circuit. As he states:

> Indeed, individual capitalists left to themselves will tend to
> undersupply their own collective needs for production pre-
> cisely because of such barriers. Individual capitalists tend
> to overaccumulate in the primary circuit and to underinvest
> in the secondary circuit; they have considerable difficulty in
> organizing a balanced flow of capital between the primary and
> secondary circuits. (1981: 97)

Harvey invokes the interventionist state as the means to entice capital investment into the secondary circuit. However, this mechanism, while important, does not answer the question of profitability—it seems to address a picture of capital accumulation and space different from the one Lefebvre has in mind. In the latter's argument, a clear impression is given of real estate's intrinsic and progressively more constant ability to siphon off capital in profitable ventures, and it is this phenomenon which must be explained, since it frames the initial contradiction in the relationship between capital accumulation and space. Characteristically, Lefebvre is no help in providing us with a precise way of explaining the profitability of investment in the built environment. It is, therefore, necessary to address this need.

The health of the secondary circuit is clearly a cyclical phenomenon which varies according to the availability of accumulated capital; Gottlieb (1976) has demonstrated the role business cycles play in such activity. Real estate, however, exists and persists over time as an attractive investment independent of such cycles. This quality arises from the very nature of property as a commodity possessed of a market within the network of capitalist social relations. While real estate is not produced in the normal way in which "nondurable" or "less durable" goods are made, it is sold as a commodity under similar market arrangements. In particular, the very same piece of land with minimal capital improvements can be utilized in a large variety of ways—so that pulverized, abstract space presents almost infinite exchange value possibilities for the turnover of land in society. That is, unlike profits from the primary circuit, the realization of value in land occurs because of its low organic composition of capital and because of the ease with which it can be transformed into alternate uses and then marketed.

Of course, the value of land is always a social product, and its ability to be turned over for a profit remains a function of the general business climate—which is, as Gottlieb (1976) reveals, a cyclical phenomenon. In addition, the market in real estate possesses institutional and state linkages which in some ways are similar to those of other commodity markets but in other ways, as with government housing subsidies, differentiate this commodity from other consumer goods. Thus the ability to convert land and to sell it is also a function of the institutional factors surrounding the regulation, subsidization, and taxation of the built environment. These must be considered in any analysis which wishes to explain the relative profitability of real estate investment. Nevertheless, the essential aspects of real estate as a commodity are its low organic composition of capital and its ability to attract investment at a level in modern society which rivals the circulation of capital in the primary circuit of industrial production. Often this results in the relentless sale and resale of property, along with its conversion to alternate uses in order for the same parcel to be turned over for a profit. For example, a particular property may start out as a house, be converted after many years into apartments, be converted again into condominiums or a cooperative, or even be torn down while still in sound condition to make way for a larger project.

The analysis of the importance of space in the capital accumulation process, therefore, involves two main questions. First, it is necessary to understand why the secondary circuit can siphon off investment from the primary circuit. Second, it is necessary to clear up the question of whether this circuit is always the site of capital formation. In addition, with regard to the first issue, there are two ways in which we can detail the action of the secondary circuit: by focusing on the institutional framework concerned with the circulation of capital in real estate, such as banks, insurance companies, and the programs of the national government, or by focusing on the activities of individuals in differentiating the variety of commodity forms which real estate (often the very same piece of land) can assume. The first approach, which is structuralist and which involves in part the relationship of the state to space, has been covered adequately elsewhere by Harvey (1975b, 1981). In what follows let us briefly review the second aspect, the importance of agency and the role which the ease in the turnover of landownership plays in drawing investment to the secondary circuit.

According to Sargent, an analysis of the real estate industry requires a look at the ways in which agents interact in the property market. As he states, however, the production of the built environment is not clearly understood:

> Surprisingly, while we know what has been happening to the shape or morphology of the American City and why, we do not fully understand how it happens. As the National Academy of Sciences reported in 1972, we know relatively little about the individual processes that lead either to the development and use of raw land or to changes in the use of developed land. (1976: 23)

Recent empirical analyses, however, especially with regard to suburban land-use conversion, have thrown considerable light on this process (Brown and Roberts 1978; Coughlin 1979; Clawson 1971; Gottdiener 1977). These studies indicate that an appropriate approach to investment in land requires a taxonomy of its different users and uses. There is no one specific type of individual engaged in the use of land to make money (see also Form 1954). Furthermore, there are several kinds of markets for land use, each with its own internal logic and constraints. Consequently, the ability to realize capital in land investment is a function of many individuals multiplied by many uses. As Brown and Roberts have indicated, in terms reminiscent of Lefebvre:

> The total supply of land is completely fixed, or inelastic. However, each individual type of use for land is completely expandable. That is, the purchaser of land buys space and theoretically *anything* can be done with that space. Each category of use—farming, housing, commerce, industry, recreation—has its own pricing structure and market. (1978: 6)

There are at least five broad categories of users involved in the turnover of land for profit: rural owners of undeveloped land, land speculators, developers, builders, and owners of developed land. Within each category there are several different types, and the same individual can participate in all five or specialize in only one. While some of these individuals are interested in rapid turnover—builders, for example—others are content to wait ten years or more before an investment in land is realized. In addition, while some land investors use the sale of other assets to finance their ventures, most use other people's money, engaging in a complex process of financing involving a variety of institutions such as banks, trust companies, savings and loan associations, and development corporations. Furthermore, each of these investors can make the same piece of real estate assume a variety of uses depending upon the social context. Finally, in addition to these direct spatial actors, there is a formidable infrastructure organized around secondary circuit activities, especially such financial agents as bankers, employees of independent loan trust companies and insurance companies, real estate agents, local government officials, planners, and so on.

The conclusion which can be reached from the above is that there are incredible numbers of ways to invest in land, and just about anyone with spare cash, regardless of class standing, can participate in the property market. This does not mean, however, that all those who invest in land make a profit. In fact, historically, while land is generally regarded as a good investment, speculators have always enjoyed mixed success in realizing large returns on their investments (Bogue and Bogue 1957). Furthermore, with some exceptions, the variety of investor and user statuses combined with the reduction of space to the commodity, land, results in continual pressure being placed upon all real estate prices to rise regardless of the general health of the economy. In this sense the competitive nature of the supply-side market for land in urban areas contributes to its high price and to the cyclical difficulties with realizing profits. At the same time, the more rapid the turnover of real estate, the faster the price will rise, and the faster the price rises the greater will be the incentive for investors to turn over most types of property. When rates of interest have been reasonable, this results in a high level of activity, which adds to the attractive appearance of investment in the secondary circuit.

Case studies of real estate activity testify to the uncoordinated nature of land development, especially when it has occurred at the rapidly expanding fringe of the metropolitan region (Clawson 1962; Harvey and Clark 1965; Sinclair 1967). There is little question that the turnover and development of land take place within a loose framework of business and institutional arrangements, so that the coordination necessary for adequate planning of growth quite simply does not exist in most areas of the United States. In his analysis of the financial structure which supports investment in the secondary circuit, Harvey concludes the following:

> The dominant impression which an analysis of institutional mediation in the urbanization process creates is of a diversity of instruments and institutions, a chaos of policies and regulatory frameworks, all of which, by some miracle, impose a certain logic and coherence on the totality of the urbanization process. This logic and coherence is not the result of a premeditated urban growth strategy, for there has been no such strategy, either at the local or the national level, these last forty years. (1975b: 137)

While there exists considerable insight behind the above observation with regard to the institutional logic manifested in the land development process, I tend to agree with Scott, who sees such a process as more anarchic than most marxists care to acknowledge (1980). It is necessary to develop this assertion more fully, and I shall do so below and in chapter 6. The very same chaos resulting from the incredibly diverse nature of land development activity is observed in the pattern of growth in the built environment. Elsewhere I have termed the curious nature of the uncoordinated yet calculated decision making associated with the development of the built environment as "planned sprawl" (1977), and its land-use pattern produces a serious cost to society (Clawson 1962; Lindemann 1976; Baldassare 1980; Real Estate Research Corporation 1974). While the determination of the price paid by society may be debated by some (Kasarda 1980; Altshuler 1977; Windsor 1979), mainstreamers have been unwilling to face the differentially carried burden which uncoordinated, secondary circuit activity produces, such as in the contemporary cases of Houston and Phoenix (Feagin 1983). Because money can always be invested with ease in the secondary circuit, such activity propels the never-ending process of property turnover and spatial restructuring, whether an area needs it or not. The major significance of this investment activity, however, is that, as Lefebvre has indicated, it is an unhealthy phenomenon. It is now possible to return to the first issue raised by the circuit analysis of capital accumulation, namely, the role of space in capital formation. Let us conclude this section by addressing it.

I have already demonstrated that, if space is considered a force of production, then it plays a theoretical part in capital formation. This must be seen as contradictory in nature. Much of the investment in the real estate market is *not* at all productive and does not always lead to capital formation. Harvey's position is that secondary circuit activity can be considered as promoting the creation of surplus value over time because it aids in some way the production of primary goods. When the secondary circuit is saturated, Harvey invokes devalorization theory to explain how the accumulation crisis is averted. The growing problems with the environmental costs of contemporary patterns of development—including congestion, pollution, overcrowding, and crime, which are all concomitant developments that accompany growth (Baldassare 1980)—indicate, however, that while real estate persists as a viable area of investment, much of this channeling of resources does *not* aid industrial production in the ways necessary for it to be a source of surplus value. In fact, in such cases, overinvestment in the built environment can actually raise the cost of industrial production and force restructuring through the relocation of certain industries, that is, by directly affecting the primary circuit of capital. Furthermore, there is a second way in which real estate investment is unhealthy. When the primary circuit is the site of overaccumulation, investment in real estate tends to avert an accumulation crisis. However, at times of underaccumulation (O'Connor 1981), such as at present in the United States, money which has been siphoned off in that way is then not available to the primary circuit, and thereby the ability of industry to recapitalize and to restructure space to suit its needs is reduced. Thus, the second circuit of real estate investment plays a very contradictory role in capital accumulation, at times aiding this process and at times hindering it, and the production of settlement space is best understood as a contingent, anarchic process which is not necessarily functional to capital's needs or explained by going outside this contradictory relation to some functionalist devalorization theory.

While capital accumulation requires the organization of space and the development of the built environment, the optimal amount of this activity cannot be realized by the chaotic financial and market arrangements comprising the secondary circuit. Consequently, this parallel sector is at the whim of the cycles in the general availability of investment funds and works by either siphoning off too much investment or too little. In this way, a mechanism which might be viewed as productive to the generation of surplus value becomes instead an active partner in the fluctuations of the waves of investment activity and the crisis base of capital accumulation. This is especially evident during boom periods of rapid growth, when there is overinvestment in real estate and speculation runs rampant. Such conditions lead to environmental blight and the underutilization of space, as well as inflation and rising interest rates due to the high level of borrowing associated with real estate investment. During periods of recession, too little investment in the built environment leads to its fixed capital—representing previous periods—acting as a barrier to future growth so that recovery is prevented.

In both these cases the role of the interventionist state becomes necessary as a regulator of investment activity and as an agent of planning. However, just as the activities of land investment vary greatly from speculator to builder to homeowner, government intervention has had to follow suit with an incredible and often crippling array of separate programs and policies, all designed to intervene in some way in the production of space. Consequently, the relationship between the state and space reproduces and multiplies the same contradictions of capitalist relations of production at levels outside the primary circuit. In short, as Lefebvre observes, secondary circuit activities have become unhealthy. More to the point, the articulation between surplus value production in the primary circuit and its material manifestation as the production of a certain built environment multiplies the contradictions of capitalism, especially those associated with the state–civil society articulation. This is so because of the central contradiction between, on the one hand, the need of primary production for modern landed property as a guarantor of capitalist relations of production and, on the other hand, the role of modern landed property as a commodity which siphons off surplus value without necessarily producing more of it. Were we living in a society which possessed a classless urban-planning capacity, such contradictions might be resolved. However, this is not the case. Thus in the United States the main contradiction of space can *never* be resolved by the state, because it lacks the capacity to control private property. The regulatory ability of government to superimpose stability on capitalist markets, which has worked fairly well for commodities, has failed to provide the same coherency for the case of spatial development itself. The price paid by this inadequacy is borne differentially by all citizens.

In summation, the following can be said about the role of space in the capital accumulation process. Clearly theories of rent and location provide only limited ways of understanding the articulation of capital and space. It is more fruitful to study the role of the secondary circuit and its array of institutions and individuals involved in the turnover of real estate for profit than it is to analyze ground rent within an urban context using nineteenth-century concepts derived from agricultural production. As I have indicated, those fractions organized around interests in real estate make sociospatial conflict a very complex affair. Furthermore, the uncoordinated pattern of secondary circuit development exacerbates the problems associated with primary circuit investment activity and contributes to the swings in economic well-being. Most important, it also helps produce sociospatial conflicts which cannot be dismissed as mere displacements of the class struggle, such as environmentalism, neighborhood activism, no-growth movements, and organized citizen lobbying for land-use reforms (see Gottdiener, forthcoming).

Thus, in opposition to marxian political economy, investment in real estate is an avenue of capital formation, but it is not always so—unproductive development of the built environment can actually contribute to higher costs in the primary circuit of production. This is especially the case for the kind of rapid, uncoordinated growth associated with boomtowns that is much celebrated as the gift of capitalism to place. It is this fundamental contradiction which exacerbates the accumulation crises of capitalism and which becomes the unhealthy situation calling for state intervention rather than the devalorization theory proposed by Harvey. However, by acting according to the many fractions of interests involved in the built environment and by creating chaotic programs, the state merely adds to the swings in investment activity. It is little wonder that such cycles explain the uneven way in which the built environment has developed (Gottlieb 1976; Scott 1980). What they do not explain is the particular form that space assumes. More specifically, the focus on investment activity needs to be supplemented with an understanding of the monopoly forces that shape settlement space, especially the state's and the economy's use of abstract space. We shall consider these in more detail in the next chapter, where I will synthesize the material in the preceding discussions in order to outline a procedure by which we can explain the contemporary form of the built environment.

The analysis in the past chapters has accomplished two goals. It has shown that, although there is virtual agreement over the *appearance* of modern settlement space, conflicting paradigms presently exist which attempt to explain that appearance. Currently, this clash is viewed by academics as one involving urban ecology, on the one hand, and a critical approach based on marxian political economy, on the other. The purpose of this chapter has been to show that the latter fails just as surely as the first.

6. Structure and Agency in the Production of Space

The past several chapters have been concerned with the limitations of the extant approaches comprising the fields of urbn science. In chapter 2 it was necessary to detail the ideological nature of mainstream work, centering as it docs on a lcgitimation of cxisting land-use patterns and their social effects by raising the causal factor of technological change to a level of preeminence. In subsequent discussions, variations on marxian approaches were considered. The essential truth of the critical perspective concerns its insistence that settlement space forms are produced by the dominant sociostructural forces controlling society. Among other things, this insight fulfills the initial promise of urban science, namely, to unlock the secrets of social organization by studying its material forms.

As we have also seen, however, there are distinct limitations among marxian approaches to settlement space as well. But our recognition of these does not in any way detract from our initial acceptance of the critical mode of reasoning as the preferred path for arriving at the truth about society. Thus the debate on the theory of space is an argument over method more than theory in that fundamental positions vis-à-vis marxian epistemology are at stake. Nevertheless, our excursion into the critical analysis of settlement space has armed us with a theory of sorts—Lefebvre's contention that no progress can be made in the project of marxism without fully accounting for space itself, that is, without introducing spatial questions and concepts directly into marxian categories of thought.

By following Lefebvre's suggestion, however, we have uncovered the essential limitations of marxism, especially in political economy and structural functionalism. It is necessary to abandon these in order to proceed with our fundamental task of understanding the production of space. Marxian political economy remains limited by its failure to transcend bourgeois categories of thought. There can be no economic analysis which is marxist unless we account for the *so-*

cial nature of capitalism. This requires the employment of dialectical reasoning and an appreciation for the simultaneous way in which marxian categories are at once social and political as well as economic. Structural functionalism is also rejected, principally because in the hands of Castells it leads away from space, away from the material environment, and toward a nominalist discourse on urban politics—one that is grounded less in a theory than in a certain fantasy regarding the revolutionary potential of the "new" social cleavages in society.

Yet, Lefebvre's theory is not very much help as a guide to spatial analysis. It remains more of an emphasis, a focus on space within the context of marxian reasoning. It is necessary, therefore, to synthesize a method based upon this emphasis. The proposed perspective understands sociospatial organization not as an outdated conceptual framework of city-based spatial forms but as a direct outcome of the relationships between economic, political, and cultural processes as they connect with the regionwide geography of metropolitan areas. This approach, called the social production of space, can be contrasted both with the orthodoxy of marxian political economy and with that of mainstream ecology, although it retains for itself transformative premises of analysis deriving from marxism. The social production of space has the following characteristics.

First, the new science of spatial forms begins with the realization that spatial as well as temporal relations are intrinsic to every aspect of social organization. According to Thrift (1983), this proposition is one tenet of the new "structurationist" school of social theory (Giddens 1979, 1981; Bhaskar 1979; Bourdieu 1977). To date this intrinsic state has been asserted but never specified, especially in terms compatible with the marxian method. In chapter 4, following Lefebvre's conception, I demonstrated the integral nature of spatial relations to the production and reproduction processes of capitalism. This specification represents an ontological break with marxism because it asserts that location, the spatial manifestation of production relations, and environmental design are all essentially involved in both the valorization and the realization of surplus value. Furthermore, the matrix of spatiotemporal relations permeates the mode of production at *every* level. This intrinsic characteristic cannot be discursively captured by any single analytical category pertinent to "space" alone. Thus, it is necessary to reject structurationist formulations which deploy an abstract, nominalist account of space circumscribed around a disembodied signified, such as "spatiality" (Soja 1984) or "locality" (Urry 1981).

These efforts merely constitute the new discourse *about* space and its importance; they fail to specify its essential qualities in terms of social relations. Yet, if spatial relations were not part of the valorization of capital, their place would be epiphenomenal in the constellation of social relations necessary to capitalist production. Thus, while clearly important, they would only be consigned to the world of appearance, and their previous neglect by marxists would be wholly warranted. However, the fact that the valorization of capital requires a spatiotemporal matrix opens up the analysis of geographical space to the very core of concerns historically pertinent to marxism. Class conflict, the reproduction of labor, the reproduction of production relations, capital accumulation, crisis formation, and so on are no longer manifestations of capitalism which can be analyzed as occurring *in* space, as marxists have shown; rather, they are *about* space. They concern spatial relations just as much as they involve relations among capital, labor, and technological change.

Having established space's intrinsic nature with regard to productive forces and relations, we can return to our observation in chapter 5 that, the moment we update marxism vis à vis space, we also transcend it. Class conflict and capital accumulation analysis both fall away as we pursue the effects of spatial relations and interests on political and economic practices. No single model of political economy, either from a marxian (Harvey 1981) or from a neoricardian (Scott 1980) perspective, can be used to deduce the present-day sociospatial patterns of multinucleated regional development. Consequently, as we make our way toward a new science of spatial production, it is necessary to cast aside all outmoded methods of thought and all categories of reasoning which no longer apply. In what follows I shall formulate a synthesis accomplishing this task which supplies a theory of the production of space in the structurationist tradition.

As a second characteristic of the social production of space, both ecologists and marxists assert that geographic and demographic phenomena are representative of social forces that are interrelated and mutually linked. Thus spatial development is understood as progressing within some specific *social* context. Marxian political economists, while subscribing to this notion, interpret this matrix as meaning the global context of the capitalist world system. They frame their analysis of localized places by showing how space has been altered by such global phenomena as the multinational corporation or the "new" international division of labor. However, this merely specifies the vertical axis of integration—it ignores the types of horizontal linkages, often contentious in nature, between groups, institutions, and holders of resources which mainstream ecologists have always sought to analyze. At the same time, ecologists—especially by ignoring the role of the interventionist state—divorce their analysis completely from the social forces interposed in space that are hierarchically structured networks of social organization. Consequently, a synthetic view of the production of space requires an integrated understanding of the three-dimensional nature of sociospatial organization as deploying hierarchical linkages to places as well as contextual or interactive relations, such as those which foster agglomeration. Furthermore, this three-dimensional array, the spatio-temporal matrix of social activities which surrounds places, involves an interrelated meshing of cultural, political, and economic forces. It cannot be specified by the reductionist arguments of either marxian political economists or mainstream ecologists.

In chapter 4, I observed that marxian structuralism attempted unsuccessfully to capture this complex intersection through a specification of three abstract systems involving economics, politics, and ideology. Over the years the critique of Althusserianism has given us a more refined approach to the state and to culture or ideology, in addition to economics. Yet, some overarching scheme linking all three systems has still to be articulated. In what follows I shall confine my efforts to draft a new theory of contemporary social organization solely to those features pertinent to the production of space, while leaving for the future a general treatment of this topic.

I view sociospatial organization as being linked by conjoined contiguous and hierarchical relations. It is the strength of this three-dimensional spatiotemporal matrix which sustains the massive, deconcentrated development of the metropolis. Thus everyday life is simultaneously particularized and touched by production relations extending across the globe; it is fragmented and hierarchically organized, atomized, and structured. It exists not only in the "corporate cities" studied by marxian political economists but in suburbs as well. In short, it is deployed across regions and nations by the very same global processes which structure each individual place. According to Mandel (1975), capitalism's phenomenal form was the factory but is now the multinational corporation. Marxian political economists associate the corporate city with the new phenomenal form; however, in chapter 7 I shall assert that they are wrong. Instead, the process of sociospatial development associated with the present phase of Late Capitalism is deconcentration, which produces a distinctive form of space—the polynucleated, sprawling metropolitan region. This can be contrasted with the implosive growth of urban concentration characteristic of nineteenth-century capitalism.

As indicated, I shall locate the production of space within the general context of an emergent theory of social organization referred to as structurationist, a theory which appreciates the role of agency, on the one hand, and structure, on the other, in the production of spatial phenomena and forms. My fundamental argument is that spatial forms are *contingent* products of the dialectical articulation between action and structure. They are *not* pure manifestations of deep-level social forces; instead, they constitute a world of appearances which must be penetrated by analysis. Before I illustrate specific applications of this approach, a final contrast with extant perspectives requires attention.

Third, and following from the preceding, it has recently become popular to draft a one-to-one correspondence between city forms and stages in the capitalist mode of production (see chapter 3). I am opposed to such a view. Two issues are involved here in the dispute about space and the periodization of capital. First, can capitalist development be considered as passing through distinct stages, and, second, do such stages manifest themselves uniquely in space? I shall argue against both issues.

In the first case, while it is possible to address the periodization of capitalist development, it must be done within the context of the long duration of its history. As Lefebvre (1973), Hirsch (1983), Jessop (1982), and Fine and Harris (1979) all contend, there has been only one historical mode of capitalism (although there are many separate formations of that mode), and its development occurs in strict continuity with the past. Distinct or qualitatively separate stages of capitalism are merely discursive conventions which can be shown to lack validity on close examination, because the basic structure of capitalism and its essential *social* relations have not changed. In the second case, as I shall demonstrate in this synthesis, developmental changes alleged by marxian "stage" theorists as contemporary— such as the hegemony of multinationals—can be shown to have existed for quite some time, often with as much social force as in the present, despite appearing in a less developed form. This means that, while it is essential to specify how capitalist organization has been altered over time, as it clearly has, it is also imperative to recognize that such transformations cannot be categorized as qualitatively unique stages: they merely represent loosely structured phases whose precise beginnings are highly debatable.

Most important, it is quite simply wrong to suppose that the link between phases of capitalist social development and spatial form is clearly demonstrable. There are no, nor have there ever been, "industrial capitalist cities," "monopoly capitalist cities," or "global capitalist cities." There are only spatial forms and modes of production linked by a contingent process and existing in various phases of

development and change. It is this process, currently one of deconcentration rather than implosion, and not the forms per se which requires our attention.

While the structural composition of capitalist development is
one explanatory source of information about spatial forms, the following text is opposed to reductionist arguments which seek to end
analysis at this level. Political and ideological forces are equally important in the production of space. Finally, because the intersection
of these social forces involves a contingent process, often with contentious outcomes, the production of space is captured best as the
complex articulation between structure and agency, which is always
in motion. In what follows, I shall proceed first by isolating those
structural aspects of capitalism most pertinent to the social production of space. These will be shown to involve certain aspects germane to all advanced industrial societies, even noncapitalist ones.
Second, particular characteristics of these structural aspects will be
discussed in detail. Special emphasis will be given to aspects specific
to capitalism as a unique mode, such as uneven social development.
Finally, this synthesis will discuss the nature of agency in the social
production of space, especially with regard to its Late Capitalist
manifestations. These voluntaristic elements involve the organization and deployment of spatial concerns—and the intersection of the
latter with the structural processes of development is shown to
produce spatial forms. I shall begin the structuralist part of this synthesis by detailing the contemporary transformations of capitalist
society most pertinent to changes in sociospatial organization. I do
not intend to canvass all the changes of the present period, only
those with the greatest impact on space. This follows from the epistemological position adopted here that the contingent process in the
production of space must always be at the center of analysis, rather
than focusing on the political economy of capitalist development
per se.

The recent sociostructural transformations which seem criti-
cally important for an understanding of the contemporary form of
settlement space coincide with changes occurring for quite some
time, but accelerating since World War II. Of these the three most important have already been identified in chapter 2. First, there is the
organization of production and administration in complex, bureaucratic structures of decision making; such a change helped integrate
the entire globe into a world system of production, marketing, and
finance that cuts across national boundaries even between east and
west. Second is the active intervention of the state at all levels of so-

ciety—on the one hand, at the federal level large-scale projects and massive sources of expenditures are structured by government, especially in connection with what Mandel (1975) calls the permanent war economy; on the other hand, at the most local level it is often difficult to separate the actions of the private and the public sectors, the two are so inextricably intertwined. Third, there is the emergence of science, technology, and a knowledge industry—involving specialized organizations of research and scientific development—as the dominant forces of production, especially given the application of advanced techniques and automation to the development of the means of labor, that is, raw material production and agriculture. Let us consider these transformations in turn.

THE EMERGENCE OF THE GLOBAL CORPORATION

Business enterprise under capitalism in the United States has evolved considerably over the past hundred years (Chandler 1977). Among the changes which are of direct interest to us is the shift from the single-product family enterprise—operating in a localized area with few plants, in which the administrative framework coexisted with the physical structure of the industrial operation—to the present-day bureaucratic, multiproduct, multiplant, multinational corporation with ownership institutionalized in shareholding arrangements, in which administration is separated from industrial work by thousands of miles in some cases (Holland 1976; Baumol 1959; Berle and Means 1932; Hymer 1979; Galbraith 1969; Means 1964; Schonfeld 1965; Williamson 1975). On the one hand, the implications of this change with regard to ownership and control, class structure, capital accumulation, and the effects of concentration have been treated by a vast and growing literature (Minty and Cohen 1972; Zeitlin 1970; O'Connor 1974, Baran and Sweezy 1966; U.S. Congress, House Committee on the Judiciary 1965; Menshikov 1969). On the other hand, the presence of multinational corporations, or what Holland calls the mesoeconomic level of economic activity (1977: 186), has been analyzed from an emergent approach now called the world system perspective, which stresses the global reach and interconnectedness of economic organization, as well as the impact of such a structure on nations, regions, and localized areas, especially with regard to the new international division of labor (Wallerstein 1979; Frobel, Heinrichs, and Kreye 1980; Rubinson 1976; Mandel 1975; Palloix 1975; Barnet and Muller 1974; Hymer 1979; Amin 1976; Holland 1976).

In brief, the implication of all these research endeavors for a science of settlement space is that the built environment must be viewed as being embedded within a complex matrix of socioeconomic organization, involving a corporate bureaucratic framework of capital accumulation on a world scale. To be sure, there are many local businesses with important functional roles within their region. However, the vast bulk of the world's resources is controlled by a global system, and any localized interests not connected directly to it must perform within the variably wide interstices between the larger matrix of economic organization. At present this integrated system of multinational corporations seems to be visibly realizing its greatest physicalist impact on spatial design through the invasion by "quaternary" information-processing or advanced corporate services into the downtown centers of our very largest cities (Gottmann 1972; Sassen-Koob 1984). However, the gleaming skyscraper headquarters and the Ginza-like districts which surround them are only the most apparent manifestations of a pervasive global influence affecting everything from agriculture to industrial production to mass culture. It is fruitless to attempt an explanation of the contemporary spread city form without a recognition of the differential way in which the activities of multinationals are deployed throughout separate places, just as it is wrong to limit any explanation only to such factors in ignorance of the more general process of deconcentration, which involves localized forces as well.

Yet, I do not wish to imply here that I subscribe to the theory of social organization deriving from the world system approach, only to emphasize its descriptive value and its assertion that every place is connected to vertical networks of business organization as well as more local sources of influence, a fact observed long ago by analysts of community decline (Stein 1960; Bensman and Vidich 1960). In chapter 2, I sketched a brief description of the way in which the functional division of space is affected by this hierarchical system with respect to the case of the central city. From this discussion it is possible to understand the limits, and the essentially metaphorical nature, of the exclusive emphasis by marxian political economists on the activities of multinationals. As observed, the complex restructuring of the central city has taken place as the consequence of a conjuncture between separate structural forces operating sociospatially. In particular, it is much more fruitful to analyze the ways in which fractions of capital—operating globally, of course—have affected every place, especially through the actions of finance capital and the combined activity of the property sector. Thus, a complete range of analysts from Gottmann to Mollenkopf have stressed the technological basis for the type of quaternary activities which make agglomeration at the city center necessary for certain social functions. In contrast, I have shown that such agglomerations are really a product of the differential spatial deployment of separate fractions of capital articulating in a complex way with urban public policy, local planning, and real estate speculation. That is, the process is more manipulative, even corrupt, and less pristine or technologically inexorable than both marxists and mainstreamers would have us believe.

THE INTERVENTIONIST STATE

The Great Depression of the 1920s and 1930s ushered in a second structural change in social organization: the de facto participation of the nation-state in the economy. This intervention has occurred in every western country since World War II (Fabricant 1950; Posner and Wolf 1967; Robson 1960; Sheahan 1963; Crosser 1960; Dillard 1948; Klein 1947; Lerner 1944; Holloway and Picciotto 1979; Crouch 1979). As we have seen in previous chapters, the forces which shape settlement space are partly political and produced by state intervention. On a purely descriptive level, it is clear that such a melding of public with private interests occurs in the following ways: price supports for products, especially agriculture; minimum wage and unemployment supports for workers; a wide variety of legislative acts which support economic activities and help structure select industries, such as housing and banking; a wide variety of programs which subsidize scientific and organizational research; vast spending programs involving projects in the built environment either under direct state auspices, such as the TVA, or under combined state-private auspices, such as urban renewal; a taxation structure which supports spending in select areas, such as single-family homes; a permanent war economy which invests billions of federal revenue dollars in a wide variety of defense-related private industries; structuration of credit, which encourages high levels of personal consumption; and, finally, state regulatory and planning agencies at every level of government.

Due to the massive extent of this intervention, the analysis of the built environment requires an understanding of how the various manifestations of state penetration in the economy amalgamate with the private incentives to produce the projects, actions, and forms of space. According to Lefebvre, the view which captures this phenomenon best focuses on the combined actions of the state and the economy in pulverizing social space through urban economic development and planning, transforming it into a commodity and then into the uniform building blocks of abstract space. Much of the work of European analysts focuses on the direct role of the state in such a process (Lamarche 1977; Lojkine 1977a, 1977b; Scott 1980; Castells 1977). Yet, it is fundamental to point out that in the case of the United States state intervention in space most often occurs through the indirect form of policy, not through active planning. Even where local planning authorities do engage in construction projects, these are often conducted by nonelective supcragencies combining public authority with private financing, such as the New York–New Jersey Port Authority. In general, the American state represents an awesome presence in land-use transformations, but the bulk of its influence is at the deep level of laws and regulations, such as zoning or tax policies, which derive from the juridical safeguards of capitalist property relations and which indirectly create the incentives that then subsidize direct action along certain lines rather than others—generally by subsidizing growth.

A number of marxian urban analysts have understood this distinction and have focused their attention on state intervention in the United States as a matter of policy (Harvey 1975b; Friedland 1980; Tomaskovic-Devey and Miller 1982). However, the conceptualization of this articulation is hampered by the limited notion of intervention for "capital in general." Among nonmarxists working in this same vein, such as Mollenkopf (1983), there is a tendency to replace economic with political reductionism and explain state intervention as essentially a political product of party competition. In contrast to extant views, I shall assert below that at the local level of the metropolitan region it is simply wrong to hypothesize a separation of the political from the economic—individuals active in the two sectors are completely intertwined by crosscutting networks. Furthermore, only recently have marxian analysts come to recognize what critics of liberalism have known for quite some time: the fractionated nature of the relationship between the state and capital, itself constituted by fractions (O'Connor 1981; Plotkin 1980). In what follows I have deemphasized the role of the state in planning, because it does not possess the same direct presence in the United States as it does in Europe. Instead, I have focused on the indirect intervention of the state through a wide variety of programs, policies, and practices which serve to subsidize the actions of certain special interests at the expense of others.

KNOWLEDGE AND TECHNOLOGY AS FORCES OF PRODUCTION

Since the classical age of economics, technological innovation condensed as a value in capital goods has always been considered a firm way in which any business could extract a greater level of production from the same share of capital and labor power. Until World War II the use of innovation and knowledge, however, possessed something of an ersatz and personal nature (Shumpeter 1939). One of the lasting structural changes of American society in the postwar period has been the organized and accelerated way in which a knowledge industry now articulates with economic activity (Rosenberg 1972; Meier 1956; Rezler 1969; Mansfield 1968; Silk 1960). There are two major ways in which the significance of such a change has been approached in the literature. First, it is considered important that technological innovation has been used as a replacement for labor, especially in semiskilled work, thus deepening the capital-to-labor ratio of industry (Carter 1970; Gillman 1957; Mandel 1975). Second, researchers point to the fact that the changing work process has helped restructure the labor force from a former predominance of blue-collar workers to the current situation, where most workers offer professional, managerial, and service skills (Poulantzas 1976; U.S. Department of Labor 1979; Bock and Dunlap 1970; Blau and Duncan 1967; Fuchs 1968; Singelmann 1977; Gartner and Reissman 1974; Braverman 1974). This second area in particular has produced direct effects on demographic deployment patterns across settlement space. We return here to the observations regarding the economic and racial segregation of metropolitan communities (Hadden and Borgatta 1965; Greer 1962; Schnore 1972) and to an important previous observation that the class structure of the United States is currently quite complex. I shall take up these topics more extensively below when I consider the relationship between contemporary transformations in social organization and the production of the new demographic pattern of spatial deployment.

THE SOCIAL PRODUCTION OF SPACE: STRUCTURAL MECHANISMS OF CAPITAL

The above structural changes are most pertinent to understanding contemporary spatial transformations, but they are not specific to capitalist societies alone. On the one hand, both the interventionist state and the accelerating role of knowledge and technological innovation in productive forces are characteristic of all advanced industrial societies. On the other, the present form of the corporation—its multinational basis—seems most characteristic of western capitalism. Yet it can be argued that communist bloc societies have approximate forms, created by the Russian state to integrate the economic activities of Eastern European countries. To be sure, there is nothing in the communist bloc comparable to the capitalist multinationals, with their global strategies to minimize labor costs and their horizontal deployment of separate functions. However, it is simply inaccurate to address the question raised by the presence of new patterns of sociospatial organization by discursively labeling them as uniquely capitalist, without demonstrating why that is so. This is an important issue to face not only for nonmarxists, whose analysis of postindustrialism can be easily dismissed as nominalist discourse (Bell 1973; Mollenkopf 1983), but also for marxists, who are all too eager to label everything which transpires in contemporary society as capitalist (Fainstein et al. 1983; Hill 1984b). In the latter case we are provided, in the main, with little more than a second nonspecific discourse which overuses the signifier "capitalist"—as in "capitalist city," "capitalist urban policy," and the like—as a shorthand substitute for more concrete analyses. Upgrading such discursive patterns requires the theoretical specification of particular elements in the production of space which are pertinent to social relations and capitalist in nature. The three main urban theories attempting such a task—those put forward by Castells, Harvey, and Scott—are hamstrung by serious limitations, as we have seen.

In what follows, I propose a fourth approach, one which specifies the capitalist nature of the production of space for the United States, but I do so within well-defined limits. First, each of the three critical approaches of marxian structuralism, political economy, and neoricardianism remains antivoluntaristic at its core. Therefore, they all commit the fallacy of functionalist reductionism in isolating the capitalist nature of the urban development process. I contend that no structuralist theory by itself can effect such a specification. My task below will be to show how the dialectical relation between structure and agency can replace previous modes of critical thought. As previously indicated, this theory will confine itself to the production of space rather than a general account of Late Capitalism.

Second, as demonstrated in chapter 5, once we take account of space it is not possible to specify sociospatial phenomena fully by marxian reasoning. Thus a new mode of critical thought is called for, one that retains the marxian dialectic but moves beyond its political economy. I have developed this argument in a series of discussions; however, space considerations do not allow me to present it here in totality. Basically, it is necessary to redefine what marxists understand the relations of production to mean and to see that they are *simultaneously* economic, political, and cultural. This implies that social phenomena are contingent rather than predetermined, following a realist epistemology, another issue which cannot be addressed at this time. The contingent nature of spatial forms means that present-day patterns are neither functional nor dysfunctional for capitalism—in fact, they are both because functional arguments are always grounded in relative perspectives. More important, spatial forms are epiphenomenal but *direct* products of deep-level, contentious forces pertinent to systems of sociospatial organization. At the surface they are produced by the articulation between agency and structure, a process which is not only relatively free from economic determinacy but which is open to continual renegotiation as the intersecting economic, political, and cultural processes battle it out in space. For this reason a study at the level of spatial forms alone, such as Gottmann's theory of the megalopolis, which fails to specify the link between morphology and particular systems of social organization, is guilty of confusing appearance with explanation. Because Nairobi and New York or Paris and London may "look" the same, they are nevertheless produced by different as well as similar processes pertinent to different systems of sociospatial organization. Urban science must be capable of piercing through appearance or form to discover the forces which produce space. Once looked for, a science of spatial differences *and* regularities linked to deep-level causes replaces the more primitive and limited understanding of positivist or reductionist thinking.

Third, contemporary marxian theory is split by a factional debate regarding an explanation for the genesis of its structural changes. While I consider their capitalist nature below, I shall avoid entering into this conflict. In fact, it might be argued that the debate over the capitalist origin of transformations leads us away from the analysis of space, away from a process that may shed new light on the larger debate. At present, three distinct approaches seek to demonstrate the capitalist nature of the structural changes associated with Late Capitalism. I shall describe them briefly, and below I shall draw upon all three rather than judge among them. One school closely follows changes in the forces of production as the principal source of all other societal transformations. This explains the current laws of motion of a capitalism propelled by deep-level changes in technological innovation and scientific progress (Mandel 1975). In contrast, a second approach views changes as occurring mainly because of the shifting interface between capital and labor, facilitated but not caused by technological advances. Advocates of this view stress the labor theory of location (Storper and Walker 1983) and/or a neoricardian approach to urbanization (Scott 1980). Finally, some marxists see capital accumulation as being the principal determining factor in its laws of motion. Changes both in the forces of production and in the new relations between capital and labor are determined by the exigencies of accumulation (Frobel, Heinrichs, and Kreye 1980; Harvey 1983). Such debates among marxists illustrate how far removed they are from understanding the dialectic and just how caught up they still are in bourgeois categories of thought, because of an insistence on isolating primal causes as a necessary condition of social theory.

Prior to recent discussions regarding the nature of contemporary capitalism, most marxists held a relatively clear picture of the structural features of capitalist society which distinguished it from more general discussions of characteristics held in common by all industrialized societies, capitalist and noncapitalist alike. This image was supplied by the theory of monopoly capitalism (Baran and Sweezy 1966), even if the theory itself was not subscribed to completely. The specifically capitalist features of contemporary society which are distinct to its path of industrialization include the concentration of industrial and financial wealth in the hands of a small fraction of the total population, an overindulgent propensity to consume as a consequence of decades of conditioning by the advertising industry and the state, and an economy with volatile rates of inflation and unemployment which is difficult to regulate.

More recently, additional structural changes have produced the present phase of capitalist society, called Late Capitalism by Mandel (1975). As indicated above, there are at least three conflicting marxian theories which account for the genesis of these changes—a debate we can fruitfully sidestep. According to Mandel the elements of monopoly capitalism, especially its characteristic concentration of wealth, have become globalized over the years so that the present depicts a phase of the past. In particular, Late Capitalism reflects the "international concentration and centralization of capital," which has in turn generated the globally based multinational corporation as the "main phenomenal form of capital" (1975: 8, 9). At the level of the forces of production, other important changes include a shift in production technology from the electromechanical to the electronic, involving the solid-state manipulation of ever more infinitesimal amounts of space and time, and the acceleration of technological innovation in general as the principal means of monopolistic profit taking. First, at the organizational level, changes include the vertical disintegration of production units and the differential spatial deployment of fractions throughout the globe—with administrative, marketing, and production activities being linked through sophisticated technology and the application of increasingly instrumental modes of decision making—and the subdivision of production itself into greatly specified skill levels of labor, thus enabling the optimal use of labor power and a global sourcing strategy for the capitalist control of costs. Second, at the level of the relations of production, new features include the penetration of capitalist social relations into virtually every sphere of daily life, aided by the state and involving the commodification of such previously traditional cultural forms of community as the family, health, education, and so on. This is sometimes called Fordism (Aglietta 1979; Hirsch 1983; Lipietz 1980), and its students suggest that Marx's nightmare of the creation of the free-standing laborer by capitalist relations may be upon us.

Certainly it is possible to devote an academic lifetime to studying these changes and debating their origins. These features are noted to convince the reader that the present moment in the United States can be analyzed according to the study of capitalist societal development more fruitfully than by paying attention to some more vague, generic category such as that of an advanced industrial society. More important, the task before us requires an examination of just how Late Capitalist transformations have affected space and, in turn, how the new spaces have articulated with Late Capitalism. Much of this discussion takes place in chapter 7, although I introduced it in chapter 2. At present I shall conclude the structural section of this synthesis by briefly tracing the phenomenal consequences of the deep-level Late Capitalist changes which are most relevant to spatial transformations. These can be summed up as follows.

First, changes in the forces of production have resulted in the progressively more footloose nature of industry, coupled with an increasingly fluid flow of capital into and out of fixed forms utilizing shifting advantages created by new technologies. On the one hand, in the United States this has produced what Bluestone and Harrison refer to as deindustrialization—the withdrawal of capital from industrial sites in this country and the transfer of production elsewhere. This has caused different fractions of capital to jockey for the control of wealth, while the activity of work itself is exported in a global sourcing strategy. As Bluestone and Harrison suggest:

Controversial as it may be, the essential problem with the U.S.
economy can be traced to the way capital—in the forms of financial resources and of real plant and equipment—has been
diverted from productive investment in our basic national industries into unproductive speculation, mergers, and acqui-
sitions, and foreign investment. Left behind are shuttered
factories, displaced workers, and a newly emerging group of
ghost towns. (1982: 6)

As fractions of capital battle each other in a global game of Monopoly, basic production flees U.S. communities, and we are beset
with plant closings. Over the last decade these have seriously dam-
aged what was once a localized everyday life based upon the working-
class neighborhood and its historic community culture (as captured
in the music of Bruce Springsteen). However, the restructuring of
capital investment according to more intensive, high-technology use
has introduced new plants with a significantly depressed need for laborers. New industries, such as information processing, together
with restructured industrial techniques have altered the relation between capital and labor in the United States. In the main, while
there are "new" jobs associated with these shifts, they do not add up
to the levels of the previous phase, and a permanent reserve army has
been generated that takes its place alongside the more pristine façades of the high-tech factories. Thus, local communities have
taken on the appearance of labor reservations, where the basic right
of work becomes a luxurious status to be competed for on a mass
scale. Such an existential, marginal condition is not limited merely
to ghetto or other poor populations, as marxists seem to suggest—it
involves everyone living under Fordist and Late Capitalist everyday
life. Consequently, traditional, humanist everyday life and the communion of neighbors are replaced by a hard-edged world of economic
struggle, where noninstrumental relations have been vaporized by
the dragon's breath of competition over scarce resources.

Second, and without question, the most prominent epiphenomenal effect of Late Capitalist changes, especially since World War II, has
been the differentiation of the social order into a structure of increasing complexity. As noted, the simple two-class model of capitalism is
inadequate. Socioeconomic forces have fragmented both the working
and the capitalist classes, so that today it is necessary to understand
the complex nature of social differentiation before any social analysis
can proceed. In the first case, the working class has been thoroughly
transformed by the ascendancy of white-collar employment. At
present, traditional blue-collar work counts for a little more than one-

third of the labor force, while white-collar and service trades consti-tute almost all the remainder. Furthermore, virtually all tasks have been converted to dual labor markets, because of the presence of a large reserve army, so that each job can be structured according to some credentialed career or be made marginal by administrative re-definition of these very same criteria. On the one hand, the refined skill levels of jobs fractionate the working class into progressively more categories. On the other, capitalist development creates new skill needs which are supplied by workers outside traditional labor ties. In both cases the balkanization of labor increases with the number of its fractions. Consequently, it is simply a mistake to go along with Castells and impute the production of these "new" social cleavages to the exogenous intervention of the state alone. The frac-tionated social order has been produced, in the main, by transforma-tions in the capitalist mode flowing from all the changes in the mode of production. These then appear in space (Friedman 1977; Cohen 1981) or are produced by space, that is, by property relations (Saunders 1978; Lefebvre 1974), as we shall see below.

In Late Capitalism, not only workers but also capitalists have become highly fractionated. As capital has penetrated and appropri-ated more and more markets and use values, the total number of in-dustries has increased geometrically. Even within the broad, generic categories of the capitalist system, such as corporate and finance capital, a wide variety of separate and often conflicting fractions is present. Thus, for example, the money market is presently a com-plex assortment of commercial banks, savings and loan associations, investment companies, independent finance companies, and mutual fund and trust companies. While in some instances such separate en-terprises may converge in a single confluent interest, there are times when they form opposing fractions that compete with each other. This is especially the case in the production of space, where separate fractions of capital fall on different sides of growth disputes, or where the finance capital infrastructure has been split over the dwindling demand for housing. This fragmentation sharply increases the need for state regulation of markets and intervention in production and credit.

Consequently, while it is possible to structurally define a seg-ment of society known as the capitalist class, it is not possible to predict how that class will behave in space or to characterize what its interest in any given situation might be. Thus, if some state theo-rist follows the structuralist paradigm and hypothesizes that inter-vention embodies the condensation of class antagonisms, it is still not possible to explain the state-space articulation because of the many fractions which comprise the essential splits over public policy. Perhaps the best way to grasp the implications of the complexity of the existing social order for the analysis of the state is to consider the following observation by O'Connor:

> In Italy, Marino Regini cannot find any clear "logic of action of the State" whether it be "capital logic," or "accumulation/ legitimation logic." The reason seems to be that state action in Italy is the result of a "spoils allotment system" of client relations, conflicts and compromises in which private actors distribute resources. Hence, state policies may be "allotments without any consistency" and not necessarily conducive to either accumulation or consensus. I believe this kind of analysis may be applicable to the U.S. as well with the major difference that the spoils allotment system works through the vehicles of well-established state agencies, congressional committees, and the legal system, rather than by more direct encounters between representatives of capital, labor, farmers, small businesses, etc., and their various fractions. (1981: 47)

Orthodox marxists are reluctant to face the importance of class fractions and their contingent clashes in the analysis of sociospatial growth, preferring instead to retreat behind a discursive argument which invokes the abstract nature of Marx's own thought (Edel 1981, 1982). However, the significance of class fractions has been fruitfully utilized in sociospatial analyses of restructuring (Longstreth 1979; Markusen 1978). The implications of this view and of O'Connor's observation above, which I concur with, will be discussed more fully below as they relate to the production of space.

A third epiphenomenal effect of Late Capitalist transformations involves the qualitative nature of active state involvement in society, as expressed by the permanent war economy with its concomitant stress on advanced technology. This has stimulated the growth of certain industries; financed capital investment in specific geographical locations, thus producing growth pole effects in particular regions; and subsidized research and development, thus increasing the scientific and technological requirements for the labor force. Since the cold war days of the 1950s, virtually half of all federal government expenditures each year have been allocated to the military and its related needs. This level of funding has had a profound effect on space, as in the construction of the system of interstate defense highways. Military-related research and production have channeled massive amounts of state spending into suburban areas at the expense of central city development, thus helping fuel the city-to-suburb demographic shift of the 1950s and 1960s. In part this emphasis has had a direct military explanation: the need to secure war-related industries and research sites from the adverse effects of proximity to large population centers. However, the very same policies have also emphasized defense spending in the sunbelt at the expense of the Northeast, a focus which cannot easily be defended by a strategic argument. Because state intervention is the product in part of political competition, its various outcomes cannot be imputed to the needs of specific class fractions alone. Consequently, the political realities underlying the location decisions for military spending assume central importance in any explanation of contemporary growth patterns (see chapter 7).

Our final effect is one that is manifested directly in the spatial patterns of land use characteristic of Late Capitalism, in what has come to be referred to as uneven development. There are two ways to consider this: as a purely economic phenomenon and as a geographical one. Clearly, the two aspects are related, and it is a mistake to separate them, especially by reifying uneven development as a spatial phenomenon. By emphasizing the locational nature of these patterns at the expense of their social origins in the present system, mainstream analysts have been guilty of ideologically masking the fundamental connection between these two dimensions of sociospatial organization. In the first case, U.S. society is and always has been unevenly developed in a demographic sense. While the majority of citizens can be ranked as belonging to a vast middle class that is possessed of a somewhat fluid capacity to increase personal income, at least 20 percent of the population exists at the poverty level and seldom participates in any sort of prosperity. In addition, American society is racially segregated—and little has been done to improve the conditions of minority groups, especially among black and Hispanic urban populations. Consequently, the metropolitan land-use pattern is made up of areas which are isolated from each other and which differ greatly in the quality of life enjoyed by their residents. This characteristic pattern of uneven development differs from the communist variety of that phenomenon (Misztal and Misztal 1984). To date, public policy has not been able to deal effectively with such sociospatial segregation, as formidable conceptual barriers stand in the way of its alleviation (Lineberry 1977; Megret 1981). From an economic point of view, capital resources have no incentive to flow toward impoverished areas. Consequently, the pattern of uneven development is reinforced and intensified by growth. As Bluestone remarks:

Those who control capital resources in the economy will tend over time to reinvest in those particular product lines, machinery, geographical areas and workers which promise the highest return on dollar investment. Conversely, investment will tend to decline in segments of the economy where potential expected profit is relatively low. The outcome is continuous growth and relative prosperity in the former sector and relative stagnation and impoverishment in the latter. (1972: 66)

As we have seen in chapter 1, the flow of economic resources and the inequitable distribution of personal wealth in the United States has had a profound effect on the differential well-being of communities. In this way, and despite economic growth, economic processes translate uneven development into spatial patterns (Thurow 1975; Reich 1981). While the bottom line of structurally induced social pathology has shifted upward toward greater levels of human decency since the nineteenth century, American cities are still little different in this regard from the sociospatial contrasts observed by Engels in Manchester (1973).

In addition to the effects of uneven social stratification on space, another aspect to economic growth in a class society is important. The capitalist development process produces external costs which must be borne by the entire community. Some of these—such as pollution, traffic congestion, blight, and crime—affect any area that is experiencing rapid, uncoordinated growth. These side effects of development are intrinsic to the very core of capitalism (Scott 1980). Because, under the existing arrangements of public policy, the private interests responsible for the external costs of growth are never called upon to remedy them, such effects constitute the major threat to the quality of life in the United States. Both O'Connor (1973) and Scott (1980) identify this form of uneven development as the central contradiction of the capitalist system, namely, the private expropriation of wealth and its social basis of production. Invariably, then, the public becomes burdened with the costs of growth. During the present phase of fiscal crisis, it has become increasingly more difficult for local areas to address this need, and the progressive erosion of the quality of life has intensified. This aspect of uneven development will be important in the discussion of urban public policy (see chapter 8).

There is a second way of understanding the sociospatial basis of uneven development characteristic of capitalism as opposed to other societies, one which was observed in chapter 2. Regional growth in capitalist economies manufactures spatial inequities. According to mainstream views of development, a self-adjusting process operates to equilibrate capital flows between regions. Thus an area which is initially impoverished can find itself at a comparative advantage — vis-à-vis labor and infrastructure costs—relative to places experiencing a boom. While capital investment initially follows the leading sector, eventually it will begin to flow back to regions that are less developed. Through competition, it is believed, the rate of investment and subsequently of profit moves back toward convergence and away from differences in spatial advantages. As indicated in chapter 2, marxian theory does not subscribe to such a view. Instead, regional development is perceived in terms of imbalance theory, as a *necessary* way in which capital accumulation takes place (Mandel 1975; Holland 1976; Amin 1976; Lipietz 1977). That is, capital works spatially to split geographic entities into unevenly developed centers and peripheries (Mandel 1975; Frobel, Heinrichs, and Kreye 1980). At the national level, for example, an analysis of the mature phase of capitalist development indicates a progressive disparity between well-off and less affluent sectors, derived from the restructuring of capitalist enterprise as part of the world system (Holland 1976). This disparity is also reflected in the new international division of labor (Cohen 1981; Frobel, Heinrichs, and Kreye 1980; Sassen-Koob 1984).

These trends suggest that uneven development is a global pattern and that imbalance theory will be the best way to capture the sociospatial effects of the growth process of Late Capitalism in the years to come. Yet, this assumption does not mean that we should subscribe to the functionalist devalorization theory of Harvey (1981). Clearly, aspects of the global nature of uneven development are associated with the other structural transformations we have considered, such as the production of split labor markets (Hodson and Kaufman 1982) and the transformation of industry by Late Capitalism (Bluestone and Harrison 1982; Tomaskovic-Devey and Miller 1982). However, while the uneven nature of capitalist development produces social and spatial effects, many of these are unintended. In chapter 2, I indicated that the restructuring of the large central cities in the United States has more to do with the global role of their corporate administrative and financial businesses than with any ties to the local region, especially with a need to devalue the surrounding built environment. Thus Lojkine, for example, has also emphasized the critical role of the big firms in restructuring the central city space of the large European communities. The relative isolation of such firms from the surrounding area's social, economic, and political activities is a result, already emphasized in chapter 2, which is at variance with ecological theory. It also suggests that the effects on the surrounding space are epiphenomenal to the location needs of multinationals. As Lojkine remarks, the behavior of the big firms can be characterized as a "privatization" of the economic infrastructure, devoid of multiplier effects for the local region, with the exception of employment (1977b: 145). Thus cities become the centers that are counterbalanced by peripheries which may be located thousands of miles away, often in third world venues. These parts of the world are tied together by the superprofits generated by uneven global development.

Large cities, however, also contain smaller and localized enterprises. Uneven development characterizes the relative way in which their prosperity has affected the surrounding area as well, but in a different sense. In particular, a kind of local imbalance theory operates by which prosperity produces blight and decay, as Scott has observed (1980; see chapter 3 above). Most marxists explain this phenomenon in terms of the logic of capital and see the devalorization of the built environment as functional for capital accumulation (Harvey 1981; Massey 1978). In contrast, I have asserted that this spatial pattern is also a consequence of the anarchy of location decisions and the uncoordinated nature of rapid secondary circuit investment. Thus, while some real estate projects are productive for capital accumulation, many are not, especially when we consider the social costs of such development as indicated above. Once large sections of the urban environment have slid into decay, it is then possible to purchase areas relatively cheaply for redevelopment. In this way the dead capital of the past, which presents a formidable barrier to development, can be obliterated and room can be made for new real estate efforts to turn over the exchange value of land. However, in the view advocated here, this process is much less functional for capital than is often thought—and, more important, it seems to operate wherever the misfortunes of capital accumulation have struck. Thus, for example, in many sections of the country factories abandoned by deindustrialization have been converted by real estate interests into shopping malls, fashionable boutiques, commercial stores, and lofts.

It is certainly doubtful whether "capital in general" has benefited by this transformation, yet profit takers in the property sector certainly have. Often the state is called in to intervene or subsidize such renewal and renovation. Both Lojkine (1977b) and Scott (1980), for example, observe that the central areas of large cities always contain small shops and family-owned businesses, most enjoying considerable if specialized trade. Such productivity constitutes a barrier to large real estate interests or growth networks looking to redevelop these areas. Thus, competitive capitalist enterprises and essentially sound housing can both be swept away, not because they have been devalorized but because they are in the way of monopoly interests manipulating the property sector. Invariably the state must be called in to intervene, on the side of the pro-growth interests, before the built environment can be turned over and resold at a profit, because many of the existing property uses have associated political constituencies which resist change. Thus central city development processes move against the locational uses of everyday business activity in favor of monopoly interests, just because more money can be made by turning over land and at the same time displacing minority and working-class community elements of the population in the name of progress. Both of these effects further enhance the sociospatial patterns of uneven development.

The history of renewal efforts and the strategic intervention of the state in favor of pro-growth networks seem to contradict the imbalance theory for intraregional comparisons. An equilibrating mechanism of sorts operates in central cities, albeit quite slowly, which is fueled by the relentless activities of the real estate circuit. We are thus left with two opposing tendencies, one which creates uneven development and the other which establishes the preconditions for equalizing the comparative advantages of locational growth. The combination of such tendencies does not, however, add up to a new equilibrium theory. The progressive effects of decay and renewal are explained by competition between fractions of capital and the ways in which the rate of surplus profit becomes equalized. Within a local context, the uneven pattern of development and its countertendencies occur because of the qualitatively different way in which fractions of capital expropriate space, including the clash between multinational monopoly interests, on the one hand, and locally based commercial interests, on the other.

As indicated above, there is an anarchic nature to the urban development process, and this produces social costs that argue against the functionalist view of the capital logic school regarding the nature of the production of space under Late Capitalism. State intervention merely exacerbates this conflict because it moves against the least powerful fraction, rather than acting in the general interest or even as a mediator, as both pluralist and Althusserian structuralists would suppose. Thus, Holland (1976) and Lipietz (1977) both possess blind faith in the ability of the state to counteract uneven development, while I view such intervention as contradictory in nature—doomed to promote growth only *within* the political and economic constraints of the existing social relations of production. In this manner the contradictory nature of state intervention is reproduced. Hence, the concept of uneven development refers in our case to the essential conflict over the expropriation of space among separate capitals and the inequitable environmental effects of the uncoordinated nature of this clash. The contentious and, therefore, political basis of the production of space will be illustrated in chapter 7, as it gives rise to new social cleavages that are specified in a manner separate from either capital logic or collective consumption theory.

In summation, uneven development in capitalist society (as opposed to its form in other modes) represents both a process of capital accumulation and a competitive relation between different fractions of capital. It is internal to the relations of production in a deep-level and multimanifested sense. These relations interact with the complex structure of the Late Capitalist social order to produce the antagonistic contradictions that are then deployed in space.

THE PRODUCTION OF SPACE: AGENCY AND CAPITALIST DEVELOPMENT

Up to this point in developing a synthesis, we have been concerned with identifying those structural features of Late Capitalism which distinguish it from previous phases and which are most important in the production of space. In an applied section I have indicated the ways in which more particular, epiphenomenal aspects of these features—such as the permanent war economy—are important to the study of sociospatial organization. While the general conditions for an understanding of comparative differences in the patterns of the built environment can be grasped by such an approach, it cannot, however, explain the production of spatial forms. To what has been said so far about structural transformations, I must add an emphasis on the specific interests which operate in society to channel the development process in those specific directions and projects which create the forms of the built environment. In short, an understanding of the production of space requires a synthetic approach which stretches across the twin poles of structure and action to unite both in a specification of the society-space articulation.

One thesis of the present discussion is that such an understanding comes from an emphasis on the specific societal interests—that is, economic, political, and social—which are organized around land itself. These include the real estate sector but also involve elements of finance and corporate capital, corrupt politicians, local booster groups, speculators, political parties in need of financial support, environmentalists, homeowners, and so on. These interests and the conflicts between them form the cutting edge of spatial changes which are spurred on by deep-level societal processes. In several previous sections I have traced out a line of discussion focused on the role of the real estate sector in this regard. Recall that attention was placed by Lefebvre on the secondary circuit of capital, which funnels excess capital into investment activities in the market for land. As discussed in chapter 3, Harvey has made good use of this concept and has developed it by specifying its structural characteristics, especially the relationship between the real estate sector, the state, and elements of the finance capital infrastructure which serve to entice capital to flow into this circuit during periods of overaccumulation. As indicated in the preceding chapter, arguments following the logic of capital fail to account for the precise manner in which secondary circuit activity is carried out. It is in this sense that a further elaboration of the central role which interests organized around land play in the production of space requires a specification of the actions of social groups in response to systemic incentives which channel re sources into the property sector.

An emphasis on property interests as the leading edge of capitalist relations in space calls for theoretical amplification in order to elevate such a notion above mere discourse or description. In what sense can this be accomplished? Once again we must face the limitation of work done in the past, work that merely refers to the actions of capitalists in a nominalist way. If capitalists are active in space, that is, in the transformation of the use values of social space to the exchange values of abstract space, how then can we specify the nature of their enterprise in a theoretical manner? Some sociologists, for example, follow Marx literally and consider individuals owning property and developing real estate as a separate class (Molotch 1976: 294). As we have seen, such a contention cannot be substantiated theoretically, because there is no class of "rentiers" in Late Capitalism. Most marxian political economists work with greater sophistication, postulating the existence of a separate fraction of capital organized around landed interests which they call property capital (Lamarche 1977; Cox 1981; Harvey 1975b). Boddy, however, has quite rightly observed that "there is no justification for distinguishing commercial capital functioning to realize the commodity *property* from that realizing any other commodity such as shoes" (1981: 279). In place of a separate fraction of capitalists, I agree with Boddy that we must consider landed interests under Late Capitalism as a separate *sector*, one that is structured around the secondary circuit of accumulation in the sense with which Lefebvre, as opposed to Harvey, conceives of that term. In chapter 5 I have specified the theoretical basis for this assertion, namely, that the value of urban land is a social product which can be exploited by anyone. Thus any individual, regardless of class, can potentially participate in the activities of the property sector, because land is a commodity which is convertible to many forms of exchange value and, in contrast to nearly every other commodity, it increases over time in its exchange value because capitalist relations require land to be expensive.

As Harvey and Boddy, among others, have also observed, the activities in the real estate market are sustained in part by a highly organized credit infrastructure attending to the needs of circulating capital. In this sense, fractions of financial, industrial, and commercial capital all combine with the state (Harvey 1975b; Hula 1980) to provide an organized structure for the property sector. The availability of credit and loans for investing in land enables capitalists and workers from any one of several fractions to engage in secondary circuit processes, making the actions associated with the property sector quite complex and often chaotic.

Having established this distinction, it remains to specify how the actions of a separate sector of capitalist development can produce the sociospatial forms of the built environment. Most often urban development is explained among neomarxists, or those nonmarxists who remain critical of ecology, as the result of activities associated with a growth coalition. In perhaps its earliest formulation, Mollenkopf and Pynoos pointed to the presence of a three-cornered relation between local politicians, bankers, and property owners or developers. These groups are bound together by a "solid coincidence of interest" in promoting growth (see also Salisbury 1964). As Mollenkopf and Pynoos note:

> Bankers and politicians get along well because, for the banker, the politician attracts depositors, provides important contacts, and ensures that no policies which are likely to hurt land values are adopted. For the politician, the banker represents a source of inside deals on development, a way of influencing mortgage decisions, and thus a way of influencing constituents, and a source of status. Hence there are many politicians on bank boards. (1972: 414)

In an earlier work (1977), I observed that what others have called growth coalitions are often composed of a select group of individuals forming a *network* which cuts across the private and public sectors, so that the two realms are indistinguishable. Thus political leaders may also be significant owners of property and may work with public advisory committees, such as zoning or variance boards, that include large property owners. Hence, public officials are also privately interested parties who work with private citizens who have public positions which can foster their private interests. In such cases, the concept of a growth "coalition" is too conspiratorial a term for what is a deep-level confluence of state-capital interests organized around the activities and ideology of growth at the local level. This phenomenon is produced by the structural way in which investment in the secondary circuit can always be considered attractive. Thus, in order to grasp the essential manner in which the property sector is the leading edge of spatial production, it is necessary to consider both the structural conditions for its activities and the ways in which separate actors—potentially from any social stratum, even the working class—coalesce into networks which then become active agents in the property sector.

In addition to the above distinction, there is a second aspect which separates what is to follow from previous approaches. Much of the development which has occurred in our large cities is a result of the actions of growth networks rather than the decisions of individual corporations, banks, and the like. Their popularity has been sustained by a general belief in the virtues of growth, especially its beneficial effects on employment levels (Friedland 1976; Mollenkopf 1975). Thus, the transformation of space always proceeds through the mediation of growth ideology. As Friedland remarks:

> In the period after World War II, major corporations and labor unions came together to forge new central city political coalitions. Organized around policies to maintain the city's economic growth and fiscal viability, the coalitions pushed forward with costly urban renewal projects, intrametropolitan transportation, industrial parks, development corporations, zoning variances, underassessments, subsidized water and power, and so on. Typically, the political coalitions were centered around strong Democratic mayors who had the partisan identification and organization necessary to deliver the city vote. (1976: 459)

In short, there are two important theoretical aspects of viewing the property sector as the leading edge of capitalist restructuring in space. First, only certain fractions of capital are involved in such coalitions. The morphology of settlement space assumes a form which is not necessarily functional for capital, only for certain fractions of that class. Because society has not reassessed the way in which it has allowed the property sector to structure the tenor of development, the production of space carries with it substantial costs as well as benefits. Second, property sector activities are the product of a complex conjuncture between institutional features of Late Capitalism and groups which come together to take advantage of spatial restructuring. Requiring ideological justification, the interests behind the property sector use the concepts of boosterism and the myth of growth to legitimate their activities. On the other side, opponents of this process counter with the ideology of no growth or community control. Consequently, the uncoordinated struggle over the production of space is enjoined at the ideological level of society as well as at the political and economic levels. In short, the clash between growth and no growth represents a basic cleavage in society, involving economic, political, and ideological practices, which remains unrecognized by most analysts of urban development. Indeed, the clash of pro growth versus no growth is as fundamental to the production of space as is the struggle between capital and labor.

In chapter 3, I indicated that certain political economists, such as Scott and Roweiss, oppose explanations for urban form which focus on the manipulatory abilities of growth coalitions. As these two remark: "From an epistemological point of view, the singling out of the property development (and finance capital) interests as the villain of the piece seems to us strained and artificial" (1978: 52). It is clear, however, that such objections miss the essential point of studying the activities of development networks. As has been shown, theorists working in the growth network tradition have all erred by hypothesizing that a separate class or even a separate fraction is involved. Thus Scott and Roweiss are correct in calling for a return to an understanding of capitalist "deep structural" relations of production in order to explain urban development. Yet, such a failing cannot be grounds for dismissing the need to identify the specific form of agency which carries out the structurally induced patterns of development, especially investment in the secondary circuit, which cuts across class lines. It is precisely the manipulation of space by powerful interests as growth networks which produces the unique features of the built environment.

Growth networks have the following characteristics which set them apart from other social agents. First, they are often combined public-private coalitions which also include elements of organized labor and which support themselves through local bureaucracies deeply dependent on growth. Thus, the activities of growth networks involve the direct intervention of the state as well as a certain political relation articulated as public support for party leadership.

Because local government requires political legitimation, it is sensitive to citizen demands. If by chance opposition to growth should aggregate to a sufficient level, it can fundamentally affect the ability of growth networks to carry out their objectives. In this sense, growth networks are not mere economic manipulators of space but are constrained by the political process. As Mollenkopf has observed, opposition to many of the activities of such groups in our large cities during the 1960s has resulted in greater visibility for their effects. Consequently, "Fewer decisions can be made behind closed doors, more diverse voices must be consulted and community interests must be balanced against business desires" (1981: 105). Thus the business climate or the relative ability of communities to offer development interests free rein in pursuing their activities has become a major consideration for businesses at the present time. In effect, localities vie for the right to be manipulated!

Second, while the same local commitment to development may exist in a wide variety of areas, the composition of growth networks can change from place to place. In some cases a coalition can include labor and, hence, elements outside the capitalist class. For such an instance, the claim that it is "capitalists" who produce the built environment requires a certain amount of circumspection. Most often it is the construction and building trade unions which actively support development and which even become successful as partners in growth networks (Friedland 1980). At times minority and civil rights groups, such as representatives of the black community, are found to be members of networks, as in New Orleans (Smith 1983). Thus, it is necessary to study the composition and behavior of growth networks according to this locational variability. In addition, it is also important to study the full range of ties from overt political coalitions to loosely structured real estate interests, which make up the growth networks boosting development. In fact, this inquiry frames a major field of new research following this transformed perspective.

Third, fractions within the capitalist class, especially among the competitive sector and those monopolists who can manipulate development, can work within these networks in different ways. Thus, the actual form which growth assumes may reflect contentious issues raised between monopolistic interests which operate outside the constraints of competitive capital and businesses merely interested in obtaining choice locations within the urban development matrix (Lipietz 1977). Most important, competition among monopolistic developers may result in the building of projects that affect each other's ability to grow, as in the overproduction of shopping centers. Often this phenomenon can be seen in suburban areas as the boarded-up and empty stores associated with shopping center blight. The tendency toward the overproduction of commercial developments invariably spreads local markets too thin, with any one of several results, such as the closing of some centers, high turnover in malls which remain open, and boom-and-bust cycles of shopping activity. Furthermore, the anarchy of production, which Marx observed operating in industry, can also be seen in the uncoordinated manner in which centers and malls are constructed. Competition which is of a speculative nature tends to pressure the real estate sector to overproduce, especially in the case of office buildings, which are often used as tax shelters. This phenomenon is especially important for small-scale developers, who operate to fill in the margins of growth or who restructure space after building by such turnover schemes as the conversion of rental housing into condominiums. In short, the relatively unbridled ability of growth networks to push development results in the irrational effects of overproduction through competition within and between fractions of capital. Importantly, this effect is relatively independent of cycles in the secondary circuit of capital accumulation, even though the intensity of competition is fueled by the general availability of capital in that circuit. For this reason, any place at any time can become the object of interest for elements of the property sector. This phenomenon and its often contentious nature form another central domain of new research, as it also helps fuel the process of deconcentration.

Fourth, in any given area, there may be more than one network which is active in manipulating public and private decision-making processes in the turnover of land. Thus, there may be competition between rival groups within the property sector. The development of space, therefore, is highly political, even if the property sector works to prevent ordinary citizens from perceiving that aspect of its nature. At times the actions of growth networks are not necessarily unopposed. Often, depending upon the socioeconomic characteristics of the community involved, coalitions may arise which seek to block the activities of development interests. The opposition between pro-growth and no-growth fractions represents a deeply rooted ideological battle over the uses of space. For this reason growth networks possess ideological as well as political and economic dimensions. Just as this organized opposition can be both political and economic, it can also attack through the ideology of no growth. In short, the interests organized around growth articulate with society at all levels, economic, political, and cultural. At present pro-growth interests generally involve both the monopolistic and highly concentrated segments of the capitalist class and the local government, because both require growth in order to survive. For this reason the concept of no growth is fought as one which threatens the very security of the country, despite the realization that alternatives to the present system of boom and bust exist (Thurow 1980; McRobie 1981). The pro-growth ideology preaches that more housing and commercial development will result in more people and greater sales, which will in turn produce more local tax revenues and more local jobs due to increased local spending. Thus everyone benefits, even those who don't need employment but who like lower taxes. The no-growth ideology emphasizes a different perspective. Development brings more people to an area than local institutions, such as schools and hospitals, can service. Thus, the downward pressure on taxes is most often overcome in the later stages of growth by the need for greater fiscal expenditures. Furthermore, increased development of land produces pollution, traffic congestion, and ultimately higher crime rates.

The significance of these clashing ideologies is that they support local efforts which constitute a portion of community politics. Quite simply, fiscal matters associated with the collective consumption problematic do not circumscribe the entire political agenda of local, county, and state politics. In addition, there are important contentious sociospatial issues concerning development which are also deeply dividing and, therefore, politically disputed at local levels of government (see Gottdiener, forthcoming). Even in cases where projects have already been built, local citizens often attempt to renegotiate the costs of growth, which they may have only recently discovered affects them adversely. Hence, the relative vulnerability of the growth networks and the conflicting nature of their separate fractions provide a second way to specify the contents of local politics in addition to issues involving fiscal disputes. Inquiry into this feature is an important source of new research on urban politics as well.

Finally, in their most amorphous forms, growth networks often work behind the scenes, in a corrupt manner, to exploit rapid development even if they do not actively advocate it. Thus, in a case study of a Long Island township (Gottdiener 1977), it was revealed that a select group of political leaders, town officials, lawyers, developers, and speculators worked in concert to exploit development for their own multiple purposes. Party leaders, for example, sought to raise funds for political campaigns by catering to independent real estate interests. Public officials took bribes in return for favorable zoning, variance, and tax decisions. Party leaders, lawyers, and speculators often worked together to obtain a small number of rezonings which made them individually wealthy. In short, the very process of development, which operates in some areas without the direct aid of a pro-growth coalition, may be exploited by a select group of local elites for party and personal gain. This can occur even in cases where there is no strong local leadership. Such networks form something like a business which makes money by virtue of control over land use rather than capital.

The degrees of freedom which enable amorphous networks of politicians and merchants to turn over a profit in land at the public's expense are provided by the relative autonomy of the secondary circuit of capital itself. Therefore, it is important to consider the actions of growth networks as part of the larger generic category of all special interests that produce and restructure space, whether they meet actively in concert or not—a feature which coalition adherents ignore because of their endemic functionalism. Thus, for example, it is often the case that large development firms have internalized many of the functions found in a typical growth coalition. Such large real estate corporations may have separate offices devoted to speculation and development, architectural design, market research, and even public relations—all employing people as liaisons to local government. Consequently, while I have used the word "network" as the best way to describe the confluence of structure and action associated with the property sector as the leading edge of spatial restructuring, I do not mean to imply that I am always referring to some back room where land deals are worked out by business owners and politicians. Often the manipulation of the environment for special interests occurs through a decision-making process which is initiated in the most professional surroundings of the corporate business world.

Invariably, through its actions, the state–property sector articulation modifies the development pattern for the worse because it is propelled by the drive for growth and because secondary circuit activity is uncoordinated. Hence, the activities of pro-growth networks constitute an additional source of uncoordinated spatial patterns alongside those stemming from the internal logic of capital accumulation (Scott 1980) or those deployed by conflict and negotiation between separate class fractions. As with other actions of the property sector, spatial outcomes have winners and losers. The latter, in particular, are those who must bear the external costs of growth—who sometimes form no-growth coalitions. Consequently, development is usually accompanied by contentious issues which can produce political conflict. The form of the built environment is, therefore, a product not only of the actions of growth networks but of the results of attempts at renegotiating those actions on the part of other groups carrying the costs of growth. This process provides the contents for the sociospatial politics which is increasingly characteristic of the local state and which supplies a dimension separate from those specified by the theory of collective consumption (Gottdiener, forthcoming; Boyte 1980; Hartman et al. 1982). Such a process creates an additional source of new topics which require investigation.

In sum, the built environment assumes a form which represents the features of Late Capitalism but which does not reflect any set of coherent sociospatial imperatives produced by that system. While the general availability of capital for the secondary circuit may govern in cyclical fashion the overall intensity of activity in the real estate sector, it cannot explain the specific form which development takes. Sociospatial patterns of development are explained by the actions of growth coalitions and networks along with the negotiations and conflicts involving those groups and other class fractions. This is frequently played out as a clash between pro- and no-growth ideologies; however, most often the property sector works unopposed—and for this reason it constitutes the leading edge of the Late Capitalist production of space. Over time the costs of this development process can be renegotiated by those asked to bear them. In such cases, and they are not many, space is once again altered to conform to the needs of other interests (Blumstein and Salamon 1979). A significant proportion of political activity at the local, county, and state levels involves just these sociospatial concerns (see Gottdiener, forthcoming). In addition, the resulting process of growth involves separate sources of irrational and uncoordinated patterns. The costs and benefits of growth produce effects on localized populations best described as uneven development. Finally, the anarchic nature of spatial development fuels a boom-and-bust cycle of growth which no one considers particularly attractive but which the present system of property relations makes impossible to change. I shall address the public policy implications of this process in chapter 8.

It is now time to illustrate how the argument synthesized above can be applied to the particular, in this case to the transformation of sociospatial changes in the United States. Before proceeding to this task, however, one additional comment suggests itself. The social production of space perspective specified by the dialectical articulation between agency and structure differs from the mainstream perspective in a central, qualitatively unique sense. Conventional theory at its core views the built environment as the outcome of myriad demand decisions made by large numbers of separate urban actors: merchants, bankers, homeowners, and the like. In my view the forms of space are produced, in contrast, by what has been specified as the articulation between Late Capitalist structures and the actions of the property sector, especially the effects of select groups and the state in channeling the flow of social development into specific places and shapes. It is the latter process—heretofore neglected as a topic of study—which forms the core of the "new" inquiries engendered by the realization that space is produced by a social process of *structuration*, so that if it is presently unguided except by callous personal gain it can nevertheless be harnessed in the future for the general good.

7. The Restructuring of Settlement Space

As early as the 1960s, Scott Greer published several books in which he called attention to the "increase in societal scale" sustaining regional urban development (1962, 1965). By this he meant the effects of technology on society, in the best mainstream tradition, and the progressive increase in the complexity of horizontal and vertical social organization which it caused. At the time, Greer observed a metropolitan area which remained differentiated by a bounded central city, on the one hand, and an expanding suburbanized hinterland, on the other. Since then, urbanized regions have matured to their present-day multicentered, unevenly developed form. Over the past two decades, the societal scale has increased through several stages of internal differentiation. Furthermore, the nature of metropolitan development is dependent as much on the growing power of oligopolistic corporations, state bureaucracies, and the many other aspects of the new sociospatial relations discussed above as it is on technology itself.

At present, regionwide deconcentration characterizes the growth patterns of settlement space. Such a process involves both agglomeration and decentralization dispersed on an expanding regional scale. Commerce, industry, cultural amenities, local political structures, and financial sources have all deconcentrated from historical city centers. At the same time, forces at work have concentrated certain functions within particular places, such as the location of financial administration and tourism within the downtown sections of cities. Linking the myriad activities across regional space are hierarchical modes of social organization meshed together by telecommunications, electronic fields of information processing, and the massive exchange of population through modes of commutation. If the present moment possesses a phenomenal form of capital—the multinational corporation—then the phenomenal form of space correlated with Late Capitalism is the deconcentrated metropolis.

Through the fallacy of hypothesizing distinct stages linked to distinct forms, such as the corporate city, marxian political economists have failed to develop an analysis equal to an appreciation of the present scale of sociospatial organization. Furthermore, political economists and marxian structuralists alike understand spatial forms as the containers of social processes, such as capital accumulation, the reproduction of labor, or world system restructuring. The epistemological position argued for by the production of space perspective asserts that sociospatial phenomena are both products and producers. Deconcentration is both a product of contemporary changes and a process of sociospatial organization which reacts back on other processes. Thus, my approach contrasts with other critical perspectives in that, while they view spatial forms as functional for capitalism—either, for example, in accumulation or in the reproduction of labor—I do not view them in this way. Certain aspects of space are functional for fractions of capital while others are not. The uncoordinated manner in which sociospatial restructuring occurs is especially dysfunctional for certain fractions of capital as well as for the working class, thus making the production of space itself one more element in the antagonistic nature of capitalist social relations.

The present chapter addresses an understanding of deconcentrated metropolitan space as a phenomenal form which stands in contrast to the impacted nodes characteristic of nineteenth-century capitalism. One purpose will be to demonstrate the operation of contemporary transformation across *all* of space, to avoid the type of limited analysis which merely focuses on the centers of urban agglomeration. In keeping with the approach adopted here, it must be remembered that the deconcentrated region was not caused by Late Capitalism. Rather, both social and spatial restructuring have been taking place conjointly and for quite some time. In fact, the hegemony of Late Capitalist relations requires the restructuring of space just as much as the latter depends on the social forces of the former.

In the *Grundrisse* (1973), Marx unveiled the relation between the city and the country as being dependent upon a subfield of the relations of production which he called modern landed property. The extension of capitalist relations to agriculture was a necessary *precondition* of urban growth. Without it, the city factories could not have enjoyed a labor pool overflowing with workers, nor could labor power be reproduced within cities at the scale necessary for industrial expansion (see Hilton 1976). Marx's style of analysis suggests that an understanding of the transformations brought about by Late Capitalism should also begin with agriculture. The new relations of production support deconcentration—they have dissolved the distinction between the city and the country and allowed industrialization's "second nature" to spill over onto the furthest reaches of the environment. Let us, therefore, begin our analysis of the articulation between Late Capitalist transformations and the form of settlement space with a discussion of the ways in which such changes have affected agriculture and the countryside.

THE TRANSFORMATION OF RURAL SOCIETY

In chapter 1, I indicated that the sociospatial dichotomies of conventional spatial analysis no longer apply to the concrete aspects of modern living. This is especially the case for the urban-rural contrast which once constituted the very backbone of Chicago School sociology. Recent research on the rural areas of modern societies concludes that they have been transformed by the pressures of Late Capitalism (Buttel and Newby 1980). In fact, there is little question that the three new sociostructural transformations associated with the contemporary phase of development—state intervention, global bureaucratic organization, and the technoscientific knowledge revolution—have thoroughly modified the agricultural process and, consequently, the social basis of rural life, which once depended upon such economic activity. According to Shover, for example, the end of World War II is considered the "great disjuncture," as it demarks the period when agriculture was changed into an industrialized, global enterprise of giant corporations that mass-produced food for a profit (1976). As Vogeler has carefully substantiated, the rise of agribusiness has meant the eradication both of the family farm and of the small town which went along with it. He observes:

> U.S. agriculture has been fundamentally transformed in the last fifty years. In 1920, when the farm population was first enumerated separately, about one American in three lived on farms. By 1977, about one person out of twenty-eight, or 3.6 percent of the nation's 216 million people, had a farm residence. This transformation has meant a massive shift in the farm population. (1981: 3)

As early as 1944, the anthropologist Goldschmidt analyzed the effect of agribusiness on the social fabric of the residential farming community. Small towns associated with family farming had more schools, doctors, religious organizations, local merchants, and in-town services and a more equitable class structure than towns tied to agribusiness. While this early study has been criticized, its results were replicated in 1977 and again in 1978 (Peterson 1977; Fujimoto 1978). As summarized by Vogeler:

> On the basis of educational, social and cultural facilities; educational attainments; socio-economic characteristics; and a range of retail businesses, the differences found in Arvin and Dinube [California] in 1944 still held in 1977. Areas with large-scale farming and undemocratic water districts had noticeably fewer towns that provided a smaller range of services. On the other hand, towns associated with small-scale farming had proportionately more elementary schools, dentists, pharmacies and medical specialists. (1981: 262)

The rise of agribusiness and its takeover of agriculture have been well documented (Hightower 1975; Danborn 1979; Berry 1972; Shover 1976). Agribusiness is comprised of highly concentrated oligopolistic interests which have restructured the organization of agriculture and the farming enterprise through the introduction of large farms and/or increased specialization of food production; the capitalization of production and a progressive reduction of labor needs at the farm level, with a concomitant transfer of food production functions from the farm into factories; adoption of the "firmlike" corporate-bureaucratic form for food production, with company interests in productivity and efficiency; a progressive integration of production into the global economic system and its commodity market flows; and, finally, the specialization of farm production itself as one part of a total conglomerate system involving the handling, merchandising, and marketing of food (Shover 1976: 149). These characteristics are in marked contrast to the farm under the earlier period of capitalist production. At present, the agribusiness industry is dominated by giant oligopolistic corporations—the small family farm is overshadowed by what has become a global enterprise of big money (Sale 1975; Hightower 1975). In addition, the proportion of the work force identified as farm labor, around 4 percent in 1970, is merely the tip of an industrial iceberg of workers deployed in other aspects of food production and distribution—as much as 25 percent of the nation's total labor force (Shover 1976). The importance of this interlocking specialization is that it is no longer shaped locationally by transport costs alone; instead, activities in support of direct farm production, such as processing, can take place in part almost anywhere, although they are found more often than not in traditional agricultural regions. Furthermore, this labor force is comprised of semiskilled blue-collar as well as white-collar service workers, with only a limited number offering skills directly related to the growing of food. This change in the labor force and in the location of farm-related activity has had a devastating effect on the small town.

In addition to becoming aware of the transformation produced by the switch from the small family farm to the multinational conglomerate with investments in agriculture, it is important to note that agribusiness has been made possible by massive state intervention since the 1930s. This state activity has taken several forms, including direct subsidies to business, subsidization of research and development, the structuring of financial sources, and the support of farm-related education. In fact, congressional acts from 1937 to 1973, such as the Bankhead-Jones Farm Tenant Act of 1937, the Agricultural Adjustment Act of 1938, the Agricultural Act of 1954, and the Agricultural Consumer Protection Act of 1973, have made agriculture the most heavily subsidized industry in America. According to Shover, for example, the Department of Agriculture, which administers the state agribusiness partnership, employs eighty-three thousand people, making it the second-largest public bureaucracy after the Department of Defense (1976). The activities supported by this department involve massive amounts of money devoted to scientific and technological research. In fact, agribusiness was made feasible by the form of technological innovation associated with Late Capitalism. In this scientific endeavor, land grant colleges have figured prominently as a means by which the state has subsidized technological innovation for the oligopolistic agribusiness interests (Vogeler 1981). In short, agribusiness is very much like any other segment of monopoly capital, only more so.

As we have already noted, the penetration and subsequent domination of agriculture by agribusiness have reduced the number of towns devoting themselves to family farm life and have irretrievably altered the rural landscape—with some resistance and much demographic uprooting of the farm population from the traditional rural town. In this manner, rural settlement space itself has been transformed into a space servicing the needs of agribusiness. This has been substantiated by a growing body of literature (Hansen 1973; Brinkman 1974; Berry 1972; Danborn 1979). Studies of agribusiness indicate that the effect of monopolistic dominance and concentration of food production has been one not of reducing greatly the total acreage under cultivation but of drastically diminishing the number of farms and of shifting the production of food away from the Northeast and Midwest to the sunbelt (Sale 1975; Coughlin 1979). As a result, those people once traditionally farming are no longer doing such work. Furthermore, the intersection between agribusiness and agriculture has not been uniform. It has taken place by virtue of the Late Capitalist form penetrating the social relations of the previous mode. This process has its spatial correlate: a kind of uneven development has occurred in which certain areas have been left behind to languish in a traditional agricultural form disconnected from agribusiness markets or financing arrangements (President's Commission 1967). Because the small holding or family farm can no longer compete with agribusiness, these unabsorbed segments have become increasingly impoverished over the years. Such areas appear as rural pockets of poverty, and it was once fashionable to blame the inferior economic conditions found there on a country "culture of poverty." From our perspective we may guess, however, that rural poverty pockets were once able to support themselves. Thus, the activities of agribusiness have produced effects on space which are largely unplanned and uncoordinated.

By way of concluding this section, it is worthwhile to reflect on the effect agribusiness has had on its functional role in reproducing Late Capitalist relations. The main result, it seems, has been as a help in freeing up land for speculation or urban development, in concert with other factors in real estate conversion. This is so because, while agribusiness does not require control of all farmland, it does prevent small farmers from working their own property at a profit. Hence it becomes more lucrative to sell the old homestead to speculators or developers if the opportunity arises—and it usually does. As Sale has observed (1975), because agribusiness is geared to the scale of the large farm, production has shifted to the sunbelt and has made the family farm in other sections of the country less feasible. This has added further to the pressures on farmers in these areas to sell to developers.

A second effect of the shift to agribusiness arises because it operates just like any other Late Capitalist industry. Consequently, it reproduces the very same needs for an industrial labor force, technological innovation, management expertise, government intervention and subsidies, and global economic policy as does the rest of Late Capitalism. In brief, then, the domination of agriculture by agribusiness means that there is now one less area where individual enterprise can escape from present-day sociospatial relations of production, and there is one additional area in which Late Capitalist relations hold sway. Thus, agribusiness aids in the reproduction of the social formation by making the same demands as industry on the labor force, on the state, and on other fractions of capital. In fact, the takeover of agriculture by agribusiness signals the hegemony of Late Capitalist relations in modern society.

In short, sociospatial transformations embodied in agribusiness have produced a progressively increasing supply of land ready for urban and suburban redevelopment, especially in the frostbelt, where large amounts of land have been converted to nonagricultural use. These transformations have reduced the number of workers permanently located on farms and have shifted the employment center of gravity in the agricultural industry to blue-collar industrialized processing and marketing plants located in cities. They have made farming less feasible as an occupation for individuals, and they have restructured rural towns that were once based upon the family farm into agribusiness centers characterized by a much more limited array of people-oriented services. In this way contemporary relations of production which structure the activities outside of agriculture also do the same within that activity, so that the hegemonic control of Late Capitalism is complete. In a sense the pristine, peopleless town produced by agribusiness is the rural correlate of present-day central city areas, because monofunctional instrumentality takes over the community as the ludic center of communion disappears. The principal result of sociospatial transformations in Late Capitalism can thus be expressed as the destruction of centralized community life—a process begun in the Middle Ages with the rise of capitalism itself.

At this moment it is necessary to leave agriculture and address our main concern, the restructuring of urban space. In chapter 2, we worked through a preliminary approach to the central city. Let us pick up the threads of that argument and proceed to apply what has been synthesized in the preceding chapters. Two provisos must be mentioned at this time. First, the following offers a mode of spatial analysis which, for the sake of brevity, will be contrasted principally with mainstream approaches. The reader will have to refer to previous discussions for the differences between my approach and other critical perspectives (see also Gottdiener 1983). Second, because both mainstream and marxian analysts seem to be almost obsessed with the city, I have chosen to deemphasize this particular site in favor of demonstrating how the forces pertinent to the production of space operate in the same way everywhere. We began this application with so-called rural areas and will continue to focus on them, paying special attention to suburbanization and frostbelt-to-sunbelt shifts. For an analysis of central city restructuring, the reader is referred back to chapter 2 and to the increasing number of volumes by critical marxists on this subject.

In essence marxists tend to interpret sociospatial changes economically—as being caused by changes in the location of jobs and industry. I view changes as a dialectical outcome of political, cultural, and economic factors which manifest themselves through the leading edge of real estate development patterns linking state intervention, forms of capital accumulation, and the manipulation of land markets. Furthermore, please note that the following discussion assumes that changes in capital accumulation, the world system, and new labor strategies, for example, highlighted by the arguments of political economists, have all played a role in the restructuring of space (see, e.g., Smith 1984; Tabb and Sawers 1984; Dear and Scott 1981). What follows stresses other factors which are equally important and which may have been at work for a longer time. More significantly, the assertion argued for here is that the articulation between state intervention and the secondary circuit of capital constitutes the leading edge of sociospatial changes, although it is not the only cause of them. Thus, for example, if the world system is consolidated around the location of finance capital in the downtown sections of New York and Los Angeles, then political and real estate incentives paved the way for that particular aspect of spatial restructuring. Economic needs and sociospatial phenomena are not only dialectically related, they are not tied together by any a priori aspect of functional necessity or logic of capital alone.

THE THEORY OF METROPOLITAN EXPANSION

As I indicated in chapter 2, urban ecology can be viewed as consisting of two distinct paradigmatic thrusts labeled as the pre— and post—World War II schools of thought. The former revolved around the work of Burgess, McKenzie, and Park, while the latter consists of Hawley and his followers. Despite the conceptual differences between them, urban ecological thought retains as its core idea a theory of metropolitan expansion which attempts to explain urban morphology. Such a focus was as true for Burgess, for example, as it is for contemporary theorists. This focus sees changes in the central city as being linked organically to spatial patterns operating elsewhere. In Burgess' view, the city starts out as a single centralized core containing all the elements of metropolitan functional differentiation. Then, through a process of decentralization and fringe area development, there is a complex deployment of functional areas across the now famous zones surrounding the central business district. Burgess conceived of this process solely in terms of horizontal, two-dimensional relations, an epistemological position preserved up to the present by other ecologists. The city grows by virtue of outward extension and succession. That is, each specialized zone extends itself by crossing the fringe and invading the area adjacent to it. The activities of the zone then dominate the region through succession, thus forcing the next outer zone further toward the periphery. In Burgess' final picture the central business district is a specialized industrial, commercial, and administrative center surrounded by a zone of transition, with the outer zones assuming specialized residential functions along with scattered local centers of economic activity. The *deus ex machina* of Burgess' model is demographic growth activated by "locomotion," which then leads to greater economic competition and functional differentiation. This in turn generates greater complexity of social organization and, finally, the areal expansion of the metropolis itself.

While Burgess' model depended for its explanatory ability on biological analogy, especially with regard to the invasion-succession cycle, his original formulation did not clearly specify the precise way in which expansion occurred. That is, with Burgess we know how the zones come to differentiate themselves, but we do not know quite why such expansion occurs or why growth needs to assume the form that it does. In this way Burgess fell victim to egocentrism, and his model could not hold up under comparative study (Schnore 1965). Despite this fact, urban ecology clings for the most part to a version of metropolitan development which derives from Burgess conceptually, which has merely replaced the notion of spatial dominance with one of functional integration, and which has retained the same class of topological relationships between the city center and the urban periphery (Bourne 1971; Berry and Kasarda 1977; Sly and Tayman 1980).

In short, conventional theory is limited to a functionalist, one-dimensional mode of causal explanation. Yet, there are two variants of conventional treatments of metropolitan expansion. The first, almost wholly atheoretical, characterizes the work of descriptive analysts of aggregate census data. The second approach, as we have already indicated, involves the postwar theoretical tradition of Hawley. In the former case, population migration is used as an independent variable and metropolitan expansion is conceived solely in terms of functional differentiation. The point here is not that migration does not affect metropolitan organization—clearly it does—but that such analyses proceed without any attempt to understand why both demographic demand-side deployment and functional differentiation have occurred in the first place. Mainstream analysts have only a primitive understanding of the associated factors and forces involved in social change, if they consider such underlying elements at all

(Biggar and Biasiolli 1978; Frey 1979; Sly 1972). Such atheoretical work can at times reach the very heights of anthropomorphic reification, where it is "functions" themselves that invade, succeed, and strive to balance each other:

> At the earliest stages of metropolitan development all the functions of the community are located in one relatively compact area; through the process of invasion and succession they move outward at the same time that formerly independent communities are brought within the dominance of the metropolitan area . . . At advanced stages of metropolitanization the lines separating ring from core and functional segregation of the two become less and less pronounced. That is, the rings increasingly take on many of the functional characteristics of the core and the core takes on many of the functional characteristics of the rings—with each there emerges a functional balance. (Sly and Tayman 1980: 122)

The above description is so generalized that it could fit just about any situation. However, it tells us nothing about metropolitan form, only that whatever is happening in space occurs with a "functional balance." By excluding any consideration of uneven development and by focusing analysis on the action of functions rather than the differential interaction of social groups, such work is ideological. Implied in the above formulation are the two processes of growth, centripetal and centrifugal, which were given a refurbished theoretical basis in the postwar ecological tradition of Hawley. In his view, society has grown complex and the bounded city form has assumed its present shape by virtue of technological innovation. In particular, such innovation has resulted in the outward migration of population, as well as in the ability of metropolitan communities to coordinate and integrate the growing complexity arising from activities spread out over progressively greater areas. In fact, for Hawley the population community can expand only by concentrating coordinating functions *within* its "nucleus," and we have seen the fallacy of this assertion in chapter 2.

According to Hawley, technological change in overcoming the friction of space is the prime causal agent of expansion, because without ease of movement a process of "cellularlike fission" arises, which he calls segmental growth, in which the regional organism fragments into a series of smaller pieces that are homologous to the whole (Hawley 1972). Segmental growth is always present to a degree, due to political fragmentation (Stephan 1971). However, for Hawley, the influence of transportation and communication innovations has countered segmental development in favor of the horizontally deployed, functional integration which remains most characteristic of metropolitan development. The mainstream explanation of regional deconcentration rests on this technologically determinist formulation. Let us examine this approach and compare it with that of the critical paradigm.

THE MAINSTREAM PERSPECTIVE ON DECONCENTRATION

Conventional analysts explain deconcentration by following the implications of the ecological model. Accordingly, early deconcentration occurred because the use of commuter railways in cities and, later, the automobile promoted the separation of residence from work and also from shops. This in turn led to the spatial differentiation of the city in terms of economic and cultural functions. Territorial displacement of the relatively wealthy, due to the ease of commutation between jobs and residences, resulted in income segregation between the poorer stratum of the population, who remained near the city center, and the more affluent, who moved to the outer reaches of the metropolis. This then led to a functional reorganization of the cities and towns within the region.

Following the work of Gras (1922) and McKenzie (1933), urban ecologists sought to analyze the expansion of the metropolitan region primarily in terms of population migration (see chapter 2). The hallmark of such work is that it attempts to fix the shift in the demographic center of gravity from the central city to the suburbs around the 1920s, that is, during the decade when widespread use of the automobile became a reality in the United States (Hawley 1956; Thompson 1947; Schnore 1957). As Berry and Kasarda have indicated, this early work failed to correct for the ability of cities to annex their suburban areas, thus hiding suburbanization which took place at an earlier time (1977: 162). Following the techniques devised by Schnore (1962), recent studies have attempted to correct for annexation. Subsequent analysis which controls for this effect indicates that centrifugal dispersal of the population has been occurring since at least the turn of the century, that is, well before the mass production of the automobile. As Berry and Kasarda note, "When the distribution of population increase is adjusted for annexation, however, faster rates of growth in the suburban ring are shown to have occurred in every decade since 1900 for every regional grouping" (1977: 186). Thus, a more enlightened analysis by ecologists of the data which control for annexation revealed that it has only been since the 1920s and 1930s that suburbs have gained population in an absolute way when compared to cities. Prior to that period, suburbanization was occurring, but it was hidden from researchers by the ability of cities to enlarge their own political boundaries. This implies that, while technology may still prove to be one explanatory factor, ecologists have always had reason to doubt their own paradigm and to look for other important variables in the production of urban form.

A second measure of the alleged effect of the auto is said by Hawley to have occurred since 1920 as deconcentration or the progressive lowering of population density across the metropolitan region, especially within the central city (1981: 61). According to Berry and Kasarda again, however, "Not until the 1950 decade do density reductions appear for any age cohorts of central cities" (1977: 191). Furthermore, these density reductions are restricted primarily to the older cities. Thus, short-distance technology cannot be the cause of deconcentration. In addition, the ecological theory of metropolitan expansion leaves unanswered the source and causes of population influx to central cities, which had to have sustained their densities during the decades since 1920, when suburbanization accelerated. As all urban historians know, many more millions of people passed *through* our metropolises than is revealed by a static look at the total population of these centers. In particular, since World War II there has been a phenomenal population exchange between whites and such minority groups as blacks within central city borders. Hence, a good deal of the urban restructuring brought about by the changes in the types of people living in central cities has been ignored by mainstreamers, except through static, descriptive analyses of census data. According to mainstreamers, such movement can be explained by the exercise of preference, that is, demand. For example, Berry and Gillard (1977) cite popular preference for small towns and lower urban densities as causing population change. This fails to mention or even discuss the involuntary pressures which have shaped the preferences of people to move despite a desire to remain where they originally lived, such as government policies, corporate restructuring, job relocations, and the like. In short, the restructuring of metropolitan regions involves forces and modes of social change more complex than the few causal factors considered by ecological theory, while this approach also displays a certain insensitivity to the social costs produced by uncoordinated urban restructuring. In fact, as the material from Berry and Kasarda suggests, the mainstream explanation of deconcentration in terms of ecological theory has always been extremely weak, even according to its own research results.

At this point we must leave the ecological paradigm once again (I shall return to it one final time in the next chapter). In order to advance a full explanation of deconcentration, it is necessary to connect the structural characteristics of the mode of production to contemporary aspects of sociospatial form. I shall do so following the production of space perspective, which highlights the role of the state–secondary circuit articulation in this process.

THE CRITICAL PERSPECTIVE ON DECONCENTRATION

Since World War II, two related but geographically separate trends have been most characteristic of the sociospatial transformations associated with Late Capitalism. These include, on the one hand, the centrifugal shift of people, industry, and commerce from the central city to suburban regions and, on the other, the differential rate of growth that has altered the traditional balance of economic power from the Northeast and Midwest to the sunbelt states of the southern rim. The essential aspect of these inter- and intrametropolitan shifts is that they represent a boom period of rapid growth, clearly of an uncoordinated nature, which has until recently been experienced in every sector of the country. The recessionary phase of the economy since 1974 is but the dark side of a once rapid expansion which enabled sectors of society associated with Late Capitalist transformations, such as the aerospace industry, banking, and real estate, to penetrate the space formerly structured by less developed capitalist relations such as labor-intensive manufacturing. Let us consider these geographical shifts in turn, beginning with the intrametropolitan changes most often labeled as metropolitan deconcentration. In what follows I shall show that the production of space has occurred in the main not because of economic processes alone but, more specifically, because of a joint state–real estate sector articulation which forms the leading edge of spatial transformations.

Metropolitan Regional Deconcentration I: Housing

There can be no doubt that the vast bulk of suburbanization was produced by locational changes of residences rather than businesses; that is, postwar suburbanization took place with housing construction independent of changes in industrial location. This does not mean that locational changes in the latter sector did not play a fundamental role in deconcentration. Nevertheless, the movement of people to suburban regions is essentially a product of the real estate and construction industries' shift to supplying massive amounts of single-family suburban housing to consumers after the war years.

In the 1930s, only 44 percent of all housing units were owner-occupied. By 1974, that proportion had become 64 percent (Agnew 1981: 465). Furthermore, the *total* number of housing units in the United States has doubled since the war, thus changing the very nature of everyday life as the American family deconcentrated into a small nuclear group housed in single-family homes (Sale 1975). During the 1970s, the real estate and construction industries were the largest in the United States, with $100 billion in revenue compared to $13 billion for the auto industry. The building of single-family homes is the largest category of this economic activity. One indication of the importance of housing is seen in the fact that real estate agents represent the nation's most numerous licensed occupation. In addition, according to Agnew, since "more than half the assets of all banking institutions are mortgage or construction loans for 'home-building', the appreciation of land results in a high turnover rate so that consumers of housing have also become the largest producers by 'trading-up' or selling their homes to buy another at a rate which accounts for as much as seventy percent of all house sales" (1981: 465). The construction and sale of single-family homes, therefore, represent a core economic activity of the United States. Furthermore, the placement of such commodities almost overwhelmingly occurs in the suburban sections of our metropolitan regions. In fact, this postwar property market boom is especially responsible for the health of the sunbelt. Over 70 percent of all housing starts in the United States during 1974 were located in this region alone. Home construction there eats up a total of 700,000 acres a year (Sale 1975).

According to a number of marxian analysts, the massive switch to single-family homeownership is a direct result of the Keynesian recovery measures which were a response to the underconsumption crisis of the 1930s and which affected the banking industry especially severely (Harvey 1975a; Stone 1975; Bradford 1979). Single-family home construction was seen both as an important, perhaps primary way in which to restabilize effective demand and as a means of rescuing the banking sector from total collapse. In addition, by enabling workers to purchase private property and to incur long-term debt, homeownership became an effective force against the labor militancy of the depression (Harvey 1975a; Agnew 1981). As an extra benefit, the suburban life produced on such a mass scale by the switch in housing form became characterized by a need for high levels of personal consumption (Galbraith 1969; Davis 1984). While this was not planned, it certainly provided the boost in effective demand necessary for stable and rapid growth in the postwar years.

The suburbanization of homeownership is almost single-handedly the consequence of active state intervention. For example, during the same year that important agricultural recovery legislation was being considered, Congress passed the Housing Act of 1934, which established the Federal Housing Authority (FHA) and the Federal National Mortgage Association (FNMA), both of which guaranteed mortgages and were intended to subsidize the depression recovery of the banking and home construction industries. Subsequent acts passed in 1937, 1949, 1954, 1961, 1968, and 1970 cemented this long-standing government involvement in the built environment. It has often been repeated by mainstream analysts that suburban development has occurred because of an insatiable demand among Americans for the single-family home. However, such massive growth would clearly not have taken place after World War II were it not for the variety of government subsidies directed toward supporting the supply of that particular form of housing. In addition to the government programs already mentioned, which propped up both a housing industry and a real estate financial framework, admissible tax deductions also worked specifically to reduce the burden of mortgage payments and local property taxes on homeowners. In 1974 the combined subsidies from tax benefits accruing to homeowners amounted to $9 billion, of which the major portion was realized by those families making more than $20,000 a year (Stone 1975). In short, property ownership is so popular in the United States because people are literally paid to participate in the real estate market.

In the previous chapter, we observed the importance of what Lefebvre calls the secondary circuit of capital accumulation, namely, the real estate sector. The flow of capital into the real estate circuit requires both an interventionist state and a freely functioning capitalist money market, both of which were put firmly in place during the Keynesian restructuring of capitalism following the depression. It is the manner, nature, and locational specificity of investment in the secondary circuit which controls the way in which settlement space develops by its very essence as the conduit of money into real estate. In fact, according to Walker, by connecting the overaccumulation cycles in capitalism with the functional role of the secondary circuit it is possible to divide urban history roughly into fifty-year stages, corresponding to the fifty-year cycles of capital accumulation known as Kondratieff waves (1981: 406). There is the mercantilist period (1780–1840), the national industrial period (1840–1890), early corporate growth (1890–1940), and the advanced corporate era (after 1940). The production of the built environment and the changes in urban form are direct products of these capital accumulation cycles. The existence of such periods with regard to the dynamics of capitalism has been widely observed for some time; the Kondratieff long waves, in particular, are based upon solid empirical evidence (Day 1976; Schumpeter 1939; Kuznets 1960; Hoyt 1933; Kalecki 1968; Mandel 1975).

Both Walker and Harvey, then, follow Gottlieb (1976) and tie the cyclical nature of capital accumulation to the stages in the production of the built environment (see Watkins 1980 for other arguments). At the apogee of each upswing in the long wave, an overaccumulation crisis is produced within the primary circuit of capital so that a voluminous surge occurs in real estate investment and a rash of speculation is touched off, thus averting the crisis temporarily. As Lefebvre has indicated, however, such property sector investment in great volumes is unhealthy if the capitalist system persists in utilizing this conduit as a mechanism to overcome accumulation crises. Eventually this activity leads to the undercapitalization of the primary circuit (Lefebvre 1974; see also O'Connor 1981), because money dumped into real estate is then not available for production in the next period. Consequently, undercapitalization of industry sets in and the downswing of the fifty-year long wave begins. The discovery of such periods helps us understand the shifting forms of the built environment, despite the complex nature of production cycles. Such a view trivializes the technologically determinist approach of mainstream analysis, which ties the production of stages in urban growth to transportation innovations alone (Borchert 1967; Adams 1970; Hawley 1981) or to changes in the structure of industry (Thompson 1965a; Watkins 1980). According to Walker, the former mainstreamers date the stages of growth from midpoint to midpoint in the long waves of accumulation, when the surge in speculation is most active, thus taking appearance for reality and advocating research with spurious correlations (1981: 422).

To return to our discussion of the housing market, the actions of state intervention and the refurbishing of the monetary infrastructure in the United States imply that the mediating features necessary for the secondary circuit to play an active role in preventing overaccumulation cycles were first in place only after the 1930s. This puts the nature of deconcentration in a slightly clearer light than that cast by Walker and Harvey. The supply-side nature of housing and real estate development has not only worked well in overcoming depression features of the economy, it has perhaps worked too well. Since the 1940s economic resources have flowed into the secondary circuit on a massive scale, and regionwide development has become perhaps the distinguishing feature of Late Capitalism. In 1949 and in every year of the 1950s, single-family home construction, for example, was phenomenal, with over 1 million units being built each year. Across the nation between 1950 and 1970, 30.5 million housing units were constructed—over 10 million units *more* than the net increase in households for that period (Berry 1973). This overextension of investment in the secondary circuit was aided by the passage of the Federal Aid Highway Act of 1956, which established the interstate system of defense highways. This program was a virtual bonanza for speculators, as it helped tear open the rural periphery to suburban development and the second home recreation market.

At present the economy has so much of its resources invested in real estate that it is committed to rescuing this sector even during the current recession, when it needs to free up capital for reinvestment in productive activity. This is illustrated especially by the activities of banks, which have worked feverishly to salvage the value of central city land, representing heavy mortgage investment (see chapter 2). Such phenomena, however, call the cyclical theory of Walker and Harvey into question. Currently, despite the depression in the housing industry, with a virtual standstill of housing starts nationwide, real estate investment is still considered to be an excellent source of profits. Thus, such investment is immune from crisis, a result counter to what Walker and Harvey suggest. As Lefebvre has indicated, the secondary circuit, from being an "accidental" means by which capital has decided to solve its accumulation problems, has now become an "essential" mode of investment activity for the Late Capitalist economy.

In short, real estate activity reflects the role of space as a source of surplus value creation as well as realization, is relatively impervious to the cycles of capital accumulation except for switches in its investment forms (from, say, suburban housing to city office buildings and malls), and represents a more fundamental process of the creation of wealth than capital accumulation theorists have understood. For example, recently in the Los Angeles area, Chevron Oil announced a $1 billion development scheme with the purchase of a 673-acre former motor speedway site. According to a local newspaper report, the oil company spent $42 million to purchase the land and began immediate construction of a residential, commercial, and industrial development which would draw additional population and jobs to the area (*Progress Bulletin*, 1981). Clearly this billion-dollar project is financed by the oil company profits defended in industry propaganda as being needed to support the further exploration for and development of new sources of energy. It is the persisting attraction of real estate as a primary source of wealth-producing investment that prevents capital from flowing back into the type of primary circuit activity which is sorely needed by the economy at the present time. Consequently, political economic arguments by marxists focusing on crisis theories of accumulation must be jettisoned in favor of a new approach to cyclical activity, based upon the production of space perspective, which asserts that real estate is a source of surplus value creation, not just realization (see the discussion in chapter 5).

The manner in which suburban residential development has occurred has been detailed elsewhere (Gottdiener 1977). This case study of the development of the Long Island region adjacent to New York City revealed the following features of this process. First, single-family home development outside the central city was transformed by organizational, production, and financing arrangements after World War II from small-scale, custom-built construction to massive developments, such as the Levittowns, consisting of several thousand homes at once. In addition, the need for large tracts was met by the conversion of agricultural land to this purpose. Between 1958 and 1978, for example, it has been estimated that twenty-two thousand square miles of land was converted from agricultural to suburban use (Brown and Roberts 1978).

Second, in the earlier stages of suburban development, speculators preceded developers. Generally, speculators are the first group to penetrate a rural area, buying up available farmland and holding it for future subdivision as early as a decade prior to actual development. Eventually this activity, along with impending suburbanization, squeezes out the remaining farms. Speculators, therefore, comprise the leading edge of unplanned metropolitan expansion. While some of them may come from the local area, many are from outside and may have international connections and financing. In all cases the combined effect of their actions can be resisted only with great difficulty by individual farmers on the projected path of suburbanization. This type of speculation has been in existence for hundreds of years, and, as Bogue and Bogue observe (1957), it does not always result in large profits. Yet, it is the appeal of potential gain and the relative ease of holding undeveloped land in areas which crave growth which sustain the vitality of this aspect of the property sector.

Third, there are also divisions of labor and geographical distinctions among developers. Those from outside the area tend to build large projects, such as malls. Some specialize in extensive residential developments, while others build apartments and office buildings. Locals, in contrast, tend to operate on a smaller scale depending upon their access to funds. One particular type of local developer with a great impact is the spot builder, that is, a constructor of individual homes who takes advantage of the economies of scale created by larger residential developments. Spot builders often work closely with local political leaders in control of zoning and variance boards in order to obtain the necessary public permission for their activities, which can otherwise violate density and even zoning restrictions. The combined effect of their actions is to fill in the margins of development and thus help create the characteristic pattern of suburban sprawl.

Fourth, local government activities, including planning efforts, zoning, and building code regulation, are all highly politicized in favor of real estate interests. As McAdams (1981) has observed in a case study of mall construction, this affinity can be explained in part as a governmental subscription to the ideology of growth. In the case of the Long Island study, more personal reasons involving the use of public office for individual and party gain were also at the base of the observed close relation between government and real estate interests. Virtually any business proposing a development in the suburban township under study was received favorably by the local political leaders. In many cases, the local government acted to subsidize growth through a variety of interventions, including zoning concessions, tax abatements, public service provisions, and the like. Even professional planners who might otherwise lobby for a selective and more rational growth policy invariably worked with developers behind the scenes, away from the public eye, in order to obtain some concessions toward better planning. Public hearings then took place after such deals were worked out, but these were little more than ideological façades which created the false impression of citizen participation. The sum total of this receptivity to development coupled with public subsidies organized by the ideology of growth is often referred to as a good business climate.

In addition, local political leaders often use public office in a corrupt manner to realize personal and party gain from their elected ability to regulate land use in regions that are growing rapidly. The close cooperation between select individuals with political influence and real estate interests takes numerous forms and seems to vary according to the type of developer, the developer's point of origin, and the type of development. Occasionally, the select group of politicians and developers will manipulate the land-use decision-making process in order to acquire permission for a project which makes them money. Although the number of these decisions is quite small relative to the cumulative weight of all land-use judgments, their strategic nature determines the tenor of development patterns for the remainder of the local area and undermines planner attempts at controlling land use.

Finally, resistance to development priorities is largely unorganized and ad hoc. This is the case despite the presence of local civic and homeowner associations, which in some instances have been active in the area for many years. In general, local areas lack any mechanisms which can provide divergent community interests with a unified perspective on growth. Although the political party can play this role, its inherent weaknesses and limited support make it more responsive to real estate interests, because those are the ones most dependent upon the unique local powers of government. Consequently, citizen opposition to development, while quite vocal at times, has little cumulative impact on the suburbanization process. Once growth occurs, however, its impact is felt unevenly by local residents. Those bearing the greater inconveniences and costs often attempt to modify the features of the built environment and make them more to their liking. This generates a renegotiation process between local residents and authorities, which often winds up with a restructuring that only exacerbates the results of uncoordinated development (Gottdiener 1977). The growth of metropolitan regions under these circumstances raises important political issues which have yet to be resolved and which, in fact, have persisted in being ignored by government policy.

The sum total of the actions organized within the structure of capitalist development finds spatial form being produced by this intersection between the local state and the secondary circuit of real estate. At this local level, in fact, there is little difference between economic and political interests—they are both articulated under the sign of growth. The end result of suburbanization is an entirely new version of settlement space. Individuals are sheltered from others with different socioeconomic statuses by residential exclusivity and spatial distance. The social space of the city's public life has been broken up and reinserted within the framework of commercial expropriation. On the one hand, everyday life transpires inside the individual suburban home, where only family members and select friends meet. On the other hand, public activities no longer take place in a ludic village center, with its particular social space and civility. They occur increasingly in the large malls or shopping centers under the auspices of the property owners. Recently, malls have added cultural events in a thinly disguised simulation of everyday city life meant to attract daily customers. Several analysts of the new organization of suburban space have commented on the displacement of public life into the commercial venue of malls. According to Feagin, for example: "Unlike downtown streets and village squares, shopping malls are private property. Shopping center owners can prohibit malls from being used for purposes [with] which they do not agree," such as political discussions, campaigning, and social interaction, especially among teenagers (1983: 22).

According to our present perspective, the indictment of suburbia comes not from a cultural critique, which cannot be developed here despite what has been said above, but from the ways in which the state–real estate sector articulation promotes uncoordinated change on a massive scale. Far from representing a direct policy of land-use planning and development, most government activity has operated behind the scenes, removed from the participation of those people most affected by suburban growth, including those who reside in the central city. Thus a certain failure of the public trust is evidenced in the uncoordinated and uneven development patterns of metropolitan expansion, which ignores the communion of social space in favor of exchange value production and reproduction. To be sure, there are strong, even irresistible incentives to live in areas outside the central city. However, the very presence of these areas does not prove that free choice has been exercised over the years by the millions of Americans now living there, as most mainstreamers like us to believe through analyses which stress only demand-side considerations. On the contrary, suburban space has been produced by the state–real estate sector articulation, which has fostered a particular form of secondary circuit activity instead of alternatives, such as planned and coordinated growth, that could just as readily have been tried and that might have preserved community values in the city as well as in the hinterland. Consequently, the present form of metropolitan expansion represents less the desires of its many residents, as ecological theory leads us to believe, than the uncoordinated activities of this leading edge of capital disguised by the ideology of growth. The outcomes of this development process are then renegotiated by those who bear its costs. Thus the sociospatial environment represents both the interests involved in the property sector and the materialized scars of the political renegotiation between the initial profit takers and the eventual users of settlement space, as the latter vainly battle to recreate some form of consociation within the hostile environment of unrelenting secondary circuit activity and its constant turnover of land.

A second spatial feature of Late Capitalism has been the decentralization of economic capacity, especially manufacturing, from the core areas to the periphery. This shift is also of two geographical natures, involving an intrametropolitan drift to the suburbs in every area of the nation and an interregional movement of industrial activity to the sunbelt and away from the "American Ruhr" of the East and Midwest. Let us consider this next.

Metropolitan Regional Deconcentration II: Industry

Virtually all analysts of industrial shifts to the suburbs note that growth represents the construction of new plants rather than a move of central city businesses to suburban locations (Watkins 1980; Rees 1978; Harrison 1974; Struyk and James 1975; Mueller and Morgan 1962; Wheat 1973). Some analysts even contend that, while central cities have lost manufacturing over the years, they continue to attract new plants. That is, the relative share of new business locations between cities and suburbs has turned in favor of the latter; however, central cities have by no means been abandoned by manufacturing, as some analysts suppose (Struyk and James 1975; McClellan and Seidenstadt 1972). According to Berry and Kasarda, central cities incurred only a 4 percent loss in manufacturing in the postwar years before 1967, while employment increased by 94 percent in the suburbs (1977: 232). Since the 1970s, analyses of national trends agree that industrial growth has virtually ceased in the central cities of the frostbelt, with the suburbs capturing the lion's share of all new plant construction, even in many sunbelt regions (Burchell and Listokin 1981; Sternlieb and Hughes 1975).

The standard mainstream explanation for contemporary patterns of industrial deconcentration focuses, as we might expect, on the effects of technology, which have changed industrial methods as well as lowering transport and communication costs (Leven 1978b; Berry and Kasarda 1977). According to James, for example:

> [Older cities] have declined because they have continued to rely on old manufacturing industries which appear to have limited potential for future growth, and which have proved vulnerable to setbacks in the centers of production in relatively newer, high technology industries. (1981: 35)

As is the case for all such explanations, institutional factors such as the interventionist state are neglected. In particular, the joint government—real estate sector activities have been largely responsible for the growth of suburban industry in all areas of the country. Kain (1970) and Craemers (1963) state, for example, that the rapidity of suburban development was particularly the consequence of a surge of new plant construction following the lifting of controls on building after the war. However, as more trenchant analyses of these changes make abundantly clear, the comparative disadvantage of the older central cities should not be interpreted as one of technological obsolescence, merely as a strong difference in the relative ability to attract new industry which worked in the favor of suburbs. As Sternlieb and Hughes observe:

> The economic problems of the Northeastern metropolises are far more complex than one could deduce from the often heard remark that the problem of the Northeast is its industrial base in a post-industrial society . . . overall, the shift and share analyses suggest that the major problem of the Northeastern metropolises is not the region's present mix of industries; the major problem is an inability to attract a share of economic activities that is commensurate with the region's historically dominant role in the American economy. (1975: 85)

In the next section, I shall examine more closely the causes of the sunbelt shift; at present, it is necessary to inquire after the factors which have stimulated the location of new plants and industries in the outer rings of metropolitan regions. Since World War II, Late Capitalist transformations have altered the business enterprise, and it has become progressively more unhinged from its dependence on the city center. Certainly this development depends to an extent on the lowering of interaction costs through technological innovation. Yet, other factors are also involved in these transformations, such as the restructuring of the world economic system since 1975 (Chase-Dunn 1984; Sassen-Koob 1984; Cohen 1981). In the main, monopoly capitalist corporations have been best able to take advantage of modern infrastructural changes that have made central city location obsolete. Due to the ease of internal financing, the administration of prices, which insures a stable market, the harnessing of technical expertise, and the administrative control over space, the large corporations of our concentrated industries have "internalized many of the economies of agglomeration" (Walker 1981: 399) which once favored the central city as the site of industry. Consequently, the shift to the suburbs reflects the growing power of the highly concentrated conglomerate business enterprise in the United States. Furthermore, increased mobility provided corporations with the ability to control labor costs by shifting organization and location, the prelude to what is presently a global labor sourcing strategy. The shift to suburban and/or peripheral global locations with cheap, organized labor is one stage in this worldwide process.

As in the case of homeownership, the location pattern of new industrial wealth in the suburbs could not have been produced without the incentives, regulations, and subsidies provided by active state intervention. Many analysts see this as a form of direct intervention. It is not. As indicated, the role of the state has been less in the form of planning than in indirect subsidies through policies aimed at aiding powerful business interests rather than developing space. Thus, the effects on metropolitan spatial patterns have been largely unanticipated and uncoordinated, because they are not the object of coherent government policy. With regard specifically to local and state governments, direct subsidies to local business which have had unplanned effects include tax write-offs, especially those which provide incentives to build new plants and new facilities rather than refurbish existing ones (Marcuse 1981; Bluestone and Harrison 1982); real estate abatements; low-interest loans; and tax-exempt development bonds. In addition, federally assisted loans have worked in concert with tax credits to discriminate against the city and in favor of the intermetropolitan shift to suburban locations (Peterson 1979). In this way, while the Late Capitalist industries came into being as a consequence of worldwide economic transformations, the present mode of sociospatial organization was partly produced by the state. In the case of intraregional location patterns, these seem to be almost wholly a mixed local, state, and federal government project. Thus, while local governments possess fundamental powers to intervene in space as regulators of land, most of these restrictions are ignored when industry wishes to enter an area—space is at the service of growth. In this manner, the direct interventionist power to plan is sacrificed so that the state can intervene indirectly to subsidize the economy through pro-growth policy.

New plant construction at the city periphery or in suburban areas was a function of several factors related to real estate development, including cheap land, lower taxes, and the presence of local boosters within government who were able to make special deals that could attract industry. Such movement inspired fiscal warfare between the city and the suburbs and between adjacent suburban areas, as each competed to make location in their area attractive. In short, while the suburbanization of industry has gone on for over one hundred years (Harrison 1974; Mills 1970; Gordon 1984), it has only been since the 1940s boom in Late Capitalist expansion that such a shift has assumed proportions large enough to affect the economic wealth of central cities and the massive deployment of population and business to the periphery. In the main this pattern has been the demand-side response of *new* industrial needs and *new* plant construction, as opposed to the kind of abandonment of the city itself which has often been alleged by critics of such patterns. However, events within the city point to the loss of many businesses because they could no longer compete with outside interests or because they were removed through urban renewal. Hardest hit in this redistribution were the older central places of the Northeast and Midwest, which lost half a million manufacturing jobs in the two decades after the war, "an average annual decline of over 1,700 manufacturing jobs per city between 1947 and 1967" (Berry and Kasarda 1977: 235). This focus on manufacturing, however, tells only half the story. As urban economies have been restructured by the shift to white-collar industries, a phenomenal growth in service positions has been generated. For the most part these have been low-paid, nonprofessional jobs employing the "working poor," that is, women, youths, and dispossessed industrial workers (see Davis 1984: 19; Gordon et al. 1982). In short, the shifts in the urban economy mean new labor relations and work force changes rather than the mere signaling of an absolute loss of jobs.

The local government–real estate sector articulation responsible for providing the supply-side component of metropolitan deconcentration can be illustrated best by the example of industrial parks. According to the Urban Land Institute (1975), literally thousands of industrial parks were set up after the 1950s by suburban municipalities in an active spatial war between local jurisdictions to attract business. Industrial parks are cleared land which is zoned and developed solely for industry. Most often, they require individual planning initiatives on the part of the local government which supplies site facilities, infrastructure requirements, and assorted incentives such as liberal tax abatements. The relatively cheap land, access to transportation routes such as interstate highways, and local government subsidies have made such places highly attractive to businesses over the years. The suburbanization of industry during the 1950s and 1960s depended heavily on the incentives made available by such areas. In addition to other benefits, local governments pushed for ambitious highway development schemes, which not only aided businesses but also opened up massive areas of the metropolitan hinterland to developers. Thus government complicity in providing the infrastructure requirements for the suburban real estate sector is quite explicit in the case of industrial parks.

When suburban areas were less mature and their fiscal burdens were less demanding, they competed well against the central city areas in attracting new industry to such parks. This, in turn, led to intense competition between suburban jurisdictions for the businesses, which aided the latter greatly. At present, due to the general slowdown in the economy, such spatial competition characterizes the development process of the entire metropolitan region. Wherever such intense competition between local jurisdictions exists, it greatly stimulates the pace of growth because of the way in which the spatial struggle translates into subsidies for development.

It is worth mentioning that, while local governments are often active partners in industrial parks, they also involve private development interests. Adjacent areas, which are held in private hands as well, invariably become highly profitable speculative investments for the development of office buildings and service centers. In short, the relative success of industrial parks provides a clear illustration of the effect of the local government–private developer linkage. While these individual developments involve planning, no comprehensive planning authority coordinates growth in the region. Consequently, their effects are largely unplanned and uncoordinated. They are a prime cause of unbalanced central city–suburban growth and, lately, figure prominently in the stratification patterns between suburban municipalities lying outside the city borders (Logan and Schneider 1981).

Despite the belief of many marxian advocates of capital logic theory, such a pattern of uneven development does not always aid capital accumulation in a direct way through the artificial production of differentials in the rate of profit between geographical locations. To be sure, vigorous spatial competition has aided business by lowering start-up and operating costs. Yet, the type of uneven development most characteristic of metropolitan growth is largely the result of uncoordinated regional expansion. Consequently, there is a certain degree of anarchy in the location decisions of businesses that is aided by local government competition for industry. The unplanned effects of this pattern have hit central city areas especially hard, because they have been unable to compete with suburban areas and have experienced an inability to expand their industrial base. Suburban areas, however, have also been affected adversely by the uncoordinated nature of growth, especially when it has been rapid. Thus the costs of development show up as traffic congestion, abandoned business locations, high turnover rates for commercial estab-

lishments, the death of older towns and centers, and increased transportation costs for workers. These very same patterns of uneven
development exemplified by metropolitan expansion are also illustrated in the rise of the sunbelt as a booming region.

Metropolitan Regional Deconcentration III: The Shift to the Sunbelt

In the previous sections, I have emphasized the importance of
supply-side factors which control the uses of space in the growth
process. In a sense this provides the important details for understanding the concept "pro-growth network," that is, the active special interests which exert monopolistic power over space and channel the development process toward certain very distinctive spatial
forms. But a focus on supply-side activities alone fails to implicate
the deep-level structural forces at work in space, forces derived from
the Late Capitalist development process which are especially involved with the needs of capital accumulation. In previous sections,
however, I have specified the effects of these forces in some detail as
stemming from certain distinct attributes of Late Capitalist social
transformations. Together these structural features and the monopolistic behavior of the local government—real estate sector coalitions
provide the two poles of the action-structure dialectic that is responsible for producing an uncoordinated development pattern. Furthermore, the materialization of this process in space, only partly
functional for capital accumulation, leads to instances of uneven
development which both aid and hinder the realization of profit
through spatial organization.

A discussion of the shift to the sunbelt can be used to highlight
these themes as well as the limitations of mainstream theory, because it has been studied as a phenomenon of place. As Mollenkopf
quite rightly observes (1981: 82), mainstream explanations stress a
demand-side view of change. They treat spatial patterns as the product of consumer preferences, that is, as the spatial effect of locational
votes by businesses and homeowners. Thus, sociospatial changes are
perceived descriptively and in demographic terms, as if the economy
functioned according to the wishes of the masses manifested in the
marketplace. For example, according to Sternlieb and Hughes:

> The pattern which we can observe in the first half of the 1970's
> is a considerable movement of *households* from the older, high
> density urban areas of the Northeast and East North Central
> states to other regions. The historic problem of the declining
> central city in most parts of the nation has been joined by the

stagnant or declining metropolis within America's heartland, the industrial belt from Boston to St. Louis . . . (1975: 5)

Such descriptive treatments of sociospatial restructuring—which constitute the bulk of mainstream analysis—are recognizable as ideological mystifications because they provide a kind of evidence, which is false, that such shifts are somehow natural or, rather, an organic representation of individual preferences. As Mollenkopf observes with regard to the work of Sternlieb and Hughes, in particular:

> In this approach, the market choices of two types of actors—producers and consumers—play a central role. Both engage in a simple utility calculation: . . . the basic argument offered by this approach is that the cities which have declined must have agglomeration diseconomies which have made them somehow less attractive to producers and consumers over the last decade or so. (1981: 82)

A second and equally limiting feature of this work is the tendency of mainstream analysts to reify place and region in making interlocational comparisons, while ignoring the social formation characteristics that are responsible for local economies (Sternlieb and Hughes 1975; South and Poston 1982; James 1981). This spatial fetishism is responsible for false regional dichotomies, such as the sunbelt-frostbelt division.

Clearly, the growth of the sunbelt region has been both distinctive and dramatic. Yet, from the perspective advocated here, it can be shown to be a product of Late Capitalist transformations which have been channeled by the state–real estate sector articulation into a booming, uncoordinated expansion—at the expense both of other areas and of all those who have been victimized by the vagaries of uneven development. Thus, between 1960 and 1970, the SMSAs of the sunbelt received 63.8 percent of the population increase among all SMSAs (Berry and Kasarda 1977: 168). In fact, between 1945 and 1975 the sunbelt doubled its population. While the manufacturing belt cities had been losing jobs and industrial strength to the suburban periphery, as we have seen, even the central cities of the sunbelt managed to capture increases in both jobs and population during that same period (Sternlieb and Hughes 1975). According to Sale, the dimensions of this growth represent a boom in the expansion of the South and West. As he indicates:

> The most recent statistics show that the southern rim continues to grow about three times as fast as the whole rest of

the country combined, and even modest projections suggest that the region will have 83.7 million people by 1980. According to the demographers, never in the history of the world has a region of such size developed at such a rate for so long a time. (1975: 166)

Once again, in the case of the sunbelt, we must differentiate between a trend which has been around for some time and the qualitatively rapid change in settlement space patterns which has occurred since World War II. Thus the southern and western states combined have been receiving a greater share of SMSA population growth than the northeast and north central states since the 1920s (Berry and Kasarda 1977: 168). Indeed, population migration patterns have been steadily trending west since the 1800s. The shift to the sunbelt, however, represents a flip-flop in the center-periphery relationship of fixed capital wealth which has *reversed* the spatial deployment of development in the United States since the depression. Some of the earliest studies to first notice this trend argued that, as the population has progressively drifted west and south, industrial wealth has followed to preserve a closeness to market centers of gravity (Fuchs 1962; Perloff et al. 1960; Thompson and Mattila 1959). However, it is now apparent that large monopolistic corporations command a greater control over their markets wherever they are situated. Consequently, they locate almost anywhere, and since the war many have preferred to situate new plants as well as new industries in relatively undeveloped regions of the sunbelt because of its recreational amenities, cheap and controllable labor, cheap land, and milder climate (Wheat 1973; Castells 1977; Watkins and Perry 1977), although the relationship between these factors and market considerations is a complex one (see chapter 3).

Just as in the case of the suburban dislocation, the rapid shift to the sunbelt since the war seems to have been accelerated by the interventionist state, especially by public policies which have stimulated defense spending, agribusiness, and those activities relying on fossil fuel combustion. Massive state spending has supported what Sale (1975) has called the "six pillars of the southern rim": agribusiness, high technology, real estate development, the military, energy, and leisure. For over three decades, in particular, the major portion of the tax dollar in the United States has gone to defense. This figure amounted to 54 percent out of every tax dollar in 1976 (Melman 1977: 181). During the war, 60 percent of the total $74 billion spending effort alone went to the fifteen states of the sunbelt (Sale 1975: 170). While defense spending dropped somewhat in the 1950s, it rose again during what some observers now call the transformation to a permanent arms economy (Kidron 1968; Melman 1970; Cook 1966; Mandel 1975). By 1970 the fifteen states of the sunbelt were receiving 44 percent of all defense spending, including over 50 percent of the Defense Department payroll; had 60 percent of the major defense installations in the United States; accounted for over 70 percent of national production in aerospace; employed more scientists and technicians than all the rest of the United States; and received 49 percent of all "pentagon research and development funds—the seed money that creates new technologies and industries" (Sale 1975: 171). There is some recent evidence that the federal spending differential between the sunbelt and the frostbelt is presently closing (Markusen, Saxenian, and Weiss 1981). Such observations, however, cannot detract from the importance of the previous pattern, which has existed for at least three decades.

The role of military spending in the capitalist economy has long been recognized as a central feature of the monopolistic stage (Luxemburg 1971; Lenin 1939; Baran and Sweezy 1966; Mandel 1975). Its significance since the 1930s has been one of increasing importance to the capital accumulation process under Late Capitalism, because of what Mandel calls the "production of the means of destruction" as a separate segment of the economy. Whether or not we can agree with Mandel's complete thesis, it is certainly the case that massive defense spending has been deployed as a *spatial* transfer of value from the Northeast and Midwest to the sunbelt. For example, Melman notes that during the two years after 1965 alone the federal government took $7.4 billion more out of New York State in taxes than it put in, while spending $2 billion more in California than it took out. In 1974 the sunbelt received $13 billion more in tax dollars than it paid, compared with a $7.5 billion outflow from New York City alone (Melman 1977: 182).

This transfer of value represents the spatial deployment of Late Capitalist needs in circumventing the barriers to development presented by the industrial infrastructure of the manufacturing belt. In part, Late Capitalist space penetrated the northeast and north central regions by developing the suburbs on an immense scale. However, the major site of the material realization of the current capitalist stage has been the previously underdeveloped regions of the South and West in the United States and the formerly undeveloped areas of the rest of the globe, such as Southeast Asia, Latin America, and the Middle East. Thus Watkins and Perry, for example, note that neither wage differentials nor the physical relocation of industry can explain the rise of the sunbelt to its present stage of industrial prominence (1977). Rather, the absence of infrastructural barriers to the development of new industry was more important; major factors included the lack of an organized labor force, cheap land, lower taxes, and a local government more receptive to the needs of industry. The very same reasons have been given to explain the flight of capital to other, less developed countries as well.

The transformation of sunbelt space, since World War II, was rapid and booming with regard to real estate development and the realization of industrial superprofits. Such a rate of expansion, however, is presently severely reduced, and we may have recently entered a new stage in Late Capitalist development, one with slower growth. The consequence of such a resource allocation process is the uneven spatial development which was described in chapter 6. This process produces metropolitan and regional spatial polarization, with the poor becoming poorer in all areas, even in the sunbelt, and the well-endowed prospering everywhere. Thus, a comparison of unemployment figures between sunbelt and frostbelt cities by Gans (1982) revealed that the level was higher for Houston than for New York. Furthermore, despite the overall uncoordinated nature of growth, many aspects of uneven development aid the capital accumulation process. That is, it is most important to distinguish between aspects of growth which are *not* functional for capitalist development, such as overconstruction of the built environment, and those aspects of uneven development which aid the process of capital accumulation. For example, in certain cases the production of disadvantaged areas, such as in the central city and in certain peripheral regions of the globe, becomes a way of making capital investment more profitable in other areas and increasing productivity levels in the advanced sector (Mandel 1975: 75–107; Soja 1980; Holland 1976; Walker 1981; Harvey 1975b, 1981; Massey 1978). Among many mainstream analysts the reified spatial manifestation of this regional process, or the "regional problem," has become the organizing idea behind understanding the production of space. That is, the concept of region becomes fetishized and elevated as the new central concern while the composition of the sociospatial growth process itself is ignored. According to Sternlieb and Hughes:

> The momentum of declining cities has been with us for a long time; however, when entire metropolitan areas are encompassed by a similar trend, we must alter our mental model of reality . . . The concept of the aging metropolis forces us to shift into a new mode of thinking; we have become inordinately accustomed to focusing on the tensions between central

city and suburbia. However, if the early 1970's are not an aberration but a benchmark of new reality, then we may have to adopt a new frame of reference: the distinctions and stresses between metropolitan areas and regions. (1975: 6)

In the preceding chapters, we have seen that what is required is not just mental soul-searching but a switch to a new paradigm of urban science in order to analyze the nature of uneven development. According to the view presented here, inequitable sociospatial patterns of economic and geographic stratification are the result of both the inherently uncoordinated way in which Late Capitalist growth processes transform society and produce space and the differential manner by which surplus value is expropriated. Second, understanding sociospatial distinctions also requires an analysis of the way in which uneven development restructures the labor force. This means studying how labor market divisions are produced (Gordon et al. 1982; Hodson and Kaufmann 1982), deployed spatially (Frobel, Heinrichs, and Kreye 1980; Storper and Walker 1984; Friedman 1977; Thurow 1975), and manifested globally (Amin 1976; Sassen-Koob 1984; Palloix 1975; Cohen 1981). Finally, if the capital accumulation process operates differentially in space, as we have seen throughout the preceding chapters, it is a mistake to fetishize this process, as mainstreamers do by conceptualizing it at the level of spatial regions. For example, the common sunbelt-frostbelt distinction is discovered to hide the dimensions of the differentiation between various sectors of the Late Capitalist social formation. Thus, the well-being of cities in the frostbelt and sunbelt is tied together by the very nature of deconcentrated sociospatial organization. As Mollenkopf observes:

Because of its insistence that cities are independent observations, the orthodox model tends to miss the quite simple point that cities like New York may benefit from the growth of cities like Phoenix. The Northeastern cities have 219 of the Fortune 500's headquarters, while the Southwestern cities have only 48. The banking resources of New York alone far exceed the combined capacity of all Southwestern cities . . . Rather than view economic activities taking place in the Southwest as competing with those of New York, it might be more accurate to say that they frequently benefit New York. The same can be said for the other Northeastern cities possessing corporate headquarters, large banking resources and plentiful advanced corporate services. (1981: 84)

The contemporary production of space process mixes a few big winners with many small losers. Spatial restructuring is uncoordinated at those levels necessary to make this outcome more equitable, consequently, the majority of citizens are compelled to live in environments which would benefit from coordinated growth. Yet, society cannot plan adequately for development because the existing relations of production prevent any attempt at altering the autonomy of private interests in control of land. This frames for us the essential contradiction of capitalist society, namely, the social basis of all wealth and its private expropriation by the capitalist class. Under the relations of production and reproduction specific to the Late Capitalist phase, this contradiction becomes manifested in an addictive dependency on growth. Furthermore, this growth is of a specific type in such a social formation. It is both rapid and uncoordinated during periods of expansion, because it is the source of superprofits. During downswings in the business cycle, it is characterized by deindustrialization and capital flight to those areas of the globe that still allow the realization of rapid development or by capital restructuring and deepening in anticipation of future upswings.

For the property sector this process involves a relentless pursuit of profitable investment through the turnover of land. In some cases this is manifested in the form of massive projects, such as large residential developments or giant office towers, constructed by those elements of the property sector which have access to large amounts of money, especially elements of finance capital and energy-related conglomerates. In other cases, the activities of the property sector show up by increasing the intensity with which existing structures are transformed into new sources of exchange value. This can occur, for example, through the conversion of apartments to condominiums and cooperatives, the demolition of low-density buildings and the construction of more profitable buildings, and the conversion of space to commercial agglomerations, such as convention halls, sports arenas, shopping centers, and malls. In all cases the activities of the property sector advance with the aid of the state. Zoning changes, variances, highway construction and other infrastructure improvements, and public policy subsidies of all kinds are but some of the ways in which the state–property sector articulation is manifested. While not all of this investment is productive and, therefore, a source of surplus value by improving the design of space as a force of production, development takes place under the sign of growth. Hence, investment in the property sector has the *appearance* of productivity and progress. In this way secondary circuit activity remains unhealthy for the activities of other circuits of capital throughout the fluctuations in the growth cycle, as the anarchy of real estate transformations relentlessly restructures space.

Whether manifested directly as a question of space or indirectly as a concern over collective consumption, the uncoordinated nature of growth provides the content for local political issues (Blumstein and Salamon 1979; Tolley et al. 1979; Boyte 1980; Laska and Spain 1980; Gottdiener and Neiman 1981; Clavel, Forrester, and Goldsmith 1980; Heskin 1981; London 1980). Due to the many interests which intersect in this process over the renegotiation of the costs of growth, outcomes are difficult to predict, and the form of space is held hostage to a process claiming neither coherency nor rationality. Yet, public policy in the United States has failed to address this issue, preferring instead to transfer resources toward those segments of society most adversely affected by the large movements of people and businesses. In the final chapter, I shall suggest that one reason for this failure of public policy is the mainstream assertion that the patterns of development are somehow optimal because they appear to be natural outgrowths of systemic forces articulating with space. Furthermore, the *political* process, which I have identified as a renegotiation over the social costs of growth, is viewed by ecologists as an "adjustment" process ontologically manifesting the equilibrating forces of social Darwinism. For these reasons, the conflict between rival paradigms over the understanding of spatial production translates into a conflict between alternative approaches to urban public policy.

8. Community, Liberation, and Everyday Life

The twentieth century has witnessed the transformation of settlement space in the United States, from the classic concentric zone central city that dominated its hinterland to a polynucleated region with a complex and hierarchical internal structure that is sustained and affected by the activities of the larger social system. Within these expanding metropolitan domains, everyday life itself has changed from that of the past. Business activity, for example, plays itself out against the backdrop of a global system of production, commerce, and finance. The insular life of the company town with a dependable market for its products has been replaced by an unsure world of international competition, merciless labor reorganization, and management pitched at volatile input and output environments.

Political life has also been transformed to fit the new sociospatial arrangements. The power of the central city is on the wane. Not only do the plurality of voters now reside in suburban constituencies, but the comparative lack of city strength hamstrings local officials, so that mayors of today have much less visibility and clout than they did in the past. If cities are still considered by politicians as capable of delivering millions of votes, then so are suburban areas. Furthermore, the halcyon days when decisions made in city back rooms affected the majority of metropolitan residents have been replaced by a more sober operating environment, which, on the one hand, locks local areas into severely constrained positions with limited resources and, on the other, requires coordination from an increasingly large number of balkanized political jurisdictions, including counties, sharing power within the metropolitan region. In short, metropolitan politics today is so different from prewar politics that we have yet to reconceptualize our thinking on the local polity in order to deal effectively with the new realities of governance.

Finally, the conditions of personal life in metropolitan environments have also been fundamentally transformed. The classic city

neighborhood of dense and localized relations has, with some no-
table exceptions, long since passed from the urban milieu, to be replaced by personalized networks of people who commute across regional space in order to experience social communion. This change
has called forth a new approach to urban sociology, one which eschews the traditional issues associated with community life in favor
of a focus on the relational networks of all metropolitan residents
(Fischer 1983; Wellman et al. 1983).

This book grew out of my deep concern that mainstream urban
science is inadequate to the task of understanding these economic,
political, and cultural transformations. Clearly the previous chapters have merely allowed us to take the first steps along the new conceptual path. In particular, I have been principally concerned here
with examining the shortcomings of approaches that purport to explain how settlement space is produced, while leaving for the moment other aspects of this reconceptualization, such as those involving local politics (Gottdiener, forthcoming) and urban culture
(Gottdiener and Lagopoulos, forthcoming). The dominant paradigm,
loosely identified as urban ecology, explains settlement space as
being produced by an adjustment process involving large numbers of
relatively equal actors whose interaction is guided by some self-
regulating invisible hand. This "organic" growth process—propelled
by technological innovation and demographic expansion—assumes
a spatial morphology which, according to ecologists, mirrors that of
communal populations of lower life forms within biological king-
doms. Consequently, the social organization of space is accepted by
mainstreamers as inevitable, whatever its patterns of internal differentiation. From such a perspective, interventions in space merely
serve to exacerbate problems by interfering with the natural mechanisms of self-adjustment, which are presumed to possess the quality
of transcendent rationality.

Against such views are numerous critics of the status quo,
including academics and city planners, who see the current pattern of regional deconcentration as being inefficient, racist, anti-
working-class, and politically impossible for local governmental
coordination. The first contribution to this debate made by the preceding chapters is that whether present-day spatial organization is
"good" or "bad" is, for the moment, *irrelevant*. The important issue,
instead, is the debate over how such patterns are produced. The combined ideological front of urban ecology, economics, and geography
dominating urban science at present possesses a false understanding
of the metropolitan development process. Consequently, it cannot
provide those interested in improving the environment with the in-

formation on growth needed by such an intervention. Yet, because they currently dominate institutional thought, ecologists are most often called upon to help formulate public policy. Let us consider one final illustration from this tradition, which we hope will eventually be exorcised from urban science. Commenting on the virtues of regional sprawl, Kasarda remarks:

> Despite the fad among city planners and academics to label suburban and exurban growth as haphazard, inefficient and undesirable, it is now becoming apparent that peripheral growth is not nearly as random or inefficient as once believed. Without guidance of any conscious master design, the suburbs and exurbs are evolving their own relatively self-sufficient hierarchy of activity centers, ranging from higher-order regional, commercial and employment centers to lower-order convenience goods and residential centers. The evolution of this multi-functional, nested hierarchy of activity centers has given rise to a new form of spatial organization—the polycentric ecological field—which has replaced the technologically antiquated primate structure of the monocentered industrial metropolis. (1980: 390)

The above quote can be contrasted fruitfully with the insights from the preceding pages. First, we note the vulgar organicism of such thought. The key word "evolution" appears several times in Kasarda's text to connote process. In such a pristine universe, a place can evolve its own spatial form of economic organization as a product of natural events, as if it existed isolated in a horizontal world, lacking connections to the larger society around it. This ignores the powerful forces of socioeconomic and political organization at work in *all* places of the social system, especially an appreciation for the actions of vested interests in space and the structural laws of motion of capitalist society. Local development then becomes the study of the intersection between agency and structure and the political attempts at renegotiating sociospatial impacts by groups whose interests were slighted by profit takers and the costs of growth. When spatial organization is discussed without reference to the social system processes which produce, sustain, and reproduce it, then places are seen to magically possess these same properties as reified features of space itself. In our view a science of settlement space forms must be based upon a knowledge of the articulation between social organization and space. Places and forms by themselves do nothing and produce nothing—only people within social organization networks possess that power. If the foregoing has had a central theme, it is that our environment is a social creation and its design can be controlled for the social good.

Second, the belief in a "relatively self-sufficient hierarchy" of places is ludicrous both in the light of world system theory and in the face of certain knowledge regarding the national system of production and distribution within the U.S. economy—admitted to have had a fundamental impact upon local space since the earliest postwar studies on the community (Stein 1960; Bensman and Vidich 1960). To be sure, commercial centers outside the older central business districts are self-sufficient as market outlets, but such horizontally constrained thinking ignores the important vertical linkages of each place to hierarchical systems of global capitalist organization.

Third, we note the "spatial Darwinism," if you will, and the technological determinism invoked in such thought to explain change. One space, the "polycentric ecological field," is actually conceived of as replacing another, the "primate structure of the monocentered industrial metropolis." This replacement in importance has allegedly occurred because the central cities have become "technologically antiquated," an assertion which flies in the face of the most primitive experience of America's world cities. A science of space cannot progress while hamstrung by such technologically determinist thought. Spatial forms cannot devour each other and succeed themselves according to some Darwinist biological analogy. The assessment of spatial well-being from a technologically reductionist perspective neglects the other sociostructural forces which transform the comparative advantages of place, especially the new international division of labor, the activities of the large firms and multinationals, state intervention, and the actions of the real estate sector. The mainstream approach would like us all to believe that central cities have lost their former importance in society. Nothing could be further from the truth: they have merely been transformed, as have all places, by the anarchic actions of Late Capitalist growth. While some of their economic functions have changed, cities have retained and even improved their significant role in the creation of wealth. Thus, of the thirty-eight central places in the United States, a recent *Los Angeles Times* report ranked the older cities of America's frostbelt, including New York, Chicago, Boston, Washington, Philadelphia, Minneapolis, and Pittsburgh, among the top ten in overall economic strength. In fact, due to the deployment of functional differentiation in space, the activities of the sunbelt and the frostbelt central cities actually complement each other economically, because each specializes in particular tasks which are then integrated by the global system of capital.

In place of the mainstream approach, I have argued for an alternate paradigm, the production of space perspective. It is characterized by the following assertions.

1. Settlement space patterns are understood as being produced by the system of social organization, which is both vertically and horizontally structured. This process involves economic, political, and cultural forces that are dialectically linked and that are understood not in terms of three distinct practices, as in the marxian structuralist approach, but through the contemporary theory of structuration, which unites structural system forces with voluntaristic modes of behavior. In the United States, the social system exhibits the characteristic features of capitalism. However, over time these features have changed as capitalism itself has developed. Consequently, it is necessary to appreciate historical change in the structure of society and to specify the diachronic phases of social development. I have pointed out above that, in opposition to marxian political economists who periodize capitalism according to qualitatively unique stages, this progression is best understood in terms of loosely overlapping phases without firm beginning and ending dates, because the essential features of capitalism as a mode of production have been preserved over the long duration of its growth. Furthermore, in opposition to marxian political economists, phases of development are not directly reflected in unique spatial forms; rather, the articulation between the mode of production and space is itself a contingent dialectical process of indistinct duration and variable effect (see number 2, below).

The present form of deconcentrated metropolitan space can be understood according to this framework as being produced by transformations in capitalism which span several periods and at least one century. Yet, accelerated sociospatial change is associated with the present phase of capitalism, called Late Capitalism, whose characteristic mode of production features began to appear hegemonically in the decades after 1920. Industrial capitalism's phenomenal productive form was the factory; its phenomenal spatial form was the city. In contrast, Late Capitalism's phenomenal productive form is the multinational corporation, and, for the case of the United States, the correlated spatial form is the polynucleation of deconcentrated space, not the "corporate city" of political economists.

2. Labeling the producing motive of space as "capitalist" does not necessarily mean, as some marxists contend, that capitalist relations are reflected directly in urban forms. Rather, it is the ongoing development of that system which comes to be materialized in space at any given time, so that observable patterns of sociospatial organi-

zation are *phenomenal* forms. Thus, the features of spatial morphology are dialectically related to structural changes in social organization. One proceeds in interaction with the other, rather than through some positivist link of social cause and spatial effect. Furthermore, and most important, sociospatial patterns are the product of contradictory, contentious processes of capitalist development, rather than being necessarily functional for capitalism or determined by some logic of capital accumulation. The most significant part of this process is the continual development of the forces of production—including not only technology and labor power but also the role of space in social organization—and the clash of these forces with existing relations of production, especially the role of the interventionist state and capital accumulation as they articulate with space. It is this contradictory development process, involving sociospatial relations at *every* level, which materializes contingently in spatial forms and which requires understanding before urban policy can be prescribed. Thus, if Late Capitalism has produced a space for itself, the deconcentrated region, then the historical process of deconcentration has helped produce Late Capitalism. Finally, in contrast to the ecologists, the forms which emerge from this process are not inexorably fated—they are social products open to enlightened redirection and better design.

3. The real estate sector, including the fraction of finance capital organized around investments in land, is the leading edge of the materialization of this Late Capitalist development process in space. It is comprised of class fractions, which often compete with each other, as well as pro-growth networks which unite otherwise disparate interests. While the actions of this sector can be concerted and organized, no overarching mechanism of coordination exists. Land is always an attractive investment, due to its malleable nature and the incentives produced by existing relations of production—it is continuously turned over and restructured as the secondary circuit siphons off capital from other forms of investment which directly aid industrial productivity. Consequently, the form which settlement space assumes is not necessarily beneficial to anyone except the self-interested profit takers of the property sector. Both capital and labor are constrained to live in an environment which is difficult to control but whose negative effects can always be transcended best by the wealthy and the powerful.

4. The mainstream paradigm explains urban development as if the state did not exist. As we have seen, sociospatial development is as much a product of the state as it is of the private sector. This aspect of contemporary society possesses similarities with noncapital-

ist countries, although both the historical circumstances and the causes of intervention differ (Misztal and Misztal 1984). In fact, so much variation exists from country to country regarding the role of the state in space that nonmarxian analyses such as neoweberianism as well as neomarxist approaches enjoy credibility (Pahl 1977; Saunders 1981). Both the cross-national and cross-paradigmatic approaches of contemporary state theories, however, do share a rejection of the mainstream approach because of its failure to specify the role of the state in space.

In the United States, state intervention is of two distinct types which operate differently at separate levels of society. For the most part, unlike its role in such countries as France and Poland, the state works indirectly through policy rather than directly through urban planning. These policies serve to subsidize at public expense the private sector production of space, while in other societies the state might itself be considered a direct producer of space, such as in socialist countries. Some of the state policies in the United States are expressly designed to support urban development and ameliorate the inequitable social circumstances of targeted populations. Other policies, such as the federal tax subsidy to homeowners or massive military spending, affect spatial patterns through indirect means. Thus the determinants of state policies differ greatly, and while most have some effect on space not every policy is functional for pursuing some particular interest in space. In short, a general theory on the intervention of the state in space for the case of the United States cannot be cast in structural functionalist terms.

In addition to national programs and policies, the local state is also involved in the production of space, principally as a regulator of land-use development or by manipulating tax powers to subsidize economic and property development. Because the fundamental ideology of municipal life involves legitimating the boosting of economic growth and because control of land is the principal power through which local jurisdictions can regulate the private sector, municipal political leaders and interests organized around the development of land often form something like a real estate development corporation, marrying government and business to create a pro-growth network. These networks are the main way in which the local turnover of land is transformed into an engine for the production of space.

Together, both types of interventionist efforts at all levels of government find the state an active partner in sociospatial change throughout the metropolis and across the nation. At present the extant theories of this relation, such as collective consumption, remain too limited to grasp its nature, just as approaches to urban social movements based upon these same extant theories fail to comprehensively treat the political process set off by the hegemonic thrust of abstract space at the expense of everyday life (see chapters 4 and 5). Currently this analytical gap is being closed by the publication of long-awaited case studies based upon the inner-city experiences of the 1960s (Katznelson 1981; Mollenkopf 1983; Friedland 1983). Aside from their ethnocentric bias, which equates the relation between the state and space with the central city experience alone, these studies are dated by their focus on the 1960s and the theories of collective consumption and the welfare state, which were more appropriate to that period. Considerably more case study efforts are currently needed on the politics of spatial production and the adjustment processes which ordinary citizens pursue politically in the face of uncoordinated metropolitan regional expansion. In fact, such considerations help define the content of a new urban political science which should replace the outdated paradigm.

5. In addition to economic and political considerations, the production of space proceeds through the deployment of ideology, specifically through the cultural fix on economic growth as the principal goal of local areas. The pro-growth ideology equates the well-being of place with its ability to foster economic development. In fact, according to some mainstream analysts (see, e.g., Peterson 1981), such a task may be the only role which places like cities can effectively play. This ideology is false in all its dimensions. Not only does growth bring with it costs as well as benefits, but the private expropriation of wealth siphons off developmental profits unequally, while leaving the burden of costs to be carried at the public's expense. At times this ideology is revealed by specific events for what it is—a thin disguise for special interests—and such pro-growth sentiments are then opposed by political interests which argue against growth. However, such political clashes have yet to call into question the central role that the emphasis on economic growth plays in social thought within the United States.

In bourgeois society, economic concerns constitute the principal subject of social inquiry; all other human considerations are secondary, if they are considered at all. Thus the hegemony of economics over political and cultural social subjects is not an inexorable outcome of some structural logic of capitalism but merely the essence of bourgeois ideology. Consequently, marxian political economy and mainstream orthodoxy possess the same ideological roots. Marxists differ from mainstreamers only through the reformist schemes proposed, which seek to ameliorate the inequities of economic patterns of development. This eludes the transformative role of social thought.

Overcoming the ideology of growth requires a concerted effort directed toward conceptualizing a theory of everyday needs linked with a theory of production under *non*-capitalist social relations. This problematic would tie together the class struggle with ideas aimed at radically transforming personal relations and community space. Such a link between Marx and his nemesis, utopian socialism, will be discussed more fully below. It is sufficient to observe at this stage that, when applied to space, revolutionary praxis moves quickly from an obsessive fix on the class struggle to an examination of the inadequacies of all social relations in everyday life—a subject which orthodox marxists do their best to avoid (Bookchin 1984; Gorz 1980). Clearly, the one should be bound up with the other in what Vaneigem calls generalized self-management (1975). Finally, the study of the ideology of growth as the cultural counterpart to the articulation between economic and political relations in space becomes a rich source of research topics for urban sociology. This type of inquiry, however, requires specification of the manner in which symbolic universes mediate material processes—a problematic handled best by sociosemiotics (see Gottdiener and Lagopoulos, forthcoming).

6. The end product of Late Capitalist growth processes is uneven development with an ever widening gap between rich and poor and with the externalization of the costs of growth to the community as a whole. Uneven development has its spatial correlates, but these are subject to constant change as a function of activities in the property sector. Thus, even in areas experiencing booming growth, widespread poverty and unemployment may be exhibited spatially as depressed or blighted ghettos. In addition, booming areas are often the site of severe environmental crises, as the cases of Houston (Feagin 1984) and Long Island (Gottdiener 1977) show. Uneven development, especially inadequate access to employment and livable wages, causes social pathologies, such as crime. Some of these problems manifest themselves in space and affect the affluent as well as the less fortunate. Furthermore, due to the uncoordinated nature of sociospatial development, conflicts manifest themselves in space and affect others as the costs of uneven growth are renegotiated. Most of the individuals harmed by this process, however, belong to the lower levels of social stratification. In both cases, the political struggle generated by uneven development provides another rich source of new research topics.

7. Contemporary transformations in the space-time matrix of social organization have fundamentally altered the conditions of lo-

cal community life. This new situation possesses the following characteristics. First, the spatial segregation of social groups has liberated the vast majority of the population from responsibility for the less advantaged, because the former no longer live in close proximity to the latter. The present is witness to the progressive marginalization and spatial confinement of those social groups least able to play an active role in the political economy. Second, and more important, the action of abstract space fragments *all* social groups, not only the least powerful, so that local community life loses the street and public areas of communion to the privacy of the home. Neighbors become increasingly estranged through a lack of common experiences, despite the superficial appearance of civility between them, as the personalized network of commuters replaces the localized community of the past, with its once dense social relations. The new areas of communion are encapsulated within social worlds engineered by the logic of consumption—the malls, shopping centers, singles bars, amusement parks, and suburban backyards.

Individuals whose principal allegiances are to personalized networks which are merely suspended in abstract, commuting space make very poor community citizens: Local political cultures in the United States, for example, are presently dying out, as manifested by low voter turnouts, low participation rates in other political activities, and an increasing social apathy. Studies of personal networks reveal the limited number of residents who are actively involved in concerns about their local environments (Wellman et al. 1983: 63). Wherever the new social relations of production and reproduction prevail, in rural as well as urban milieus, local communities are transformed into privatized domains devoid of street interaction, with limited services and limited use of public space. This process and the dimensions of contemporary community relations provide the content for the new subjects of urban sociology. What is still needed is a greater awareness of the type of problematic discussed above, regarding the ideology of growth.

In sum, the new paradigm proposed by this discussion treats economic, political, and cultural phenomena converging on settlement space in a manner which elevates new concerns to the center of urban inquiry and redirects thought away from a narrow fix on economic development. In place of explanations for the production of space based upon the study of the actions of large numbers of economic actors making marginal decisions about transport and product costs, we need to closely observe the actions of the large firms and the combined private-public networks organized around the secondary circuit of space, which manipulate space in pursuit of profits and superprofits. In place of a focus on political negotiations typified by pluralist mechanisms of adjustment played out equitably within a neutral state framework, we need to examine the political struggle of unequals lying at the core of everyday adjustments to the uneven manner in which sociospatial development proceeds. Furthermore, in place of the neutral state itself, we need to specify the operation of special interests—including relatively autonomous state managers themselves—in the political arena, especially with regard to the triple articulation of the state, civil society, and space.

Finally, in place of a narrow fix on tracking down the minute differences between residents of places and their respective personal networks, we need to address the larger questions of modernity—marriage, divorce, child rearing, aging, the nature of work, mutual aid—that is, the new social relations comprising everyday life experiences within the deconcentrated metropolitan environment. This is especially the case for all aspects of social reproduction, including the family, work, subcultural networks, political struggles, and the quality of community life.

The differences between the dominant mainstream urban paradigm and the paradigm proposed to supplant it can be illustrated one final way, this time with regard to a question held in abeyance at the beginning of this chapter, namely, their respective public policy implications. In recent years, severe problems of a sociospatial nature have progressively arrived at the forefront of interest. The metropolitan region, or the polycentric ecological field, if you will, was discovered by census analysis to be stratified by income, race, and lifestyle. Many of the issues associated with the built environment, such as crime, traffic congestion, pollution, fiscal shortfalls, declining educational quality, mismatches between job opportunities and labor force locations, the flight of industry, and the declining tax base of the central cities, are being analyzed more and more from a sociospatial perspective and from the organizing idea of uneven development. We can, therefore, separate conservatives from progressives among urban analysts precisely by inquiring whether they view these sociospatial development patterns as good or bad. Most ecologists would follow Kasarda and endorse, on the whole, the intra- and intermetropolitan changes as indicating the spatial needs of contemporary society and the social Darwinism of place. Therefore, if the sunbelt has risen to its present stage of prosperity while the frostbelt has fallen on hard times, it is believed that there is something intrinsically beneficial provided to business by the former—that is, a proper "business climate"—and there is something innately bad about the built environment of the latter.

This blaming of the victim, which ignores the *global* and *national* operation of the state and the economy in producing changes by the geographical transfer of value, is at times quite explicit. Thus Suttles, in particular, has been interested in pointing out that central cities of the urban heartland need to transform their character or their "values" and cater more to the interests of the average American in order to again become attractive places to live. As he indicates:

> Many of the old central cities of the urban heartland continue to be important centers of the performing arts, expensive shops, higher education, and exposition halls for sports, art, and natural history. However, most of these amenities have a rather narrow appeal, and while they make life more livable for the cultured and young singles, they do little to hold the masses of people who depend heavily on the local tavern, ball park, school district, parish or church for their entertainment and social life. (1977: 529)

Yet, the central city once nurtured the exact type of everyday life for the working class which is described in the above quote. Far from exhibiting some innate preference of the working class, the absence of average American residential areas in the central city is the consequence of sociospatial incentives produced by supply-side interventions in space, comprising the combined economic, political, and ideological forces unleashed by capitalism since at least the 1960s. Clearly the "masses" would not have left their old neighborhoods unless they were encouraged to do so by the new transformations of settlement space, which have been specified in great detail, so that what are apparently the demand-side voluntary decisions observed by ecologists are understood instead as being structured by the social forces articulating with space through the property sector.

The social production of space seeks to understand the operation of these larger forces in order to make the kind of public policy recommendations which can reverse the hardships of sociospatial change. The above quote represents sentiments which wish to substitute a *value* problematic for the question of uneven development. This is a common aspect of mainstream public policy recommendations for disadvantaged people as well as places. Such an ideology succeeds through the spatial fetishism of place, which takes surface appearance for reality and which sees behavior as emanating from subject voluntarism alone. Mainstream ecology divorces thought from concentrating on the historical processes which have produced the demographic deployment patterns of society and the geographical transfer of value at the core of uneven development, created by the supply-side actions of the public and private interests organized around the property sector and industrial production. Invariably, among other mainstream public policy prescriptions aimed at changing values but not social forces, anti-working-class sentiments soon surface. Thus declining cities are advised to muzzle militant unions and alter the "values" of municipal employees so that they can adjust to a more spartan life-style. The heartland cities and regional victims of uneven development are also advised to restructure their business climate by providing more incentives for companies to locate there, ostensibly by making local taxpayers provide corporations with generous abatements. In effect, disadvantaged places are exhorted to subsidize future capitalist development in order to overcome the problems produced by that very process in the past.

In these and other sentiments, it is always the place itself which is somehow unworthy, and therefore it is always the place itself which must "acquire new values," "turn over a new leaf," or "repent" by some collective act of *local* will in order to regain the lost state of grace. In short, the ecologists, as Protestant missionaries, visit the working people of America's central cities, as New Guinean savages, and prescribe for them a plan to attain salvation which involves transforming themselves and their settlement space into attractions that can once again bring back the "big birds" of capitalism under the ideological sign of promoting economic growth. This cargo cult approach to urban public policy and the well-being of community places, however, can possess credibility only by ignoring the massive, multibillion-dollar transfer of value enacted by a multinational economy and the interventionist state, which is ongoing and which is implemented by a wide variety of agricultural, military, land development, labor force, industrial, and extractive resource programs. If one wishes to ignore the impact of this historical process and its inequities, there is still ample reason to appreciate the way in which it is related to the spatial production of settlement forms. Upon this analytical and theoretical bottom line rests our call for a new explanatory paradigm.

In 1980 the President's Commission for a National Agenda for the Eighties unveiled its *Urban America in the Eighties*—the policy proposals for urban regions. This is a remarkable document because it provides evidence of the amount of work presently necessary to unmask the ideological misconceptions fostered by mainstream urban analysis, even though its policy proposals have never been enacted. The document is well salted with selectively chosen references and facts. It prides itself on debunking certain myths. It presents explanations for growth patterns with the self-assurance of science. Yet, it is hopelessly twisted in its assumptions and recommendations, because it relies exclusively on the outdated paradigm of mainstream urban analysis. In the words of Glickman, "The commission completely misunderstands the nature of US urban policy" (1981: 507). However, that apparent misconception performs an important function. The report is a model for what both Althusser and Lefebvre call a representation (Marx's *Darstellung*), that is, the articulation of ideology with knowledge, a combination of ideas functional for ruling-class interests with institutionally produced statistics and "scientific facts." In its highly developed arguments, the report reaches the very summit of spurious reasoning—it exemplifies, quite clearly, the fact that we are presently involved in an intense ideological battle over the control of space.

The "new" urban agenda, however, warrants study, despite the fact that it has passed quietly from the present scene. It is a document which can help detail the way in which the basic causes of problems in this society come to be displaced by sophisticated yet mystifying arguments, so that their origins can no longer be recognized. What are its essential features?

First, the report acknowledges and documents the present-day development patterns of society, but it then assigns them a natural ontological status. Social organization, according to the report, develops through certain immutable laws, and these affect place. Public policy should be formulated to aid existing development patterns rather than counter the flow of growth. In short, we are asked by organicist reasoning to accept the status quo as natural, not to inquire whether vested interests are behind the observable patterns. Second, the report is remarkable as a neoconservative document for the attention which it pays to the poor. This is a new dimension of such an ideology. It documents quite accurately the hardship of uneven development and the increasing gap between the relatively affluent and the growing numbers of the underclass in our metropolitan regions.

Such an observation is combined in the report with the first feature as the basis for its policy prescriptions. These are at once an alleged critique of previous urban policy and the foundation for a new agenda. In the past, it is argued, policy has been directed toward place. This has countered the trend of sociospatial transformations which have made the central city technologically obsolete. Instead, policy should go with the flow and follow contemporary social changes by acknowledging uneven development and by directing itself toward the people affected by such patterns. More specifically, a people-oriented urban policy would, above all, help individuals travel or move to those areas better suited to provide them with employment. In this way, urban policy becomes an adjunct of the economic forces changing society, and individuals become mere cogs in the global sourcing strategy of mobile, multinational capital, which does not possess a shred of responsibility for local community life itself.

The President's Commission report has been deservedly criticized by urban analysts, but few have recognized that it is a document in an ideological war. According to Gans, it skirts the essential issue of the cause of uneven development:

> The unfortunate fact is that the report avoids the real issue. We are now living in a society with a slowly but steadily increasing number of unemployed, underemployed, and intermittently employed people, and thus also with a rising percentage of Americans who are in danger of becoming economically useless. (1982: 19)

No amount of people-directed programs can possibly counter the structural forces presently at work in American society. As Gans suggests, the report is totally asociological about the ability of the poor to move (1982: 18). More significantly, this document ignores the inherently basic nature of growth under capitalism, which produces uneven development regardless of where it occurs. Thus, in areas that are presently booming, unemployment rates are comparably as high as they are in areas experiencing decline. In fact, growth has a marginal impact on the local unemployment rate. While new jobs are created by development, these are invariably the kinds of positions which cannot alleviate the deprived condition of the underemployed and unemployed work force (Tomaskovic-Devey and Miller 1982). In short, the report wishes to pass off the ideology of growth as a natural solution to social problems while ignoring the uneven and inequitable nature of that process. For example, according to Bluestone and Harrison:

> There is a widespread tendency to view an entire region as though it were homogeneous. This is reflected in the media's obsession with the "Sunbelt-Frostbelt" imagery. However, evidence has been uncovered of extraordinarily uneven development within regions, including the Sunbelt. (1982: 33)

It is precisely for this reason that urban policies have always countered development trends not by seeking to alter root causes but by attempting to support programs which helped the disadvantaged regardless of where they lived. In effect, the President's Commission ignored the historical record of social programs in this country in a bold *political* attempt to abandon the societal priorities of the past twenty years, under the ideological distortion that they had not worked (1980: 507–508). In this way the plight of all those people adversely affected by the uncoordinated patterns of sociospatial development has been turned into a politicized issue over public policy philosophies. Unfortunately, such a casting away of public responsibility characterizes the very essence of neoconservative influence in the federal government and its policies up to the present moment.

The most remarkable aspect of the report which announced the "new" urban agenda is its lack of implementation. As such it remains an important document of neoconservative ideology. What, then, has become of urban public policy in this country? To a great extent it has simply disappeared from the scene. As is clear from the above, neoconservative ideology ultimately seeks to legitimate the status quo. This implies giving the development process virtual free rein under the ideological claim that growth fosters the good of all, so that attempts at countering trends by government merely detract from the system's own ability to follow the path best for it. In this light, the prescriptions of the "new" urban agenda would have served to strengthen existing developmental patterns. A second-best outcome from this perspective would be, of course, to do nothing, and that is precisely what has occurred. At present there is no concerted national attempt at managing sociospatial growth, nor has there been such a policy in place for some time.

The United States has increasingly become a society organized to fight those deprived of the benefits of development, as opposed to one which attempts to discover its root causes and alleviate its problems. At present the U.S. prison population is the highest in history, with an estimated 500,000 inmates nationally. Most of those behind bars are members of minority groups; hence, parallels between the United States and South Africa are not far off in this regard. The social control mechanisms now deployed to manage the large numbers of marginalized people in this country possess a spatial component which has been relatively effective. First, the sheer scope of segregation in society, both within central cities and in suburbs, means that the most disadvantaged groups are also the most isolated. Despite countersegregating programs, such as busing, neighborhoods throughout the metropolitan region remain stratified by race and class. The lack of contact between separate social groups makes it easier for the state to manage discontent by spatially and selectively deploying its agents and institutional mechanisms of social control. Through the neglect of root causes, social pathology in these areas

turns inward, and murder, drug addiction, and family problems become characteristic of life in economically deprived areas, as studies
on the emotional impact of unemployment now show (Hansen,
Bentley, and Skidmore 1981). Lefebvre observes:

> Cities are transformed into a collection of ghettos where indi-
> viduals are at once "socialized", integrated, submitted to ar-
> tificial pressures and constraints . . . and separated, isolated,
> disintegrated. A contradiction which is translated into anguish,
> frustration and revolt. (Martins 1982: 171)

Second, there is an insidious political implication to the observation that current affairs no longer require a national urban policy.
It seems that a neoconservative political strategy which favors business and the relatively well-off population of suburban homeowners
no longer needs to address the economically depressed workers in
company towns or central city constituencies at all in order to win
national elections. Economic trends which are already in place favor
the future prosperity of the already affluent, so that doing nothing in
the way of urban policy becomes the most Machiavellian of political
strategies. This aspect is brought to light once cognizance is taken of
the spatial impact of neoconservative economic policies. Thus, tax
policies aid the more well-to-do, and their depreciation allowances
encourage relocation to the suburbs along with the building of large
commercial shopping malls, thereby further aiding the development
of the suburban infrastructure. Increases in defense spending will
also aid the sunbelt and the suburbs at the expense of the older central cities. According to Glickman:

> The major thrusts of the administration's programme are to
> take back the public sector gains won by the poor in the past
> 20 years, to re-establish higher profit margins and the U.S. role
> of military supremacy, and further to shift economic activity to
> the south, west and the suburbs (the administration's political
> power base). (1981: 510)

In short, the neoconservative strategy advocates a public policy which
strengthens the political power of people and places benefited by the
lines of flow of deconcentration.

From all accounts, the neoconservative strategy uniting political appeals with trends in sociospatial development is working, and
some liberals also seem eager to try it. The twin drivers of ideological control—namely, the threat of communist expansion and the
threat of domestic crime—both generate enough support for military spending and domestic policies which stimulate central city

flight, even among the working and underclass elements of the population who stand to benefit least by them. The blind faith encouraged in the support of economic growth prevents workers from questioning the inequitable nature of rapid development and the underlying control of surplus wealth by giant international conglomerates, many of which invest increasingly in overseas economies. Finally, the social Darwinism behind sunbelt-frostbelt distinctions makes it appear that members of the working class in depressed areas are themselves to blame for what are in fact structural changes in U.S. capitalism. An ideological emphasis on promoting an "improved business climate" and "aggressive business competition" has served to mask quite effectively the role of the state as a subsidizer of monopoly interests, the takeover of business by giant conglomerates, and the uneven results of growth even in areas which are momentarily extolled for exhibiting the "right" attitudes. In the end, society is forced to grow at a rapid rate in certain isolated sectors, because that is the only way in which the monopoly capitalists, with their high organic composition of capital, can achieve the profits they need to sustain their far-flung operations. But that very pattern of growth produces the extremes of uneven development, which then makes it necessary to produce even more in order for the trickle-down public policy to work. The entire globe, advanced countries and their underdeveloped cohorts, is thrown onto a merry-go-round of perpetual boom-and-bust cycles which destroy the globe's resources at an alarming rate and push future generations into a debt-financed process of growth that can never become solvent.

Many analysts of the left-liberal persuasion, recently and quite rightly, have become alarmed at the extent to which present economic policies have served to spatially consolidate a neoconservative political power base which affects both political parties. Unless opposition forces are able to mobilize interests in their own defense, it is feared that the current transformations in society will place the course of future development inexorably on the path to a divided country, one that exhibits increasing disparities between the working well-off and the marginally employed or working poor. There is a growing consensus that one alternative to the status quo is the concept of economic democracy (Carnoy and Shearer 1980; Thurow 1980; Clavel, Forrester, and Goldsmith 1980). According to Carnoy and Shearer, this concept refers to the transfer, in part, of the control of economic decision making to the workers and the public. Most important, under this policy the public would have a greater say in the investment decisions currently sustaining deindustrialization and capital flight. Such a program would require more reinvestment of capital in local areas. In addition, it might encourage worker buy-outs in cases where conglomerates have shut down existing plants (Glickman 1981: 515; Hansen, Bentley, and Skidmore 1981). Finally, economic democracy would reestablish an effective voice for labor in negotiating increases in both indirect and direct wages, thus reversing the recent policies of neoconservatives, which have led to progressive polarization of the quality of life for rich and poor.

There is little question that measures to combat deindustrialization are sorely needed at this time in the United States. Current public policy programs are merely adjuncts of the needs of multinational conglomerates, whose policies impoverish workers and farmers in this country in pursuit of superprofits through the organized world system. A strong domestic policy curbing the activities of powerful, vested economic interests would reestablish the measure of balanced development sorely needed to overcome uneven and uncoordinated growth patterns. Yet, the left-liberals' response to the current situation in part reflects the ideological straitjacket within which all critical thought has recently been trapped—namely, the fallacy that our problems are only economic ones and that a left-liberal political economy is necessary to counter the neoconservatism which is presently hegemonic. As observed, this left-wing approach preserves the same subject of bourgeois social thought, economic growth equated with social well-being, while avoiding a shift to a more transformative social subject, the radicalization of community life paired with the class struggle.

In effect, such a program falls into the trap set for it by conservative ideologues, who claim that the liberals have had their chance and have been running the country for too long as it is. They contend that it is now time to give conservatives their opportunity even if their policies, such as the recent President's Commission report, are only thinly disguised Machiavellian projects in favor of sustaining present-day growth patterns. The reformist programs of the left are in this sense the best legitimation for the right's current use of government offices. Unlike conservatives, who are mobilized directly in favor of the ruling class, reformers wish to ignore the class struggle over ownership of the means of production. The latter, instead, believe in the fantasy that giant multinational conglomerates will be inclined to share greater control over decision making in a happy marriage with the working class. The ultimate fantasy of the left is that economic democracy can be achieved through democratic means, that is, through the reelection of the liberal coalition, which actually has always shown itself vulnerable to conservative challenges, especially when economic times improve. In this sense, and as Bookchin (1984: 9) observes, the call for economic justice is merely a logical extension of the bourgeoisie's call for juridical and political equality; it does not attack the fundamental inadequacies of all bourgeois social thought.

The failure of left-liberal thought lies with its reliance on marxian political economy. This approach focuses attention on the large firms, the multinationals, the world system, and the structural inability of local municipalities to control the economic resources which are the source of public welfare. Measures to counteract the power of concentrated, globally situated wealth have become the principal response of radical reformers advocating local control of economic resources.

To be sure, this problem is central to the issues arising from the nature of space under Late Capitalism. It is, however, not the only one which must be faced. Giving up political economy as the ideology of left-liberalism means abandoning its narrow focus on the central city. A truly transformative agenda would address inequitable sociospatial processes occurring in suburban and farming areas as well as downtown. It would involve the middle class as well as minorities. Finally, it would question the very nature of community life in every location. This means, in particular, raising to the forefront issues of culture and politics associated with the family, life-cycle needs, the nature of work, male-female relations, structures of political decision making, the role of new technologies, the nature of ethnic and racial relations, modes of satisfying needs other than consumerism, environmental management, and so on, in addition to economic considerations regarding societal growth. Such concerns are important once we broaden the potential base of left-liberalism from its domination by an urban and urbane elite.

At the bottom line, however, the fact remains that although we know what needs to be done, it is not entirely clear how we can accomplish it. Ultimately, calls for the transformation of social relations must face up to directly challenging the property relations which lie at the core of capitalism as a system of social organization. This is the point beyond which transformational acts have yet to pass, and it makes the schemes of left-liberals appear utopian because any moves to alter property relations in the United States are always closely monitored and controlled.

For example, economic democracy as a left-liberal reformist strategy has its spatial analogue, namely, the call for greater resident control of land-use planning and development. In fact, the environmental movement of the 1960s and 1970s has worked in just this area in ways that are independent of but complementary to the needs addressed by advocates of economic democracy, because they concern the self-management of space. According to Popper:

> The early proponents of land-use reform were a loose coalition of environmentalists, city planners, land-use lawyers, some state and federal officials, a few progressive business people, and citizen activists of all sorts. They had concluded that the objectional results of the development boom were caused primarily by zoning, particularly as administered by local governments. So when, in the late 1960's, a larger segment of the public began to perceive the seriousness of the nation's land-use problems, the vanguard of the reform movement had already worked out a solution. (1981: 12)

In the minds of reformers, land use was controlled by special interests at the local level, including business and government leaders. Only independent agencies at higher levels of government could regulate land use in a manner which would stand apart from special interests. This "centralized regulation" strategy called for the creation of regulatory bodies which would not have links to land development interests but which could administer, under well-defined laws, the development of land for the greatest good.

The thrust of the land reform movement, therefore, did not question existing property relations but was merely aimed at obtaining greater control over land development decisions in the public interest. This goal was not a uniformly perceived priority of the monopoly capital sector, and the national drive for a land-use policy act did not achieve success. In studying the 1974 failure of the act to pass the House, Plotkin found that vested economic interests were not actively involved in pressing for passage; thus "corporations do not gain advantages from the state automatically" (1980: 412). According to students of this effort (Popper 1981), greater success was enjoyed by the reform movement itself at local and state levels. There regulatory practices more restrictive of land uses were adopted. However, in the absence of a coordinated national mandate, these local reforms varied greatly from place to place and even within the very same region in their effectiveness. Further, in the absence of extending liberatory ideas from land to space itself, such reform efforts will never achieve transformative control over local planning and design.

The preceding has treated left-liberal thought that emphasizes political economy at the expense of a more global analysis quite disparagingly. On the basis of what has been said here, how can we overcome the contentious ideological battle between the two opposing political philosophies, which see themselves as politicizing public office once victory is attained at the polls? To begin with, it is necessary to recognize that there can be no social programs which advance democratization which do not also take account of space. Lefebvre advocates the extreme view of this observation. He claims that sociospatial praxis must directly address the property relations at the very core of the capitalist mode of production. Thus, using this criterion, economic democracy can be categorized as a reformist measure. It advocates the democratization of control over industrial production but does not seek to change ownership patterns except through incremental measures, such as "more local control of capital," rather than the takeover of local space itself. In fact, some of its advocates pledge that its measures will actually make the capitalist system work better (Glickman 1981: 515). However, only by seizing a space can an effective social praxis be realized. This means an activist approach to placement as well as economic decision making and the advocacy of local control of local resources. Worker empowerment and self-management must be extended to space itself and cannot be confined to the factory. Such a transformative approach has yet to be worked out.

In contrast to the utopian schemes of left-liberal reformers, there is another form of utopianism which once addressed the evils of capitalist growth. Plans for independent socialist communities advocated long ago by Fourier and Owen, for example, and once criticized as utopian by Marx himself, point the way toward addressing all the questions associated with the revolutionary transformation— issues of community, culture, politics, and economics. In a sense, by linking spatial change to social restructuring, the utopian socialists were correct and Marx was wrong. The former's utopianism lay not with their holistic approach to the evils of industrial life, such as their desire to transform the family and relations between the sexes, as might be supposed, but with their failure to extend the notion of a liberated social space back toward the working class of the central cities, which the utopians had abandoned. Yet, their schemes speak to us now in a period when such concentrations of labor no longer exist, while the quality of local community life languishes for lack of control over the means of social development. It should always be remembered that along with capitalist growth come new cultural and political forms, so that suburbanization, for example, has transformed the family, relations between the sexes, and political practice as surely as any purposely planned community scheme. In fact, the relation between spatial change and its effects on everyday social affairs remains an undeveloped but important topic of the new urban sociology (see, e.g., Hareven 1982; Pred 1981).

Quite clearly, the present moment contains the embryonic forms of the new social transformation. The best examples of these are the communities across the globe following the ideas of Fritz Schumacher (see McRobie 1981), because they have transcended political economy. However, the concrete, holistically conceived ideas about technological alternatives to capitalist growth are disparate and are fragmented from other important social transformations, such as those alternative life-style communes with new forms of culture and politics. Consequently, Marx's caution against the utopian communities of his time is as trenchant now as it was then. At present, alternative social forms which focus on technological or environmental change alone can never provide a basis for the thorough transformation of society (see, e.g., Bookchin 1984). Such communities are mere enclaves existing in what Lefebvre calls privileged space—a space made possible by the balance of power relations in society, which requires the subjugation elsewhere of the working class. Such privileged spaces also exist in affluent suburban communities and city enclaves of the well-off, who seem capable of guarding their everyday life against the social pathologies which afflict adjacent areas.

The revolutionary transformation requires the extension of the new sociospatial relations to the *un*-privileged spaces—those areas where the exigencies of daily living affect everyday experience but remain beyond the control of local residents, such as the factory, the workshop, the school, the street, the less affluent community. The pursuit of such a project requires a strategy of generalized self-management which unites ownership and control relations in the workplace with those of the home. As Lefebvre remarks:

> The reconstruction of the "low to high" of social space, previously produced from "high to low," implies general self-management, that is, at the various levels, complementing that of the units and instances of production . . . Only in this way can the socialization of the means of production include the issue of space. To do otherwise, to define "socialist space" as natural space or as communes living on a privileged space or by "conviviality," is to confuse the end with the means, the goal with the stages; it is, in other words, abstract utopianism. (Quoted in Martins 1982: 294)

The new political agenda organized around what can be called sociospatial praxis can make progress only through a clean break with past notions which focus on some abstraction called the working class, which ties change only to social movements of industrial workers with a large demographic impact, or which fragments concerns into issues of community control or environmental quality alone. Nascent movements of a transformative nature, such as the cultural needs of youths, minorities, and women, also deserve our attention. Above all, the new ideas currently being worked out by the generic push for alternative social movements require some time to mature before we can expect them to solve our immediate strategic needs for political changes (see Bookchin 1984; Castells 1983; McRobie 1981; Gorz 1980). It is this need and this agenda centering around a sociospatial praxis which must be embraced by left-liberalism as it seeks to integrate the factory with the farm and the central city with the suburb.

At present, the neoconservative ideology, backed up by the interests of monopoly and competitive capitalists as well as elements of the working class, seems not only to characterize popular political control but is reflected in the status quo of uncoordinated public policies. While economic interests may prefer greater centralized planning, it is not as pressing a priority as some reformers may think. Both economic and spatial control have been consolidated in the hands of the private sector without any respectable challenge to that authority from the working class. In the absence of any concerted movement to alter the property relations of society, which underpin both economic and spatial development, reform measures seem destined to fulfill the profit-making needs of monopoly capital, if they experience any success at all. We are left with a situation within which fractions belonging to the complex social order will jockey for positions of advantage during the yearly progress of socio-economic growth.

Combating neoconservative public policy at present involves challenging commonly held beliefs about the role of growth in solving the problems of society. Until now, social thought about such a project has been straitjacketed by the ideology of growth, a property marxists share with mainstreamers. This ideology masks several real aspects of current patterns of development that are fatal to its premises. First, because sociospatial development in the United States is uncoordinated, growth invariably brings with it significant problems. Pollution, traffic congestion, rapidly rising prices, housing shortages and the consequent increase in the price of shelter, overcrowding, high crime rates—especially violent attacks of a random nature—and the overdevelopment which leads to blight are but some of the side effects of growth. All the developed areas which are most often touted by neoconservative ideologues as personifying the "right" type of business climate, such as Houston, suffer greatly from these and other costs of growth. Most important, through the mechanism of this ideology, those costs are internalized by individuals themselves. The belief in the benefits of expansion has become a mechanism of social control, personified perhaps by worker acceptance of the long ride home through congestion, noise, and smog.

In addition, the ideology of growth ignores the fact that uneven development is an intrinsic part of the Late Capitalist growth process. Thus growth can create new jobs, but it can do so only within the constraints of capitalist relations of production. Hence, such expansion is confined to specific sectors of the labor force and does not alleviate the rate of unemployment. This is especially the case for the high-tech industries, which have been specifically touted as the solution to our structural employment problems (Tomaskovic-Devey and Miller 1982; Benson and Lloyd 1983). Some of the most rapidly growing areas of the country also have high unemployment rates, even with strong multiplier effects from the leading-edge industries influencing other sectors of the local economy. Booming development creates a large segment of the local population that is relatively well off, especially people imported to endogenously created jobs from other areas. However, there is a certain impoverishment of workers produced by the uncoordinated manner of growth which is a *structural* feature of this process. Most important, the newer, capital-intensive industries have less of a demand for workers than previous types of production; thus, as Benson and Lloyd (1983) observe, there is little hope that workers displaced from jobs today will be brought back into the fold of prosperity by the technological innovations of tomorrow.

There is a third and final effect of growth ideology. Pro-growth advocates ignore completely the role of the state in affecting the geographical transfer of value which sustains development. Thus the phrase "right business climate" is often used as a pseudonym for "hefty government incentives." At present there is intense spatial competition between local areas for new businesses. Often areas which have become growth centers have achieved that status as a consequence of massive government spending. In addition, areas which attract new businesses generally have made sacrifices to extend publicly supported subsidies to the business community. Far from representing the social Darwinist outcome of competitive survival, this state-economy-space linkage is a local version of socialism for the growth sectors of business. On the aggregate, that is, when state intervention is recognized at all its levels, it becomes clear that the private and public spheres have merged into a kind of amalgam which is neither capitalism nor socialism but a U.S. variant of the welfare state—one that works in the interests of the monopoly sector, because it pursues growth under the existing property relations. Even noncapitalists, therefore, subscribe to the social relations of the existing system because they are believed to bring prosperity and jobs. Invariably, the rapid swings of development characteristic of Late Capitalism make those industries which are healthy due to a lack of competition, such as those in the highly concentrated multinational monopoly sector, comparatively better off. At the same time, businesses immersed in the competitive environment which keep their profit-making edge through innovation fail to find locational opportunities that can overcome their sector's constraints. The outcome of this process is a version of social inequity afflicting the capitalist class as well as its workers. Thus, the family farm, which has evolved over the years as a highly efficient enterprise, is currently being driven out of existence by a state–monopoly sector conjuncture in agribusiness. Such unevenly produced inequities, with their profound social implications, are ignored by advocates of growth.

The civic boosterism behind pro-growth proponents merely conceals the special interests that wish to capitalize on the public subsidization of development so that superprofits can be realized. There is considerable historical evidence to substantiate this claim, especially from studies of the local government–real estate sector relation. A more contemporary example would be the notorious "enterprise zone" proposal for inner-city aid. As originally conceived by Peter Hall, it advocated the public creation of special places within the central city where vigorous competition between businesses and entrepreneurs could be fostered, in the manner of the commercial and light industrial success of Hong Kong. In the United States this conception was transformed into a plan self-evidently created to meet the needs of speculators and industries lusting after a public means of attacking the social rights gained by labor over the years and hungry for a new scheme by which to turn over devalorized city land for a profit (Goldsmith 1982).

Through the ideological devices of conventional thought, the causes of society's problems are advocated as their cures. The long-lived special interests operating behind this status quo enjoy the initial profit taking each time that space is turned over or restructured. By this assertion I do not mean to imply that all mainstreamers are actively involved in the machinations of these special interests or that all conventional analysts are insensitive to the condition of the less fortunate. On the contrary, most urban analysts are removed academically from direct roles in the growth process. Yet, by failing to define the problems of sociospatial development as *intrinsic* to the deep-level relations which produce them and by fostering a mode of analysis which relies on an explanatory paradigm that is ideological, mainstreamers support the conventional outlook toward sociospatial change.

The desire to forge an analysis which recognizes the importance of special interests as well as structural forces comes from experience with empirical work. The discovery that space is a *political* product of intended and unintended actions implies that the possibility exists for a more intelligent design and use of the environment by confronting the narrow, vested interests surrounding the ownership and control of land. While the marxian approach to space remains undeveloped, it persists as the most fruitful tradition that we currently possess, because of its sensitivity to the monopolistic forces which produce abstract space. This requires changing the existing property relations of society and redesigning both the workplace and the community accordingly. However, this is a sensibility which seems as alien to other marxists of a more theoretical bent as it is to mainstreamers.

The misrecognition of the transformational nature of collective seizures of space by marxian thought, which seeks to deemphasize such a sociospatial praxis, is fundamentally important to overcome. In part, local efforts at controlling social space have failed because of the fractional nature of the social interests which are deployed in space. That is, the inability of community-based political activists to aggregate into a social force rests with the essentially spatial nature of such groups. While interests may be shared by individuals living in separate locations, their lack of proximity under the conditions of sociospatial domination makes them think as strangers. Such attitudes are, of course, reinforced by the fetishism produced by existing property relations, which promote individualistic modes of consumerism, especially with regard to limiting local community attachments. Building communality across neighborhoods as well as across occupational categories—or within them for that matter—remains a formidable task, but one which is restrained by ideological mind-sets alone rather than by any fragmentation due to some allegedly innate territorial imperative (Suttles 1973).

A second reason for the limited impact of sociospatial political action also has its origins in everyday life—in this case, the multiplicity of concerns which have to be faced by local community organizations to varying degrees. Thus, for example, Kotler lists no fewer than forty-one separate issues which have been placed on the agendas of community organizations (1979: 40). Because priorities vary from place to place, it is not always possible for separate neighborhood groups to agree over the right way to address these issues or even their respective importance. But, despite the formidable barriers to political aggregation, recent years have witnessed the growth of national movements, especially those of neighborhood activists (Boyte 1980) and of tenants (Heskin 1981). To date, however, sociospatial praxis has yet to make its way into the articulated political strategies of traditional social movements.

Left-liberal thought has tended to downplay the importance of all user social movements to the primacy of workplace transformations. What is needed, however, is an integration of one with the other around the maturing ideas associated with general self-management. At present sociospatial confrontation among all class fractions comprises a considerable portion of the contents of local politics, especially in the ideological battle between pro-growth advocates and those developing a sensibility which calls for balanced growth and coordinated planning. In the debate on the theory of space, the structuralist impulse has served to reinforce the peripheral status of sociospatial confrontation and its embryonic call for community self-management. This has been accomplished by discursively labeling Lefebvre's approach "historicist" and by specifying the theoretical significance of such actions as a displaced form of the class struggle within the field of consumption. Yet, as Harvey once observed (1976), such confrontations call the real property relations at the very core of the capitalist mode of production into question, and capitalism can ill afford this.

So far, state intervention and the exercise of power have confined the volatility of spatial users to isolated and multiply manifested incidents. Urban marxian thought has failed to appreciate fully that underlying all these disparate cleavages are the property relations of capitalism, as well as a system which reproduces the primacy of spatial exchange values over spatial uses. A greater recognition of the transformational role of sociospatial praxis requires a redirection of marxian thinking. At present the language of sociospatial liberation necessary for such a task has yet to be invented, as we are overburdened with the categories of political economy. Without the new vocabulary, spatial practice is perceived as representing an accident of collective behavior. The present moment is one in which the absolute space of political and economic domination reigns hegemonically over the social space of everyday life. Everywhere the built environment signifies the instrumental and functional nature of construction, while the use values of space, both communal and personal, retreat further and further away from public experience. Currently there is only a faint glimmer of realization that it is necessary for the users to reclaim space and to reassert design according to the multiple purposes of social space (Goodman 1971; Sale 1980; Hartman et al. 1982; Whyte 1980). Thus, sociospatial thought must be redirected away from an analysis of the economy toward the transformation of social relations, which requires a return to the struggle for a balanced community life deploying transformative social relations in space. This project, tying production and consumption relations together in a liberated space, remains undeveloped in radical thought. If the urban revolution began in the ghetto streets and through the People's Park, then we have only ourselves to blame for not carrying the struggle, both utopian and strategic, inside the middle-class privacy of our own neighborhoods.

References

Adams, J. 1970. "Residential Structure of Midwestern Cities." *Annals of the Association of American Geographers* 60: 37–62.

Aglietta, M. 1978. "Phases of U.S. Capitalist Expansion." *New Left Review* 110: 5–42.

———. 1979. *A Theory of Capitalist Regulation*. London: New Left Books.

Agnew, J. 1981. "Home Ownership and the Capitalist Social Order." In Dear and Scott 1981.

Alcaly, R., and D. Mermelstein, eds. 1977. *The Fiscal Crisis of American Cities*. New York: Vintage.

Alihan, M. 1938. *Social Ecology*. New York: Columbia University Press.

Alonso, W. 1964. *Location and Land Use*. Cambridge, Mass.: Harvard University Press.

———. 1971. "Equity and Its Relation to Efficiency in Urbanization." In J. Kain and J. Meyer, eds., *Essays in Regional Economics*. Cambridge, Mass.: Harvard University Press.

Althusser, L. 1970a. *On Lenin and Other Essays*. New York: Vanguard.

———. 1970b. *For Marx*. New York: Vintage.

———. 1971. *Lenin and Philosophy*. New York: Monthly Review Press.

Altshuler, A. 1977. "Review of the Costs of Sprawl." *Journal of the American Institute of Planners* 43: 207–209.

Amin, S. 1976. *Accumulation on a World Scale*. New York: Monthly Review Press.

Anderson, J. 1973. "Ideology in Geography: An Introduction." *Antipode* 5: 1–6.

Anderson, M. 1964. *The Federal Bulldozer*. Cambridge, Mass.: MIT Press.

Armstrong, R. 1972. *The Office Industry*. Cambridge, Mass.: MIT Press.

———. 1979. "National Trends in Office Construction, Employment and Headquarters Location in the U.S. Metropolitan Areas." In P. Daniels, ed., *Spatial Patterns of Office Growth and Location*. New York: John Wiley and Sons.

Baldassare, M. 1980. *The Growth Dilemma*. Berkeley and Los Angeles: University of California Press.

Bandyopahyay, P. 1982. "Neo-Ricardianism in Urban Analysis." *International Journal of Urban and Regional Research* 6: 277–282.

Baran, P., and P. Sweezy. 1966. *Monopoly Capitalism*. New York: Monthly Review Press.

Barnet, R., and R. Muller. 1974. *Global Reach*. New York: Simon and Schuster.

Baumol, W. 1959. *Business Behavior, Value and Growth*. New York: Macmillan.

Beauregard, R. 1984. "Structure, Agency and Urban Redevelopment." In Smith 1984.

Beckmann, M. 1968. *Location Theory*. New York: Random House.

Bell, C., and H. Newby. 1976. "Community, Communion, Class and Community Action." In D. Herbert and R. Johnson, eds. *Social Areas in the City II*. London: John Wiley and Sons.

Bell, D. 1973. *The Coming of Post-Industrial Society*. New York: Basic Books.

Bellush, J., and M. Hausknecht. 1967. *Urban Renewal: People, Politics and Planning*. Garden City, N.Y.: Anchor Books.

Bensman, J., and A. Vidich. 1960. *Small Town in Mass Society*. New York: Free Press.

Benson, I., and J. Lloyd. 1983. *New Technology and Industrial Change*. New York: Nichols Publishing.

Berle, A., and G. Means. 1932. *The Modern Corporation and Private Property*. New York: Macmillan.

Bernard, J. 1962. *American Community Behavior*. New York: Holt, Rinehart and Winston.

Berry, B. 1962. "Cities as Systems within Systems of Cities." *Papers and Proceedings of the Regional Science Association* 13: 147–164.

———. 1967. *Geography of Market Centers and Retail Distribution*. Englewood Cliffs, N.J.: Prentice-Hall.

———. 1968. *Theories of Urban Location*. Resource Paper 1. Washington, D.C.: Association of American Geographers.

———. 1971. "Internal Structure of the City." In Bourne 1971.

———. 1973. *The Human Consequences of Urbanization*. New York: St. Martin's Press.

Berry, B., and D. Dahman. 1977. *Population Redistribution in the U.S. in the 1970's*. Washington, D.C.: National Academy of Sciences.

Berry, B., and Q. Gillard. 1977. *The Changing Shape of Metropolitan America*. Cambridge, Mass.: Ballinger.

Berry, B., P. Goheen, and H. Goldstein. 1968. *Metropolitan Area Definition*. Washington, D.C.: Government Printing Office.

Berry, B., and J. Kasarda. 1977. *Contemporary Urban Ecology*. New York: Macmillan.

Berry, B., and K. Smith, eds. 1972. *City Classification Handbook*. New York: John Wiley and Sons.

Berry, W. 1972. *The Unsettling of America*. New York: Avon.

Berube, M., and M. Gittel. 1969. *Confrontation at Ocean-Hill Brownsville*. New York: Praeger.

Bhaskar, R. 1979. *A Realist Theory of Science*. Leeds, Eng.: U.K. Book Publishing.

Biggar, J., and F. Biasiolli. 1978. "Metropolitan Deconcentration: Subareal In-Migration and Central City to Ring Mobility Patterns among Southern SMSA's." *Demography* 15: 589–603.

Blau, J., M. LaGory, and J. Pipkin. 1983. *Remaking the City*. Albany: State University of New York Press.

Blau, P., and O. Duncan. 1967. *The American Occupational Structure*. New York: John Wiley and Sons.

Blaug, R. 1968. "Technical Change and Marxian Economics." In D. Horowitz, ed., *Marx and Modern Economics*. New York: Monthly Review Press.

Block, F. 1980. "Beyond Relative Autonomy: State Managers as Historical Subjects." *Socialist Register 1980*: 227–242.

Bluestone, B. 1972. "Economic Crisis and the Law of Uneven Development." *Politics and Society* 2: 65–82.

Bluestone, B., and B. Harrison. 1982. *The Deindustrialization of America*. New York: Basic Books.

Blumstein, J., and L. Salamon, eds. 1979. Special Issue on Growth Policy in the Eighties. *Law and Contemporary Problems* 43.

Bock, D., and J. Dunlap. 1970. *Labor and the American Community*. Englewood Cliffs, N.J.: Prentice-Hall.

Boddy, M. 1981. "The Property Sector in Late Capitalism: The Case of Britain." In Dear and Scott 1981.

Bogue, A., and M. Bogue. 1957. "Profits and the Frontier Land Speculator." *Journal of Economic History* 17: 1–23.

Bollens, M., and H. Schmandt. 1965. *The Metropolis*. New York: Harper and Row.

Bookchin, M. 1984. *The Ecology of Freedom*. Palo Alto: Cheshire Books.

Borchert, J. 1967. "American Metropolitan Evolution." *Geographical Review* 57: 301–332.

Boulay, H. 1979. "Social Control Theories of Urban Politics." *Social Science Quarterly* 59: 605–638.

Bourdieu, P. 1977. *Outline of a Theory of Practice*. New York: Cambridge University Press.

Bourne, L., ed. 1971. *Internal Structure of the City*. New York: Oxford University Press.

———. 1975. *Regulating Urban Systems*. London: Oxford University Press.

Bourne, L., and J. Simmons. 1978. *Systems of Cities*. New York: Oxford University Press.

Boyer, B. 1973. *Cities Destroyed for Cash*. Chicago: Follett Publishing Co.

Boyte, H., ed. 1979. Special Issue on Neighborhood Activism. *Social Policy*.

———. 1980. *The Backyard Revolution*. Philadelphia: Temple University Press.

Bradford, C. 1979. "Financing Home Ownership: The Federal Role in Neighborhood Decline." *Urban Affairs Quarterly* 14: 313–336.

Bradford, D., and H. Kelejian. 1973. "An Econometric Model of the Flight to the Suburbs." *Journal of Political Economy* 8: 566–589.

Bradshaw, T., and E. Blakeley. 1979. *Rural Communities in Advanced Industrial Society*. New York: Praeger.

Braverman, L. 1974. *Labor and Monopoly Capital*. New York: Monthly Review Press.

Brinkman, G. 1974. *The Development of Rural America*. Lawrence: University Press of Kansas.

Brodsky, H. 1973. "Land Development and the Expanding City." *Annals of the Association of American Geographers* 63: 159–166.

Brown, H., and N. Roberts. 1978. "Land Owners at the Urban Fringe." Unpublished paper, York University, Canada.

Burchell, R., and D. Listokin, eds. 1981. *Cities under Stress*. New Brunswick, N.J.: Rutgers University Press.

Burgess, E. 1925. "The Growth of the City: An Introduction to a Research Project." In Park, Burgess, and McKenzie 1925.

Burns, L., and W. Pang. 1977. "Big Business in the Big City: Corporate Headquarters in the CBD." *Urban Affairs Quarterly* 4: 533–544.

Buttel, F., and H. Newby. 1980. *The Rural Sociology of Advanced Societies*. London: Croom Helm.

Campbell, A., and J. Dollenmeyer. 1975. "Governance in a Metropolitan Society." In A. Hawley and V. Rock, eds., *Metropolitan America in Contemporary Perspective*. New York: John Wiley and Sons.

Carchedi, G. 1975. "On the Economic Identification of the New Middle Class." *Economy and Society* 4: 1–86.

Carnoy, M., and D. Shearer. 1980. *Economic Democracy: The Challenge of the 1980's*. White Plains, N.Y.: M. E. Sharpe.

Carruthers, E. 1969. "Manhattan's Office Building Binge." *Fortune* 80: 114.

Carter, A. 1970. *Structural Change in the American Economy*. Cambridge, Mass.: Harvard University Press.

Cassidy, R. 1972. "Moving to the Suburbs." *New Republic*, June 22, pp. 20–23.

Castells, M. 1968. "Y-a-t-il une sociologie urbaine?" *Sociologie du Travail* 1: 72–90.

———. 1975. "Advanced Capitalism, Collective Consumption, and Urban Contradictions." In L. Lindberg et al., eds., *Stress and Contradictions in Modern Capitalism*. Lexington, Mass.: D. C. Heath.

———. 1977. *The Urban Question*. Cambridge, Mass.: MIT Press.

———. 1978. *City, Class and Power*. New York: Macmillan.

———. 1980. *The Economic Crisis and American Society*. Princeton: Princeton University Press.

———. 1983. *The City and the Grassroots*. Berkeley and Los Angeles: University of California Press.

———. 1984. "Crisis, Planning and the Quality of Life." In Smith 1984.

Chandler, A. 1977. *The Visible Hand*. Cambridge, Mass.: Harvard University Press.

Chapin, F., and S. Weiss. 1962. *Factors Influencing Land Development.* Chapel Hill, N.C.: Institute for Research in Social Science.

Chase-Dunn, C. 1984. "Urbanization in the World System: New Directions for Research." In Smith 1984.

Christaller, W. 1966. *Central Places in Southern Germany.* Englewood Cliffs, N.J.: Prentice-Hall.

Clark, C. 1951. "Urban Population Densities." *Journal of the Royal Statistical Society*, Series A, vol. 114: 490–496.

Clark, G., and M. Dear. 1981. "The State in Capitalism and the Capitalist State." In Dear and Scott 1981.

Clavel, P., J. Forrester, and W. Goldsmith. 1980. *Urban and Regional Planning in an Age of Austerity.* New York: Pergamon Press.

Clawson, M. 1962. "Urban Sprawl and Speculation in Urban Land." *Land Economics* 28: 99–111.

———. 1971. *Suburban Land Use Conversion in the U.S.* Baltimore: Johns Hopkins University Press.

Cohen, G. 1978. *Karl Marx's Theory of History.* Oxford: Oxford University Press.

Cohen, R. 1981. "The New International Division of Labor, Multinational Corporations and the Urban Hierarchy." In Dear and Scott 1981.

Coleman, J. 1976. "Liberty and Equality in School Desegregation." *Social Policy* 6: 9–13.

Coleman, J., S. Kelly, and J. Moore. 1975. *Trends in School Segregation, 1968–73.* Washington, D.C.: Urban Institute.

Comte, A. 1875. *System of Positive Policy.* New York: Burt Franklin.

Cook, F. 1966. *The War Torn State.* New York: Macmillan.

Coughlin, R. 1979. "Agricultural Land Conversion in the Urban Fringe." In M. Schnept, ed., *Farmlands, Food and the Future.* Ankeny, Iowa: Soil Conservation Society of America.

Cox, K. 1978. "Local Interests and Urban Political Processes in Market Societies." In K. Cox, ed., *Urbanization and Conflict in Market Societies.* Chicago: Maaroufa.

———. 1981. "Capitalism and Conflict around the Communal Living Space." In Dear and Scott 1981.

———. 1982. "Housing Tenure and Neighborhood Activism." *Urban Affairs Quarterly* 18: 107–129.

Craemers, D. 1963. *Changing Location of Manufacturing Employment, 1947–1961.* New York: National Industrial Conference Board.

Crosser, P. 1960. *State Capitalism in the Economy of the U.S.* New York: Macmillan.

Crouch, C., ed. 1979. *State and Economy in Contemporary Capitalism.* London: Croom Helm.

Danborn, D. 1979. *The Resisted Revolution.* Ames, Iowa: Iowa State University Press.

Davie, M. 1937. "The Pattern of Urban Growth." In G. Murdock, ed., *Studies in the Science of Society.* New Haven: Yale University Press.

Davies, J. 1966. *Neighborhood Groups and Urban Renewal.* New York: Columbia University Press.

Davis, I. 1980. "Seven Requirements Determine the Success of Downtown Revitalization Projects." *Journal of Housing* 37: 448–449.

Davis, M. 1984. "The Political Economy of Late-Imperial America." *New Left Review* 143: 6–38.

Day, R. 1976. "The Theory of Long Waves: Kondratieff, Trotsky, Mandel." *New Left Review* 99: 67–82.

Dear, M., and A. Scott, eds. 1981. *Urbanization and Urban Planning in Capitalist Society.* New York: Methuen.

Debord, G. 1961. A tape-recorded talk delivered May 17, reprinted in K. Knabb, ed., *Situationist International Anthology.* Berkeley: Bureau of Public Secrets, 1981.

Dillard, D. 1948. *The Economics of John Maynard Keynes.* New York: Prentice-Hall.

Dobriner, W. M., ed. 1958. *The Suburban Community.* New York: G. P. Putnam's Sons.

———. 1963. *Class in Suburbia.* Englewood Cliffs, N.J.: Prentice-Hall.

Douglas, A. 1925. *The Suburban Trend.* New York: Century Co.

Duncan, O. 1961. "From Social System to Ecosystem." *Sociological Inquiry* 31: 140–149.

Duncan, O., et al. 1960. *Metropolis and Region.* Baltimore: Johns Hopkins University Press.

Duncan, O., and A. Reiss. 1950. *Social Characteristics of Rural and Urban Communities.* New York: John Wiley.

Duncan, O., and L. Schnore. 1959. "Cultural, Behavioral, and Ecological Perspectives in the Study of Social Organization." *American Journal of Sociology* 65: 132–146.

Duncan, S. 1981. "Housing Policy, the Methodology of Levels, and Urban Research: The Case of Castells." *International Journal of Urban and Regional Research* 5: 231–253.

Dunleavy, P. 1979. "The Urban Bases of Political Alignment." *British Journal of Political Science* 9: 409–443.

———. 1980. *Urban Political Analysis.* London: Macmillan.

Edel, M. 1977. "Rent Theory and Labor Strategy." *Review of Radical Political Economics* 9: 1–15.

———. 1981. "Capitalism, Accumulation and the Explanation of Urban Phenomena." In Dear and Scott 1981.

———. 1982. "Home Ownership and Working Class Unity." *International Journal of Urban and Regional Research* 6: 205–221.

Edmonston, B. 1975. *Population Distribution in American Cities.* Lexington, Mass.: D. C. Heath.

Edwards, R. 1975. *Contested Terrain.* New York: Basic Books.

Engels, F. 1973. *The Condition of the Working Class in England.* Moscow: Progress Publishers.

———. 1979. *The Housing Question.* Moscow: Progress Publishers.

Fabricant, S. 1950. *The Trend of Government Activity in the U.S. since 1900*. Princeton: Princeton University Press.

Fainstein, N., et al. 1983. *Restructuring the City: The Political Economy of Urban Redevelopment*. New York: Longmans.

Fainstein, S., and N. Fainstein. 1978. "National Policy and Urban Development." *Social Problems* 28: 124–146.

―――― and ――――. 1980. *Urban Political Movements*. Englewood Cliffs, N.J.: Prentice-Hall.

Fava, S. 1956. "Suburbanism as a Way of Life." *American Sociological Review* 21: 34–37.

Feagin, J. 1983. *The Urban Real Estate Game*. Englewood Cliffs, N.J.: Prentice-Hall.

――――. 1984. "Sunbelt Metropolis and Development Capital: Houston in the Era of Late Capitalism." In Sawers and Tabb 1984.

Fellmuth, R., ed. 1973. *Power and Land in California*. New York: Grossman.

Fine, B. 1979. "On Marx's Theory of Agricultural Rent." *Economy and Society* 8: 243–250.

Fine, B., and L. Harris. 1979. *Re-Reading "Capital."* London: Macmillan.

Firey, W. 1945. *Land Use in Central Boston*. Cambridge, Mass.: Harvard University Press.

Fischer, C. 1976. *The Urban Experience*. New York: Harcourt, Brace, Jovanovich.

――――. 1983. *To Dwell among Friends*. Chicago: University of Chicago Press.

Form, W. 1954. "The Place of Social Structure in the Determination of Land Use." *Social Forces* 32: 317–323.

Frey, W. 1979. "Population Movement and City-Suburban Redistribution: An Analytic Framework." *Demography* 15: 571–588.

Friedland, R. 1976. "Class Power and Social Control: The War on Poverty." *Politics and Society* 6: 459–490.

――――. 1980. "Corporate Power and Urban Growth: The Case of Urban Renewal." *Politics and Society* 10: 203–224.

――――. 1983. *Power and Crisis in the City*. New York: Schocken Books.

Friedman, A. 1977. *Industry and Labor: Class Struggle at Work in Monopoly Capitalism*. London: Macmillan.

Friedman, J., and J. Miller. 1965. "The Urban Field." *Journal of the American Institute of Planners* 31: 312–320.

Frobel, F., J. Heinrichs, and O. Kreye. 1980. *The New International Division of Labor*. New York: Cambridge University Press.

Fuchs, V. 1962. *The Changing Location of Manufacturing in the U.S. since 1929*. New Haven: Yale University Press.

――――. 1968. *The Service Economy*. New York: National Bureau of Economic Research.

Fuguitt, G., and C. Beale. 1978. "The New Patterns of Non-Metropolitan Population Change." In K. Taueber, J. Bumpass, and J. Sweet, eds., *Social Demography*. New York: Academic Press.

Fuguitt, G., and T. Heaton. 1980. "Dimensions of Population Redistribution in the U.S. since 1950." *Social Science Quarterly* 61: 508–523.

Fuguitt, G., and H. Voss. 1979. *Growth and Change in Rural America.* Washington, D.C.: Urban Land Institute.

Fujimoto, I. 1978. "The Communities of the San Joaquin Valley." In U.S. Congress, Senate, *Priorities in Agricultural Research of the U.S. Department of Agriculture,* 95th Congress, 2d session, part 2. Washington, D.C.: Government Printing Office.

Gaffney, M. 1967. "Land Rent, Taxation and Public Policy." *Papers and Proceedings of the Regional Science Association* 23: 141–153.

Galbraith, J. 1969. *The New Industrial State.* Boston: Houghton Mifflin.

Gale, S., and E. Moore, eds. 1975. *The Manipulated City.* Chicago: Maaroufa Press.

Gans, H. 1967. *The Levittowners.* New York: Pantheon.

———. 1982. "Political Straddling." *Society* 19: 18–20.

Gappert, G., and H. Rose, eds. 1975. *The Social Economy of Cities.* Urban Affairs Annual Review 19. Beverly Hills: Sage Publications.

Gartner, A., and F. Reissman. 1974. *The Service Society and the Consumer Vanguard.* New York: Harper.

Gettys, W. 1940. "Human Ecology and Social Theory." *Social Forces* 18: 469–476.

Giddens, A. 1973. *The Class Structure of Advanced Societies.* New York: Harper.

———. 1979. *Central Problems in Social Theory.* Berkeley and Los Angeles: University of California Press.

———. 1981. *A Contemporary Critique of Historical Materialism.* Berkeley and Los Angeles: University of California Press.

Gillman, J. 1957. *The Falling Rate of Profit.* London: Dennis Dobson.

Gist, N., and S. Fava. 1974. *Urban Society.* New York: Crowell.

Glickman, N. 1981. "Emerging Urban Policies in a Slow Growth Economy: Conservative Initiatives and Progressive Responses in the U.S." *International Journal of Urban and Regional Research* 5: 492–527.

Glucksmann, M. 1974. *Structuralist Analysis in Contemporary Social Thought.* Boston: Routledge and Kegan Paul.

Goldschmidt, J. 1944. *As You Sow: Three Studies of the Social Consequences of Agribusiness.* Montclair, N.J.: Held, Osmund Co. Reprinted 1978.

Goldsmith, W. 1982. "Enterprise Zones: If They Work, We're in Trouble." *International Journal of Urban and Regional Research* 6: 435–442.

Goodall, B. 1972. *The Economics of Urban Areas.* New York: Praeger.

Goodman, R. 1971. *After the Planners.* New York: Simon and Schuster.

Gordon, D. 1977a. "Capitalism and the Roots of the Urban Crisis." In Alcaly and Mermelstein 1977.

———. 1977b. "Class Struggle and the Stages of Urban Development." Watkins and Perry 1977.

———. 1984. "Capitalist Development and the History of American Cities." In Tabb and Sawers 1984.

Gordon, D., et al. 1982. *Divided Workers: The Historical Transformation of Labor in the U.S.* New York: Cambridge University Press.

Gorz, A. 1980. *Ecology as Politics.* Boston: South End Press.

Gottdiener, M. 1977. *Planned Sprawl: Private and Public Interests in Suburbia.* Beverly Hills: Sage Publications.

———. 1983. "Some Theoretical Issues in Growth Control." *Urban Affairs Quarterly* 17: 55–73.

———. 1984. "Debate on the Theory of Space: Towards an Urban Praxis." In Smith 1984.

———. Forthcoming. *Metropolitan Politics: Neo-Marxism, Neo-Weberianism and the Theory of the Local State.*

Gottdiener, M., and A. Lagopoulos, eds. Forthcoming. *Meaning in the City: An Introduction to Urban Social Semiotics.* New York: Columbia University Press.

Gottdiener, M., and M. Neiman. 1981. "Characteristics of Support for Local Growth Control." *Urban Affairs Quarterly* 17: 55–73.

Gottlieb, M. 1976. *Long Swings in Urban Development.* New York: National Bureau of Economic Research.

Gottmann, J. 1972. "Urban Centrality and the Interweaving of Quaternary Activities." In G. Bellad and J. Tyrwhiit, eds., *Human Identity in the Urban Environment.* Baltimore: Penguin.

Gramsci, A. 1971. *Selections from the Prison Notebooks of Antonio Gramsci.* New York: International Publications.

Gras, N. 1922. *Introduction to Economic History.* New York: Harper and Row.

Green, D. 1980. "Urban Subcenters: Recent Trends in Urban Spatial Structure." *Growth and Change* 11: 29–40.

Green, M., B. Moore, and B. Wasserstein. 1972. *The Closed Enterprise System.* New York: Bantam.

Greer, S. 1962. *The Emerging City.* New York: Free Press.

———. 1965. *Urban Renewal and American Cities.* Chicago: Bobbs-Merrill.

Guest, A. 1973. "Urban Growth and Population Densities." *Demography* 10: 53–69.

———. 1975. "Population Suburbanization in American Metropolitan Areas, 1940–1970." *Geographical Analysis* 7: 267–283.

Habermas, J. *Legitimation Crisis.* Boston: Beacon Press.

———. 1979. *Communication and the Evolution of Society.* Boston: Beacon Press.

Hadden, J., and B. Borgatta. 1965. *American Cities: Their Social Characteristics.* Chicago: Rand McNally.

Haddon, R. 1970. "A Minority in a Welfare State Society." *New Atlantis* 2: 80–133.

Hahn, H. 1971. *Urban-Rural Conflict.* Beverly Hills: Sage Publications.

Hannerz, U. 1969. *Soulside.* New York: Columbia University Press.

Hansen, G., M. Bentley, and M. Skidmore. 1981. *Plant Shut Downs, People and Communities: A Bibliography.* Logan: Utah State University Press.

Hansen, N. 1973. *The Future of Non-Metropolitan America*. Lexington, Mass.: D. C. Heath.

Hareven, T. 1982. *Family Time and Industrial Time*. New York: Cambridge University Press.

Harloe, M., ed. 1977. *Captive Cities*. New York: John Wiley and Sons.

Harris, C., and E. Ullman. 1945. "The Nature of Cities." *Annals of the Academy of Political and Social Science* 242: 7–17.

Harrison, B. 1974. *Urban Economic Development*. Washington, D.C.: Urban Institute.

Hartman, C. 1974. *Yerba Buena*. San Francisco: Glide Publications.

Hartman, C., et al. 1982. *Displacement: How to Fight It*. Berkeley: National Housing Law Project.

Hartman, C., and R. Kessler. 1984. "The Illusion and Reality of Urban Renewal: San Francisco's Yerba Buena Center." In Tabb and Sawers 1984.

Harvey, D. 1973. *Social Justice and the City*. Baltimore: Johns Hopkins University Press.

———. 1975a. "The Political Economy of Urbanization in Advanced Capitalist Societies: The Case of the U.S." In Gappert and Rose 1975.

———. 1975b. "Class-Monopoly Rent, Finance Capital and the Urban Revolution." In Gale and Moore 1975.

———. 1976. "Labor, Capital and Class Struggle around the Built Environment." *Politics and Society* 6: 265–295.

———. 1981. "The Urban Process under Capitalism: A Framework for Analysis." In Dear and Scott 1981.

———. 1983. *The Limits of Capital*. London: Macmillan.

Harvey, D., and L. Chatterjee. 1974. "Absolute Rent and the Structuring of Space by Financial Institutions." *Antipode* 6: 22–36.

Harvey, R., and W. Clark. 1965. "The Nature and Economics of Urban Sprawl." *Land Economics* 41: 1–6.

Hauser, P., and L. Schnore, eds. 1965. *The Study of Urbanization*. New York: John Wiley and Sons.

Hawley, A. 1950. *Human Ecology*. New York: Ronald Press.

———. 1956. *The Changing Shape of Metropolitan America*. Glencoe, Ill.: Free Press.

———. 1972. "Population Density and the City." *Demography* 9: 523–524.

———. 1977. "Urbanization as a Process." In Street et al. 1977.

———. 1981. *Urban Society: An Ecological Approach*. 2d ed. New York: John Wiley and Sons.

Heilbroner, R. 1965. *The Limits of American Capitalism*. New York: Harper and Row.

Herbert, D. 1972. *Urban Geography: A Social Perspective*. London: David and Charles.

Heskin, A. 1981. "The History of Tenants in the U.S.: Struggle and Ideology." *International Journal of Urban and Regional Research* 5: 178–203.

Hightower, J. 1975. *Eat Your Heart Out*. New York: Crown Publishers.

Hill, R. 1974. "Separate and Unequal: Governmental Inequality in the Metropolis." *American Political Science Review* 68: 1557–1568.

———. 1977. "Capital Accumulation and Urbanization in the U.S." *Comparative Urban Research* 2: 39–60.

———. 1984a. "Fiscal Crisis, Austerity Politics and Alternative Urban Policies." In Sawers and Tabb 1984.

———. 1984b. "Urban Political Economy." In Smith 1984.

Hilton, R., ed. 1976. *The Transition from Feudalism to Capitalism*. London: New Left Books.

Hindness, B., and P. Hirst. 1975. *Pre-Capitalist Modes of Production*. London: Routledge and Kegan Paul.

Hirsch, J. 1981. "The Apparatus of the State, the Reproduction of Capital and Urban Conflicts." In Dear and Scott 1981.

———. 1983. "The Fordist Security State and New Social Movements." *Kapitalistate* 10: 75–87.

Hirst, P. 1979. *On Law and Ideology*. Atlantic Highlands, N.J.: Humanities Press.

Hodson, R., and R. Kaufmann. 1982. "Economic Dualism: A Critical Review." *American Sociological Review* 47: 727–739.

Holland, A. 1976. *Capital versus Region*. New York: St. Martin's Press.

———. 1977. "Capital, Labor and the Regions." In H. Folmer and J. Ooskehaven, eds., *Spatial Inequalities and Regional Development*. The Hague: Nijhoff.

Holloway, J., and S. Picciotto. 1979. *State and Capital: A Marxist Debate*. Austin: University of Texas Press.

Horkheimer, M. 1972. *Critical Theory*. New York: Herder and Herder.

Hoyt, H. 1933. *One Hundred Years of Land Values in Chicago*. Chicago: University of Chicago Press.

Hughes, E. 1928. "A Study of a Secular Institution: The Chicago Real Estate Board." Ph.D. dissertation, University of Chicago.

Hula, R. 1980. "Housing Lending Institutions and Public Policy." In D. Rosenthal, ed., *Urban Revitalization*. Urban Affairs Annual Review 10. Beverly Hills: Sage Publications.

Hymer, S. 1972. "The Multinational Corporation and the Law of Uneven Development." In J. Bhagwati, ed., *Economics and the World Order*. New York: Macmillan.

———. 1979. *The Multinational Corporation*. Cambridge, Eng.: Cambridge University Press.

International Journal of Urban and Regional Research. 1982. Special Issue on Enterprise Zones 6.

Isard, W. 1956. *Location and Space-Economy*. Cambridge, Mass.: MIT Press.

Ive, G. 1974. "Walker and the 'New Conceptual Framework' of Urban Rent." *Antipode* 7: 20–30.

James, R. 1977. *Back to the City*. Washington, D.C.: Urban Institute.

———. 1981. "Economic Distress in Central Cities." In Burchell and Listokin 1981.

Jessop, B. 1982. *The Capitalist State.* New York: New York University Press.

Jiobu, R., and H. Marshall. 1969. "Urban Structure and the Differentiation between Blacks and Whites." *American Sociological Review* 36: 638–649.

Kain, J. 1968. "Housing Segregation, Negro Employment and Metropolitan Decentralization." *Quarterly Journal of Economics* 82: 175–197.

———. 1970. "The Distribution and Movement of Jobs and Industry." In M. Ursofsky, ed., *The Metropolitan Enigma.* Garden City, N.Y.: Anchor Books.

Kalecki, M. 1968. *Theory of Economic Dynamics.* New York: Monthly Review Press.

Kasarda, J. 1972. "The Theory of Ecological Expansion: An Empirical Test." *Social Forces* 51: 165–175.

———. 1980. "The Implications of Contemporary Redistribution Trends for National Policy." *Social Science Quarterly* 61: 373–400.

Kasarda, J., and G. Redfearn. 1975. "Differential Patterns of City and Suburban Growth in the U.S." *Journal of Urban History* 2: 43–66.

Katznelson, I. 1976. "The Crisis of the Capitalist City: Urban Politics and Social Control." In W. Hawley et al., eds., *Theoretical Perspectives on Urban Politics.* Englewood Cliffs, N.J.: Prentice-Hall.

———. 1981. *City Trenches.* New York: Random House.

Keat, R., and J. Urry. 1975. *Social Theory as Science.* London: Routledge and Kegan Paul.

Kidron, M. 1968. *Western Capitalism since the War.* London: Macmillan.

Klein, L. 1947. *The Keynesian Revolution.* New York: Macmillan.

Koopmans, T., and M. Beckman. 1957. "Assignment Problems and the Location of Economic Activities." *Econometrica* 25: 53–76.

Kotler, M. 1979. "A Public Policy for Neighborhoods and Community Organizations." In Boyte 1979.

Kuznets, S. 1960. *Capital in the American Economy.* Princeton: National Bureau of Economic Research.

Lamarche, F. 1977. "Property Development and the Economic Foundations of the Urban Question." In Pickvance 1977a.

Lange, O. 1963. *Political Economy.* Vol. 1. New York: Pergamon Press.

Laska, S., and D. Spain, eds. 1980. Special Issue on Back to the City. *Urban Affairs Quarterly* 15.

Lefebvre, H. 1939. *Dialectical Materialism.* London: Cape.

———. 1968. *Le droit à la ville.* Paris: Anthropos.

———. 1970. *La révolution urbaine.* Paris: Gallimard.

———. 1972. *La pensée marxiste et la ville.* Paris: Casterman.

———. 1973. *The Survival of Capitalism.* London: Allison and Busby.

———. 1974. *La production de l'espace.* Paris: Anthropos.

———. 1979. "Space: Social Product and Use Value." In J. Freiberg, ed., *Critical Sociology: European Perspective.* New York: Irvington Publishers.

Leinsdorf, D., et al. 1973. *Citibank.* New York: Grossman.

Lenin, V. I. 1939. *Imperialism: The Highest Stage of Capitalism.* New York: International Publishers.

Lerner, A. 1944. *The Economics of Control*. New York: Macmillan.

Leven, C. 1978a. "Growth and Nongrowth in Metropolitan Areas." *Papers and Proceedings of the Regional Science Association* 41: 101–112.

———, ed. 1978b. *The Mature Metropolis* Lexington, Mass.: D. C. Heath.

Lindemann, B. 1976. "Anatomy of Land Speculation." *Journal of the American Institute of Planners* 42: 142–152.

Lineberry, R. 1977. *Equality and Urban Policy*. Beverly Hills: Sage Publications.

Lipietz, A. 1977. *Le capital et son espace*. Paris: Maspero.

———. 1980. "The Structuration of Space, the Problem of Land, and Spatial Policy." In J. Carney, R. Hudson, and J. Lewis, eds., *Regions in Crisis*. London: Croom Helm.

———. 1982. "Towards a Global Fordism?" *New Left Review* 132: 33–48.

Lipsky, M. 1970. *Protest in City Politics*. Chicago: Rand McNally.

Logan, J., and M. Schneider. 1981. "The Stratification of Metropolitan Suburbs, 1960–1970." *American Sociological Review* 46: 175–186.

Lojkine, J. 1977a. "Contribution to a Marxist Theory of Capitalist Urbanization." In Pickvance 1977a.

———. 1977b. *Le marxisme, l'état, et la question urbaine*. Paris: Centre de Sociologie Urbaine.

London, B. 1980. "Revitalization of Inner-City Neighborhoods." *Urban Affairs Quarterly* 15: 373–487.

Long, L., and D. DeAre. 1983. "The Slowing of Urbanization in the U.S." *Scientific American* 249: 33–41.

Longstreth, F. 1979. "The City, Industry and the State." In C. Crouch, ed., *State Economy in Contemporary Capitalism*. London: Croom Helm.

Losch, A. 1954. *The Economics of Location*. New Haven: Yale University Press.

Lukács, G. 1971. *History and Class Consciousness*. Cambridge, Mass.: MIT Press.

Luxemburg, R. 1971. *The Accumulation of Capital*. New York: Monthly Review Press.

Mandel, E. 1971. *The Formation of the Economic Thought of Karl Marx*. London: New Left Books.

———. 1975. *Late Capitalism*. New York: Velos.

Manners, G. 1974. "The Office in the Metropolis." *Economic Geography* 50: 93–110.

Mansfield, E. 1968. *The Economics of Technological Change*. New York: Norton.

Marcuse, P. 1981. "The Targeted Crisis: On the Ideology of the Urban Fiscal Crisis and Its Uses." *International Journal of Urban and Regional Research* 5.

Markusen, A. 1978. "Class, Rent and Sectorial Conflict: Uneven Development in Western U.S. Boomtowns." *Review of Radical Political Economics* 10 (Special Issue on Uneven Development): 117–129.

Markusen, A., A. Saxenian, and M. Weiss. 1981. "Who Benefits from Intergovermental Transfers?" In Burchell and Listokin 1981.

Marshall, H. 1979. "White Movement to the Suburbs: A Comparison of Explanations." *American Sociological Review* 44: 975–994.

Martindale, D. 1962. *The City*. New York: Collier Books.

Martins, M. 1982. "The Theory of Social Space in the Work of Henri Lefebvre." In R. Forrest, J. Henderson, and P. Williams, eds., *Urban Political Economy and Social Theory*. Epping, Essex, Eng.: Gower Press.

Marx, K. 1964. *Pre-Capitalist Economic Formations*. New York: International Publishers.

——. 1967. *Capital*. Vol. 3. New York: New World.

——. 1973. *Grundrisse*. New York: Vintage.

Massey, D. 1977a. "Towards a Critique of Industrial Location Theory." In R. Peet, ed., *Radical Geography*. Chicago: Maaroufa.

——. 1977b. *Industrial Location Theory Reconsidered*. London: Milton Keynes, Open University Press.

——. 1978. "Survey: Regionalism: Some Current Issues." *Capital and Class* 6: 106–125.

Massey, D., and A. Catalano. 1978. *Capital and Land*. London: Edward Arnold.

Massey, D., and R. Meegan. 1978. "Industrial Restructuring versus the Cities." *Urban Studies* 15: 273–283.

Mayer, H. 1969. "The Spatial Expression of Urban Growth." Resource Paper 7. Washington, D.C.: Association of American Geographers.

Mazie, S. 1972. *Population Distribution and Public Policy*. Vol. 5. Washington, D.C.: Government Printing Office.

McAdams, C. 1981. "A Power Conflict Approach to Urban Ecology." *Urban Anthropology* 19: 295–318.

McClellan, K., and P. Seidenstadt. 1972. *New Business and Urban Employment Opportunities*. Lexington, Mass.: D. C. Heath.

McKenzie, R. 1925. "The Ecological Approach to the Study of the Human Community." In Park, Burgess, and McKenzie 1925.

——. 1933. *The Metropolitan Community*. New York: McGraw-Hill.

McRobie, G. 1981. *Small Is Possible*. New York: Harper and Row.

Means, A. 1964. *The Corporate Revolution in America*. New York: Macmillan.

Megret, A. 1981. "Achieving Equity in an Era of Fiscal Constraint." In Burchell and Listokin 1981.

Meier, R. 1956. *Science and Economic Development*. Cambridge, Mass.: MIT Press.

Melman, S. 1970. *Pentagon Capitalism*. New York: Columbia University Press.

——. 1977. "The Federal Rip-Off of New York's Money." In Alcaly and Mermelstein 1977.

Menshikov, S. 1969. *Millionaires and Managers*. Moscow: Progress Publishers.

Milgram, G. 1967. *The City Expands: A Study of the Conversion of Land from Rural to Urban Use.* Washington, D.C.: Government Printing Office

Miliband, R. 1973. "Poulantzas and the Capitalist State." *New Left Review* 82: 83–93.

Mills, E. 1970. "Urban Density Function." *Urban Studies* 7: 5–20.

———. 1972. *Studies in the Structure of the Urban Economy.* Baltimore: Johns Hopkins University Press.

Mingione, E. 1977. "Pahl and Lojkine on the State: A Comment." *International Journal of Urban and Regional Research* 1: 24–36.

———. 1981. *Social Conflict and the City.* New York: St. Martin's Press.

Minty, M., and J. Cohen. 1972. *America Inc.: Who Owns and Operates the United States.* New York: Dell.

Misztal, B., and B. Misztal. 1984. "Urban Social Problems in Poland: The Macrosocial Determinants." *Urban Affairs Quarterly* 19: 315–328.

Mollenkopf, J. 1975. "The Postwar Politics of Urban Development." *Politics and Society* 5: 247–296.

———. 1981. "Paths toward the Post-Industrial Service City: The Northeast and the Southwest." In Burchell and Listokin 1981.

———. 1983. *The Contested City.* Princeton, N.J.: Princeton University Press.

Mollenkopf, J., and J. Pynoos. 1972. "Property, Politics and Local Housing Policy." *Politics and Society* 2: 407–429.

Molotch, H. 1976. "The City as a Growth Machine." *American Journal of Sociology* 82: 309–332.

Mueller, E., and J. Morgan. 1962. "Location Decisions of Manufacturers." *American Economic Review* 52: 204–218.

Muller, P. 1976. "The Outer City." Resource Paper 75-2. Washington, D.C.: Association of American Geographers.

———. 1981. *Contemporary Suburban America.* Englewood Cliffs, N.J.: Prentice-Hall.

Muth, R. 1969. *Cities and Housing: The Spatial Pattern of Urban Residential Land Use.* Chicago: University of Chicago Press.

Myrdal, G. 1957. *Economic Theory and Underdeveloped Regions.* London: Duckworth.

National Office Market Report. 1980. Houston: Office Network.

O'Brien, T., and A. Ganz. 1972. "A Demographic Revolution: The Impact of Office Building and Residential Tower Development in Boston." Boston: Boston Redevelopment Authority.

O'Connor, J. 1973. *The Fiscal Crisis of the State.* New York: St. Martin's Press.

———. 1974. *The Corporations and the State.* New York: Harper and Row.

———. 1981. "The Fiscal Crisis of the State Revisited." *Kapitalistate* 9: 41–61.

Offe, C., and V. Rouge. 1975. "Theses on the Theory of the State." *New German Critique* 6: 137–145.

Pahl, R. 1970. *Patterns of Urban life.* London: Longmans.

————. 1975. *Whose City?* Harmondsworth, Sussex, Eng.: Penguin.

————. 1977. "Stratification and the Relation between States and Urban and Regional Development." *International Journal of Urban and Regional Research* 1: 7–16.

Palen, J. 1981. *The Urban World.* New York: McGraw-Hill.

Palloix, C. 1975. *L'internationalisation du capital.* Paris: Maspero.

Park, R. 1925. "The City: Suggestions for the Investigation of Human Behavior in the Urban Environment." In Park, Burgess, and McKenzie 1925.

————. 1936. "Human Ecology." *American Journal of Sociology* 42: 1–15.

Park, R., E. Burgess, and R. McKenzie. 1925. *The City.* Chicago: University of Chicago Press.

Perloff, H., E. Dunn., E. Lampard, and R. Muth. 1960. *Regions, Resources and Economic Growth.* Baltimore: Johns Hopkins University Press.

Perloff, H., and L. Wingo, eds. 1968. *Issues in Urban Economics.* Baltimore: Johns Hopkins University Press.

Peterson, G. 1979. "Federal Tax Policy and Urban Development." In B. Chinitz, ed., *Central City Economic Development.* Cambridge, Mass.: Abt Associates.

Peterson, P. 1981. *City Limits.* Chicago: University of Chicago Press.

Peterson, S. 1977. "The Family Farm in California." Technology Task Force Report. State of California.

Pickvance, C. G., ed. 1977a. *Urban Sociology: Critical Essays.* New York: St. Martin's Press.

————. 1977b. "From Social Base to Social Force." In Harloe 1977.

————. 1982. *The State and Collective Consumption.* London: Milton Keynes, Open University Press.

————. 1984. "Spatial Policy as Territorial Politics." In G. Rees, ed., *Political Action and Social Identity.* London: Macmillan.

Plotkin, S. 1980. "Policy Fragmentation and Capitalist Reform: The Defeat of National Land-Use Policy." *Politics and Society* 9: 409–442.

Popper, F. 1981. *The Politics of Land-Use Reform.* Madison: University of Wisconsin Press.

Posner, M., and S. Wolf. 1967. *Italian Enterprise.* Cambridge, Mass.: Harvard University Press.

Poulantzas, N. 1973. *Political Power and Social Classes.* London: New Left Books.

————. 1976. *Classes in Contemporary Capitalism.* London: New Left Books.

Pred, A. 1973. *Urban Growth and the Circulation of Information: The U.S. System of Cities, 1790–1840.* Cambridge, Mass.: Harvard University Press.

————. 1977. *City Systems in Advanced Economies.* London: Hutchinson.

————, ed. 1981. *Space and Time in Geography.* Stockholm: C. W. K. Gleerup.

President's Commission for a National Agenda for the Eighties. 1980. *Urban America in the Eighties.* Washington, D.C.: Government Printing Office.

President's National Advisory Commission on Rural Poverty. 1967. "The People Left Behind." Washington, D.C.: Government Printing Office.

Preteceille, E. 1973. *La production des grands ensembles*. Paris: Mouton.

——. 1977. "Equipments, collectifs et consomption sociale." *International Journal of Urban and Regional Research* 1: 101–123.

Protash, A., and M. Baldassare. 1983. "Growth Policies and Community Status." *Urban Affairs Quarterly* 18: 397–412.

Pye, R. 1977. "Office Location and the Cost of Maintaining Contact." *Environment and Planning* 9: 149–168.

Pynchon, T. 1968. "Journey into the Mind of Watts." In A. Blaustein and R. Woock, eds., *Man against Poverty*. New York: Random House.

Quante, W. 1976. *The Exodus of Corporate Headquarters from New York City*. New York: Praeger.

Ratcliff, R., et al. 1979. "The Civic Involvement of Bankers." *Social Problems* 26: 298–313.

Real Estate Research Corporation. 1974. *The Costs of Sprawl*. Washington, D.C.: Government Printing Office.

Rees, A., and G. Schultz. 1970. *Workers and Wages in an Urban Labor Market*. Chicago: University of Chicago Press.

Rees, J. 1978. "Manufacturing Headquarters in a Post-Industrial Urban Context." *Economic Geography* 54: 337–359.

Reich, M. 1981. *Racial Inequality: A Political Economic Analysis*. Princeton: Princeton University Press.

Review of Radical Political Economics. 1978. Special Issue on Uneven Development 10.

Rey, P. 1982. "Class Alliances." *International Journal of Sociology* 12: 2.

Rezler, J. 1969. *Automation and Industrial Labor*. New York: Random House.

Richardson, H. 1972. *The New Urban Economics*. London: Pion.

Riesman, D. 1957. "The Suburban Dislocation." *Annals of the Academy of Political and Social Science* 314.

Robson, W. 1960. *Nationalized Industry and Public Ownership*. London: Allen and Unwin.

Romanos, M. 1976. *Residential Spatial Structure*. Lexington, Mass.: D. C. Heath.

Rosdolsky, R. 1980. *The Making of Marx's "Capital."* London: Pluto Press.

Rosenberg, N. 1972. *Technology and American Growth*. New York: Harper.

Rosenthal, D., ed. 1980. *Urban Revitalization*. Urban Affairs Annual Review 18. Beverly Hills: Sage Publications.

Rossi, P., and R. Dentler. 1961. *The Politics of Urban Renewal*. New York: Free Press.

Roweiss, S. 1981. "The Urban Land Question." In Dear and Scott 1981.

Rubinson, R. 1976. "The World Economy and the Distribution of Income within the States." *American Sociological Review* 41: 631–659.

Sale, K. 1975. *Power Shift: The Rise of the Southern Rim and Its Challenge to the Eastern Establishment*. New York: Random House.

——. 1980. *Human Scale*. New York: Perigee Books.

Salisbury, R. 1964. "The New Convergence of Power in Urban Politics." *Journal of Politics* 26: 775–797.

Sargent, C. 1976. "Land Speculation and Urban Morphology." In J. Adams, ed., *Urban Policy Making and Metropolitan Dynamics*. Cambridge, Mass.: Ballinger.

Sassen-Koob, S. 1984. "The New International Division of Labor in Global Cities." In Smith 1984.

Saunders, P. 1978. "Domestic Property and Social Class." *International Journal of Urban and Regional Research* 11: 233–251.

———. 1979. *Urban Politics*. London: Hutchinson.

———. 1981. *Social Theory and the Urban Question*. London: Hutchinson.

Sawers, L., and W. Tabb, eds. 1984. *Sunbelt/Snowbelt*. New York: Oxford University Press.

Sbragia, A. 1981. "Cities, Capital and Banks: The Politics of Debt in the USA, UK and France." In K. Newton, ed., *Urban Political Economy*. London: Francis Pinter.

Schnore, L. 1957. "Metropolitan Growth and Decentralization." *American Journal of Sociology* 63: 171–180.

———. 1961. "The Myth of Human Ecology." *Sociological Inquiry* 31: 29–43.

———. 1962. "Municipal Annexations and Decentralization, 1950–1960." *American Journal of Sociology* 67: 406–417.

———. 1963. "The Socio-Economic Status of Cities and Suburbs." *American Sociological Review* 28: 76–85.

———. 1965. *The Urban Scene*. Glencoe, Ill.: Free Press.

———. 1972. *Class and Race in Cities and Suburbs*. Chicago: Markham.

Schnore, L., and H. Winsborough. 1972. "Functional Classification and the Residential Location of Social Classes." In Berry and Smith 1972.

Schonfeld, A. 1965. *Modern Capitalism*. New York: Oxford University Press.

Schumpeter, J. 1939. *Business Cycles*. New York: Harper.

Scott, A. 1976. "Land and Land Rent: An Interpretative Review of the French Literature." In C. Boord et al., eds., *Progress in Geography*. London: Edward Arnold.

———. 1980. *The Urban Land Nexus and the State*. London: Pion.

Scott, A., and S. Roweiss. 1978. "The Urban Land Question." In Cox 1978.

Seldon, H. 1975. *Land Investment*. Homewood, Ill.: Dow Jones–Irwin.

Sennett, R., and J. Cobb. 1972. *The Hidden Injuries of Class*. New York: Knopf.

Séve, L. 1978. *Man in Marxist Theory and the Psychology of Personality*. London: Harvester Press.

Shannon, F. 1945. *The Farmer's Last Frontier*. New York: Farrar and Rinehart.

Sheahan, J. 1963. *Promotion and Control of Industry in Postwar France*. Cambridge, Mass.: Harvard University Press.

Shevky, A., and W. Bell. 1975. *Social Area Analysis*. Stanford: Stanford University Press.

Shover, J. 1976. *First Majority–Last Minority*. DeKalb: Northern Illinois University Press.

Silk, L. 1960. *The Research Revolution*. New York: McGraw-Hill.

Sinclair, R. 1967. "Von Thunen and Urban Sprawl." *Annals of the Association of American Geographers* 57: 72–87.

Singelmann, J. 1977. *The Transformation of Industry*. Beverly Hills: Sage Publications.

Singer, H. 1936. "The 'Courbe des Populations': A Parallel to Pareto's Law." *Economic Journal* 46: 245–263.

Sly, D. 1972. "Migration and the Ecological Complex." *American Sociological Review* 37: 615–628.

Sly, D., and J. Tayman. 1980. "Metropolitan Morphology and Population Mobility." *American Journal of Sociology* 86: 119–138.

Smith, D. 1973. *The Geography of Social Well-Being in the United States*. New York: McGraw-Hill.

Smith, M. 1979. *The City and Social Theory*. New York: St. Martin's Press.
———. 1983. "Managed Growth and the Politics of Uneven Development in New Orleans." In Fainstein et al. 1983.
———. 1984. *Cities in Transformation*. Urban Affairs Annual Review 26. Beverly Hills: Sage Publications.

Smith, W. 1970. *Urban Development: The Process and the Problems*. Berkeley and Los Angeles: University of California Press.

Soja, E. 1980. "The Socio-Spatial Dialectic." *Annals of the Association of American Geographers* 70: 207–225.
———. 1984. "The Spatiality of Social Life." In D. Gregory and J. Urry, eds., *Social Relations and Spatial Structure*. London: Macmillan.

Solow, R. 1973. "On Equilibrium Models of Urban Location." In M. Parkin, ed., *Essays in Modern Economics*. London: Longmans.

South, S., and D. Poston. 1982. "The U.S. Metropolitan System." *Urban Affairs Quarterly* 18: 187–206.

Spencer, H. 1909. *Principles of Sociology*. New Haven, Conn.: Archon Books.

Sraffa, P. 1960. *The Production of Commodities by Commodities*. New York: Cambridge University Press.

Steedman, I. 1977. *Marx after Sraffa*. London: New Left Books.

Stein, M. 1960. *The Eclipse of Community*. New York: Free Press.

Stephan, G. 1971. "Variation in County Size: A Theory of Segmental Growth." *American Sociological Review* 36: 451–461.

Sternlieb, G., and R. Hughes, eds. 1975. *Post-Industrial America: Metropolitan Decline and Inter-Regional Job Shifts*. New Brunswick, N.J.: Rutgers University Press.
——— and ———. 1981. "New Dimensions of the Urban Crisis." In Burchell and Listokin 1981.

Stone, M. 1975. "The Housing Crisis, Mortgage Lending and the Class Struggle." *Antipode* 7: 22–37.

Storper, M., and R. Walker. 1983. "The Theory of Labor and the Theory of Location." *International Journal of Urban and Regional Research* 7: 1–41.

———— and ————. 1984. "The Spatial Division of Labor: Labor and the Location of Industries." In Sawers and Tabb 1984.

Street, D., et al., eds. 1977. *The Handbook of Contemporary Urban Life*. San Francisco: Jossey-Bass.

Struyk, D., and F. James. 1975. *Inter-Metropolitan Industrial Location*. Lexington, Mass.: D. C. Heath.

Suttles, G. 1973. *The Social Construction of Community*. Chicago: University of Chicago Press.

————. 1977. "Changing Priorities for the Urban Heartland." In Street et al. 1977.

Tabb, W., and L. Sawers, eds. 1984. *Marxism and the Metropolis*. 2d ed. New York: Oxford University Press.

Taueber, K., and A. Taueber. 1964. "White Migration and Socio-Economic Differences between Cities and Suburbs." *American Sociological Review* 29: 118–129.

Taylor, G. 1915. *Satellite Cities: A Study of Industrial Suburbs*. New York: Appleton.

Therborn, G. 1978. *What Does the Ruling Class Do When It Rules?* London: New Left Books.

Theret, B. 1982. "Collective Means of Consumption, Capital Accumulation, and the Urban Question." *International Journal of Urban and Regional Research* 6: 345–371.

Thompson, E. 1978. *The Poverty of Theory, and Other Essays*. London: Merlin.

Thompson, Warren. 1947. *The Growth of Metropolitan Districts in the U.S., 1900–1940*. Washington, D.C.: Government Printing Office.

Thompson, Wilbur. 1965a. *A Preface to Urban Economics*. New York: John Wiley and Sons.

————. 1965b. "Urban Economic Growth and Development in a National System of Cities." In Hauser and Schnore 1965.

Thompson, Wilbur, and J. Mattila. 1959. *An Econometric Model of Post-War Industrial Development*. Detroit: Wayne State University Press.

Thrasher, F. 1963. *The Gang*. Chicago: University of Chicago Press. Originally published 1927.

Thrift, N. 1983. "On the Determination of Social Action in Space and Time." *Environment and Planning* 1: 23–57.

Thurow, L. 1975. *Generating Inequality*. New York: Basic Books.

————. 1980. *The Zero-Sum Society*. Cambridge, Mass.: MIT Press.

Tolley, G., et al. 1979. "The Urban Growth Question." *Law and Contemporary Problems* 4: 211–238.

Tomaskovic-Devey, D., and S. Miller. 1982. "Recapitalization: The Basic Urban Policy of the 1980's." In N. Fainstein and S. Fainstein, *Urban Policy under Capitalism*. Urban Affairs Annual Review 22. Beverly Hills: Sage Publications.

Topolov, C. 1973. *Capital et propriété foncière*. Paris: Centre de Sociologie Urbaine.

Turner, J. 1978. *The Structure of Sociological Theory*. Homewood, Ill.: Dorsey.

United States, Congress, House Committee on the Judiciary, Antitrust Subcommittee. 1965. *Interlocks in Corporate Management*. Washington, D.C.: Government Printing Office.

United States, Department of Housing and Urban Development. 1980. *Council on Development Choices for the 1980's*. Washington, D.C.: Government Printing Office.

United States, Department of Labor. 1979. "Employment Projections for the 1980's." Bulletin 2030. Washington, D.C.: Government Printing Office.

Urban Land Institute. 1975. *Industrial Development Handbook*. Washington, D.C.: Urban Land Institute.

Urry, J. 1981. "Localities, Regions and Social Class." *International Journal of Urban and Regional Research* 5: 455–464.

Vance, J. 1977. *This Scene of Man*. New York: Harper's College Press.

Vaneigem, R. 1975. *Revolution in Everyday Life*. London: Situationist International.

Vining, D., and A. Strauss. 1977. "A Demonstration That the Current Deconcentration of Population in the U.S. Is a Clean Break with the Past." *Environment and Planning* 9: 751–758.

Vogeler, I. 1981. *The Myth of the Family Farmer: Agribusiness Dominance of U.S. Agriculture*. Boulder: Westview.

Von Thunen, J. 1966. *The Isolated State*. New York: Pergamon.

Walker, R. 1975. "Contentious Issues in Marxian Value and Rent Theory." *Antipode* 7: 31–54.

———. 1981. "A Theory of Suburbanization." In Dear and Scott 1981.

Wallerstein, I. 1979. *The Capitalist World Economy*. New York: Cambridge University Press.

Warner, S. 1962. *Street Car Suburbs*. Cambridge, Mass.: Harvard University Press.

Watkins, A. 1980. *The Practice of Urban Economics*. Beverly Hills: Sage Publications.

Watkins, A., and R. Perry. 1977. *The Rise of the Sunbelt Cities*. Beverly Hills: Sage Publications.

Weber, A. 1899. *The Growth of Cities in the 19th Century*. New York: Macmillan.

Weissman, H., ed. 1969. *Community Development in the Mobilization for Youth Experience*. New York: Association Press.

Wellman, B., et al. 1983. *Network as Personal Communities*. Research Paper 144. Toronto: Center for Urban and Community Studies, University of Toronto.

Wheat, L. 1973. *Regional Growth and Industrial Location: An Empirical Viewpoint*. Lexington, Mass.: Lexington Books.

Whyte, W. 1956. *The Organization Man*. New York: Doubleday.

———. 1980. *The Social Life of Small Urban Spaces*. Washington, D.C.: Conservation Foundation.

Williams, O. 1971. *Metropolitan Political Analysis.* New York: Free Press.

Williamson, O. 1975. *Markets and Hierarchies: Analysis and Anti-Trust Implications.* New York: Free Press.

Wilson, J. Q. 1967. *Urban Renewal: The Record and the Controversy.* Cambridge, Mass.: MIT Press.

Windsor, D. 1979. "Critique of 'The Costs of Sprawl.'" *American Planning Association Journal* 45: 279–292.

Wingo, L. 1961. *Transportation and Land.* Washington, D.C.: Resources for the Future.

Wood, R. 1959. *Suburbia: Its People and Their Politics.* Boston: Houghton Mifflin.

———. 1961. *1400 Governments.* Cambridge, Mass.: Harvard University Press.

Wright, E. 1978. *Class, Crisis and the State.* London: New Left Books.

Wright, E., et al. 1982. "The American Class Structure." *American Sociological Review* 47: 709–726.

Zeitlin, M. 1970. *American Society Inc.* Chicago: Markham.

Index

Agribusiness: effect of, on space, 231–235. *See also* Late Capitalism

Althusser, Louis: and Castells, 110–114; and Marxian thought, 111–114

Bookchin, Murray: approach of, to community, 171; and critique of political economy, 282

Burgess, Ernest W.: concentric zone model of, 32; location theory of, 30–33

Capital: in general, 90–92; fractions of, 90; circuits of, 96; second circuit of, 97, 183–194; property sector of, 176–183, 219–225, 261, 268; stages of, periodization of, 199–200; and spatial form critique, 207. *See also* Capital accumulation; Finance capital; Growth networks

Capital accumulation: and urban space, 86–109; in work of Harvey, 87–91; Lefebvre's approach to, 124–125; and second circuit, 243–245. *See also* Capital; Marxian political economy

Castells, Manuel: approach of, to city, 21; and Althusser 110–114; comparison of, with Lefebvre, 116–156 passim; and theory of space, 115–120; and urban sys-

tem, 118; and theory of collective consumption, 118, 119, 136–137; approach of, to urban social movements, 139, 147–150

Chicago School: basis of approach of, 27–30; and moral order, 28; and neglect of culture, 29; and concentric zone model, 32–33; and ecological location theory, 32; contributions of Park, Burgess, and McKenzie to, 33; critique of, 34–35

City form: bounded, 5; Burgess model of, 7, 32–33; polynucleated realm model of, 14; critique of Marxian conception of, 20, 199–200, 207; neoricardian approach to, 100–109; and growth coalitions, 220–226

Class conflict: Marxian approach to, 73, 74; and location theory, 75–92; and accumulation, 87; in work of Harvey, 90–91; and spatial praxis, 126; and the state, 133–134; and space 160–166; and housing classes, 166–170; and growth networks, 223–224. *See also* Urban social movements

Collective consumption: critique of, 115, 120, 139–143; and the state, 118–120; and housing classes, 167. *See also* Castells, Manuel; Urban social movements

Community: and stratification, 11;